Housing Allowances for the Poor: A Social Experiment

Westview Replica Editions

This book is a Westview Replica Edition. The concept of Replica Editions is a response to the crisis in academic and informational publishing. Library budgets for books have been severely curtailed; economic pressures on the university presses and the few private publishing companies primarily interested in scholarly manuscripts have severely limited the capacity of the industry to properly serve the academic and research communities. Many manuscripts dealing with important subjects, often representing the highest level of scholarship, are today not economically viable publishing projects. Or, if they are accepted for publication, they are often subject to lead times ranging from one to three years. Scholars are understandably frustrated when they realize that their first-class research cannot be published within a reasonable time frame, if at all.

Westview Replica Editions seem to us one feasible and practical solution to the crisis. The concept is simple. We accept a manuscript in camera-ready form and move it immediately into the production process. The responsibility for textual and copy editing lies with the author or sponsoring organization. If necessary we will advise the author on proper preparation of footnotes and bibliography. The manuscript is acceptable as typed for a thesis or dissertation or prepared in any other clearly organized and readable way, though we prefer it typed according to our specifications. The end result is a book produced by lithography and bound in hard covers. Edition sizes range from 200 to 600 copies. We will include among Westview Replica Editions only works of outstanding scholarly quality or of great informational value and we will exercise our usual editorial standards and quality control.

Housing Allowances for the Poor:
A Social Experiment
M. G. Trend

This volume is the story of a rural welfare agency that successfully operated a housing program based on participant self-reliance and trust. In 1972, the U.S. Department of Housing and Urban Development (HUD) undertook a large research effort designed to test the feasibility of using direct cash assistance, given in the form of a monthly housing allowance, as a means of helping low- and moderate-income families obtain decent housing on the open market. Dr. Trend focuses on one of eight agencies that HUD selected to design and implement their own approaches to this program. Using participant observation, case studies, surveys, and statistical techniques, he examines the development and execution of the North Dakota program over a two-year period, discussing the reasons why the program developed as it did, defining success criteria, and comparing the performance of the North Dakota agency with the other organizations that participated in the experiment. Among his conclusions: the project was run primarily as an income-transfer program, rather than as a pure housing program, and its local acceptance was dependent on an approach that coincided with the existing value system of the population within the program area.

M. G. Trend is senior analyst at Abt Associates Inc., where he directs case studies for 31 legal services projects. He received his Ph.D. in social anthropology at the University of Minnesota. Dr. Trend is associate editor of *Human Organization*, a journal of the Society for Applied Anthropology.

O'Hare had a little notebook with him and printed in the back of it were postal rates and airline distances and the altitudes of famous mountains and other key facts about the world. He was looking up Dresden, which wasn't in the notebook, when he came across this, which he gave me to read:

> *On the average, 324,000 new babies are born into the world every day. During that same day, 10,000 persons, on an average, will have starved to death or died from malnutrition. So it goes. In addition 123,000 persons will die for other reasons. So it goes. This leaves a net gain of about 191,000 each day in the world. The Population Reference Bureau predicts that the world's total population will double to 7,000,000,000 before the year 2000.*

"I suppose they will all want dignity," I said.
"I suppose," said O'Hare.

— Kurt Vonnegut, Jr.
Slaughterhouse Five

Housing Allowances for the Poor: A Social Experiment

M. G. Trend

Westview Press
Boulder, Colorado

A Westview Replica Edition

All rights reserved. No part of this publication may be reproduced or transmitted in any form or by any means, electronic or mechanical, including photocopy, recording, or any information storage and retrieval system, without permission in writing from the publisher.

Copyright © 1978 by Westview Press, Inc.

Published in 1978 in the United States of America by

Westview Press, Inc.
5500 Central Avenue
Boulder, Colorado 80301
Frederick A. Praeger, Publisher and Editorial Director

Library of Congress Number: 78-52057
ISBN: 0-89158-057-3

Printed and bound in the United States of America

For R.C.K.

Contents

Preface
List of Figures
List of Tables

1 INTRODUCTION   1
   About This Book   1
   The Eight AAE Sites   10
   Experimental Design   27
   Glossary   36
   Notes   41

2 NORTH DAKOTA: THE PLACE, THE PEOPLE
   About North Dakota   45
   The Contracting Agency   73
   Notes   77

3 BEHIND CLOSED DOORS: THE PLANNING PROCESS   83
   First Contacts   83
   Initial Preparation   87
   The Orientation Session   89
   Writing the First Plan   90
   The Critique   95
   Revising the Plan   96
   The Final Conference   98
   Notes   99

4 STAFFING: PATTERNS AND STRATEGIES   101
   Staffing Strategies   107
   Communication   113
   Notes   114

5 THE AGENCIES AND THE COMMUNITY:
   IT AIN'T GONNA BE THAT WAY   117
   A Low Profile Approach with Landlords   117
   Discouraging Welfare Referrals   120
   Handling the LHAs   123
   Relations with the Federal Government   125

6 PARTICIPANT FLOW   127
   Mrs Feist: "Anything you want to ask, ask..."   127
   About Mrs. Feist   128
   Hearing About the Program   129
   Applying   129
   Screening and Certification   130
   Computing the Allowance   131
   Awaiting Selection   132
   Being Selected   132
   The First Session   133

        The Second Session 134
        The Third Session 139
        Issuing a Payment 139
        Commentary 140

7   PROGRAM HISTORY 141
        Introduction 141
        The Issue of Outreach: The Early Optimism 145
        The Rise of Phase-In Monitoring 160
        The Rise of the Enrollment Session 172
        Getting the Last Ones In 180
        A Broader Vision: Towards Regionalized Housing Authorities 189
        Steady State Operations 198
        Notes 210

8   PARTICIPANT CASE STUDIES 211
        Introduction 211
        "My History is Very Poor." Mrs. Erko 212
        "If I Can Just Keep On Like This, At Least I'll Be Even..." Sally Klein 225
        "If I Could Just Get Those Numbers Straight..." Edward and Roxanne Kunst 235
        "If You Can Get It, Take It." The Maddings 239
        "I Don't Want To Be On This Thing My Whole Life..." The Webbers 243
        "If They're Out Talking About Me, They're Leaving Other People Alone." Alice Sadowski 249
        "You'd See Them With The Gravy Running Down Their Chins..." Peter Barnes 254
        The Participants Revisited 258
        Commentary 274
        Notes 282

9   ANALYSIS AND COMMENTARY 285
        Program Goals 285
        The View of the North Dakota Agency 313
        Commentary: The Housing Allowance Approach 318
        Notes 325
        Epilogue 329

APPENDIX A 331
APPENDIX B 343
APPENDIX C 355
BIBLIOGRAPHY 364
ABOUT THE AUTHOR 369

List of Figures

1-1 Percent of Families Below Poverty Level 16
1-2 Percent Minority in Urbanized Areas 18
1-3 Percent of Housing Units Renter Occupied 20
1-4 Percent of Units Lacking Plumbing Facilities 22
1-5 Rental Vacancy Rate in Urbanized Areas 22a

2-1 The Project Area 53
2-2 Mental Map from North Dakota 66
2-3 The Mental Map from Minnesota 67
2-4 The Ignorance Surface from North Dakota 68

3-1 North Dakota Proposed Organization Chart, Strategic Plan 93

4-1 North Dakota Proposed Organization Chart, Detailed Plan 101
4-2 North Dakota Maximum Staffing Pattern (Official Version) 104
4-3 North Dakota Maximum Staffing Pattern (Unofficial Version) 104
4-4 North Dakota Staffing Pattern: May, 1974 106

9-1 Rank Ordering of Sites by Income Changes and Certification Stringency 316
9-2 Rank Ordering of Agencies by Elaborateness of Application Forms and by Income Changes 317

List of Tables

1-1 U.S. Regional Data and the AAE Sites 13
1-2 Program Areas of the Eight AAE Sites 14
1-3 Eligible Population and Housholds Enrolled in the AAE 17
1-4 Updated Housing Market Information on AAE Program Areas 23
1-5 Summary Table--Characteristics of the AAE Sites 28

9-1 Enrollment Process: Planned vs. Actual 287
9-2 Comparison of Demographic Characteristics of Eligible and Applicant Populations at Each Agency 292
9-3 Mean Initial Payment to Recipients 296
9-4 Attaining Financial Feasibility 296
9-5 Plan Distribution of Households 297
9-6 Actual Distribution of Households 298
9-7 Percentage of Movers and Non-Movers 299
9-8 Rent Burdens at Enrollment 301
9-9 Rent Burdens at Payment Initiation 302
9-10 Gross Rent at Enrollment and at Payment Initiation 303
9-11 Enrollee Termination Rates and Reasons for Termination 312
9-12 Incidence of Changes in Income Data by Site 315

Preface

In June, 1973, I answered an ad in the Minneapolis paper for a research job. The company which placed the advertisement was named Abt Associates Inc. It was located in Cambridge, Massachusetts, and I called them collect.

Two people flew out from Boston to interview me. The firm had a contract with the federal government to evaluate an experimental program that had to do with housing.

A week later, I was flown to the East Coast for some more interviews. I came back the same evening and felt like Cinderella. The one-day trip seemed extravagant to me and still does.

Abt Associates wanted an anthropologist to spend 10 months observing an agency trying to get a new program running. They called me back and asked if I would rather go to Oklahoma or North Dakota. I said North Dakota. I forget the reason for that.

I wound up staying for more than a year because my contract was extended for 90 days more. I had a good time and learned more than I expected. My family thrived, too.

Afterwards, I continued to work for Abt Associates and moved to Massachusetts, which is where I live now--in Concord. Last August made it three years that I've been out here. Mostly, I've been doing a lot of writing that all has to do with the project I was hired to work on in 1973.

I have several acknowledgements to make. I owe a lot to the staff of the North Dakota Experimental Housing Allowance Project, to the participants with whom I came into contact, and to various North Dakota state and local officials who aided me in the original research effort. Special thanks go to the project director, Gottfried Kuhn, who helped insure that my relationship with his agency would be a smooth one. I appreciate his careful criticisms of the case study from which this book draws heavily. I wish him well in his retirement.

I am grateful to Dr. William Hamilton, my contract manager, who gave me permission to use the quantitative data base from the evaluation effort.

This book was originally submitted to and accepted by the University of Minnesota as my Ph.D thesis. Thanks go to my advisor, Professor Robert C. Kiste; to Professor Eugene Ogan, who chaired my final examination; and to the others on my committee. The comments and suggestions were welcome. I think I took most of those offered.

The manuscript was edited by Shari Ajemian. Joyce Stamps prepared the typescript. I thank them both.

This book is my own work. The opinions expressed here may not necessarily reflect those of Abt Associates Inc., or the federal agency which sponsored the effort. No official endorsement should be inferred.

M. G. Trend
9 September 1977
Concord, Massachusetts

Housing Allowances for the Poor: A Social Experiment

1. Introduction

ABOUT THIS BOOK

    This book is about a public agency that participated in a social experiment sponsored by the U. S. Department of Housing and Urban Development (HUD). The Administrative Agency Experiment (AAE) is one of three research efforts that constitute the Experimental Housing Allowance Project (EHAP)[1]. Authorized by the Housing and Urban Development Act of 1970, the experiments were designed to test the concept of using direct cash payments to help low-income households secure decent housing.

    The three-part experimental program was undertaken to answer several policy questions concerning this type of public assistance. These included:

1. Is direct cash assistance a feasible and desirable way of helping low-income households in need of better housing?
2. If direct cash assistance is made a part of the national housing policy, how might such a program be administered?
3. In what form should the housing allowance payments be given?
4. What effect do housing allowances have upon improving the local housing stock?

As a study in <u>management issues</u> associated with housing allowance programs, the AAE was directed toward answering the second of the above questions. Accordingly, HUD selected eight agencies, located in different parts of the country, to design their own versions of a housing allowance program. A naturalistic research design* was adopted whereby the eight con-

---

*A naturalistic experiment is one which does not have control groups.

1

tracting agencies (as they came to be called) were given leeway in planning programs which were intended to serve up to 900 households at each of the sites.

Once the completed plans had been approved by HUD, the contracting agencies were given permission to create the administrative agencies which would try to implement the programs as planned.

Abt Associates Inc., a private research firm based in Cambridge, Massachusetts, was chosen by HUD to be the evaluation contractor for the AAE. Over a three-year period, the company would be responsible for monitoring the progress of the eight agencies. At the end of this time, the researchers would write a series of reports assessing the effectiveness of the different approaches and the AAE as a whole. The agencies themselves would no longer exist and the remaining participant families would have been transferred long ago to the local housing authorities in the eight areas.

A wide variety of quantitative and qualitative data was collected to assist the evaluation. The precise methods are described later in this chapter. Of significance was that each administrative agency had an on-site observer (OSO) assigned to it for at least one year. The OSO was usually an anthropologist. His job was to collect the qualitative ("soft") data that would augment the quantitative ("hard") data. The latter is more traditionally associated with policy research.

The Social Service Board of North Dakota was one of two welfare agencies that participated in the AAE. I was hired by Abt Associates to be the OSO for the North Dakota site. On a daily basis, I observed the newly-created agency as the staff administered the program their director had designed.

Program operations began in July, 1973. This date marked my appearance on site as well. For the following thirteen months, I lived in Bismarck, the headquarters of the agency.

When I left Bismarck at the end of July, 1974, the agency had attained its stated goals. By most measures, the program had been a success. As planned, the agency had reached its target of 400 participating households. Program costs were running well below the limits set by HUD. Indeed, the agency had accumulated a surplus of funds. Survey responses from a large sample of participants indicated that almost all of them were enthusiastic about the program. The AAE was unusual in that it allowed recipients to select their own housing as long as it was <u>rental</u>

housing and met certain criteria of standardness. Many of the respondents had volunteered that the thing they liked most about housing allowance is that they allowed people to keep their <u>dignity</u>.

For those who had decided to move when they entered the program, the preliminary data collected by Abt Associates showed a moderate improvement in housing quality. For those who had decided to remain in their existing housing, rent burden was reduced by the monthly cash allowance.

Things were beginning to wind down when I left for Massachusetts to join the analysis staff of Abt Associates. The North Dakota agency was three months into the "steady-state period." According to the rules of the program, no new applications could be accepted after the first seven months of operations. Ninety days after that, all enrollees in the program had to find housing and fulfill other requirements if they were to receive a housing allowance at all. The agency was preparing to transfer the empty program openings to the four local housing authorities operating within the program jurisdiction. This was according to the regulations.

Although I was not on site for most of the steady-state period, I was able to follow the progress of the North Dakota project by reading the agency's reports to HUD, and by having occasional telephone conversations with the staff. I also made two field visits during 1975, one in January and one in May. This gave me another opportunity to observe agency activity first-hand and to maintain contact with several participant families whose progress I had been following for about a year.

My impressions remained positive. The North Dakota operation seemed to be marked by a smoothness that was matched by few of the other agencies. The agency director, a senior official in the state welfare system, had been faced with a difficult task. He had planned and administered a coherent effort that satisfied several potential critics.

For HUD, it was important that the agency be run in a financially responsible manner while still serving a cross section of the eligible population. Informally, at last, some of the analysis staff at Abt Associates were skeptical that a poverty program could be run in such an easy-going manner as at the North Dakota agency. Applicants <u>declared</u> their own income. This information was used to provide the basis for figuring out the amount of the individual housing allowance. Outside verification of the applicants' statements was not required. Few counseling services were offered to enrollees. Prospective participants inspected their own units for standardness. They themselves were responsible for negotiating a rental agreement with their landlords.

The AAE was a potentially controversial program for the local area. One of the risks was that the general public would view the program as a government giveaway, yet another waste of the taxpayers' money. The trust that the agency planned to place in its clients was also something that could be looked upon with disfavor by the more conservative elements in the community.

At the same time, the agency director wished to avoid associating the AAE with any sort of welfare program. This was no mean feat, since the contracting agency was itself a welfare organization. The director felt that a new program--if it got tagged with a welfare label--would probably fail to attract applications from the working poor. People in North Dakota are no different than people elsewhere: being on the dole is being stigmatized. Attracting non-welfare segments of the population was of importance to the AAE. The program had been designed to serve a broader sector of people than the usual one for assistance programs. Income limits for program eligibility had been set relatively high.

In retrospect, the North Dakota program seems to have been a kind of a balancing act between potentially conflicting requirements. The criteria for "success" was multiple. This thesis shows that while the North Dakota effort was a balancing act of sorts, it was not a haphazard one. The how and why of the agency's success must be illustrated, commented upon, and measured.

The Argument

In order to understand the reasons why the North Dakota agency succeeded, it is necessary to define the things that "success" could mean, both in the view of HUD and within a local context. Once the criteria for making a judgement have been set, it is then possible to show how the program was operated so that failure did not occur.

The quickest way for a local program to fail was for an agency to have too few participants in the program. This could happen if there were too few eligible households applying, or if too many enrollees failed to find housing within a sixty to ninety day time limit. A successful program had to avoid these twin pitfalls. Early in the course of the AAE, the

Jacksonville, Florida, project was plagued by a high termination rate. Operations were suspended, a new approach was planned. After being re-funded, the Jacksonville agency resumed its work. The initial effort was the subject of a special report.[2]

Financial difficulties could also limit agency success. The funding method required that agencies monitor their administrative expenditures carefully. Also, high-payment households had to be balanced off by low-payment households. By doing these two things, a local agency could stay within their budgets and thus attain <u>financial feasibility</u>. Generous funding by the federal government made it difficult for an agency to run completely out of money. However, four of the eight agencies did not manage to make up their initial operating deficits and hence did not become feasible in the true, balance-sheet sense of the word.

Another criterion of program success is more analytic. It speaks to the stated intent of the AAE: improving the housing situation of participants. All of the agencies were required to set housing standards and to use some form of inspection to insure that those in the program were not living in poor quality housing. The degree to which participants improved their living situation--something that can be measured on a variety of indices--provides some sense of how well the program was operating at a particular agency.

Agencies were also given the responsibility of serving a demographically representative sample of eligible households within their respective program areas. The degree to which this was achieved can be measured by matching the characteristics of enrollees and recipients against those of the larger population.

Local acceptance of the program, both by the community and by those receiving the assistance, can also be viewed as important to an agency. All of the AAE organizations were wary of negative publicity. An unpopular program can make administration difficult when community operation is required.

In like fashion, a social program that gives financial assistance to those in need, but which is intensely disliked by the recipients, has also failed in its mission. One of the reasons that housing allowances were proposed is that this form of assistance was thought to be a dignified alternative to the stigma--real or imagined--of public housing projects. Participant attitudes can be assessed by examining survey and interview responses.

In short, the North Dakota agency tried to meet a series of goals that included:

1. Achieve full participation
2. Attain financial feasibility
3. Improve the living situation of recipients
4. Serve a cross-section of eligible households
5. Gain the acceptance--or at least avoid the rejection--of the program by the local community
6. Maintain the dignity of program participants.

The North Dakota experiment was a coherent effort that fit well in the local area. The program was built on the idea that most of the participants were honest and capable of managing their own lives with a minimum of interference from public agencies. Giving social services that were not needed was seen by the new staff as a way of making people dependent. People who couldn't manage for themselves were, in turn, people who were different from other North Dakotans. The agency's approach to housing allowances held that recipients were average people who lacked but one thing: enough money to get decent housing. This attitude, as it was reflected by the staff that ran the program, went a long way toward allowing participants to keep a feeling of dignity.

The appeal of the AAE "message" was enhanced, no doubt, by the homogeneity of the population within the program area. Almost all were white, literate, even middle-class. They subscribed to the same set of values that the agency staff members did. Unlike many other sites, in the North Dakota program area one has to look for evidence of a "culture of poverty" that can make the administration of any assistance program difficult.

A very high percentage of those enrolled in the North Dakota experiment were able to meet all the requirements and receive payments. The majority of the recipients did not move to different units. The improvement in housing was in the form of reduced rent burden. Since the agency was required to impose a housing standard, the goal of full participation was made easier by a good, modest, housing stock.

Having a high rate of enrollees success in the housing market helped other aspects of the program as well. Full registration made financial feasibility possible. Every active participating household released additional funds from HUD under the terms of the contract.

Careful monitoring and a program approach that avoided wholesale referrals of high-payment welfare recipients also insured the fiscal viability of the experiment.

Demographic balance was easier to achieve in North Dakota than at any other site. As noted previously, the population was almost entirely white; hence, over-subscription by minorities was not the problem it was at other sites.

The agency also tried to reduce administrative expenditures whenever possible. The management style resulted in more than mere financial feasibility. It resulted in austerity. When coupled with a low public profile, the likelihood of adverse community reaction was lessened.

In the foregoing ways, the North Dakota agency achieved it successess. The effort was largely the result of a single individual, the program director. He wrote the plans and ran the agency. As a native of the state, he was familiar with the values of North Dakotans and the images they have of themselves. While the chance to have a housing allowance project was offered by outsiders, the actual form that the program would take was determined by an insider.

As a senior official within the contracting agency, the director knew how to use the resources of the welfare organization to good advantage. At the same time, he avoided those aspects of public assistance that he did not want associated with the new program. His experience also meant that the contracting agency was willing to let him run the program his own way.

The director recruited young, enthusiastic staff members who were willing to implement the program as he had envisioned it. In this way, little was lost in the translation from plans to action.

Certain skills in project and financial management were also possessed by this individual. The North Dakota experiment was able to run with a minimum of difficulty. There was a sense of purpose. Fiscal austerity itself fit well within the North Dakota value system.

The experimental effort approached North Dakotans --inside and outside the program--in terms of their own values and culture.

The Structure of This Book

The first part of this chapter has laid out the arguments upon which the remainder of this book rests. Further illustration and analysis will be required to convince the reader that the position taken is a valid one.

The remainder of this chapter is taken up with the details of the AAE, the requirements imposed by HUD, the other participating agencies, the data sources used, and the role of the OSO. Also included is a glossary of technical terms used in the experiment. Acronyms abound. I have tried to minimize these as much as possible by using only the most important ones as a convenient shorthand. These neologisms are explained once in the text, or else in the form of a starred footnote at the bottom of the page in which the terms appears. The glossary, then, is an aid to the forgetful, who I imagine will include most of those who do not have to use government Newspeak on a daily basis.

The second chapter describes the setting in which the North Dakota AAE operated. The description focuses upon the program area (which comprised four counties), the people, and their values. This chapter shows that there is a distinctive Great Plains culture, of which North Dakota is a variant.

Chapter 3 is an account of the launching of the project. The narrative begins in March, 1973, when the Social Service Board was first approached by HUD. Since I was not on site at the time, this period has been reconstructed on the basis of in-depth interviews with the original staff members. In addition, certain "historical memoranda" from the agency, from HUD, and from Abt Associates, all proved useful in doing this task. The chapter shows the planning process, the meetings between various parties, and the red tape that had to be dealt with before the housing agency could be created.

Chapter 4 outlines the staffing strategy used by the program director once the required plans had been approved and the contracts signed. The timetable of the experiment was such that the program had to get underway quickly if the North Dakota agency was to make use of the full seven month enrollment period.

Chapter 5 breaks away from a strictly chronological approach in that it gives the agency director's intentions for handling the outside community and then uses certain events to illustrate how the welfare offices were actually discouraged from sending over their caseloads for enrollment in the AAE. This prevented the director from losing control of the program at a very early stage of its development.

The sixth chapter continues the abstractions that began a few pages earlier. Here, "Mrs. Feist"

--a fictitious participant--applies, enrolls, and becomes a recipient. The purpose of the piece is to orient the reader to how the agency operated vis-a-vis the participants. Using a "typical participant," such as "Mrs. Feist," is useful in that the reader can become acquainted with everyday operations of the agency before he has to deal with larger issues that had to do with the program itself.

The seventh chapter is an historical narrative. This part of the book shows how the program developed over time.

Sub-headings are used to denote different phases of the experiment. Coverage begins wiht the start-up of the agency and ends with the preparations for the final year of the project. Due to the short-term nature of the AAE, the life span of an agency and a social program was compressed into a period of three years.

Case histories of seven participant households make up the eighth chapter of the book. These families are followed over a year's time. The experiences of each household are described and then analyzed to ascertain the effect of the program upon a small, disparate, but intensely observed sample.

Much of the material for this book was drawn from a case study I wrote for the evaluation. The North Dakota agency is studied in isolation from the other projects in the AAE. The final chapter departs from this mode. The North Dakota "outcomes" are measured against those of other sites. This provides the reader with an opportunity to see how the North Dakota approach worked relative to the ones employed by other agencies. The comparison cannot be strictly controlled, however, due to the naturalistic research design that was used. If the AAE had been designed as a more traditional piece of evaluation research, it is likely that anthropologists would not have been stationed on-site and this work could not have been written in its present form.

Since the analytic chapter is the final one, conclusions to the book are given. Backed by both qualitative and quantitative data, the arguments presented earlier in this chapter may remain assertions, but they are at least documented and analyzed assertions.

Lastly, there are three appendices. The first contains a chronology of significant program events that took place during the coverage period of this book. Usually, these are program milestones of some sort. Also included are materials on the backgrounds of each staff member. The second appendix contains relevant forms and documents used internally by the agency. The third appendix contains forms used by Abt Associates Inc. for purposes of the analysis.

A Note On Style

In writing this book, I have attempted to portray the character of agency operations and to elucidate the underlying, motive philosophy behind the North Dakota effort as well. In order to give a rounded impression of the agency, staff activities, and the milieu in which operations occurred, I have employed certain novelistic, or filmic techniques[3]. This account of the North Dakota AAE is told in narrative fashion. In the main body of the book, italics are used either to offset my own reflections, or to report certain incidents at which I was physically present.

There are two exceptions to the above rule. In the fictitious story of "Mrs. Feist," italics are used whenever the agency and "Mrs. Feist" are interacting. In the participant histories, my presence is much more visible. I have elected to keep myself in boldface **type**. This reflects the conditions under which the data for this chapter were gathered. Whereas I was at the agency on a daily basis, I visited the participants every few weeks. I was a guest. The participants reacted to me in a much more obvious fashion than the agency people who had gotten used to having me around. Italics are frequently used to denote final visits.

Given that this book uses local context and culture as an explanation vehicle, I have used localisms wherever appropriate and whenever they are not confusing. For example, terms of address and reference may not appear to be consistent--at first glance. This is not the case, however. I found that males tend to refer to each other by their last names--much like in the military--while females, at least until middle age, are referred to by their first names. With this in mind, the usage becomes consistent, though different from many other parts of the country. Retaining such localisms gives a more correct rendering of North Dakota reality--at least as it presented itself to me.

THE EIGHT AAE SITES

The design of the Administrative Agency Experiment

was such that not only were eight public organizations chosen as contracting agencies, but also, they were matched pairs of four different types. The eight agencies selected to participate in the AAE are listed and categorized as follows:

> Local Housing Authorities (LHAs):
>   Tulsa Housing Authority (THA)
>   Housing Authority of the City of Salem, Oregon (HAS)
>
> Public Welfare Agencies:
>   Durham County Department of Social Services (DSS)
>   Social Service Board of North Dakota (SSB-ND)
>
> State Organizations supervising housing programs:
>   Commonwealth of Massachusetts Department of Community Affairs (DCA)
>   State of Illinois Department of Local Government Affairs, Office of Housing and Buildings (DLGA-OHB)
>
> Interjurisdictional Organizations:
>   Jacksonville Department of Housing and Urban Development (JHUD)
>   San Bernardino County Board of Supervisors

The contracting agencies were charged with the responsibility of writing a series of plans for their version of the AAE and creating a new agency to implement the program. In most cases, personnel from within the contracting agencies were also responsible for heading the newly-created agencies.

Selection of the contracting agencies was an involved process that stretched out over the better part of a year. The central office of HUD, located in Washington, D. C., contacted the regional HUD offices and asked them each to recommend candidates for an AAE site within their own jurisdictions. In making the final choices, the central office employed several criteria.

One of the most important determiners was the competency of the contracting agencies themselves. All of the organizations which were offered a site by HUD had impressive track records in running public programs of various types. Indeed, this was probably how they first came to the attention of the regional HUD offices.

Another important criterion was the willingness of the local governments to accept an experimental program operating within its jurisdiction. One agency, located in the state of New York, advanced to the stage of writing the preliminary plan, only to discover that the local government would not grant the necessary approvals. The organization was dropped from consideration and another one substituted in its place.

Other factors beyond agency type influenced the final selections. These included agency location, population characteristics, housing markets and stock, and the character of the proposed program area. These key site characteristics are discussed in detail so that the place of the North Dakota agency within the total scheme of the AAE can be easily visualized.

Regional Data

There are nine census regions within the United States. Six of these areas had an AAE site. This dispersion was planned so that a wide variety of populations and housing markets would be served by the experiment and thus provide a test of direct cash assistance in different settings. In the Middle Atlantic, East South Central, and Mountain regions, there were no sites. The omission of the second of these regions is the most serious. The area is largely rural, ranks the lowest in overall housing quality and percentage of public funds spent on public welfare, and has the highest incidence of poverty. As shown in Table 1-1, the North Dakota site is from among the most rural of the regions which were represented in the experiment.

Of the 248 urbanized areas in this country, approximately 200 were included within the census regions that had an AAE site. However, the size of the particular urbanized areas in which the eight sites were located is more restricted.

Large cities were excluded from consideration by HUD. It was felt that the impact of a program which would serve 900 households in any one locality would not prove to be a meaningful test of cash allowances. Cities of this type have large housing markets which could easily absorb this number of people looking for better housing. Also, there would be potential problems in managing such a program.

Extremely rural areas were excluded for the opposite reason. As Table 1-2 shows, the North Dakota site had the smallest population. The program area spanned four counties and the largest city within its boundaries was less than 35,000. It was felt that a program area with fewer than 100,000 would have too small a housing market to absorb the low-income enrollees without causing inflation which

TABLE 1-1

U.S. REGIONAL DATA AND THE AAE SITES

Census Regions	% Urban	Median Family Income	% Families Below Poverty	% Direct General Public Welfare*	% Housing Units Lacking One or More Plumbing Facilities	Number of Urbanized Areas in Region	AAE Sites
Northeast							
New England	76.4	10,613	6.7	9.2	3.5	24	Springfield
Middle Atlantic	81.7	10,395	7.9	9.4	2.9	26	
North Central							
East North Central	74.7	10,560	7.5	4.5	4.0	48	Peoria
West North Central	63.7	8,982	10.1	6.2	5.8	20	Bismarck
South							
South Atlantic	63.6	8,539	14.0	4.6	9.5	40	Durham, Jacksonville
East South Central	54.6	7,166	21.0	.6	16.5	14	
West South Central	72.7	7,964	16.8	.4	7.7	40	Tulsa
West							
Mountain	73.2	9,070	10.9	4.5	4.0	14	
Pacific	86.0	10,600	8.3	11.0	1.8	22	Salem, San Bernardino

Source: U.S. Census 1970, Public Use Sample

*Percent of total local revenues spent on Public Assistance, a proxy for priority given to welfare expenditures.

would negate the effect of the housing allowances. Further, rural areas also tend to have high percentages of home owners. This would make it even more difficult for participants to find housing, had such areas been included. (The AAE was designed as a program for renters.)

While there was no strictly rural site, four of the agencies had program areas that included rural portions. The four sites are: Durham, Salem, Peoria, and North Dakota. Of these, North Dakota approximated a truly rural area most closely. The counties which make up the program area in North Dakota have only fifteen people per square mile, which ranks them among the lowest population densities in the country. However, four small population centers, which contained the bulk of the people in the counties, had much higher densities, up to 2400 people per square

TABLE 1-2

PROGRAM AREAS OF THE EIGHT AAE SITES*

Agency Location	Population of Program Area**	Geographic Areas Included in Program Jurisdiction	Type of Urban/ Rural Situation
Salem, Oregon	93,041	Salem Metropolitan area	Medium sized city with adjacent growth area (10 mile radius)
Springfield, Massachusetts	472,917	Springfield Metropolitan area (4 cities and 15 surrounding towns)	Area of multiple, medium sized cities and towns
Peoria, Illinois	196,865	City of Peoria and Fulton County (rural) and Woodford County (rural)	Medium sized city with nearby rural areas
San Bernardino, California	547,258	Valley portion of San Bernardino County (includes 10 incorporated cities and towns and an equal number of unincorporated places)	Area of multiple medium sized cities
Bismarck, North Dakota	104,187	Four rural counties (Burleigh, Morton, Stark and Stutsman) each with one major city	Small cities and towns with surrounding rural areas
Jacksonville, Florida	545,900	Consolidated City of Jacksonville (includes all of Duval county)	Large Metropolitan area
Durham, North Carolina	132,681	Durham County (includes city of Durham as well as rural portion of county)	Medium sized city with adjacent rural area
Tulsa, Oklahoma	342,000	City of Tulsa	Large Metropolitan area

* Population figures taken from agency estimates in Detailed Plans, with the exceptions of Durham, which is the 1970 Census total for the County of Durham (Durham Plan used city data only); and Salem, which is the 1970 census total for the urbanized area of Salem (Salem plan used SMSA data).

mile. Taken in all, the eight program areas are in no way unrepresentative of the country as a whole, barring the existence of metropolitan areas in excess of 600,000 people.

Population Data

The sites encompassed a variety of populations demographically and economically. One salient indicator of population characteristics for a public assistance program is the percent of families below the poverty level as defined by the 1970 Census. Such statistics provide a rough indication of the relative need for housing assistance among the sites. There is one important qualifier, however. The 1970 Census defined "poverty" for a four-person family as being less than $3,473 in annual income. For the housing allowance experiment, the eligibility limits were set much higher, almost twice as high. While the precise income limits varied from site to site in order to reflect local conditions, a family of four could still qualify for a payment if it made as much as $7,000 per year.

Figure 1-1 shows that in the city of Bismarck*, 7.4 percent of the families were below the poverty line. This is about midway between the extremes in the AAE.

The number of households below the poverty line is not a good indicator of the true number of households that were eligible to participate in the AAE. This is due to two reasons. First, as was previously mentioned, the eligibility limits for income were set high. This would tend to expand the number of eligibles. However, the exclusion of homeowners from the program meant that the number of eligible households was correspondingly reduced. Each agency was required to estimate the number of households who could theoretically be served by a program such as the AAE if enrollment had not been limited. Most of the agencies erred on the high side, a factor which influenced the course of the program in many instances. More reliable estimates are given in Table 1-3.

---

*One of the difficulties in analyzing the North Dakota site is that it contains no Standard Metropolitan Statistical Area (SMSA). Hence, reliable statistics are difficult to obtain and often must be extrapolated. In much of the background material, site characteristics refer to the city of Bismarck, rather than to the North Dakota, or "Bismarck" site.

15

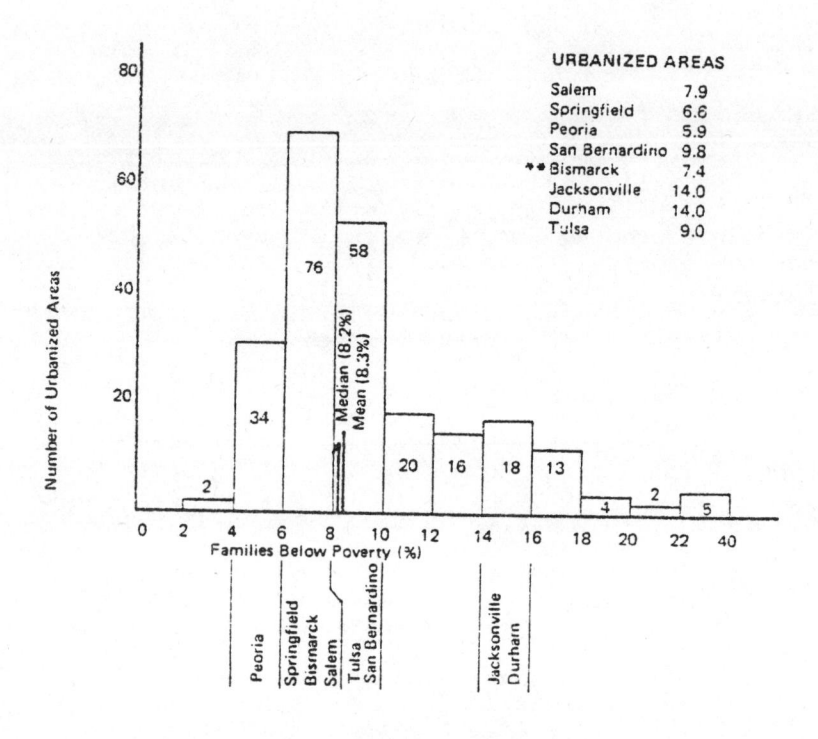

Figure 1-1: Percent of Families in Urbanized Areas Below Poverty Level*

Source: County and City Data Book, 1972 (Based on 1970 Census) Determination of Median Not Weighted by Population.

* As defined for 1970 Census.

** City of Bismarck.

TABLE 1-3

ELIGIBLE POPULATION AND HOUSEHOLDS ENROLLED IN AAE

Site	Eligible Households In Program Area	Eligible Households as % of Total Households in Program Area	Enrolled Households	Enrolled Households as % of Total Eligible Households
Salem	6,993	12%	1,108	16%
Springfield	21,054	15%	1,209	6%
Peoria	6,049	11%	1,445	24%
San Bernardino	22,369	14%	1,004	4%
Bismarck	2,673	9%	499	19%
Jacksonville	21,177	13%	1,035	5%
Durham	6,764	17%	732	11%
Tulsa	10,702	9%	1,068	10%

Source: 1970 Census of Population (data from Fourth Count Population - one in one hundred Public Use Sample are combined). "Eligible Households" are limited to renter households.

The North Dakota agency had both the fewest number of eligible households and the lowest percentage of eligibles relative to the population-at-large. It also had the largest program area. This meant that this particular agency faced the possibility of having a genuine shortage of enrollees.

A final population statistic is the percentage of minorities residing within the program areas. Segregated housing markets can pose problems for a housing program where the recipients are not living in a concentrated housing allowance project. Because of this, HUD wanted at least some of the sites to have a significant number of minorities.

In Figure 1-2, the eight sites are compared to the other urbanized regions in the country:

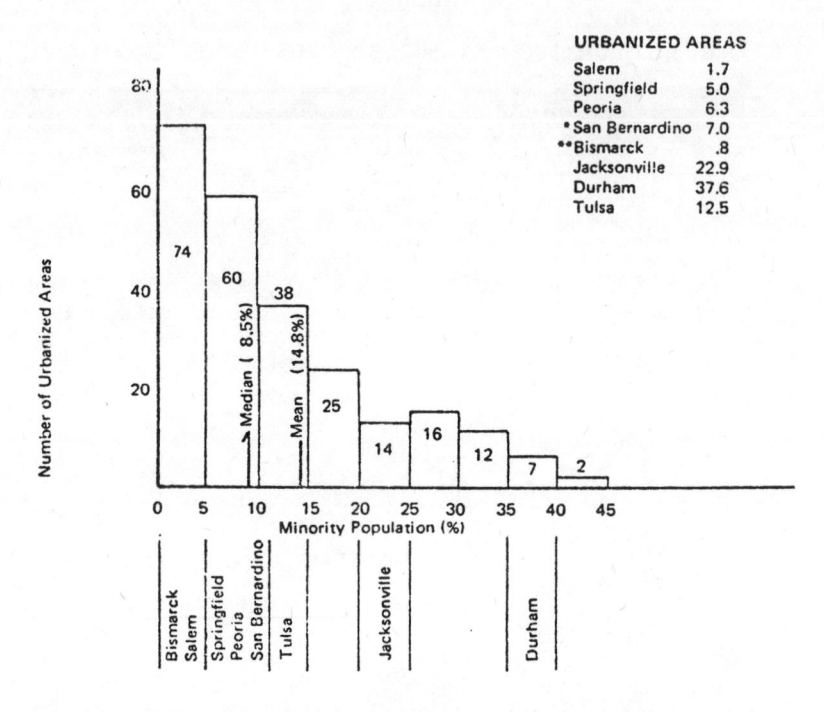

[Bar chart showing Number of Urbanized Areas vs Minority Population (%):
- 0-5%: 74 (Bismarck, Salem)
- 5-10%: 60 (Springfield, Peoria, San Bernardino) — Median (8.5%)
- 10-15%: 38 (Tulsa) — Mean (14.8%)
- 15-20%: 25
- 20-25%: 14 (Jacksonville)
- 25-30%: 16
- 30-35%: 12
- 35-40%: 7 (Durham)
- 40-45%: 2]

URBANIZED AREAS
Salem	1.7
Springfield	5.0
Peoria	6.3
*San Bernardino	7.0
**Bismarck	.8
Jacksonville	22.9
Durham	37.6
Tulsa	12.5

Figure 1-2:   Percent Minority In Urbanized Areas
              (Negro and Others)

Source: County and City Data Book, 1972 (Based on
          1970 Census) Determination of Median Not
          Weighted by Population.

* Figure for San Bernardino underestimates minority
  population, urbanized area has additional 16% of
  "Persons of Spanish Lanugage or Spanish Surname."

** City of Bismarck.

For the most of the AAE sites, "minority" meant black populations; however, for the San Bernardino site, the most significant minority group was persons of Spanish language or Spanish surname. The North Dakota and Salem program areas are unusual in that they are almost entirely white. In the case of North Dakota, this was due to a quirk in the program regulations which excluded Amerindian reservations for reasons explained later in the text.

Housing Market Characteristics

The AAE required that all households receiving payments live in housing that was "decent, safe, and sanitary." Participating agencies were required to set standards that met the minimum housing requirements of other leased housing programs run by the federal government. The physical condition of "typical" modest housing in the program area, and the availability of that housing--as expressed by the rental vacancy rate--provide data points which may give some prior indication of how difficult it would be to secure acceptable housing in any given site.

Figure 1-3, on the following page, shows the percentage of units within a site that were renter as opposed to owner-occupied. The figure compares the site proportions to those of the other urbanized areas within the country.

The national mean proportion of rental housing is 37.4 percent of all units. Most of the sites are close to this figure. There are two exceptions: Peoria, at 30.9 percent, is slightly below the national median, while Durham, at 53.0 percent, is substantially above it. The city of Bismarck, again taken as representative of the site as a whole, is almost exactly at this mid-point.

The above statistics do not indicate the physical quality of the housing units. While "standardness" is difficult to measure, one proxy measure for it which is used by the census is the percentage of units which are lacking some or all indoor plumbing facilities. It should be stressed, however, that this represents a very lenient standard that was far less stringent than any of those imposed by the agencies. Figure 1-4 compares the sites against the urbanized areas in the country.

The North Dakota site shows one of the higher incidences of housing that lacked basic plumbing facilities--3.3 percent. However, more updated data shows that the census overstated the number of such dwellings. Below, the sites are ranked according to the 1970 Census (Column A) and according to more recently available information (Column B):

HOUSING QUALITY

Lower % substandard	A. Census Sources	B. Information from updated sources*
↑	San Bernardino	Salem
	Salem	City of Bismarck
	Tulsa	San Bernardino
	Springfield	Tulsa
↓	Durham	Springfield
	Peoria	Durham
Higher %	City of Bismarck	Peoria
substandard	Jacksonville	Jacksonville

* See Table 1-4 for sources

URBANIZED AREAS

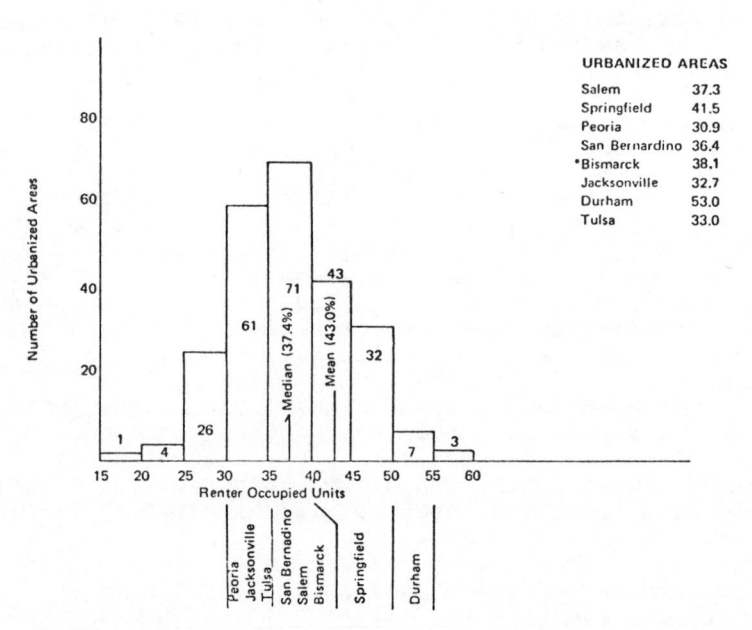

Salem	37.3
Springfield	41.5
Peoria	30.9
San Bernardino	36.4
*Bismarck	38.1
Jacksonville	32.7
Durham	53.0
Tulsa	33.0

Figure 1-3 Percent of Housing Units in Urbanized Areas Renter Occupied
Source: County and City Data Book, 1972 (Based on 1970 Census) Determination of Median not Weighed by Number of Units
*City of Bismarck

While most of the sites experience only minor reordering, the city of Bismarck, which has housing stock that is typical of the remainder of the North Dakota program area, moves up sharply from having one of the highest percentage of units that lack plumbing facilities, to having one of the lowest. The correctness of the rating, based upon updated sources, was confirmed independently by a "windshield survey" conducted by Abt Associates Inc. at each of the sites. The consensus of the evaluators, and the OSO as well, was that the area had modest housing stock. Absent were slum dwellings, on the one hand, and housing in the $50,000-plus range, on the other. This would prove to be an important factor when enrollees were trying to find new units that would meet the agency's standards.

Another factor which could have a bearing on a housing allowance program is the rental vacancy rate in a locale. Irrespective of the presence or absence of segregated housing patterns, or the quality of the stock itself, program enrollees would potentially face a difficult time locating decent units if the rental markets were "tight." "Tight" and "loose" are relative terms. According to a variety of sources, a 5 percent vacancy rate is the rule of thumb established for a workable housing allowance program.[4] Figure 1-5 shows the census-derived vacancy rates for the AAE sites as compared with other urbanized areas.

At the time of the census, the AAE sites tended to be around the median for rental vacancy rates. The two exceptions to this were Tulsa, which has a good housing stock, and Jacksonville, which has a poor one.

The rental vacancy rate is something which is subject to extreme fluctuation. Loss of population can loosen the market, as can new construction. Conversely, a rapid rise in population, if there is no corresponding building boom, can result in a shrinking market for anyone who is looking for a new place to live. In the case of Jacksonville, for instance, an influx of military personnel into the area during the first few months of the program probably reduced the supply of good units considerably.

The more recent data show some minor reordering of the sites relative to each other. Detailed information as the the nature of the market is given in Table 1-4. Briefly, the more recent sources suggest a rank ordering as follows:

21

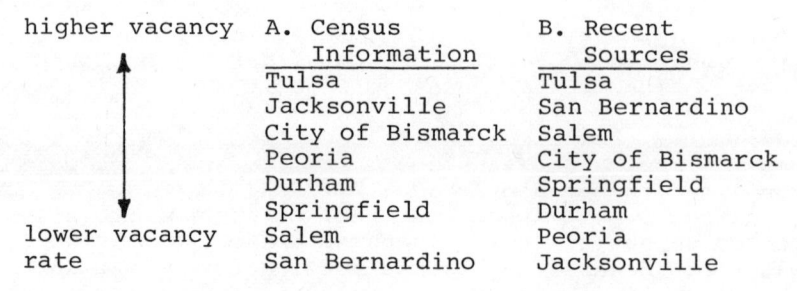

```
higher vacancy   A. Census              B. Recent
      ↑             Information              Sources
      |          Tulsa                   Tulsa
      |          Jacksonville            San Bernardino
      |          City of Bismarck        Salem
      |          Peoria                  City of Bismarck
      |          Durham                  Springfield
      ↓          Springfield             Durham
lower vacancy    Salem                   Peoria
rate             San Bernardino          Jacksonville
```

The newer data sources do little to affect the ranking of the North Dakota site. Similarly, neither the census rental vacancy rate (7.4 percent), nor the more recent rate (6.1 percent) vary much from the mean of the urbanized areas in the United States (6.8 percent). However, as this chapter points out, Bismarck, the state capital, was rising in population, as were the other cities in the program area. It is possible that even the 6.1 percent figure quoted above is much too high.

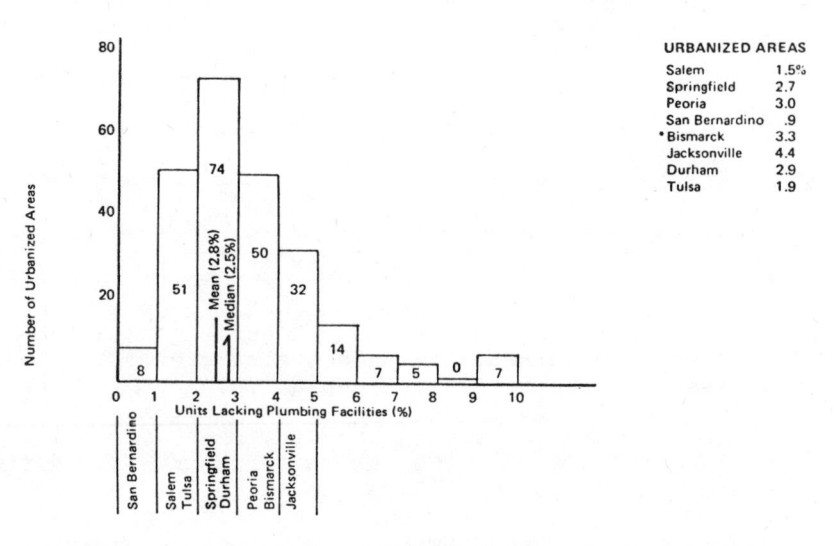

URBANIZED AREAS
Salem   1.5%
Springfield   2.7
Peoria   3.0
San Bernardino   .9
*Bismarck   3.3
Jacksonville   4.4
Durham   2.9
Tulsa   1.9

Figure 1-4:   Percent of Units in Urbanized Areas Lacking Some Or All Plumbing Facilities

Source: County and City Data Book, 1972 (Based on 1970 Census)   Determination of Median Not Weighted by Total Number of Housing Units

URBANIZED AREAS	
Salem	5.7
Springfield	5.9
Peoria	6.6
San Bernardino	5.6
*Bismarck	7.4
Jacksonville	11.6
Durham	6.1
Tulsa	13.1

*City of Bismarck
Source: *County and City Data Book, 1972 (Based on 1970 Census)*
Determination of Median Not Weighted by Population
Mean Not Available

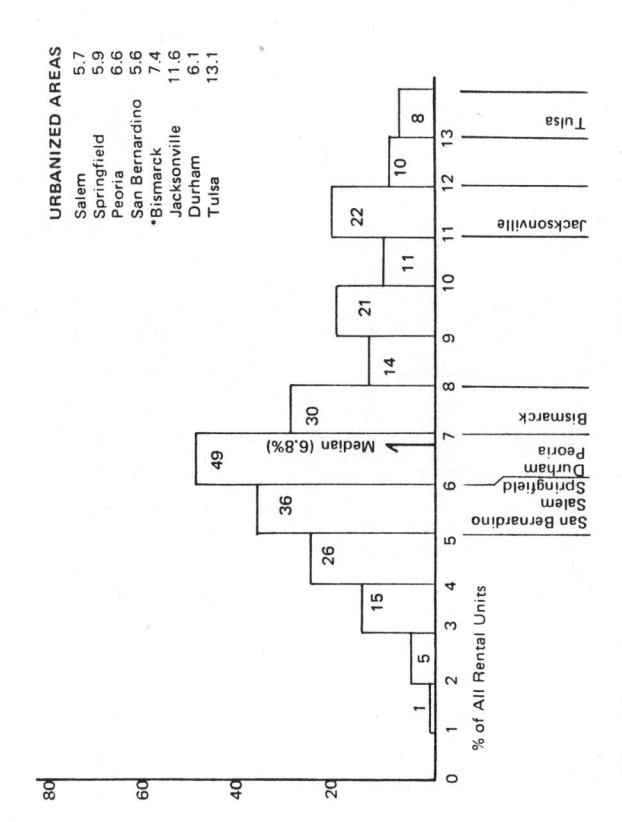

Figure 1-5 Rental Vacancy Rate in Urbanized Areas

22a

Table 1-4

UPDATED HOUSING MARKET INFORMATION ON AAE PROGRAM AREAS

Agency	Housing Condition	Availability
Salem	Housing generally good, 1974 study estimates 8 percent of total occupied units substandard, many single family structures.[1]	Rental vacancy rate was at its peak at start of AAE; postal survey in March, 1972, indicates rental vacancy rate of 7.2 percent; postal survey (for apartments only) in October, 1972, reported apartment vacancy rate of 10 percent.[3]
Springfield	Housing stock old in the city (sixty percent over forty years old); City Planning Department estimated (1973) that fifteen percent of all occupied units in city were substandard, and that as high as thirty percent to forty percent were substandard in central city neighborhoods; many multiple unit structures.[4]	1970 rental vacancy rate for city was 6.2 percent; most of the vacent rental units are in old buildings, many substandard.[5]

Salem

1. *Regional Housing Statistical Profile*, Regional Housing Program, 1974.

2. *Housing Market Analysis, Salem, Oregon*, Department of Housing and Urban Development (HUD), Federal Housing Administration (FHA), Economic and Market Analysis, March 1, 1972.

3. *Neglected Housing Needs, A Low Income Regional Housing Analysis*, September, 1973.

Springfield

4. *Problems, Progress and a Program*, Third Edition, Springfield City Planning Department, April, 1974.

5. 1970 *Census of Housing*.

Agency	Housing Condition	Availability
Peoria	Housing stock in central city neighborhood is generally old (fifty percent over thirty years old); very high percentage lacking plumbing in these areas, many multiple unit structures.[6]	Rental vacancy rate for city was estimated at 4.5 percent (July 1970), most in older units.[7]
San Bernardino	Housing fairly new, much built after WWII, suburban, single family detached; also large number of new multfamily apartments have improved area's stock.[8]	Overbuilding of rental units 1970-73 has increased rental vacancy rate of almost twelve percent (October 1973);[9] however, general deficiency of low rent units for families with income under $5,000.[10]

Peoria

6. *Tri-County Regional Housing Report, Peoria, Tazewell and Woodford Counties, Illinois,* December 1973.

7. *Analysis of the Peoria, Illinois Housing Market* (as of July 1, 1970) HUD, FHA. Economic and Market Analysis Division.

San Bernardino

8. *Analysis of Riverside-San Bernardino, California Housing Market,* (as of October 1, 1973), HUD, FHA, Economic and Market Analysis Division.

9. *Ibid.*

10. *Housing,* East Valley Planning Agency, August, 1971, San Bernardino County Planning Department.

Agency	Housing Condition	Availability
Bismarck	City of Bismarck is typical of area; generally good standard housing, many single family structure.[11]	Housing study (1971) reports rental vacancy rate of 6.1 percent, most vacant for rent are standard.[12]
Jacksonville	Jacksonville Area Planning Board reported the following in 1972 housing study: "Housing in Jacksonville has relatively low median value and the average unit is of mediocre quality, estimate fifteen percent of all occupied units are substandard,"[13] 1970 Census suggests much higher percentage for center city areas.[14]	A rental vacancy survey conducted by City Community Renewal Program (1973) for twenty-five percent of city's rental units concluded that four percent would be most realistic assessment of vacancy rate and that eighty percent of these were of such low rent that they were probably substandard.[15]

Bismarck

11. *Bismarck Housing Analysis,* Harmon, O'Donnell and Henninger Associates, Inc., Denver, Colorado, May 1972.

12. *Ibid.*

Jacksonville

13. *Housing Market and Needs Analysis,* Jacksonville Planning Board, July 1972.

14. *1970 Census of Housing.*

15. "Jacksonville Rental Vacancy Survey," Jacksonville Community Renewal Program, January 24, 1973.

Agency	Housing Conditions	Availability
Durham	Estimate based on City Planning Department data indicates that fourteen percent of city's occupied units fail to meet city's minimum standards;[16] estimate of substandard units for rural county areas was nineteen percent.[17]	1972 housing market study estimated rental vacancy rate of six percent; vacant units in central city areas are generally substandard;[18] inadequate supply of vacant standard housing for low income families was cited as major problem for city during the '70s.[19]

Durham

16. "Substandard Housing in Durham" Durham Morning Herald editorial, November 17, 1973, based on Durham City Planning Department figures.

17. "Rural Housing Problems in the Triangle J Region and Prospects for Their Solution," July, 1973.

18. *Analysis of the Durham, N. C. Housing Market* (as of January 1, 1972), HUD, FHA, Economic and Market Analysis Division.

19. *The Housing Needs of Low and Moderate Income Households in Durham, 1967-75,* Morton Hoffman and Co., May 1968.

Agency	Housing Condition	Availability
Tulsa	Housing generally good, large amount of multi-family apartment constructions 1970-72 has improved stock; housing study undertaken in 1971 estimated that 8.6 percent of all occupied units in the "Central Sector" of the city were substandard.[20]	Very high rental vacancy rate; 1972 housing market study estimates rental vacancies at 13.6 percent; also noted that if units of marginal and substandard condition were removed from the stock, the rental vacancy rate would still be twelve percent.[21]

26

Tulsa

20. *Regional Housing Study, Volume II,* Indian Nations Council of Governments, June, 1971.

21. *Analysis of Tulsa, Oklahoma Housing Market* (as of January 1, 1972) HUD, FHA, Economic and Market Analysis Division.

Disregarding any changes in the tightness of the housing market that may not have been reflected in published materials, it can be said that, as a whole, the AAE sites had rather ordinary rental vacancy rates. Except for Tulsa, none of the sites had a great surplus of good units and none but Jacksonville had a dire shortage, either.

Summary

Overall, the eight AAE sites were rather ordinary in a statistical sense. On almost every measure, the sites occupy a mid-range on the indices for urbanized areas. Geographic coverage is not complete, although it is nearly so. The most serious omissions seem to be cities over one-half million people and a site—other than Jacksonville—in the deep South that had poor housing and an impoverished citizenry.

Compared to other sites, North Dakota had an ethnically homogeneous population, a sparsely populated but expansive program area, and a good housing stock. The rental market was characterized by a medium vacancy rate which was possibly declining. These were features beyond the agency's control. When combined with the agency's philosophy and administration, these factors shaped the outcome of the North Dakota experiment.

EXPERIMENTAL DESIGN

Although the AAE was a naturalistic experiment, it was not unstructured. Agencies planned their own versions of a housing allowance program, but were constrained by rules and regulations set forth in a planning guide furnished by Abt Associates Inc. Variation was encouraged. The task of Abt Associates Inc., as the evaluation contractor, then became to identify what variations occurred and, if possible, what differences they made.

TABLE 1-5: SUMMARY FILE - CHARACTERISTICS OF THE 8 AAE SITES

Location of Administrative Agency	Contracting Agency	Character of Site			Demographics				Housing			
		Location	Population of Program Area	Density (Geographic Character)	% Families Below Poverty	% Minority	No. Eligible Population (Households)	Eligible Households as % of Total Households	% Rental	Condition % Lacking Plumbing	Rental Vacancy Rate [3]
Salem, Oregon	Housing Authority of City of Salem	Pacific West	93,041	Medium Sized city with adjacent growth area	7.9%	1.7%	6,993	12%	37.3%	1.5%	7.2%
Springfield, Massachusetts	Commonwealth of Massachusetts Department of Community Affairs	New England	472,917	Area of multiple medium sized cities and towns	6.6%	5.0%	21,054	15%	41.5%	2.7%	6.2%
Peoria, Illinois	State of Illinois Dept. of Local Government Affairs Office of Housing and Buildings	East North Central	196,865	Medium sized city with nearby rural areas	5.9%	6.3%	6,049	11%	30.9%	3.0%	4.5%
San Bernardino, California	San Bernardino County Board of Supervisors	Pacific West	547,258	Area of multiple medium sized cities	9.8%	23.0%[1]	22,369	14%	36.4%	.9%	12.0%
Bismarck, North Dakota	Social Services Board of North Dakota	West North Central	104,187	Small cities and towns with surrounding rural areas	7.4%	.8%	2,673	9%	38.1%	3.3[2]	6.1%
Jacksonville, Florida	Jacksonville Department of Housing and Urban Development	South Atlantic	545,900	Large metropolitan area	14.0%	22.9%	21,177	13%	32.7%	4.4%	4.0%
Durham, North Carolina	Durham County Department of Social Services	South Atlantic	132,681	Medium sized city with adjacent rural areas	14.0%	37.6%	6,764	17%	53.0%	2.9%	6.0%
Tulsa, Oklahoma	Tulsa Housing Authority	West South Central	342,000	Large metropolitan area	9.0%	12.5%	10,702	9%	33.0%	1.9%	13.6%

Sources: All sources for information in this summary table are found in text of this chapter.

[1] includes 16% "Persons of Spanish Language or Spanish Surname"

[2] more recent housing studies of Bismarck indicate that 1970 census over stated degree of standardness in city's housing.

28

Structured observation--both direct and indirect--was used. A variety of instruments were developed. These were complemented by participant observation. In order to give some form to the data collection and analyses, a set of fourteen administrative "functions" were postulated. These would categorize the activity at each of the agencies for comparison purposes.

Functions

The analytic functions were used for three purposes: planning, budgeting, and evaluation. The following provides a brief definition of each function:

1. Start-up: those administrative and organizational activities undertaken by an agency in preparation for the operation of the experiment.
2. Determination of the Eligible Population: an estimation of the number and type of all households within a program area who may be eligible for program participation.
3. Outreach and Screening: the dissemination of information about the program to those potentially eligible for participation, accepting applications, and reviewing the applications to identify those who may be enrolled in the AAE.
4. Phase-In: the planning and monitoring of participants' enrollment in the program to assure that the enrollees are demographically representative of the eligible population-at-large and that enrollment is timed to avoid disruption of the housing market.
5. Enrollment: processing potential recipients from application to signing of certain documents outlining their rights and responsibilities under the program.
6. Certification and Recertification: the verification of household size and income as reported at application.
7. Counseling: the provision of information and services to enrollees and recipients which assists them in participating in the experiment.
8. Payment Operations: the selection of a payment method and the disbursement of housing allowances to recipients.
9. Audit and Control: the accounting procedures required to budget and control government funds for the experiment.
10. Management Support: the administrative tasks and procedures undertaken to insure the viability of the experiment.

11. Maintenance of Records: the collection of data and keeping of records required to document the experiment.
12. Inspection: the examination of a unit to determine if it meets health and safety standards.
13. Relations with Suppliers and Others: the communications between the agency and other market related groups, such as landlords, with whom enrollees and participants may be in contact.
14. Termination: the completion of the experiment, including the transferral of all remaining recipients to other housing programs and the phase-out of program activities.

Two of the above functions, the determination of the eligible population and termination, were of minor concern for the evaluation. The first was done by the agencies during the planning stages. It was a one-time sort of thing, accomplished under great time pressures, and would tell HUD little about housing allowances that could be used for a national program. Termination was similarly not intended as a part of the analysis at all. HUD was interested in how to run a program, not in how to close one down. Thus, while each agency would run the program for three years, the evaluation would focus only upon the first two of them. The collection of data would be thereby limited in time and scope.

Data Collection

Six different types of data were collected from both agencies and participants. They are:
1. Agency management reports.
2. Operating forms used by agencies for each applicant participant and enrollee.
3. Surveys of participants.
4. Secondary site data.
5. Sampling of agency records.
6. Direct observation of agency activities and interviews with agency staff, members of the community, and selected participants.

The first type of data, agency management reports, were required by HUD and Abt Associates. Each month, agency directors prepared and submitted a progress narrative that was organized according to the relevant administrative functions. These reports also included certain budgeting and scheduling forms. In preparing this book, they were used to check the impressions I had at certain times as they were recorded in my field notes.

Another source of management data was the time sheets that each agency staff member filled out on a weekly basis. Hours worked were allotted to the administrative functions. These data have proved useful in making cost estimates.

The agencies also used a set of operating forms, designed by Abt Associates, to provide data on each participant at each stage of participation. These forms include: an application form, a certification and recertification form, an enrollment form, a payment initiation form, and a termination form. Samples are included in Appendix C. Taken together, these forms provide demographic, economic, and housing information on all applicants, enrollees, recipients, and terminees, regardless of the status that any particular household achieved. Since all agencies used the same set of forms, the data are comparable across sites and are used for the analysis section of this book.

A sample of participating households was surveyed three times at each site. The interviews were conducted at program enrollment, six months later, and then, eighteen months after the initial survey. The original sample at each site was large enough--about 150 households--so that even with normal attrition, the outcomes could still be statistically significant. At each agency, the OSO selected the households randomly. No one at the agency knew who was in the sample. Interviews were conducted by locally-hired people. The survey instruments were used to collect data on participants' attitudes toward their housing, their neighborhoods, the program, and the AAE staff.

Each interviewed household also had its dwelling inspected by the Abt Associates researchers. The first inspection, done on the original unit, provides a baseline against which subsequent changes in quality can be measured.

Community data were collected by the OSO. In addition to the usual census material, the observer was often able to locate locally-commissioned studies and other published materials that were not readily available outside of the program area. This was useful for obtaining a more rounded picture of the local area since, in most cases, the observers were not "natives."

Under the agreements made with HUD, the site observers were to be allowed access to agency records. The degree of access varied from agency to agency. In North Dakota, the files were completely open. This proved to be a valuable resource. One of the features of bureaucracies is that they leave "paper trails". The opportunity to use unobtrusive measures to test field hypotheses is probably much greater than when the anthropologist works in a non-literate society.

The final source of data, direct observation and interviewing, made up the bulk of observer-generated materials. Field notes were kept. In addition, observers completed a series of "function logs." These were submitted at regular intervals. The logs helped structure the observations so that they would be compatible with the quantitative data which was organized according to the fourteen analytic categories previously mentioned.

Staff members were interviewed at their convenience, both in response to special requests made by the analysis working in the home office of Abt Associates, and also at the initiative of the site observer. Local officials, realtors, and landlords were also interviewed in much the same manner.

Analytic Products

Three types of reports were envisioned as the final products of the evaluation. The first of these comprised a series of comparative, functionally-based reports. These were to be dependent upon the quantitative outcomes of each experiment. Each report was to look at a group of related administrative functions. While the focus of each report was subject to change, the working titles were:

> The Enrollment Process, which includes program advertising ("outreach"), application-taking, certification of income and household size, eligibility determination, and providing enrollees with information about their rights and responsibilities under the program.
>
> Participant Services, which includes providing housing information and all other non-financial aid to participants, often in the form of counseling.
>
> Payment Operations, which includes all activities necessary to disburse housing allowance payments to participants.
>
> Program Management, which includes all activities associated with planning, staffing, controlling, and monitoring an agency or a program.

To complement this comparative approach, a series of <u>site case studies</u> was designed. These case studies were to give a more holistic presentation of how the program operated at each of the sites. Local environment was to be taken into account, something which was impossible in the function-based reports. Thus, if a given agency seemed to have a high degree of success in getting minorities into the program, the reasons for this could be explored in the case study. The observer/author was not bound by the analytic functions for his explanations, and a more interpretative approach could be used.

The third type of report consisted of <u>policy</u> recommendations which outlined varions design alternatives for a national housing allowance program. It was to attempt to integrate the function, quantitatively-based reports with the more qualitative case studies. The intent of this report was to describe the "best practices" for attaining policy objectives.

The analysis of the AAE has not been concluded yet. The described reports are in their draft stages. This book relies the most on the case study for the North Dakota agency. However, in order to give a more complete presentation, I have drawn on the other reports and on the quantitative data base as well.

The Role of the Observer

Doing evaluation research is different from the usual work that anthropologists do. This has been the subject of several articles in recent literature.[5] Nevertheless, a few words are in order to clarify the role of the anthropologist in a particular research project, the Administrative Agency Experiment.

The main difference between the traditional role and the one the anthropologists were assigned for the AAE was that the OSOs were not independent agents pursuing their own research. The eight of us were part of an interdisciplinary team. Most of the Abt Associates staff was located in Cambridge. The data we collected were not, originally, for our own use--as this excerpt from a training manual shows:

> Abt staff located in Cambridge, Massachusetts will analyze the data according to the research design. Every effort should be made by the OSO to distinguish between

hir* job of <u>OBSERVATION</u> and <u>DATA COLLECTION</u> and the evaluation role or the Abt analysts in Cambridge.[6]

The OSOs were envisioned as recording devices—a far cry from Edward H. Spicer's hopeful vision of anthropologists finally getting "their hands dirty with value choices under circumstances that force them to experience the process as responsible policymakers."[7] Rather, the job description was closer to a more pessimistic one that I recently expressed as the anthropologist as "go-fer."[8] We were expected to provide the soft, mushy, observational grist for the quantitative analytic mill.

In reality, the job gradually worked out to be something between the two extremes. It was soon found that complete, "objective" detachment from the site situation was neither attainable nor desirable. While the OSOs dutifully completed their logs, there was still the problem of interpretation. A log entry or field note could describe a new procedure and give the reasons why it was adopted. However, the consequences of a policy change lay outside the realm of "pure" observation.

The site observers were asked to analyze and to speculate. Debriefing sessions, held periodically at the Cambridge offices, resulted in new homework assignments for many of us. We had to write additional, topical papers on issues relevant to our sites. The distinction between "observer" and "analyst" blurred.

The observers left the sites in late summer, 1974. Instead of simply disappearing—as had been the original plan for avoiding "site bias"—most were retained as consultants to write the case studies. I elected to work at the home office, and eventually assumed responsibility for designing the case studies.

The former OSOs still continue their association with Abt Associates. The site perspective seems to remain critical regardless of the different analytical techniques—qualitative and quantative—that are used on the data.

The extent of the continued use of anthropologists, now that they are no longer at the sites, remains a surprise when one considers our original contracts. Shortly before I wrote this introduction, the "site consultants" completed a three-week stay in

---

*"Hir" is a neologism sometimes used in Abt Associates documents in place of the allegedly sexist "his," or the supposedly more awkward "his/her."

Cambridge. Their task was to assemble and interpret the site data for an upcoming report.

Looking back, I guess it could be said that we were naive in accepting a role that specified only observation and little analytic thinking. It worked out all right, though. Maybe this book shows this.

GLOSSARY

Term	Meaning
Abt Associates Inc. (AAI)	The research firm chosen by HUD to evaluate the Administrative Agency Experiment.
Administrative Agency	The organizations that gave housing allowances to participants.
Administrative Agency Experiment (AAE)	That part of the Experimental Housing Allowance Project designed to answer questions about the administrative issues involved in running a housing allowance program.
Agency Program Manual (APM)	A planning guide and rule book given to each agency in the AAE.
Annual Contributions Contract	The funding mechanism for each AAE agency.
Applicant	One who applied to the AAE, regardless of his/her technical eligibility.
Audit and Control	One of fourteen administrative functions. See page 31.
Brooke Amendment	A federal law which states that no one in a low-income housing project can pay more than 25 percent of his/her net income for rent.
C*	Rent estimates for standard housing at each site.

Term	Meaning
(re)Certification	The verification of applicant statements regarding income, assets, and household size.
Contracting Agency	Any of the eight agencies which were contacted by HUD and agreed to participate in the AAE.
Counseling	An administrative function. See page 29.
Demographic profiles	Target goals which each agency had to meet for minorities, sex of head of household, and other demographic characteristics.
Detailed Plan	The final plan submitted to HUD by each of the agencies. It outlined the approach that would be taken.
Equal Opportunity (EO)	Training received by agency staff and procedures followed to make certain that no discrimination would occur in the AAE.
Functions	Any of fourteen analytic categories created to capture organizational behavior for purposes of the evaluation.
Eligible Applicant	Any applicant who met the eligibility requirements for participation in the AAE.
Enrollment	An analytic function. See page 29.

Term	Meaning
Enrollment Period	A period, usually six to eight months in length, during which an agency could take people into the program.
Evaluation Contractor	Abt Associates Inc.
Experimental Housing Allowance Project (EHAP)	A three-part social experiment, funded by HUD, which was designed to test the concept of housing allowances. Also, EHAP was the term used by many AAE agencies to refer to the Administrative Agency Experiment. See page 1 for further clarification.
Fair Market Rents (FMRs)	The equivalent of C* for the new Section 8 housing program.
Financial Feasibility	A state which is achieved when an agency pays back its initial operating deficit and incoming money exceeds that which is paid out.
Government Accounting Office (GAO)	An arm of Congress responsible for auditing government programs.
Government Technical Representative (GTR)	An individual responsible for monitoring a local social program. GTRs are representatives of a sponsoring federal agency.
Housing Search Period	The sixty to ninety day period during which an individual enrollee had to find standard housing in order to qualify for benefits.

Term	Meaning
Inspection	An administrative function. See page 30.
Letter of Award	An official notification, given by HUD, that informed an agency that it had been chosen to have and AAE site.
Local Housing Authority (LHA)	A local organization, usually county-based, which is authorized to administer HUD programs.
Maintenance of Records	An analytic function. See page 30.
Management Support	An analytic function. See page 29.
North Dakota Department of Social Services (ND-DSS)	The state level welfare organization in North Dakota, the contracting agency for the North Dakota AAE.
Outreach	An analytic function. See page 29.
Phase-In	An analytic function. See, page 29.
Planning Grant	Money received from HUD that allowed an agency to write the plans required for the AAE.
Post-payment Terminee	Any individual who left the AAE after receiving at least one housing allowance payment.
Pre-payment Terminee	Any individual who left the AAE before receiving any benefits.

Term	Meaning
Prudent Person Concept	A welfare term that refers to the judiciousness of the agency staff member who checks income statements made by a person applying for public assistance.
Public Housing Agency (PHA)	Any public organization, regardless of the size of its jurisdiction, which administers housing programs to clients.
Quality Control (QC)	A field review technique used by welfare agencies as a means of auditing the accuracy of the eligibility determination and income certification mechanisms.
Recipient	Someone who is receiving program benefits. Also called a "participant".
Rent Burden	The proportion of household income which goes for rent and utilities.
Screening	An administrative function. See page 29.
Section 23	That part of the housing law which made it possible for the AAE to be funded. Also, Section 23 authorizes an LHA to lease housing on the private market.
Section 8	A new HUD housing program which use housing allowance approaches. It superceded Section 23.
Selected Applicant	An individual who had applied, been found eligible, and been invited to enroll in the AAE.

Term	Meaning
Steady-State	That period, after the first nine months of the AAE, after which no new applicants could be accepted into the program.
Strategic Plan	The preliminary plan, outlining an agency's proposed strategy, submitted to HUD by all AAE agencies.
Termination	Leaving the AAE; also, preparation made by the AAE agencies for ceasing operations at the end of thirty-six months of operations.
U.S. Department of Housing and Urban Development (HUD)	The sponsor of the AAE.
Work Incentive Program (WIN)	A vocational training program for public assistance recipients. Mandatory for all AFDC mothers who have no children under six years of age.
Zero Income	The state of having no income.
Zero Payments	Exceeding the eligibility limits of a program so that no benefits will be forthcoming.

NOTES

1. The two other experiments in the Experimental Housing Allowance Project are:

   1. The Housing Allowance Demand Experiment (HADE) which tests the effect of housing allowances on consumers. HADE provides allowances to 1200 households selected at random in each of two large cities (Pittsburgh, Pennsylvania and Phoenix, Arizona). The allowances are given in several different forms, with

differing requirements. Information is also collected on 600 "control" families which do not receive allowances. The evaluator for the experiment is Abt Associates Inc.
2. The Housing Allowance Supply Experiment (HASE) which focuses upon the market effects of housing allowances. Approximately 9,600 families in South Bend, Indiana and Green Bay, Wisconsin were selected for participation. The program includes both renters and homeowners. Information is collected on the changes that occur in the housing market and responses by housing suppliers, due to the existence of a large-scale housing allowance program. The evaluator is the Rand Corporation.

2. William L. Holshouser, Jr., Report on the Selected Aspects of the Jacksonville Housing Allowance Program, (Cambridge, Abt Associates Inc., 1976). The report concludes that the Jacksonville experiment was plagued by a welfare image which an inadequate outreach effort could not overcome. A disproportionate number of the program applicants were poor blacks. The program image made it hard for these individuals to secure adequate housing in a market that was highly segregated and had low-quality stock. Further, because of an anti-welfare bias in the local area, many housing suppliers would not cooperate with the program.

3. With one exception, however. Since this book is social science research, and not fiction, I have deliberately "flattened" the personalities involved. Two-dimensional characters, in my opinion, allow one to focus better on the program and the agency.

4. I am unable to place the origin of the five percent minimum rental vacancy rate as a prerequisite for a workable housing allowance program. Herbert Gans, in an article entitled, "A Poor Man's Home Is His Poorhouse," states that: "In cities where the vacancy rate is below five percent, insufficient units would be available to enable slum dwellers to take advantage of the allowance." (New York Times Magazine, March 31, 1974), p. 49.
    Robert C. Weaver, a former secretary of HUD, makes a similar assertion in "Housing Allowances," (Land Economics, LI 3, August, 1975.)

5. See Allan F. Burns, "An Anthropologist at Work," (CAE Quarterly, Volume VI, No. 4, pp. 28-34), and Charles A. Clinton, "The Anthropologist as Hired Hand," (Human Organization, Vol. 34, No. 2, pp. 197-204).

6. Abt Associates Inc., On-Site Observers' Handbook, (xerox 1972), p. I-3. Ironically, the manual was written by two of the first anthropologists hired on the project. The distinction between data collection and evaluation is, in the last analysis, an untenable one.

7. Edward H. Spicer, "Anthropology and the Policy Process," (pp. 118-133) in Michael V. Angrosino, ed., Do Applied Anthropologists Apply Anthropology? (University of Georgia Press, Athens, Georgia, (1976), p. 132.

8. See my "The Anthropologist as Go-fer," (A paper presented in the symposium entitled Observational Research in Evaluating Public Policy Paper presented at a meeting of the Society for Applied Anthropology, St. Louis, Missouri, 1976).
   In it, I argue that the field ethnographer is more likely to become a data clerk than he is a "policy maker."

2. North Dakota: The Place, The People

ABOUT NORTH DAKOTA

    When I lived in Minneapolis, North Dakota seemed like a hinterland, peopled by wheat farmers in overalls and by rednecked cowboys. Conservative. Always voting Republican so we could stay out of war. Another thing, people were always coming *from* North Dakota to find jobs. No one I ever heard of left Minnesota to go to North Dakota. It was always the other way around. In the seven years I lived in the Twin Cities, I never actually visited the state, although I had driven through it on the way to the West Coast.

    My friends, when they heard I had decided to take a year's job there, made the necessary, the *required* disparaging remarks. I later found out that Montanans, too, make jokes about North Dakota, and that North Dakotans make jokes about themselves.

    North Dakota exports grain and people. In a forty-year period, from 1930 to 1970, the relative population ranking of the state declined steadily, from thirty-sixth in the nation to forty-fifth.[1] The decrease in population has been reflected in actual numbers, too. From a high of approximately 681,000 in 1929, just before the beginning of the Great Depression and the Dust Bowl, the 1970 Census reported that only 617,761 were now residing in the state. It is not so much that North Dakota has failed to show an increase in its population; rather, the rest of the country has grown dramatically. During the same forty-year period, the total population of the United States increased 65 percent, from 123 million to 203 million.

    The causes of the slow, steady population loss are largely economic. A local source comments:

...World War I with its inflation did not bring prosperity to our state, partly because we could not profit from war industries as did many other states, and partly because we had poor wheat crops between 1914 and 1919 except in 1915, and in that year the wheat price was low. Even with the shortage, wheat was not permitted to rise very much because the federal government set the price at $2.20 when the cash price would have been $3.06.[2]

Post-war deflation and lack of industrial development, the latter continuing to the present, insured that the state would not grow. North Dakota remains an agricultural state, with almost one-third of its employed males being agricultural workers. Principal crops include wheat and cattle, operations which require vast amounts of land. The state is large enough and the population dispersed enough so that only one Standard Metropolitan Statistical Area (SMSA) exists: Fargo. Since the definition of an SMSA specifies a population of at least 50,000 people*, the city barely qualifies.

Population Characteristics

More than 97 percent of North Dakotans are white. The largest single minority are Amerindian. While this ethnic group comprises approximately 79 percent of the non-white population, their actual numbers are less than 14,000.[3] Census figures state that 10,642 Amerindians live in rural areas, but are not engaged in farming.[4] This indicates that most are on a handful of reservations located in various parts of the state. Another thousand or so are in agriculture. The remainder--less than 2000 individuals-- live in cities.

The concentration of minorities upon small geographic areas makes North Dakota appear more homogeneous than it really is. A visitor to rural Emmons County, located in the south-central portion of the state, would probably see no minority families. In contrast, Amerindians are in the majority in Sioux

---

*SMSAs are large urbanized areas for which detailed census statistics are available.

County, which lies just across the Missouri River. This is the location of the Fort Yates reservation. The state's black population is also concentrated in small pockets, wherever there are military installations.

Among the white population some subtle settlement patterns can be observed. The eastern portion of the state is Scandanavian and Lutheran, especially in the Red River Valley that borders Minnesota. As one travels westward, the population becomes more heavily Catholic, the residents there being descendants of the so-called "German Russians" who came over in a later immigration. For all groups, the traditional religions hold sway. Presbyterians, Congregationalists, Methodists, and Unitarians are few. A local writer notes that:

> This "liberalism" in religion has had little appeal to North Dakotans. Others of the native American group like Disciples of Christ, Churches of Christ, Assemblies of God and the various Pentecostal groups tend to be quite conservative. These groups have had very little success in North Dakota because the traditional faiths have more than met the conservative needs and desires.[5]

The writer also states that native-born Americans living in North Dakota were also more likely to move out of the state, thus leaving a residue of immigrants. Indeed, during the days of the Dakota Territory, almost one-half of the people living in what is now North Dakota were born outside of the United States.

Compared with the rest of the United States, North Dakotans have been, and still remain, economically disadvantaged. Per capita income in 1969 was $2,469, a figure which ranked forty-first in the nation.[6] In the immediate area, only South Dakota placed lower. Most of the other poor states are located in the South.

Just as the population characteristics vary within North Dakota, so does income. In 1970, the median income for all families in the state was $7,838[7]. The mean income, which is much more subject to skewing if the distribution is uneven, was somewhat higher: $9,086.[8] Median income for both rural, non-farm families and for rural, farm families was somewhat lower than the state as a whole. The figures are $7,157 and $6,733 respectively[9]. City dwellers are much better off, with a median annual income of just over $9,000 for a typical family[10].

The greatest disparity of income is not between rural and urban people, however. This distinction is reserved for the difference in economic opportunity of whites as compared to Amerindians. While the general census figures indicate that white males in North Dakota have a median annual income of $5,000,[11] a special study of Amerindians shows that males of this group have a median income of almost $2,000 less,[12] Thus, the most dramatic stratifier seems to be race, which is followed only distantly by residence.

In all, it would appear that North Dakota is a poor state, with certain elements within the population being still more economically disadvantaged. Nevertheless, the smallness of the minority population is such that the low socio-economic indicators are reflective of the white population, rather than the status of any other group.

The Land

Driving west on I-94 out of Minneapolis and towards Bismarck is unsettling. The rises level off, and trees become shrubs. The illusion is one of progressive subtraction. If Minnesota is forest and well-watered farm land, then North Dakota is sky over a dessicated bumpy plain.

Country Road-Burleigh County

*It was July, and the temperature was over 100°.
I stopped my car--it was close to overheating anyway
--around lunch time. A metal sign outside the West
Fargo motel-restaurant advertised a steak with the
price of a room. The parking lot was filled, and I
squeezed my small car in next to a pick-up truck. I
noticed that it had an empty gun rack attached to the
inside of the back window. The other cars in the lot
were practical Fords and Chevies, and a few Buicks.
It didn't even look like Volkswagen country. Entering, I was conscious of my long hair and beard.*

*Inside, the place was comfortably crowded, and
men sat hunched over drinks at the long wooden bar.
In another huge room, the steam tables were set up.
I filled up on franks, kraut and beans for a buck and
a half. The crowd was mixed, but male. Truckers in
jeans and long-sleeved shirts sat at their tables.
Men in business suits talked among themselves. No
overalls. The jukebox in the next room had country-western coming out of it: "Satin sheets to lie on,
satin pillows to cry on." The beer cost forty-five
cents extra. I looked up at the high ceiling, and I
felt like I was eating in a furnished airplane hangar...*

North Dakota is a geographical oddity, an area that isn't even "supposed" to be there in the first place. Except on the eastern edge where it is separated from Minnesota by the Red River, there are no natural boundaries; they are all surveyed--conventional, not natural. Eric Sevaried, a North Dakota Hall of Fame notable, recalled how as a school boy he had traced a map of the "meaningless rectangle" that is the state and asked, "Why are we here on the cold flat top of our country. What am I doing here?"[13]

The state's counties are also rectangles, smaller ones within the larger. Roads, too, seem to run at right angles, and small population centers erupt regularly in response to the crossing of any two of them. The smaller the road, the farther away from the arterial highways which follow the old railroad lines, the more insignificant the town. Settlement size is relative in North Dakota. Regional trade centers are usually from 10,000 to 15,000 in population.

It is the native who recalls the state when it is cold. In winter, the out-of-state license plates on the cars of tourists passing through to either coast are not seen. Fewer travelers venture out. The feeling of isolation can become one of desolation.

If August midday can reach 108°, enough to soften the pavement noticeably, then -40° is possible in

January. Winter storms can kick up suddenly, and vision is restricted by "snow-fog"--windblown, dry snow that lies along the roadbed to be stirred up by the tires of passing vehicles. Cars creep along at a treacherous 35 miles per hour, and drivers hope that they won't get behind a semi. The solution then is to barrel through on the left hand lane. The consolation is that the road does not curve.

During other parts of the year, travel is routine, but distances are long. The visitor usually sees the countryside through the tinted glass of an air conditioned automobile, although eventually, by driving far enough and long enough, even the unacquainted become aware of the subtle difference in the open scenery. Contrary to popular outside opinion, the Great Plains bear no resemblance to a billiard table.

The harsh climate of North Dakota, coupled with the relatively level terrain, has had a limiting influence upon the state's economy. Elwyn B. Robinson, an historian, has noted that there are four different regions in North Dakota[14]. In the easternmost corner of the state, there is flat area which is devoted to wheat and mixed-farming operations. There, from the edge of the Red River Valley to the Missouri River, which is located along a north-south axis in the center of the state, most agriculture is based upon wheat. Once this dividing line is crossed, the terrain gets drier and a little more rolling. Wheat and cattle-raising compete for top billing. Finally, in the little Missouri River Valley near the Montana border, wheat gives way almost completely to cattle ranching.[15]

The growing season for the state is 130 days. Wheat needs only 100 days to mature and does best on an annual rainfall of no more than thirty inches. More moisture than this increases crop loss from disease and other factors as well. In good years, the entire area has optimum conditions that produce high-protein durum wheat. Yet, there are times when the rainfall is less than the commonly-thought ideal minimum of fourteen inches. The western third of the state has below this amount of rainfall about one-third of the time and this may account for the increase in beef-cattle operations there. In contrast, the eastern third of the state suffers droughts only about 8 percent of the time. The conditions in the central portions lie between these two extremes.

Except for the few remaining homestead farms of from 160 acres to roughly 400 acres, most farms are large and mechanized. The size of present-day agricultural operations had its forerunners in the large "bonanza" farms of the previous century. Bonanza farms, usually of 1000 acres or more, were consolidated holdings, run by out-of-state corporations. This situation was made possible by large amounts of cheap railroad lands that were made available as the Dakota Territory became settled. By 1889, when the territory was divided into North and South Dakota, and admitted to statehood simultaneously, the bonanza farms were in full operation. This type of farming was successful because it raised single crops and could "effectively use a large labor force by adopting large-scale, efficient machinery."[16]

Rising land values, increased taxes and, much later, laws restricting the ownership of farms by corporations all combined to doom the exploitative bonanza system. However, some of the characteristics of this era still pertain to agriculture in North Dakota. For example, while most agricultural holdings are now in the hands of North Dakotans, the markets still lie outside the state. Minneapolis/St. Paul are seen by many North Dakotans as being exploitative agents for the Eastern big-money interests. The dependency upon one or two crops still remains. The good years are countered by the bad. The land itself, while no longer held by outside corporate interests, is still unevenly distributed.

Parallels can be seen in the state's cattle industry as well. In the late 1800s the Marquis de Mores tried to set up a meat-packing plant in the western part of the state which would compete with St. Paul. The enterprise failed, in part due to the lack of cooperation from the railroads. Today, St. Paul remains the major shipping point of North Dakota beef.

In 1970, the statistics indicated that North Dakota farms were approaching the size of the bonanza holdings. The average farm had 930 acres, and increase of almost 200 acres in a decade.[17] In contrast, the average farm in the United States as a whole is less than 400 acres. Improved highways, which made North Dakota farmers more mobile, have encouraged the reconsolidation of farmlands. Increased mechanization has also contributed to this trend. Finally, more marginal operations, unable to compete in a modern market, were driven out of existence and incorporated into more efficient, existing operations. As Robinson has offered:

In North Dakota over two-fifths (of the farms) had less than 500 acres in 1959. For much of the state, however, a father-and-son partnership, a typical arrangement, could handle from 640 to 1,280 acres in a grain-and-livestock operations and some family farms had 2,000 to 4,000 acres. Such farms were much more profitable because they could make fuller use of expensive agricultural machinery.[18]

For those forced off the land, this has meant a move to the city, whether in North Dakota, or elsewhere. Yet, according to the North Dakota Economic Atlas[19], the state lags badly in manufacturing and service industries. In 1969, the North Dakota Legislative Assembly passed legislation to permit the state, county, and city governments to offer tax exemptions in order to encourage businesses to relocate. Some have, but many are related to agricultural industries. Recently there has been much news about the possibility of having a coal gassification industry that would take advantage of the extensive lignite deposits located in the western parts of the state. North Dakotans are split on the issue. Most would welcome the increased economic opportunity, but many fear that the end result would be a "one-time crop" that will be "harvested" to the advantage of outsiders. That is, the East would benefit, while North Dakota would be left with a strip-mined landscape.

The Program Area

Among the eight AAE sites, North Dakota had the largest program area. It comprised four quasi-rural counties: Stutsman, Burleigh, Morton, and Stark. Compared with other areas in North Dakota, they are unremarkable except that all are bisected by Interstate 94. Each of them also has a small city within its boundaries. The cities range in size from 11,000 to 34,000 people, and grew up as trade, governmental, and later, medical centers along the railroad line that brought the original homesteaders to this part of the country years ago.

The car started to overheat again about two hours later. I pulled off the freeway near Jamestown. Conveniently, it was within the project area. Mac's Cafe and Lounge was dark, and done in black vinyl. No one was there except the bartender, a slight man

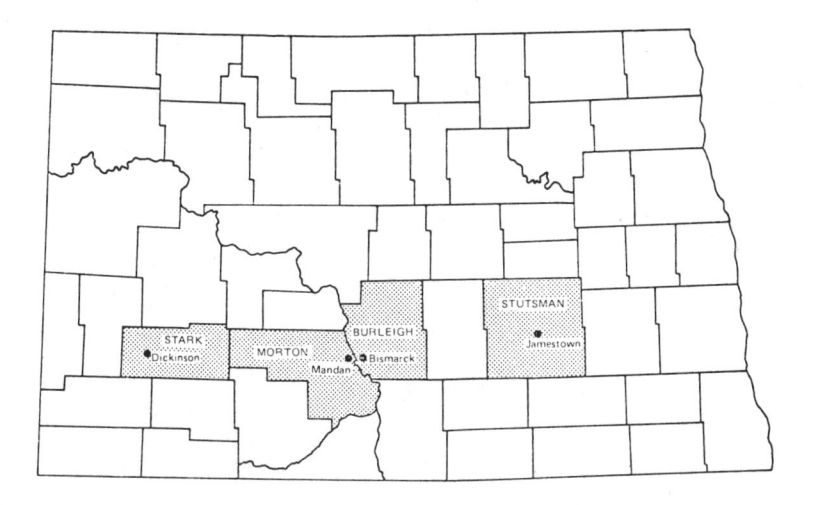

Figure 2-1 The project area

*with a moustache. We made conversation, and he told
me that he was a colonel in the Air National Guard.
North Dakota would be the third largest nuclear power
in the world if it seceded from the Union, he said.
We talked about hunting for a while, and he showed
me a half-grown Labrador he was going to train. A
woman walked in carrying a bowl of soup. She had just
had a tooth extracted and couldn't eat anything solid.
They knew each other, and began to talk.*

    Stutsman County, the easternmost part of the program area, is located in the middle of wheat country. Over one-half of the farms are strictly cash grain or other field crops. In addition, general farming operations account for about one-fifth of the remaining agricultural endeavors. The county also has a fair amount of forest and woodland, most of which is confined to the James River Valley. By North Dakota standards, the area is well watered.

The transportation network is excellent, the county being crossed in a north-south direction by U.S. Highway 81, as well as the previously-mentioned east-west I-94.

The majority of the population in Stutsman County is not in the rural areas, or even in small towns. More than 15,000 people--over 65 percent of the county residents--may be found within the Jamestown city limits.[20]

Jamestown is one of the more progressive and Republican cities within the program area. Because of its location and freight services, there is a fair amount of manufacturing. There are at least three firms which employ over 100 people each. One is a bakery, another is a gear works, and the last is a mobile home manufacturer.

In 1970, the census-derived rental vacancy rate was 5.2 percent, the tightest in the program area.[21] During 1973, a rapid expansion of industry probably reduced this figure substantially.

The median family income in 1970 was a reported $8,286 per year, a rather average figure.[22] However, 10.7 percent of the families in the city were below the poverty level, the highest among for four cities.[23] This may, in part, account for the quick acceptance that the program received here.

Regardless of the economic conditions of a minority of city residents, several improvements have taken place. These have been in the form of new building projects. Most notably, the city has built a new Civic Center, probably in emulation of Bismarck. Federal funds have made this possible and now, local residents here can see Johnny Cash, too.

Due to program constraints, Kidder County, which is interposed between Burleigh and Stutsman counties, was not included in the experiment. With slightly over 4,000 people, the jurisdiction is almost entirely rural and would have provided an excellent test of a housing allowance program in a place where there are no concentrations of people. Unfortunately, the county has such a small population that there was no local housing authority to whom the households could be transferred after the experiment was over.

Finally, Bismarck. I tried the Covered Wagon, just off the main drag. It was a package store in front, and the horseshoe bar was in back. The young bartender seemed anxious to talk to me. He mentioned my English car parked outside, and offered that his mother was from Coventry. His father married her after World War II. Now, he was retired from the Armed Forces and sold carpeting.

His rolled shirtsleeves bothered me. In high school all the motorcycle hoods carried their cigarettes that way. Maybe he doesn't smoke, I thought idly.

I left, unloaded the car, did some shopping and picked up my wife and son at the airport. They had left Minneapolis only an hour before.

The city/county dichotomy is extreme in Burleigh County. Bismarck, at 34,000, is the state capital, and over 85 percent of the county residents live there.[24] Although this is still wheat country and crops are important, Bismarck has drawn people off the farms and from various parts of the state. The city is the fastest growing one in the state, and planners envision that Bismarck will become the hub of North Dakota life within the next twenty years.[25] Already, the business of Bismarck is government, and according to a 1972 survey,[26] over 4,200 individuals are employed in this area.

Accordingly, an ambitious urban renewal program has been undertaken, and the plans include a mini-mall in the downtown shopping district. (Jamestown is now also considering a similar undertaking.) A multi-million dollar civic center has been completed and is now in use. Because of its proximity to Minneapolis/St. Paul, Bismarck is able to draw name entertainers.

According to the 1970 Census, the city vacancy rate was 7.4 percent three years before the program was scheduled to begin.[27] Yet, it is doubtful that this figure is accurate, taking into account the rapid growth of the city. During the first year of the experiment, the units listed for rent in the weekend edition of the Bismarck Tribune shrank from three full columns to less than a sixth of this. While this unobtrusive measure is an imprecise one, it probably indicates that the rental housing supply could not keep up with the demand that had been generated by increased population.

Economic indicators suggest that Bismarck residents were financially well off compared to the rest of the program area residents. The median household income was $9,756, and only 7.1 percent of the families were below the poverty level.[28] However, as a capital city, the cost of living was higher than in other parts of the program area. The median contract rent was eighty-eight dollars per month, nine dollars a month more than Jamestown, its nearest competitor.[29]

Mandan, across the Missouri River, is more of a blue collar town. A large oil refinery is located there, and the Burlington Northern Railway is also a

Oil Storage Tanks-Mandan

substantial employer. In many respects, Mandan has been stunted by the existence of Bismarck, only six miles away. The city is about one-third the size of Bismarck and has only 55 percent of the population of Morton County.[30] As a poor sister city, the lower rents attract a fair number of commuters who work across the river. More than 25 percent of the Morton County residents work outside of its boundaries.[31]

The rental vacancy rate in Mandan was listed as appreciably higher than Bismarck's--8.3 percent according to census data.[32] Ironically, though more units seemed to be available, few people from Morton County responded to the program. Some of the staff members at the agency would later note that Mandan was "different" from the areas lying east of Morton County. The population is more ethnically German-Russian and Catholic. Politically, it votes Democratic, but conservatively so.

Morton County also marks the beginning of beef country, as the land gets drier and poorer. Signs in Mandan announce "Where the West Begins." Diagonal street parking seems to reinforce this claim. Many of the staff felt that those in the western part of the state were more individualistic and less inclined to accept outside help.

Much the same can be said for Dickinson, located in western Stark County. Here, signs inform the traveler that "This is Beef Country." And so it seems, as ranches spread out and herds of white-faced Herefords graze beneath the steel powerline transmission towers.

With 12,500 people out of a total county population of 19,690, Dickinson had the second highest vacancy rate of the four cities: 8.1 percent.[33] Being also German-Russian, Catholic, and blue-collar, Dickinson would prove slow to respond to the program. Economic statistics, however, showed that there were many in the area who could have benefited from the AAE. Although Dickinson residents have the highest income of any of those in Stark County, the median family income in 1970 was calculated to be only $7,835, the lowest in the urban portions of the program area.[34] The percentage of those under the poverty level, 9.7, was the second highest of the four cities.[35]

Housing Quality in the Four Cities

Throughout the area, in the small cities at least, one fact seems to hold true: the existing housing, whatever its availability, is well kept. By East Coast standards, single-family units are small. They are usually frame buildings on medium- or small-sized lots with clean, carefully tended lawns. From outside appearances, one would suspect that any substandardness would be the result of deficiencies that were built-in, not the result of neglect. This is especially true of older buildings, those constructed before 1945 and the advent of uniform building codes.

State Capitol

The two eastern cities also have a sprinkling of new, multi-family garden apartments. No high-rises, residential or otherwise, are found in the area. The structures are built close to the plain and sit there, crab-like. An exception is the state capitol building which looks, appropriately enough, like a grain elevator. If nothing else, the low population insures that deterioration found in high density areas does not exist; it simply cannot. There are not enough people to populate a slum, much less create one.

Outside the four cities, home ownership is high and rental units fewer. It is also more likely that a house in the country would be judged substandard because it would not have the required indoor plumbing facilities. In Jamestown, for instance, the census shows that only 4.5 percent of all units lacked this amenity, while almost one-fourth of the units located elsewhere in the county were similarly unequipped.[36] Further, of the ninety-six units for rent within the city at the time the census was taken, all but seven had full plumbing.[37] The image of the ramshackle, owner-occupied farmhouse is a not-uncommon reality even in the more well-off areas in the state. Yet these would be the people that the AAE, because it was a renters' program, could not serve.

Modest Housing in One of the Four Cities

North Dakota Character

Several traits and values seem to distinguish the residents of the Great Plains, which include North Dakotans, from those who live in other parts of the country. These values and behaviors include a high value that is placed upon individualism, self-sufficience, and integrity. Countering these is an inclination toward cooperation and even collective action. In addition, intense localism is set off by a feeling of inferiority. Egalitarianism contrasts with feelings that there the "big guys" and the "little guys." "We" are always the latter. Finally, all of the above often find their expression in a blunt kind of male dominance.

The roots of these traits and values are laid historically in the physical and cultural isolation of the area. Dependency, based upon economic exploitation and the weather, also had an influence. These factors continue to be salient to this day, although the leading edge of them has been tempered somewhat by increased communication. All but the weather, that is. Nobody has done anything about that. Mark Twain was right.

Frederick Jackson Turner, in his now-classic essay on the importance of the frontier in the history of this country, wrote:

> Up to our own day American history has been in a large degree the history of the colonization of the Great West. The existence of an area of free land, its continuous recession, and the advance of American settlement westward, explains American development.[38]

The Great Plains was the last major frontier. The day of the free, or cheap, land is gone. Most North Dakota land goes for at least $200 an acre. Even the rocky stuff in the western part of the state sells for $75. It was good while it lasted.

The first exploitation of the area which is now North Dakota came as early as 1801. A small trading post was located on the Red River. This marked the real beginning of the buffalo fur trade. The center of it was located in Pembina County, one of the original counties in the Minnesota Territory. It reached as far west as the Missouri River, about the center of the present-day state, and as far east as Lake Itasca, which is now in Minnesota.

The rise of St. Paul insured that the entire area would become a colony of the United States, rather than one of Canada. Supplies could be brought in, and the buffalo robes ferried out, much more cheaply than they could by way of Hudson Bay. The markets, then, were established early in one of the same Midwestern cities where they exist today. St. Paul, and later Minneapolis, was the gateway to Chicago and the rest of the civilized world. By 1847, the herds had been decimated in the middle portion of the Minnesota Territory. Bison could no longer be found east of the Missouri River.

Iowa's admission to the Union in 1846 was followed by Minnesota's in 1858. This spurred the creation of Dakota Territory in 1861, which was to exist until 1889, when it was divided along a surveyed axis to form North and South Dakota. As soon as the territory was legally defined, small settlements began to spring up in its eastern regions. The Yanktons had conveniently ceded large amounts of land in the vicinity. Agriculture began to be practiced. Up until this time, only some of the Amerindian tribes and a few fur traders had bothered much with it. The debut of Dakota agriculture was delayed somewhat, however. A drought ran from 1862 to 1868 and crops were poor.

In the interim, and for a while thereafter, much of the economic activity centered around the harvesting of the remaining bison. The Union Pacific Railroad, which came in 1869, sealed the doom of these animals. It split the last herd in a north-south fashion. The destruction of the southern herd was accomplished in 1878, while the northern one lingered into the 1880s. Afterwards, a bone trade flourished. Men in wagons picked up the bones from the plain, hauled them into town, where they were shipped out by railroad to be ground into fertilizer.

The empty land in the western part of the territory was quickly converted, like many parts of the Great Plains to the south, into a grazing range for cattle. Conveniently, a local market already existed --the U. S. Army, which was busy "pacifying" the more stubborn tribes. It was only with the development of more railroad that it became feasible to ship cattle to the St. Paul stockyards.

While the beef business was being established, Dakota Territory was coming into its own agriculturally:

In 1870 Dakota Territory produced 170,460 bushels of wheat, 133,140 bushels of corn, 4,118 bushels of barley, 50,471 bushels of potatoes, and 114,327 bushels of oats. By 1879 Dakota was able to produce 2,275,000 bushels of wheat.[39]

By the 1880s, the economic value of the area was recognized and this, more than anything else, meant statehood at the end of the decade.

The production figures are impressive when one considers that the population of the northern portion of the territory consisted of perhaps 10,000 people. In addition to this population base, there were "two newspapers, two hundred miles of railroad, much steamboat traffic, and United States courts."[40] A fortunate set of circumstances, partly technological in nature, combined to produce an exploitative boom that by 1890 had increased the population of North Dakota "by more than 1,000 percent--from an estimated 16,000 to 191,000."[41]

Besides improvements in machinery, a key to North Dakota development and economic dominance by Minneapolis lay in a new milling process. By grinding the grain loosely, separating the rather brittle bran of the spring wheat, it was possible to reprocess the flour so that the color did not differ from that made from winter wheat. Minneapolis became a milling center. More railroads were built. Besides the large "bonanza" farms, homesteading operations were begun by settlers arriving from the East and various parts of Europe. They had been lured by an advertising campaign that was underwritten by the Northern Pacific Railroad. The company sent its agent as far as London, England. Advertisements were printed in several languages and distributed over Europe.

The homesteaders' life in North Dakota was a bleak one:

> On the North Dakota frontier the railroad made pioneering less primitive and hastened the bringing in of conveniences. But the railroad, by the rapidity with which it brought people to the unsettled country, must have increased the emotional shock...All of the settlers except the German-Russians came from humid regions, and were awed by the vast, open, almost barren prairie. It increased their sense of isolation and loneliness. And long winters added to their hardships.[42]

For most of the settlers, it meant learning new farming techniques that could exploit the environment: "Their victory lay in adapting themselves to the prairie-sod houses and dugouts for shelter, fish and game for food, mutual helpfulness and self-reliance, and a concentration on wheat..."[43]

As Kraenzel has pointed out, both the humid area farming techniques the settlers brought with them and the limited amount of homesteading land acreage that could be held--also suited only for moist regions --made survival that much harder.[44] It must have done wonders for the work ethic. The reliance upon a single crop, and the severe drought which periodically impeded the development of the Great Plains as a whole, made agriculture a risky business in North Dakota.

North Dakota was particularly harder hit by the residue of humid-area social institutions than were states such as Montana, which were settled later, after adaptation had taken place:

> The smaller average size of the county in North Dakota is directly traceable to the importation of humid-area beliefs...These patterns were all predicated on humid-area ideas--a much denser population, more churches, schools, towns and cities than the area could afford.[45]

This resulted in the so-called "Too-Much Mistake" that has afflicted North Dakota--booming, building, and then failing.[46]

In addition to the difficulties posed by nature, isolation, and inappropriate land tenure and social institutions, the North Dakota farmers had to face exploitation when it came time to sell their crops in the fall:

> When they finished threshing, the men would haul their wheat to town and lay in supplies for the winter. They followed a wagon track across the prairie and sometimes marked the way with piles of sod or with willow sticks...In town, as many as 100 men with wagons or sleighs might be waiting to sell their loads. Grain buyers were often not too honest, and cheated farmers in weighing and grading the wheat. The buyer graded by merely looking at a sample and biting a kernel or two, often grading too low and taking off too much for dockage...With his grain sold, the settler would buy large quantities for supplies, for trips to town were dangerous in winter.[47]

Yet, the major reason for the exploitation was that the markets were located outside of North Dakota and farmers were at the mercy of Minneapolis. Rural or local elevators belonged to Minneapolis firms, and independents colluded with the larger owners to make sure that the prices did not rise. In response, farmers formed cooperatives and the progressive movement captured North Dakota as it did many other agricultural states. North Dakota, however, ran after the dream harder.

One of the upshots of the progressive movement in North Dakota was the creation of an agrarian socialist state during World War I. The Bank of North Dakota and a state-owned grain elevator remain as vestiges of this social experiment. The depression of 1921 forced the Bank of North Dakota to try to sell its bonds to Eastern financiers. The conditions were that the bank confine its activities to state institutions and government. Further, the expansion of socialistic enterprises was to go no further. The offer was refused. However, lack of capital and countervailing political winds meant that an ambitious home-building program could not be realized. The Nonpartisan League, the maverick political party that tried to implement the reforms, dwindled away. It was revived briefly during the Great Depression, when a reformist governor imposed an unsuccessful grain boycott in an effort to boost sagging prices and declared a more successful moratorium on mortgage foreclosures in order to save thousands of North Dakotans from bankruptcy.

Downtown Bismarck Today

The inability of North Dakotans to control their own destiny is symptomatic of conditions on the Great Plains. Kraenzel, in his <u>Great Plains in Transition</u>, states:

> Supported by Midwestern cities, newspapers, radio, tanker trucks, streamliners, and financial ties, this westward thrust of humid-area civilization exerts a constant pressure...The residents of the Plains are...like pawns. Twice, in the last two world wars, the residents of the region have patriotically overextended themselves to raise bumper crops, each time with the help of more than the usual amounts of rainfall. At present, these residents are in the second postwar period of painful readjustment to the decline in such production, a decline made more pronounced by a reduced precipitation. Since the economy of the Plains is chiefly agricultural and without local controls to govern price or volume of production as there are in the case of many industrial areas, the residents are at the mercy of forces outside the region.[48]

Eric Sevareid, a native of Velva, in the eastern part of the state, recalls the leveling effects of the weather upon which a good crop depended:

> Food harvest meant that my father would have to leave his office in the back of the bank, remove his hard white collar, change to overalls, and taking my older brother with him, go help out on one of the bank's farms by driving the four-horse binder, while Paul, who was big for his age, would struggle with the shocks. Hired man or town banker, wheat was the common denominator of his democracy. It made all men equal, in prosperity or wretchedness.[49]

Implied in the above quote is a spirit of cooperativeness in time of mutual need. One is dependent upon individual resources for daily survival. Yet when a group effort is needed, one is forthcoming. The cooperative side of the duality is more characteristic of wheat-growing enterprises. In cattle ranching areas, the individualistic side of the coin is more predominant. The culture there is more "masculine," with "great emphasis on strength, fortitude, and ability to take punishment without complaint."[50] Individuality, egalitarianism and isolationism are responses to the settlement patterns in cattle ranching which dictate sparse settlement if natural resources are to be exploited.

In contrast, wheat farmers, though their holdings may be large, do not operate their enterprises in isolation and are affixed to a single spot on a daily basis--the farm house. High labor demands come in spurts, usually during the harvest. Wheat prices were less stable than cattle prices and this, too, led to the forming of collectives. With a farm, there is much that can be gained by cooperation. Only with water rights is this sort of mentality found among ranchers.[51]

The tensions between individualism and cooperation, eqalitarianism and the knowledge that some--at least from the benefits they reap--are more fit than others, can be formulated into a dualistic "credo" for the entire Great Plains:

1. It is good to do things by yourself, without help;
2. ...but when you do need help, it is good to have someone around to give it.
3. People who can't make it on their own should be helped;
4. ...but those who take help from the government tend to be lazy...
5. ...although, the government should help out in time of need.[52]

This sort of dualism would be operative in the AAE and nowhere is it more fully expressed than in some of the participant case histories, where a sample of the AAE recipients tell their own stories about what it is like to be on a new form of public assistance.

The historic dominance of the "masculine" culture traits is often ascribed to the rigors and necessities of the frontier. Yet, an equally convincing case can be made that the so-called "cowboy" culture is a result of dependency, a feeling of inferiority. Kraenzel describes the actions of Plains people as being a form of "minority behavior" that characterizes people on the prod--the fighting at a drop of a hat and internal competition that can negate the effects of cooperation and leaves them open to even more outside exploitation.[53] Wheat or beef, the markets still lie to the east and the Twin Cities are the outposts of the big-money interests. The isolation of the area, equidistant from either coast and sparsely populated, has precluded the formation of an idiom of self-expression.

North Dakota sources recognize that the feelings of inferiority have left their mark on North Dakota character:

> Many North Dakotans felt that either the state was in a weak and inferior position in the nation or that it was so held by the majority of Americans. They felt alienated from the mainstream of American life, as if they were looked down upon as inferior by the rest of the American people...People of rural state, they felt like country cousins toward the city folk of the nation.[54]

The feelings of inferiority are real and have been subject to empirical investigation. If one assumes that negative feelings about one's state are a cause or an effect on a negative self-image, then a probing of North Dakotans should give concrete evidence of how they feel about the area in which they live. This has been recently done by two British geographers who combined survey data with cartographical methods.[55] The resulting "mental maps" graphically illustrate such things as the geographical preferences of the sample population under study. Figure 2-2 illustrates the residence preferences of a sample of North Dakota students.

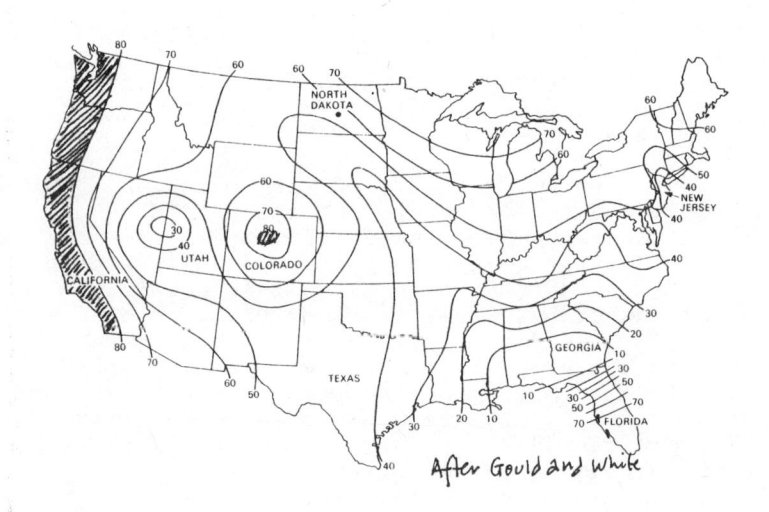

Figure 2-2 Mental map from North Dakota.

In the previous representation, the higher-numbered isobars indicate those places which the sample preferred to live. The positive image of Colorado and California is not unusual, especially in Midwestern maps, nor is the high rating given to southern Florida. The North Dakota mental map is unique in that it was the only area of the country where the locals queried consistently rated other areas of the country much higher than they did their own. One may think of North Dakota as a "sink-hole" from the native point of view. This "depression" is formed by the high ratings that North Dakotans assigned to Minnesota, the West and far West, and to Colorado.

Figure 2-3 illustrates that a sample of Minnesota students agreed with the North Dakotans' assessment of this Great Plains state.

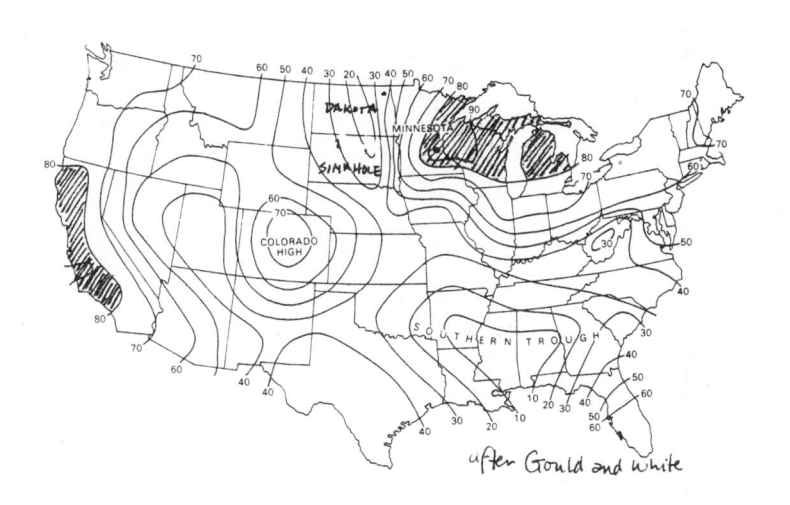

Figure 2-3 Mental map from Minnesota.

While the Minnesota mental map also shows a Colorado and California "high," the positive rating that the Minnesotans gave to their own state is much more of a normal pattern. In the other states where this mapping was done--California, Alabama, Pennsylvania, and Illinois--the respondents invariably rated their own area the highest, followed by certain "glamour spots," which varied from group to group. The one universal seemed to be that all of the groups surveyed responded that the Dakotas were unattractive, places where one would not want to live.

Mental maps can also be used to illustrate the isolation of North Dakota. In Figure 2-4, the lack of knowledge that North Dakotans have of the East is illustrated:

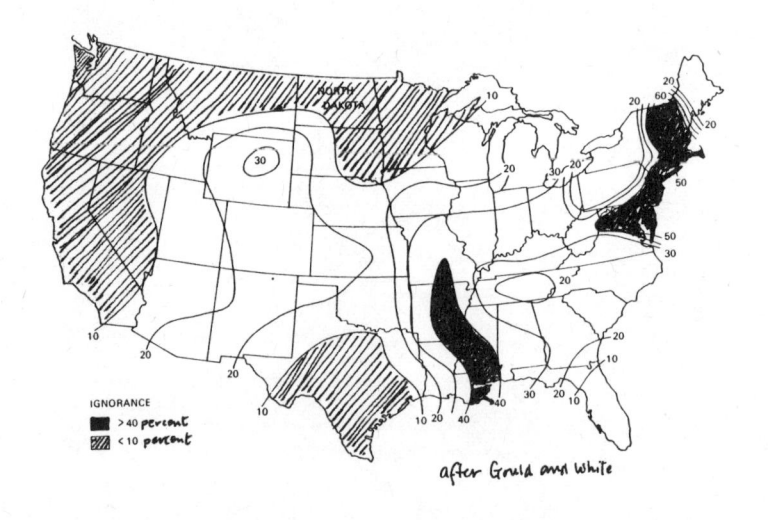

Figure 2-4 The ignorance surface from North Dakota.

In the above representation, the isobars represent the percentage of students who failed to locate a state correctly on a blank map. Thus, the lower-numbered isobars indicate familiarity with a region. Other maps, not reproduced here, indicate that this lack of knowledge is in part due to travel. Most of the North Dakota students sampled had confined their visiting solely to the upper midwest and the West. However, only about 50 percent had been as far west as the Montana border and considerably less than this to California. The heightened knowledge of western geography, as noted in the above figure, may have been also due to the positive image that this region had for the North Dakotans in the sample.

North Dakota Today

North Dakota remains a colony. Now that coal gassification is a possibility, it seems as though the state will be less of an agricultural colony and more of a mineral one. Just as the cooperative-forming residents protested the controlled wheat prices, a movement is underfoot to insure that the strip-mining of the lignite deposits will allow some benefits to accrue to the natives. If this is not to be, then most North Dakotans would probably prefer that the coal fields continue to lie underneath the soil. Organization against encroachments from the outside seems to come too little, and too late. If this resource is wrested from the locals, there may be a resurgence of the old resentments.

For now, the people of the Great Plains are forthright and accommodating. William Inge, a playwright originally from Kansas, has called them "sweet." The label applies to North Dakotans as well as to the others. It is the land of literalism. Verbal contracts are still honored here. A person's work is good.

Maybe we're a little gullible," he said. "Born and raised in the upper midwest, we're taught to trust each other. We assume a stranger is honest until he proves otherwise. In metropolitan areas they assume a stranger is a crook until he proves otherwise."

H---- cited the case of a farmer who wrote a $30,000 check to a man he'd just met a few hours earlier. The swindler, who never revealed his name, promised to invest the money at fifteen percent interest, and then left the state, H---- said.[56]

Relationships are still conducted face to face. "Visit" is a verb, as in "to visit." It is almost never a noun. One "visits" rather than "pays a visit."

It is then that business gets transacted. Drop by, exchange pleasantries, and mention what you want, or rather, what you'd like to see happen. Success seems directly proportional to one's personal reputation for straightforwardness and competence.

Individual initiative is valued, the type that says "You can make it if you try." This attitude is evident in spite of the fact that wages are atrociously low and the lack of union activity is used as a drawing card to tempt relocating manufacturers. In North Dakota, we can do the same job cheaper and more dependably. Strikes are almost unheard of; the $2.00 an hour job is alive and well and living in North Dakota.

Farms are getting larger now, and there is a ready supply of labor that migrates to the small cities. Those who want to stay have to take whatever work is available. Having an education increases the chance that the individual will leave the state. There aren't the mega-universities or the industry to support specialists.

Individualism has its ironic overtones. It is conformist in its expression. If North Dakotans are individualistic in the Frontier Tradition, they are individualistic <u>together</u>. It's not, "You can't run me." Rather, "<u>I don't</u> want to be told." In truth, the individual doesn't <u>need</u> to be told because he probably is doing what's expected of him.

The people are joiners.[57] American Legion Clubs, Elks, Moose, and Eagle Lodges swell. Membership seems to be related to social station. Strivers, and those who have already made it, join the Elks.[58] The Moose is full of truck drivers. Characterizing the Eagles is more chancy--in one city they draw the elderly oom-pa-pa crowd, while in another, the young adults hang out there. At the same time, the existence of social stratification is denied.

"*Oh, I don't know, I never did believe much in that 'class' stuff. I'm just a person.*"

The respondent is a participant who has just gotten a raise when the company was bought up and unionized. His dream is a place in the country with land enough for a few horses.

"*Well, do most of your friends have the same kind of job, do the same kind of things and belong to the same lodge as you?*"

"*Sure...*" A silly question.

"*Yes!*" his wife agrees emphatically.

Bruce Severy, a young teacher from Los Angeles, wanted to get away from it all, and secured a job in Drake. He didn't join in, didn't socialize, and was

perceived as an intellectual snob. In the middle of
the school term, he assigned books by Kurt Vonnegut,
Jr. The members of the school board confiscated the
books and burned them. Severy called it culture
shock, the outside world was appalled, the townspeople
thought everyone should mind their own business, that
it was an internal matter. Today, Severy works in a
Grand Forks hospital and writes articles and poems
about his experiences in North Dakota. He never understood what it was all about, only that he threatened
them:

FOR EDWARD GIBBON

kids cruise in cars of lust

scream obscenities learned
from parents after church.

Christians are drunk again.
and out crucifying, again.

recoiling from the terribles.

while ladies and teachers
hide at canasta.

play for nickles and dimes.

concern (dilute)
is spreading like broth

around bones of the witches
in the small town stew.[59]

When the "individualists" do conform, life
appears harmonious and well integrated. Placidness
reigns, unlike the Dustbowl Thirties. The choices
are laid out, the roles defined. It's still a male-
dominated game, something out of the <u>Imperial Animal</u>.[60]
Women follow men, their groups and clubs are pale
imitations and usually do not even have a meeting
place.
    Only men belly-up to the bar, quaff beers and
play "The Jars," a game of chance where you rip
strips of paper from a card to hit a winner. The
men stand ankle deep in the discarded stubs. They
know what wheat is bringing a bushel and the price
of beef per hundred weight. The system works beauti-
fully if you're white and the Plains equivalent of a
"Good Ole Boy." It doesn't work so well if you're

71

an Indian and can't get served; or if you do get served, you can still get rousted waiting in front of the bus station for a ride back to United Tribes Employment Training Center.

If the possibilities aren't as attractive as Outside, neither are they as horrifying. The old trusting values still hold, even as North Dakota changes. The Covered Wagon Bar, the Silver Dollar, and even the Paper Dollar. Women enter in threes and fours and more. "Whiskey and ditch!" someone yells. On the other hand, there are fancy clubs on the Strip. Universal yet incongruous names--the Dockside, the Orient, the Playmoor and the Townhouse. Rock bands make the circuit--one had a midget that sang and played guitar. Or maybe it was a dwarf. Lounges are made up to be something they aren't--like maybe a ship--and the lights on the ceiling are supposed to be stars. A mechanical nozzle gizmo dispenses an exact ounce and a quarter into a plastic disposable glass. In the male vernacular, making the rounds of those joints is called "Checking the Traps."

The American Legion

The mass media mixes with the ghost of William
Langer,* the Dust Bowl, and the Great Depression.
Read the out-of-town newspapers, yes. Watch the X-
rated movies, that too. Even if you have to look
away from the eyes of pickets at <u>Last Tango</u>. But it's
still Ford and Chevy land, practi<u>cal count</u>ry. Leave
that rich kid Z-car back East, or in California,
wherever they drive those things. It's a long wait
if that Peugeot Diesel breaks down in Minot. There
is no real sports car set. Be showy, if you are
young and you must. But do it with a modified Detroit
offering with wide tires that can be squealed down
Main Street.

    A car overcomes isolation. Put on 20,000 miles
a year,[61] and it's still normal driving. Remember,
there's all that visiting to do, all that basetouching.
But the car never leaves North Dakota, except maybe
for an occasional trip to the Twin Cities to visit a
relative who left it all.

    *"What kind of jobs do they have here, anyway?
Maybe I ought to move down there for a while. Take
advantage of my G. I. Bill. Go to bartending school.
I'm getting nowhere working at the State Pen."*

    The Plains are the Great Leveler, the Fractional
Denominator, the Cottage Cheese Factory, at times.
And yet, the radio: "A Bigger Better Country You
Can't Find...."[62]

    Perhaps the greatest service the housing allow-
ance project provided to the residents was to allow
them to keep their feeling of independence. No, it
isn't welfare, it's from the state, an experiment.

    The Practical Ones, would occasionally retort:
"How much is it costing us taxpayers for these 400
families?"

    Another denizen of the classless society who had
been left out: "What about home<u>owners</u>? We need a
break, too."

THE CONTRACTING AGENCY

    The Social Service Board of North Dakota is com-
posed of seven "civilian" members who are appointed
by the governor with the consent of the state senate.

---

*A Non-partisan League governor during the 1930s.

The organization is an outgrowth of the Public Welfare Board, a non-salaried supervisory body established during the 'thirties to distribute state and federal funds made available for relief purposes. County welfare boards, in turn, were created to administer social programs and money at the local level.

It is the board which is the official agency for any welfare activity in North Dakota that is not the express responsibility of any other state-level organization. Through an executive director, a welfare professional appointed by the Board, this group of citizens controls the activities of the North Dakota Department of Social Services. In 1973, the Department had about 250 employees, most of them fulltime, many of whom worked at the Bismarck headquarters in the capitol building. The budget was a large one. For the two year period ending on June 30, 1973, the Department of Social Services had received a total of more than $42.8 million. Of this, $40.6 million had been disbursed, leaving a surplus of somewhat more than $2.2 million.[63]

The Social Service Board had a local and national reputation of being a fiscally responsible organization. Careful spending was a tradition with them. As a strong, state-supervised, county-administered welfare agency, a commitment had long ago been made toward progressive welfare administration.

Although assistance payments and simple social services are still administered by the county, there has been a tendency toward regionalization and increasing state-level control. Since the mid-1960s, North Dakota has had eight Area Social Centers (ASSCs). Each center has a specified territory. Within its boundaries, the ASSC supervises the local county welfare offices and provides the more costly services that would not otherwise be available because of sparse population. This approach represents one solution to the problem posed by a state which is geographically large yet has only 617,000 people. It is in this manner that high quality services can be conveniently and economically provided. ASSC resources are available to any North Dakotan, regardless of economic station.

While the state handles matters in an even-handed matter, things are not quite so uniform at the county level. Locals often complain that there are easy counties and hard counties. Recipients sometimes feel that the more conservative welfare directors are not responsive to people's needs and tend to deny aid even in the most deserving of cases. Nowhere is this more apparent than in the giving of General Assistance.

This money comes solely from the county and is used
for emergency situations only. Since no federal or
state funds are involved, decisions made by the county
welfare office cannot be appealed. As a result, during fiscal year 1973, Stutsman ounty disbursed over
$14,000 in general assistance, while Stark County gave
out $3,500.[64] Both have approximately the same population, and both were within the program area. Conservative welfare offices reflect the philosophy of
the local area; the liberal county directors argue,
however, that it is the director's job to educate
members of the community, that people do have an obligation toward their less fortunate fellow residents.

Aid to Families with Dependent Children (AFDC)
payments have been high in spite of the fact that
North Dakota is not a rich state. AFDC grants have
consistently been in the top ten or fifteen states,
while income has usually ranked in the bottom fourth
or fifth. In 1973, a family of four could receive
$315 per month.[65] Before double digit inflation, it
was liveable.

At the same time, the Department of Social Services has been an efficiently-run organization. The
Social Service Board, like its predecessor, the Public Welfare Board, has been free of outside political
influence. Members are still non-salaried, although
they do receive expenses, and must account to the
state legislature every two years.

In keeping with the rather austere outlook of
North Dakotans, money spent must be carefully accounted for and justified. Although at the time the AAE
began, the state was eligible for seventy-one dollars
in federal welfare funds for every twenty-nine dollars
raised locally, the state has never made a business
out of dealing with the federal government.[66] Indeed,
the North Dakota Department of Social Services and
the Social Service Board would probably never have
agreed to run a housing allowance experiment had not
one of the senior employees taken a special interest.

At the time of HUD's initial contact, Gottfried
Kuhn was the most senior person in the North Dakota
welfare system. He represented the liberal end of the
spectrum within the department. Indeed, this was
  occasional criticism: "The only trouble with Gottfried is that he'll give the world away with a fence
around it--if you let him."

The Agency Director

Through the years, he had worked his way up and had had increasingly more to say. With his prodding, North Dakota, always a leader in welfare innovation, had become one of the first states to institute the "flat grant." Under this system, the recipient is given a fixed sum of money each month and then is allowed to budget according to personal needs. Previously, separate allowances had been given for food, clothing, and housing.

While working at the county level, Kuhn had also trained a number of individuals who eventually went on to occupy high positions at the state level. One of his "graduates" promoted the acceptance of the "simplified method of eligibility determination," which lets the applicant declare his or her own income and assets. The recipient retains a feeling of dignity, not being subject to rigorous third party cross-checking.

Although the state was able to operate an efficient assistance payments system under this humane method, changes in federal regulations no longer permit this sort of freedom. In 1973, North Dakota had AFDC error rates ranging from one-fifth to one-third of the national average.[67]

If Kuhn, in his thirty-eight years with the state, was a social liberal, his management of financial matters was conservative. One of his first moves as Benson County welfare director at the very beginning of his career was to outlaw the use of cash in the office. He felt that it was too hard to keep track of and provided temptation where it was needed least. During the course of the experiment, when confronted by changing rules and techniques, his response often was to say that he didn't care which methods were used, only that he wanted a "clear audit trail."

This apparent unconcern for procedure is not quite accurate, however. During both the planning and operations phases of the experiment, Kuhn expended his energies trying to run a program that would fit rural area, allow him to test his own concepts, and still remain financially feasible.

76

NOTES

1. U. S. Bureau of Census, Statistical Abstract of the United States, (U. S. Department of Commerce, Washington, D. C., 1974), Table 13.

2. Roscoe L. Lokken, North Dakota, (Valley City College Press, Valley City, North Dakota, 1974), pp. 44-45.

3. U. S. Bureau of the Census, Census of the Population: 1970; SUBJECT REPORTS, Final Report PC (2) -1F, American Indians (U. S. Government Printing Office, Washington, D. C., 1973), Table 4.

4. Ibid., Table 4.

5. Richard M. Lunde, "North Dakota and Its Immigrants," (The North Dakota Teacher, November, 1962), p. 27.

6. U. S. Bureau of the Census, Statistical Abstract of the United States, Table 627.

7. U. S. Bureau of the Census, Census of Population: 1970: General Social and Economic Characteristics, Final Report PC(1)-C 36, North Dakota, (U. S. Government Printing Office, Washington, D. C., 1972), Table 57.

8. Ibid, Table 57.

9. Ibid, Table 57.

10. Ibid, Table 57.

11. Ibid, Table 47.

12. U. S. Bureau of Census, American Indians, Table 4.

13. Eric Sevareid, "You Can Go Home Again," (pp. 279-298) in Brian R. Goodey and R. J. Eiden, eds., Readings in North Dakota Geography, (North Dakota Studies, Bismarck, 1968), p. 281.

14. Elwyn B. Robinson, History of North Dakota, (University of Nebraska Press, Lincoln, 1966).

15. See also, Melvin E. Krazek, North Dakota: A Human and Economic Geography, (North Dakota Institute for Regional Studies, North Dakota Agricultural College, Fargo, 1956).

16. Hiram M. Drache, The Day of the Bonanza, (North Dakota Institute for Regional Studies, Fargo, 1964), p. 91.

17. Bureau of the Census, Statistical Abstract, Table 1015.

18. Elwyn Robinson, History of North Dakota, pp. 445-446.

19. North Dakota State Planning Agency, North Dakota Economic Atlas, (N. D. State Planning Agency, Bismarck, 1969).

20. U. S. Bureau of the Census, Census of Population: 1970; General Population Characteristics, Final Report PC(1)-B-36, North Dakota, (U. S. Government Printing Office, Washington, D. C. 1971), Table 16.

21. U. S. Bureau of the Census, Census of Population: 1970; Detailed Housing Characteristics, Final Report HC(1)-B-36 North Dakota, (U. S. Government Printing Office, Washington, D. C., 1972, Table 1.

22. U. S. Bureau of the Census, General Social and Economic Characteristics, Table 107.

23. Ibid., Table 107.

24. U. S. Bureau of the Census, General Social Characteristics, Table 40 and General Population Characteristics, Table 16.

25. In spring, 1975, the county began an informal census. According to the Burleigh County Auditor, the county had reached 45,000 people. Most of this gain was registered in Bismarck, which gained approximately 4000 people.

26. Bismarck Champber of Commerce, "North Dakota:" Community Data for Industry, (brochure, complied 1973), unpaginated.

27. U. S. Bureau of the Census, <u>Housing Characteristics</u>, Table 1.

28. U. S. Bureau of the Census, <u>General Social and Economic Conditions</u>, Table 107.

29. U. S. Bureau of the Census, <u>Housing Conditions</u>, Table 1.

30. U. S. Bureau of the Census, <u>General Population Characteristics</u>, Table 40.

31. U. S. Bureau of the Census, <u>General Social and Economic Conditions</u>, Table 119.

32. U. S. Bureau of the Census, <u>Housing Characteristics</u>, Table 1.

33. U. S. Bureau of the Census, <u>General Population Characteristics</u>, Table 16.

34. U. S. Bureau of the Census, <u>General Social and Economic Characteristics</u>, Table 107.

35. <u>Ibid</u>, Table 107.

36. U. S. Bureau of the Census, <u>Housing Characteristics</u>, Tables 18 and 29.

37. <u>Ibid</u>, Table 18.

38. Frederick Jackson Turner, "The Significance of the Frontier in American History, in George Taylor, ed., <u>The Turner Thesis Concerning the Role of the Frontier in American History</u>, (Problems in American Civilization, Boston, 1949), p. 1.

See also, Nelson Klose, <u>A Concise Study Guide to the American Frontier</u>, (University of Nebraska, Lincoln, 1964), for a series of criticisms of the Turner thesis.

39. Lokken, <u>North Dakota</u>, p. 31.

40. Robinson, History of North Dakota, p. 132.

41. <u>Ibid</u>., p. 134.

79

42. *Ibid.*, p. 156-157.

43. *Ibid.*, p. 157.

44. See Carl Frederick Kraenzel, *The Great Plains in Transition*, (University of Oklahoma Press, Norman, 1955).

Though published over twenty years ago, this book remains the definitive one on the Great Plains region as an exploited whole.

See also, K. Ross Toole, *The Rape of the Great Plains*, (Little, Brown and Co., Boston, 1976).

45. Kraenzel, *The Great Plains in Transition*, p. 175.

46. Robinson, *History of North Dakota*, passim.

47. *Ibid*, pp. 162-163.

48. Kraenzel, *Great Plains in Transition*, pp. 6-7

49. Eric Sevareid, *Not So Wild A Dream*, (Alfred A. Knopf, New York, 1946), p. 4.

50. John W. Bennett, *Northern Plainsmen* (Alline, Chicago, 1971), p. 178.

51. Some writers have argued that the North Dakota propensity toward cooperatives is due to the ethnic stock of the state--Scandanavians in the east and German-Russians in the west. Robert P. Wilkins, in The Non-Ethnic Roots of North Dakota Isolationism (pp. 206,221, *Nebraska History*, Vol. 44, No. 3, September, 1963), notes that the Scandanavians were "socialists," and that the German-Russians had an "anti-capitalist bias" (pp. 206-207). However, the ecological demands of farming versus ranching seem to be a more powerful explanation of the cooperative mentality one finds in eastern North Dakota, which is heavily Scandanavian and wheat-raising.

Other writers have commented upon the similarity between the individualistic Great Plains Amerindian culture and the ranching culture which replaced it. See, Joe B. Frantz and J. E. Choate, *The American Cowboy*, (University of Oklahoma Press, Norman, 1955), *passim*.

52. Bennett, *Northern Plainsmen*, p. 282.

53. Kraenzel, *The Great Plains in Transition*, p. 228.

54. Robinson, *History of North Dakota*, p. 550.

55. Peter Gould and Rodney White, *Mental Maps*, (Pelican Books, London, 1974), see especially, pp. 93-130. The maps were taken from pp. 98, 103, and 121, respectively.

56. The incident occurred in Minot, North Dakota, and the article was reprinted in newspapers throughout the state. It appeared in the *Dickinson Press* on November 8, 1974 under the title, "North Dakota is prime area for con men."

57. In Bismarck, the Lloyd Spetz American Legion Post #1 has approximately 2700 members. North Dakota is the only state to have three posts among the twenty largest. North Dakota also has the highest percentage of eligible veterans who belong to this organization. The figure approaches 70 percent.

58. In 1973, the initiation fee for the Elks in Bismarck was $100. For the Moose, it was $25. Both lodges in the capital city had over 3000 members. The Eagles were much smaller, but had recently undertaken the construction of a new aerie.

59. Bruce Severy, *Crossing Into the Prairies*, (Scopcraeft Press, Grand Forks, 1973), p. 21.

60. Lionel Tiger and Robin Fox, *The Imperial Animal*, (Dell Publishing Co., New York, 1972).

61. This is the average number of miles driven by North Dakotans in 1973, according to a variety of sources.

62. The line is from a frequently-played radio jingle advertising North Dakota as a tourist attraction.

63. Social Service Board of North Dakota, *Social Services in North Dakota*, (Report, 1973), Table 10.

64. *Ibid.*, Table 2.

65. The maximum figures are set by the state legislature during their biennial meetings. According to a recent conversation with the agency director, the new limit for a family of four was set at approximately $365 in 1974. This figure compares favorably with the more industrialized states, such as Massachusetts.

66. The matching fund ratio is tied to state income figured over a three-year period. For the 1974 fiscal year, North Dakota experienced the most rapid increase in per capita income of any state in the nation. Cattle prices were high in 1973. The wheat harvests for both 1973 and 1974 were excellent. The market price was helped by the Soviet grain deal. Due to the increase in income, the state was scheduled to have its federal contributions reduced. The eventual ratio will be approximately 58:42.

67. On January 1, 1974, all state began an intensive eighteen-month effort to reduce the ineligible AFDC case rates to no more than 3 percent, and the eligible overpaid case rates to no more than 5 percent. North Dakota has been one of the few states to achieve the required tolerance rates. Previous to this effort, the error rates (April to September 1973) were as follows:

Source: U. S. Department of Health, Education and Welfare SRS Circular, December 20, 1973.

	Cases with Errors as a Percent of Total Cases			Amount of Payment Error as a Percent of Total Payment		
	Ineligible	Eligible But Overpaid	Eligible But Underpaid	Ineligible	Overpaid	Underpaid
National Average	10.2	22.8	8.1	8.9	7.1	1.4
North Dakota	1.9	8.4	1.9	0.8	1.8	0.1

3. Behind Closed Doors: The Planning Process

FIRST CONTACTS

Gottfried Kuhn first heard about the housing allowances in November, 1972, when he was the Director of Economic Assistance for the Department of Social Services. The U. S. Department of Agriculture (USDA) had sent a memorandum stating that housing allowance payments were not exempt as income for determining food stamp eligibility.

Kuhn figured that some bureaucrat somewhere was flexing his muscles. In any case, the letter did not apply to on-going programs within the state: "I threw it in File 13," he later admitted.

"File 13?"

"The wastepaper basket."

The importance of the memo changed in early 1973 when the Department of Housing and Urban Development contacted the Social Service Board of North Dakota to see if they would be interested in participating in the AAE.

From HUD's point of view, North Dakota would be a desirable addition in several respects. If the Social Service Board agreed to the proposal, it would mean that only one more welfare agency would have to be chosen to complete the matched-pair design of the AAE. At the time, two other social service agencies were also being considered. One was in the Northeast, the other in the South. Whichever one was eventually chosen, North Dakota would provide geographic contrast and balance.

Most of the other sites had a city as their primary project area. By far, a Great Plains agency would be the most rural one in the experiment. The location also insured that HUD's Region VIII* would

---

*Region VIII consists of Wyoming, Montana, the Dakotas, Colorado, and Utah, and is headquartered in Denver.

have representation. Previously, a city in Colorado had been considered as a possibility, but homeownership there was almost 90 percent, and HUD doubted that the small rental market could absorb several hundred participants looking for new housing. Finally, the North Dakota Department of Social Services came highly recommended by the U. S. Department of Health, Education and Welfare.[1] If failure occurred, it would not be because of shoddy administration.

HUD was already familiar with the general area. During the first round of awards, Basin Electric Power Cooperative in Bismarck had submitted a housing allowance proposal that was almost accepted. It called for an experiment that would cover four counties, but there was no other similar agency with which to pair it, so it was not selected. The Morton County Housing Authority had also applied, but the size of the jurisdiction, coupled with its low population (20,310), made the operation of a large-scale social program within its borders inappropriate.

The first meeting with the Department of Social Services* personnel was held in Bismarck on March 7, 1973. Five senior people from the department represented the Social Service Board. Representatives from HUD-Washington and HUD-Denver had flown in to make the presentation. An analyst from the evaluation contractor** was also on hand to answer technical questions about the project. Since the AAE was an experiment, reporting and monitoring requirements would be much heavier than in a normal social program.

After the presentation, the North Dakota people were interested, but doubted that they could participate. Although the North Dakota legislature was in session, the group felt certain that no further spending of state funds would be approved. Furthermore, the session was about to end, and there was no time to present anything to the legislative committee.

The HUD representative assured them that the money involved would be entirely federal, and that even the planning period would be covered. The important thing was the time constraint: a new agency would have to be created within ninety days of the Letter of Award.***

---

* Hereinafter referred to as "the department."

**Throughout this book, "evaluation contractor" is the term used to denote Abt Associates Inc.

***The official HUD notification that an agency had been selected for the AAE.

If that was the case, they replied, there would probably be no problem, although they would still need approval from the Committee of the Budget. It would be at least a week before anything could be done; the group wanted time to look at the project in greater detail. They felt that three months would be ample time to set up an agency, even with the two required planning conferences.

HUD still had one concern: the size of the housing market. The Bismarck-Mandan area has only 50,000 people. They were worried that there might be the same problem as with the rejected Colorado site, although there did seem to be a balance between home owners and renters.

The day before, the HUD team had met with the director of the Burleigh County Housing Authority. He believed that Burleigh and Morton counties were large enough to have a meaningful experiment and pointed out that there were almost 500 families on his waiting list alone. Most of these were living in adequate units, he said. The problem was that they were paying high rent. A quick, informal telephone survey of realtors had turned up 150 adequate vacant units after only a few calls. The director was sure that there were still more vacancies in the area. Later in the day, the director of the neighboring Morton County Housing Authority estimated that even a small town like Glen Ullin might have as many as fifteen units for rent.

The HUD people were still unsure. Finally, someone suggested that the project area might extend a hundred miles in either direction along I-94. Four of the five counties had operative Section 23 agreements.* This meant that there would be no trouble in transferring the participants to other housing programs when the experiment was over.

Such a move would have its advantages. By including four counties, the total population would be over 100,000. This was twice that of the Bismarck-Mandan area; I-94 would make the project area easy to service since the highway cut across the area in an east-west fashion.

---

*Section 23 is that provision of the Housing Act of 1937 which allows the establishment of local housing agencies and empowers them to lease existing units from private landlords.

A copy of the Agency Program Manual (APM) was left with the North Dakota people. It explained the program and the experimental constraints more fully. If the Social Service Board agreed to participate the thick book would serve as the sole planning guide for the new agency.

Thor Tangedahl, the executive director of the Department of Social Services, gave Kuhn the responsibility for making the decision as to whether North Dakota should participate. The free market philosophy behind housing allowances intrigued Kuhn. As director of economic assistance, he was sensitive to the high visibility those receiving assistance were forced to accept. In the supermarkets, food stamps recipients could be identified by the dully colored coupons they used to pay for their groceries. With subsidized housing, the units were often architecturally distinct and concentrated in a small area. In Bismarck, for example, welfare families lived in look-alike townhouses located in the south side. Many AFDC mothers resided there and local wits referred to the project as "Sin City." The AAE seemed to get around this visibility problem, although participants would not be completely anonymous, due to the lease requirement.

Kuhn also felt that the experiment would be a chance for the department to administer a program aimed at a population that was primarily non-welfare. If the new agency was managed carefully, the uneven image that the system had at the county level could be avoided.

From a personal point of view, Kuhn liked the idea of an experiment. As an undergraduate, he had majored in one of the social sciences, anthropology, at the University of North Dakota. The AAE undoubtedly appealed to these instincts. If he had input into the planning, he reasoned, it might give him the opportunity to test some of his own concepts in a program that was aimed at a broad spectrum of people. Most of the Social Service Board programs were administered solely on the basis of need and touched only a few of the state's residents.[2]

The question was still where to run the project. Grand Forks could handle the 700 households HUD had talked about, except that the housing picture was confused by an air base. Fargo was the only SMSA in the state, but it was too far east, and the housing market spilled over into Minnesota. He considered the Devil's Lake area, and then rejected it. It was too sparsely poulated, and whoever ran the program would have to relocate there for a couple of years.

Kuhn met again with the other departmental officials. He thought that it would be worthwhile for the state to participate, and agreed that the four-county area made sense. "Who's going to run it?" he asked.

Nobody volunteered. One of the members suggested a team approach. Kuhn was unimpressed, and argued that one person should have the sole responsibility. That way, if anything went wrong, somebody could be accountable.

Tangedahl asked Kuhn if he would be willing to head the agency himself. Kuhn thought for a minute, and then replied that he thought he'd lose too many benefits, especially if he lost his accumulated sick leave by transferring to a new agency, even if it was one that he created.

The group thought that everything could be arranged. They could call it a horizontal transfer.

Kuhn accepted, reasoning that he would retire after the program was over. That would give the Social Service Board a chance to choose a replacement to fill his present position.

With Kuhn heading the North Dakota Experimental Housing Allowance Project*, the new agency would operate freely. As the most senior person in the welfare system, he would report only to Tangedahl. A less experienced person would have been stuck somewhere in the departmental hierarchy. Kuhn would also have a free hand in designing his own program as he had requested.

INITIAL PREPARATIONS

There were still a few things to be settled. Kuhn wanted to staff up cautiously in case things didn't pan out. If he hired a full staff, and then HUD backed down, he would be left with a public relations problem. Also, he wanted to use young people for client contact positions. They would be more quickly available anyway, and would bring a fresh outlook to the new agency. If the AAE were run by a welfare organization, it shouldn't <u>look</u> as if it were.

---

*In North Dakota, as at many other sites, the AAE and the administrative agency were both known as the Experimental Housing Allowance Project (EHAP).

He also had to go to the Emergency Commission to get permission to spend the federal funds. The legislature had recessed until the next biennium, and the appointed commission acted in its stead.

On March 23, 1973, the Social Service Board was awarded the planning grant, and Kuhn felt he could act. Since HUD was talking about 700 households, he asked the Commission for approval to spend up to $1.8 million. It was only a guess, but he wanted to be high enough so that he wouldn't have to go back again. Later, the number of slots was cut to 500, and then to a final 400. He scaled down his estimate to $1.2 million.

Since the project had been endorsed by the Social Service Board and involved no state funds, the Emergency Commission approved the expenditure. Kuhn was also given permission to borrow up to $40,000 from departmental funds for the planning period. His only worry was that the cash flow from the federal government would not be a smooth one.

In April, he recruited the first three members of his staff. First, he talked to the wife of the former departmental director. She agreed to come on as a secretary for an indefinite period of time. Once she was no longer needed, she would "retire" again. Kuhn reasoned that she would be insurance against over-staffing. If there was an unexpected lull, he could let her go and not hire a replacement.

The Agency Program Manual seemed to indicate that someone with a statistical background would be needed for all phases of the program. Kuhn drove north to the Devil's Lake area, where a services delivery demonstration project was underway. He knew a few of the younger staff, and asked two of them if they'd be interested in a possible three-year appointment. Neither of them wanted to leave the project, but one of the fellows recommended a former classmate who had a M.A. in economics. His name was Greg Simonson. The friends said that Greg was between jobs now and was helping out on his father's farm near Minot. They were sure he would be interested.

The final hire was for the position of assistant director. Theoretically, it was optional, but Kuhn thought the job would be a necessary one. The program area was over 300 miles across, and he thought that 1,000 or 2,000 people might apply. Also, he had no idea how many landlords and community groups might call the agency for program information.

He knew that in his own division, Bob Barr would soon be available. Barr's job was being phased out due to federal cutbacks. Kuhn was familiar with his work at the Capitol and also as a former appeals referee* and caseworker within the system. Barr could write the counseling, or "software," portion of the plan.

Kuhn made him an offer, but cautioned that nothing was really set for sure. Later, Barr recalled: "Gottfried said that it would all happen pretty quick. I guess it did. He told me on Tuesday, and three days later we were on our way to Washington."

THE ORIENTATION SESSION

The meeting with HUD was an orientation session for the last three agencies chosen for participation in the AAE. The group from HUD was larger than before, and the North Dakotans met the assistant GTR,** Joe Queenan, for the first time. His job was to supervise the production of the plan and to provide technical assistance to the writers when necessary. Once the experiment was underway, he was to step back and assume a monitoring role. Normally, a more senior person would have had this task, but the Denver GTR turned the job over to his younger trainee.

The last group of agencies had an advantage over the earlier ones: the Agency Program Manual had evolved into a stable document. The first agencies had to use a manual that was constantly being revised and amended as questions concerning operations and interpretation of regulations came up.

Still, it wasn't perfect: "You had to adjust to it and work with it," Kuhn recalled. "The definitions were a little bit difficult and I still think they are." The problem was that the manual was built around fourteen analytic functions. In many ways, they did not reflect working reality: "There was even a question of the chronological order in which the functions were set up." Kuhn later said. It

---

*Assistance recipients are entitled to appeal any action taken by the welfare board. At the "fair hearing," an official from the North Dakota Department of Social Services acts as a judge, or "appeals referee."

**"GTR" is an abbreviation for Government Technical Representative. GTRs are usually based in the regional HUD offices and provide expertise to local organizations running HUD programs.

would have been easier if the Agency Program Manual had been designed around the actual order of client services.

WRITING THE FIRST PLAN

After the meeting, the North Dakota representatives and Joe Queenan returned to Bismarck to write the first version of the plan. The task was to meet the constraints dictated by the design of the experiment and yet come up with a coherent philosophy behind their effort.

Kuhn was still cautious about spending money. He located an unused room in the state capitol and furnished it with a borrowed table and rented chairs. If HUD decided to cancel the contract, the Social Service Board would not be out anything.

The original staff remembers this as a happy time. Joe would come down on a Tuesday and then return to Denver at the end of the week. "We'd work like hell, and then Greg and Joe and I would go out for a few beers," Barr recalled.

Five of them sat around the table and tried ideas out on each other. Kuhn especially liked it because "nobody tried to take credit for anything." Paula Ovre, the secretary, came up with several suggestions; because of her husband's past employment, she was familiar with the state system and where to tap in on it.

If the long work sessions drew them together, so did the philosophy that the director and the assistant GTR shared: minimizing administrative costs in a project that was already hampered somewhat by its comparatively small size and large program area. Most of the other AAE sites had concentrated populations and were intended to serve more than twice the number of North Dakota's 400 projected participants.

To handle the two outlying counties, Kuhn decided to use "satellite centers." This would mean that two extra counselors would have to be used: there was no other way to handle the project area. He wanted to locate the branch offices in Dickinson and Jamestown, where Area Social Service Centers already existed: "...both of these centers are centrally located within these cities and counties, and are, thus, readily accessible to various demographic and socio-economic groups."[3] Still, the counselors' salaries would increase the costs per enrollee. With only 400 households in the program, the employees in the outlying counties would probably be underworked. The tradeoff was between economy and rapid processing, and service.

The strain between these two desires was paradoxical. Kuhn's central goal was participant-oriented: "...to maximize the satisfaction or utility which each household derives by its participation in the experiment."[4] The means by which the goal could be achieved were administrative: he wanted to have the agency as small as possible. The use of satellite centers was one case where there was a basic conflict: without the centers, only Bismarck-Mandan people would get into the program, but with them, the administrative costs would rise, thereby reducing the "efficiency" of the program.

There were still some economies which could be managed, however. As an offshoot from the state welfare organization, they could tie into the state check-writing system instead of setting up their own. The cost could be nominal, and the system was dependable: in all the time Kuhn had been with the department, there was only one occasion when the checks were delayed.

Using a mail-in application with self-declaration of income and assets was another possibility. HUD had told them that having participants do their own certifications of financial status was something that would be interesting to test. The earlier Social Service Board experiment in using the "simplified method of eligibility determination" had been successful and this gave Kuhn confidence. In his opinion, the method was both sound and inexpensive.

Most people, the earlier experiment had found, were forthright about their financial situation. Staff time could be cut by the use of this method, since interviews were avoided. In some situations the face-to-face interview was faster, however: if someone made an unbelievable statement, the interviewer could ask the applicant right then, instead of having to make a telephone call or write a letter.

The key to the successful use of the simplified method lay in the agency and whoever reviewed the applications there. A certain expertise is required. The reviewer must be experienced enough, judiciousness is "prudence," and the control exercised by the reviewer is known as "the prudent person principle" in the welfare circles.

Kuhn decided that putting a self-declaration system into operation would be no problem. The department had already developed forms for rural areas that could be adapted for AAE use.

Doing the planning tables proved to be the most critical task. The characteristics of the eligible population had to be accurately figured, since it was from here that the average housing allowance could be calculated and program costs estimated. Census statistics were spotty, as the proposed program area had no SMSA within its boundaries.

The planners decided to use those renters who were "living under inadequate conditions" for the eligible population. This group included those who were living in units that lacked some or all plumbing facilities, those with more than 1.25 persons per room, and those paying more than 25 percent of their income for rent.

Queenan had earlier suggested that state income tax figures be used to provide accurate information of the "income-eligible population," and that they employ a different method for determining who were paying too much of their income for rent. He suggested that thirty-one percent of disposable income would be a reliable index. This was eventually rejected by HUD. The eligibility limits would be set individually at each site. Those families earning up to 125 percent of the poverty level would probably be eligible. The agency had to use census figures and conform to the Brooke Amendment[5] stipulation that families spend no more than 25 percent of their adjusted gross income on housing.

The original method was adopted again. The planning staff estimated that there were 3788 renter households in the area that would be eligible. They thought that as many as 1000 might apply. This was a figure that was roughly comparable to the participation rate in other programs within North Dakota. Besides, they figured they would use low-key outreach methods to advertise the program. If there were to be only 400 openings, they didn't want to cause bad feelings by turning people away. Word would get around, and that would kill the concept of housing allowances within the state.

In order to help with the financial planning, HUD had intended to develop rental cost figures for units of various sizes in each program area. These were known as C* figures—the "Cost of Standard Average Rentals." Since HUD had not given them these yet, the planners made up their own. All of them were familiar with rent levels, and they agreed on a schedule which would range from $115 a month for a single person household to $230 a month for a six person household. Using these figures, an average monthly rent of $137.40 was arrived at. Then, by subtracting one quarter of the monthly income of the "average" participant, the average housing allowance payment was set at $100 per month. Making up the planning tables was like using a cookbook; the instructions were given in the Agency Program Manual. Simonson and Queenan did all the figuring.

Once the application volume estimates were made, the group could produce an organization table. Barr and Kuhn drew upon their knowledge of work loads. The Agency Program Manual seemed to indicate that counseling and eligibility determination should be kept completely separate. If that was the case, then two of the specialized eligibility control technicians* would be needed.

The rest of the staffing pattern was unremarkable. They estimated on the high side and assumed that their outreach would be overly successful. Thirteen full-time positions were budgeted, although Kuhn had decided that he wouldn't fill all the openings until he knew if their estimates were right.

Beyond the costing details of the plan, there was also the commitment to the idea of the experiment itself. Queenan suggested a strong research design which would actually test different techniques for

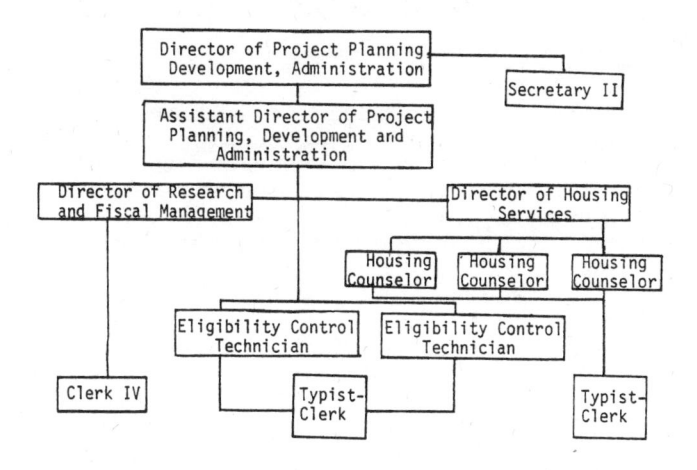

Figure 3-1 North Dakota Proposed Organization Chart, Strategic Plan

---

*Eligibility control technicians are clerical workers who specialize in computing payments for assistance recipients. Unlike caseworkers, they have no counseling duties.

the delivery of housing services. Those in Stark, Morton, and Burleigh counties would be the control group which would utilize stricter, more conventional methods. Those in Stutsman County would make up the experimental group for any testing that would be done.

The suggestion was accepted. The staff felt that Joe, besides providing statistical data, was also the expert about HUD. They had never worked with a housing agency before, and didn't know what was expected of them: "Without Joe, there wouldn't have been any program."

The area of inspection was something which interested all of them. A basic question could be whether the participants themselves would be capable of deciding the condition of their units. "Decent, safe, and sanitary," had been the phrase that was bandied about during the orientation session; Stutsman County participants would be the group to use self-inspection.

The standards had to be reasonable, they figured. If the amount of the actual housing allowances was around $100, then participants would be living in older, less expensive units. They didn't want to set the inspection criteria so high that this part of the housing market was eliminated.

The group settled on eight points which would determine if a unit was adequate. It had to be structurally safe. There had to be running water and plumbing facilities. The kitchen had to have a sink and a connection for a stove. The wiring had to be safe. The heating plant had to be in good working order. There could be no overcrowding. These criteria, especially the requirement for a flush toilet, would eliminate some of the rental housing in the truly rural areas.

The effectiveness of different counseling techniques was something else that would be easy enough to test. The three control counties would have individual counseling sessions, while Stutsman County people would be counseled in groups.

The projected 400 program openings were apportioned amongst the four counties according to the number of eligible households that resided within each jurisdiction. Burleigh County was assigned 170 openings, Morton County, 90, while Stark and Stutsman were given 70 each.

Finally, the North Dakota people wanted to develop their own forms in lieu of the required ones. In particular, they wanted to collect housing information on the applicants. That way, they could have a baseline against which to compare subsequent changes in housing quality. The AAE was an experiment, but they also wanted to do their own analyses.

The plan was typed only nineteen days after they had begun working on it. Kuhn was dissatisfied with it. He felt that not enough financial information had been given to them to allow them to estimate costs accurately. In the transmittal letter he apologized for the "shortcomings in the text and cost analysis table."[6]

Copies of the report were sent to HUD and to the evaluation contractor for review. The Bismarck plan, like most others, suffered from sketchiness which reflected both the limited time period allowed for planning and the lack of reliable census figures for the area. Later, the staff, and the assistant GTR as well, would say that they were satisfied with the length of the planning period, but would have liked more hard data to have been supplied to them, perhaps by the evaluation contractor. That way, they could have spent more time reading literature about rural areas and working on the philosophical aspects of the plan.

THE CRITIQUE

On May 10, five days after the submission of the plan, the Strategic Plan* review conference was held in Washington, D. C.

Several suggestions were made. The most frustrating criticism of the plan was that the design had to be altered. "No experiments within experiments," they were told. The AAE was a naturalistic experiment and would approximate an actual program. North Dakota would have to decide what kind or inspection it wanted. Some of the other agencies were already using agency inspection. It was suggested that the agency could use self-inspection. It would be cheaper, anyway.

In their review of the cost section, HUD asked if administrative expenditures could be reduced. Kuhn replied that they would try and noted that

---

*The first plans produced by the agencies were called "Strategic Plans," because it was in these documents that the agencies' strategies, or approaches to a housing allowance program, were laid out.

reliance upon self-inspection would account for some savings. A reduction of from $500,000 to $400,000 was suggested as a rough goal. Later, Kuhn estimated that the least they could run the agency on was somewhat more than this--$460,000. If there were any further cuts, North Dakota would have to withdraw.

Another criticism of the plan was that the description of local conditions was too spotty. At the very least, there should be a discussion of the vacancy rates. Furthermore, the eligible population would have to be recalculated on the basis of the entire population, not just those renters "living under inadequate conditions."

Finally, if the agency planned on using a special application form, HUD wanted to approve it before it was put in use. It would have to contain all the necessary information required by the experimental forms already in use at the other sites.

The North Dakota agency requested that six weeks be allowed for the recruitment and hiring of staff. As it was now, most of Kuhn's hires were emergency appointments. Filling the lower level positions would require that the full State Merit System* procedures be followed.

REVISING THE PLAN

Writing the second, or "Detailed" plan took another twenty-six days. "Gottfried had much more input into the second plan. It became much more his thing," Queenan recalled.

The experimental control group was eliminated.[7] More participant self-reliance was substituted in its stead. Counseling was largely eliminated; services would be given only if asked for, or if there was an obvious need. Self-inspection for all program units was adopted with only one exception, mobile homes. This type of structure made up a significant portion of the rural housing. Since mobile homes are not of conventional construction and can have unique structural problems, the staff wanted these to be checked by the state building inspector.

Most of the people who would be applying could take care of themselves, Kuhn felt: "They manage other areas of their lives, so why not this one?" Ideally, the strengths in the persons would be emphasized, rather than the structure of the experiment or the program.

---
*The Civil Service system in North Dakota

From his past experience, Kuhn knew that it was easy to make people <u>dependent</u>: "If you deliver counseling services because <u>you</u> decide that they need this and <u>you</u> went and counseled them and they had to sit still because they couldn't do anything else, then of course, I think you would find great need for it. They couldn't escape." The task was to keep the participants independent.

He didn't want to bother any landlords, either. If they were interested in the experiment, they would have to initiate the calls. The agency would not post a list of their available units. The participants would have to find these on their own.

The philosophy was still unstated, but coherent: most participants' problems were strictly financial, and that was what the allowance was for. The agency would run the AAE as an income transfer program.

Queenan and Simonson recalculated the eligible population as HUD had suggested. According to the census figures, 7,000 households might be "income eligible." They doubled their application estimate to 2,000 people and felt more confident that they would need two eligibility control technicians. The low-profile outreach became even more important, since they still assumed a one-third response rate.

They also halved the number of female-headed households to be enrolled. Instead of the 18 percent they had estimated earlier, they settled on 10 percent, since that was their proportion in the general population. These changes later turned out to be planning errors. Ironically, they had been inspired by the reviewers' insistence that a more accurate estimation of the potential eligibles be made.

The C* figures were finally ready. A local "panel of experts" had been assembled to estimate housing costs in the project area.[8] The resulting figures were somewhat lower than those the agency had used. When coupled with the new average income of the intended participants, it meant that the average housing allowance payment was lowered.

Bob Barr designed the new application form, while Kuhn rewrote the management section. Since strict experimental controls were no longer the point of the experiment, the director wanted more of his own stamp on things. The section was by far the longest of any in the plan, and it reflected his basic managerial concern of fiscal responsibility. From past experience, he knew that the only thing which could really hurt the program would be lack of money. Thus, a special emphasis would be placed upon program monitoring.

Work on a self-inspection form was also begun, although it would not be completed until the program was almost underway. The planners had consultations with the Bismarck building inspector to gather information which would allow them to fashion a minimum standard which complied both with the Section 23 leased housing requirements and with the city building codes. The result of this work would be a two-page checklist that was written in non-technical language so that the average participant could use the form himself. It contained a series of about thirty questions that could be answered in a yes or no fashion. Most of the questions were about the basic soundness of the unit.

There were still a few things to do. The housing authorities would have to be told to secure approval from the municipalities within the four county area. He had been in touch with the local directors, and they were enthusiastic about the program. He doubted that there would be any problems.

Finally, Queenan edited the plan so that it would have only one style. One of the problems with the first plan had been that it looked as if it had been written by five different people, as indeed it had.

THE FINAL CONFERENCE

My first meeting with the North Dakota staff was in Washington, D. C. It was in June, 1973, a month before I was scheduled to report on site. My purpose in attending was to be introduced to the people I would be observing for the next year. They were in Washington to have the final version of their plan reviewed by HUD-Central. Three of the then four staff members came to the meeting. The secretary stayed home in Bismarck.

We sat around a table in a room that glared from the fluorescent lights above. The criticisms were minor, and centered around the dollar figure in the planning tables that were in the back of the document. One of the HUD men drew away from the conversation and filled sheet after sheet with calculations.

In turn, the remaining HUD members asked questions: "Why are there so few American Indians in the profile? You've got them here at zero-point-seven percent."

"North Dakota has a large Indian population, but most of them are on reservations. These are outside of the program area."

"I _thought_ that was the reason," the woman replied. Her head nodded vigorously. "But I had to be sure. Someone's going to ask about that, and I wanted to have an answer." A quiet reminder--the Indians were long ago shunted onto confined areas. Occasionally, the Human Calculator would interrupt, "This seems a little high...".

Back to figures and the sheets of paper again. The North Dakota group was unintimidated. Every criticism was answered with a genuine offer of aid to see where the error in logic was. It was an exercise in rationality, the earnest outlanders and the skeptical cosmopolitans.

Finally, "You're not going to check on them at all?" A series of half nods. "You think your _prudent person_ concept will work, huh?" More nods, and a silence that begins to get heavy. The tenseness dissolves in self-conscious laughter among the cosmopolitans.

The ritual is over. They still have to adjust some minor cost estimates, but the plan is intact. Bob Barr, the future assistant director, asks if I need any help finding an apartment, and I tell him I've already got one lined up. We exchange telephone numbers and addresses. He promises to send me a copy of the plan.

Fittingly, the package gets lost in the mail. The 400 miles between Bismarck and Minneapolis are longer than the maps indicate.

Kuhn was pleased. The North Dakota group was free to return to Bismarck; the agency would be a reality in less than a month. They would easily meet the ninety day limit. Kuhn still had to interview the job applicants who were on the Merit System Register. He still had to secure some office space. There was enough money left in the planning grant to purchase all the office equipment, and he figured he could pay a year's rent in advance.

NOTES

1. See: Department of Health, Education and Welfare, "Administrative Review of Social Services, (DHEW report for North Dakota, 1965), for an example of the high regard in which the North Dakota welfare system was held.

2. In April, 1974, North Dakota had only 4,455 families receiving AFDC. Source: Department of Health, Education and Welfare, "Public Assistance Statistics (DHEW, SRS 75-03100, April, 1974), Table 4.

3. North Dakota Experimental Housing Allowance Project, Strategic Plan (xerox, May, 1973), p. 14.

4. Ibid, p. 1.

5. The modified Brooke Amendment states that residents of public housing may not pay rent in excess of 1) 25 percent of their adjusted income, 2) five percent of their gross income, or 3) allotted welfare housing payment, whichever is greater. (Public Law 93-383, 88, Stat. 633). In public housing, rents are fixed by the housing authority. In the AAE, however, actual rents were determined by the private market. Hence, rent estimates for acceptable housing (C*) were used in the payment formula: $HAP = C^* - .25 Y_{net}$, where Y_{net} is adjusted income.

6. North Dakota Experimental Housing Allowance Project, Strategic Plan, cover letter.

7. Ironically, experimental controls would prove to be something that the AAE lacked when it came time for analysis. One other agency, Durham, had also proposed a strong experimental design. Like the North Dakota agency, it was not allowed to put these plans into effect.

8. The "Delphi method" was used as a way of eliciting information from locals who had a knowledge of housing conditions in the four-county area. For a detailed explanation of this method see, O. Helmer, Social Technology (Basic Books, New York, 1966).

4. Staffing: Patterns and Strategies

On page four of the North Dakota Detailed Plan is a very ordinary organization chart.[1] It looks like this:

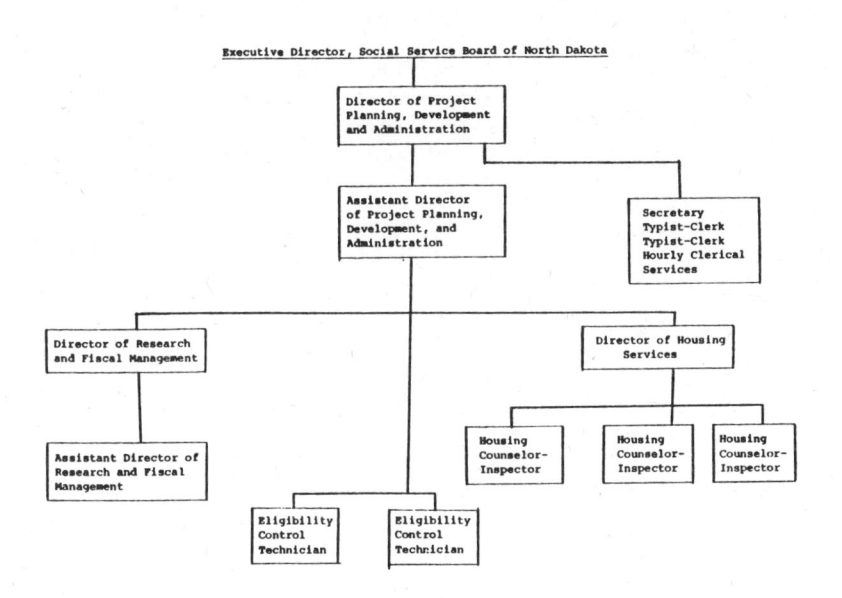

Figure 4-1. North Dakota Proposed Organization Chart, Detailed Plan

The chart was a requirement. Page I-35, Section 6.1 of the APM states that the planners must present "a full organization chart showing every staff position, whether agency, volunteer or subcontractor."[2]

Inevitably, hierarchies are depicted. They remind one of the idealized kinship diagrams that anthropologists use, but vertical distance is authority instead of generations.

In the above representation, only the specific titles are unusual. They have a certain pompousness about them. Thus, Kuhn becomes the Director of Project Planning, Development and Administration; Barr, the <u>Assistant</u> Director of Project Planning, Development and Administration, while Simonson is titled the Director of Research and Fiscal Management.

Even in the planning stages, the North Dakota agency was envisioned as a small one. This was dictated by the director's early estimation of workloads. If organization tables are fictions, bureaucracies require that they be reasonable ones. It almost seems as if the designers worked from project size to staff size and then arranged people in a pyramid.

In moving from the Strategic* to the Detailed Plan, one can see some streamlining. For example, all of the secretaries have been brought directly under the control of the director. Sound management principles dictate this: the planned agency is too small to have secretarial specialists. The new arrangement looks "neater," somehow, but it is only a paper change. There are still at least four levels of command shown, while the maximum size of the agency is given at a dozen or so. If Kuhn and the others had planned to use volunteers or had subcontracted some of the agency activities, perhaps the elaborate organization table would have "made more sense" on paper. But it is still an acceptable design; it doesn't look any different than most of the organization charts that appear in the specific and detailed plans of the other AAE agencies.

The table doesn't tell much of anything, then. Instead of listing the personnel and their duties, it stacks them like the progressively smaller layers on a wedding cake. Four or five layers are the maximum one can have with a mere dozen people if he still wants to keep the idea of a hierarchy.

At least one reviewer, more familiar with organization tables than with North Dakota, was skeptical. After apparently looking at the organization table on page 48 of the Detailed Plan, and then at the accompanying map on page 19, he concluded that the program area was too large for such a small staff:

---

* See page 93 of this book for a diagram.

> Huge geographic area suggests a high probability of program management problems... Agency has been totally laissez faire re: participants...participants will initiate much of the program delivery requests to which the <u>agency will attempt to respond</u>.

This note, pencilled on one of the copies of the Detailed Plan, pointed out an area which many thought would be a focal point for the analysis:

> Handling a large rural expanse is the most obvious challenge the North Dakota agency will face.

There was nothing in the plan to insure the anonymous critic. There was nothing about strategies, nothing about style, nothing about the idiom in which business was to be conducted.

In the director's opinion, the success of the North Dakota effort would depend upon the centralized management that was written into the Detailed Plan, but which charts do not really show. Only one person would be responsible for policy decisions. At the same time, the small size of the agency insured that a more informal and interactive agency would be substituted for the formal hierarchy. Nevertheless, official documents would show the structure indicated in Figure 4-2 on the following page.

In actual practice, however, the lines of authority seemed to resolve themselves into a different configuration, which is shown in Figure 4-3. There are several reasons why this pattern emerged.

Kuhn was interested in financial feasibility and kept tabs on a series of demographic profiles by consulting directly with Greg Simonson. The position of director of research and fiscal management did not involve the making of policy. The work was specialized in nature, and Barr had no training in the area of financial management and thus would not supervise this aspect of agency operations.

Barr's expertise was in eligibility determination and in counseling. He was given the task of overseeing the workers in these two areas. The rule was not absolute: Kuhn would often talk to the counselors directly, especially when one had a client who appeared to need extra help in order to participate. The initial elimination of the proposed position of director of housing services made communication more direct. All of the four counselors were on equal footing.

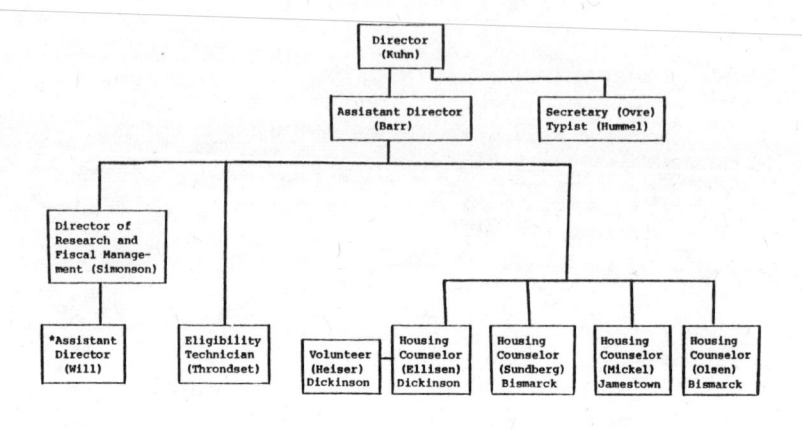

Figure 4-2. North Dakota Maximum Staffing Pattern
(Official Version)

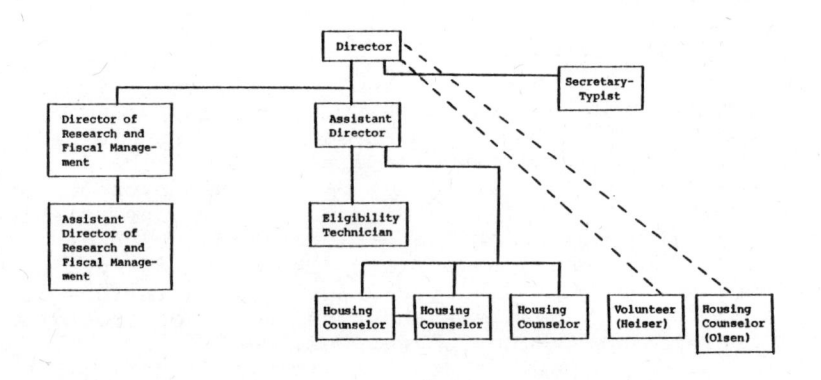

* a clerical position

Figure 4-3. North Dakota Maximum Staffing Pattern
(Unofficial Version)

Olsen, the only male among the counselors, tended to bypass Barr on a regular basis. This seemed to reflect a fact of life about North Dakota: females deferred to the nearest male, whereas with men there was more of a choice. Also, the ecology of the office arrangement may have had something to do with this. The North Dakota Experimental Housing Allowance Project occupied a suite of four offices. Olsen's room was physically closer to Kuhn than it was to Barr. The assistant director had a small cubicle in the largest room, the one which housed most of the Bismarck staff.

The Stark County office had an outreach volunteer who was a longstanding friend of Kuhn's. He reported directly to the director on the state of affairs in the westernmost county in the project area. Kuhn was concerned about lagging enrollment and wanted the volunteer's expert opinion on such matters. Also, the satellite center housing counselor was young and female. The issue was never resolved as to who reported to whom out there. The Stark County counselor assumed that her boss was the volunteer, while the volunteer swore it was the other way around.

As staff resigned or were terminated, the organization contracted, and the agency became more compact from a formal organization point of view. In September, one of the counselors left and was not replaced. At the end of the following month, Mrs. Ovre, the head secretary, announced her resignation, as expected. In November, Kuhn's friend left Dickinson to go south for the winter. In March, the two satellite center counselors were terminated, and the offices were served on an itinerant basis by Olsen and Barr. Finally, the typist-clerk, Dolores Hummel, asked permission to work half-time. These changes meant administrative costs were reduced at the North Dakota agency. At this point, the staff had six and one-half full-time positions, and the office was reorganized.

Barr was no longer assistant director. Instead, he was put over Olsen, and made the director of housing services. The new pattern now had only three levels of authority and approximated the reality of informal office organization, although Olsen still felt free to report directly to Kuhn. The graduated hierarchy was no longer in evidence, and the new structure reflected the single-manager office the North Dakota agency really was:

```
                    ┌──────────┐
                    │ Director │
                    │  (Kuhn)  │
                    └──────────┘
```

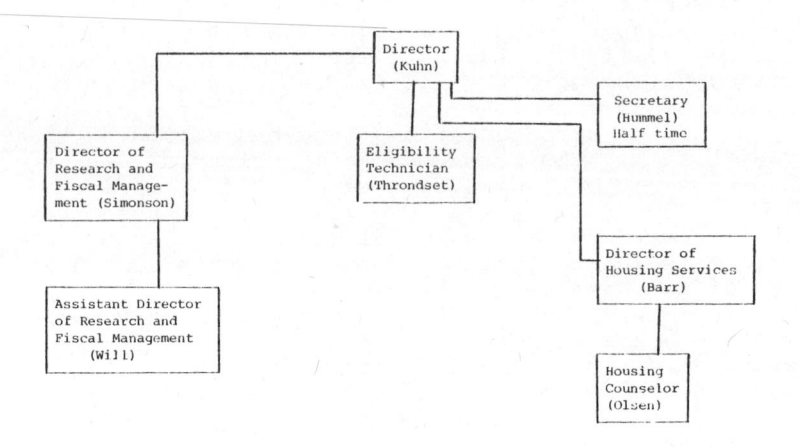

Organization chart showing:
- Director (Kuhn) at top
- Secretary (Hummel) Half time
- Director of Research and Fiscal Management (Simonson)
- Eligibility Technician (Throndset)
- Director of Housing Services (Barr)
- Assistant Director of Research and Fiscal Management (Will) — under Simonson
- Housing Counselor (Olsen) — under Barr

Figure 4-4. North Dakota Staffing Pattern, May, 1974

This would continue to be the official organization table for the agency. Kuhn did not intend to change this until the last six months of the experiment when he planned to reduce the staff until it resembled the skeleton crew who wrote the original plans.

Organization charts, formal or informal, are one of many realities. They usually satisfy that one under which management operates, but there are other viewpoints. Once, the site observer gave each person in the agency several strips of paper, each with the name of a staff member on it. He asked them to arrange the pieces in "any way that makes sense." Barr, Kuhn and Simonson duplicated the official organization table.

In contrast, the secretaries moved the names around until they mimicked the flow of paper in the office. The counselors were a mixed lot. Bob Olsen's arrangement looked like those of the three managers. The Jamestown counselor separated the names according to the analytic functions, with her cohorts in one pile, the managers in another, the financial monitors in a third, and the secretaries in a fourth. A similar pattern was followed by the other satellite center counselor. The eligibility technician produced a design that looked like the spokes of a wheel. Her name was next to those with whom she had close personal relationships--other women.

The figure the eligibility technician assembled seemed to have elements of the office hierarchy in it. The supervisory positions were held by males; the clerical positions by other females. As convivial as the group was, coffee breaks--long, drawn-out affairs--also seemed to reflect North Dakota social life: men with men and women with women.

Coffee at the Red Owl

STAFFING STRATEGIES

The director was cautious in his hiring. The planned members of staff would have been hired only if his earlier estimate of the application rate had proved correct.

Staff members were terminated as soon as the peak workload was over. Even so, he felt that he had hired one counselor too many. Because of the agency's low public profile, Bob Barr's job was in many ways superfluous, and he could be freed to help with the enrollment sessions. Before Kuhn had to make the change, one of the counselors conveniently moved out of the area, and he did not hire a replacement.

In all other cases, Kuhn was able to work unneeded employees back into the state system if that was what they desired. The limited job tenure was something he had made clear in the beginning.

In addition to this cautious hiring pattern, Kuhn pursued a definite strategy as to what sort of person would be hired for which position. Kuhn hired experienced people for the secretarial jobs and deliberately chose inexperienced people as counselors.

Betty Throndset, the sole eligibility control technician, was one of those with experience. She had been one of the first "ECTs" in the welfare system. For the past seven years, she had been doing that sort of work at the state and county levels.

"I didn't want to get hung up or experience any problems in determining technical eligibility as far as financial status was concerned," Kuhn later explained. She was expected to be accurate and quick. Further, separating the client contact and eligibility aspects of casework meant that payment determinations could be done dispassionately. At least that was the theory in the North Dakota welfare organization.

On a more practical level, paper processing could now be handled in the central Bismarck office. The mails could be used to relay payment information to the satellite center counselors.

During the course of the experiment, Betty handled most of the certifications and felt that she could process a maximum of seventy-five per week. The flow of applications was such that this maximum was seldom exceeded. When it was, Barr was able to help out.

In time, Barr began to resemble a utility infielder. Since he had helped write the plan, he was familiar with program regulations. He had supervised eligibility work before, and he could do counseling as well.

Yet, at least at first, Kuhn kept open the possibility that he would have to hire a second eligibility control technician. If the full 2000 applications had surfaced, there would have been no other choice. "You'd probably be asking me why I didn't hire six counselors, too," he confided. This was when the observer was asking him how he knew that the original staff he hired would probably be enough. He pleaded past experience and lucky guesswork.

Kuhn gave his personal secretary, Delores Hummel, the choice of remaining at the Capitol or following him to the EHAP job. She had been with him for several years, and elected to come along.

The housing counselors were the only other professional positions which had to be filled: "I didn't look for experience. I didn't want experience in the working background." The reason was simple enough: if the AAE was not supposed to look like a welfare program, one way of ensuring this would be to hire as counselors people from outside the welfare system. That way, he wouldn't have to ride herd on them. It was also a philosophy of his: I've hired inexperienced people for over thirty years, brought them on board, and got them acquainted with their job and their assignment. It wasn't that threatening to me to hire an inexperienced person and start them out."

Another time, in a more glib vein, he noted: "I've been around here for thirty-eight years. Hell, my institutional memory is long enough for the whole staff."

There were some trade-offs involved: newer people tended to make mistakes that were unpredictable. They hadn't been socialized by the welfare system. Also, having inexperienced people increased the chances that Kuhn could push his vision of the AAE. The younger people wouldn't have anything with which to compare the AAE.

The first counselors hired were those in the main office. Bob Olsen and Kris Sundberg quickly accepted the offer. Olsen had been working for the Workmen's Compensation Bureau for the past two years. Sundberg had been a social worker for a year in Crookston, Minnesota.

The counselor for the Jamestown post, Peggy Mickels, was hired in late July, two weeks after the first two. She had just been graduated from the University of North Dakota in Grand Forks.

The only difficulty that remained was finding someone for the Dickinson opening. None of the counseling positions paid well, and those in the satellite centers were for ten months only. Branch offices were expensive to operate, and Kuhn saw no reason for having a full-time person in the outlying counties after the initial enrollment period was over. Kuhn had been lucky in finding someone for Jamestown so quickly.

The first two applicants he interviewed from the Merit System Register were unsatisfactory, as far as he was concerned. Although the job was a temporary one, Kuhn insisted on professionalism. Whomever he hired had to be willing to move on in the system. Although Kuhn made no promises of future employment for the young counselors, he wanted to use the AAE as a training ground for future social workers.

A week passed, and program applications had already started to come in. He waited a little longer, and then toyed with the idea of having one of the Bismarck counselors service the western office one day a week. Then, he tried to talk to Joe Heiser, the retiring director of the Stark County Welfare Office, into accepting the position.

Heiser took the job, reconsidered, and then declined. He argued that the pay would not make up for his lost Social Security benefits. Instead, he would be happy to stay on as a temporary outreach volunteer.

Kuhn called the department's director of personnel and told him that the position was open again. He hired Siri Ellisen, a young woman who had been a business major at the University of North Dakota. Her background in psychology was strong, and he felt that she was "professional" enought to qualify. It was already August, the first month of the enrollment period.

The only other position left to be filled was that of assistant director of research and fiscal management. It was actually a clerical position. Here, the difficulty was the low pay, a little over $300 a month. Simonson was given the responsibility for finding the proper person. An older woman accepted, thought it over, and then declined the job. The pay was too low. In September, he found someone willing to take the position. Jane Will had worked at a finance company and had the required financial background.

The North Dakota agency was staffed up at last.

Training

For the original staff of four, there was little formal training which could be done. They had attended the HUD planning workshop during the spring and then went through the intellectual exercise of actually producing the required agency plans within a limited time period. Kuhn and Barr were both veterans of the Department of Social Services. Paula Ovre's husband had been a former executive director of the department. Only Simonson had limited experience with social programs, and his job was largely technical. The four of them trained the rest of the staff.

The clerical workers needed the least amount of training. Their skills were largely transferable. All that was required was a familiarization with the forms to be filled out and the office procedures to be used. In addition, they were required to read the APM from cover to cover.

Training the eligibility technician was more involved. Her work was closely related to the financial aspects of the AAE. Accurate eligibility determinations were critical, especially with Kuhn's emphasis on fiscal matters.

Betty's skills were not as transferable as those of the secretarial staff. The welfare and social security programs with which she had been involved all had different requirements. To perform her job correctly, she had to be conversant with a new set of rules.

In order to facilitate this, the two secretaries decided to make up fictitious cases, using blank agency application forms. Betty would then do the determinations, and the results would be discussed with Simonson and Barr, who acted as trainers.

Often, the family situations depicted were unlikely. For example, one of the "applicants" had a disabled wife who was drawing social security benefits, and had recently taken a foster child into the home.

The "correct" deductions* had to be taken. The household was given a double deduction because of the disability, and the foster child was counted as a family member, since he or she probably would have been resident in the domestic unit for the required ninety days.

In cases where there was a question about the eligibility rules, Barr, Simonson, and Betty would consult the APM. If the manual was unclear, the agency director would be asked for his interpretation of the regulations. If a question still remained, Kuhn would then give permission to contact the assistant GTR. Throughout the experiment, the director insisted that he approve any contacts with HUD representatives initiated by the agency. Thus, he would be aware of any changes in policy that were made. "You have to do it that way. Otherwise you lose control of the program," he said.

The dry runs also gave them a change to judge the adequacy of the mail-in application form they created. It wasn't perfect: Barr realized he had

---

* The amount of the housing allowance was based on net income which was the total income less certain deductions. Special deductions were also allowed if the applicant was over sixty-two or disabled.

made a mistake in asking the "amount" of life insurance the family had. Only the cash value of the policies could be counted against the $6000 asset limitation for participating households.

The role-playing sessions were held at odd times, whenever Barr and Simonson were free. New agency forms were also developed. One of them was a payments matrix. Once the household's net income was determined, Betty found the maximum payment allowed by simply running her fingers down the rows and across the columns. A similar utilities matrix was also manufactured. This table showed the estimated average cost of heat and electricity for families of various sizes. This was an important innovation which probably increased the accuracy of payments. In the AAE, the amount of the housing allowance could not exceed the rent paid. C* figures had utilities included. However, local practice was such that the tenant often paid these himself. In cases where the contract rent charged was below C*, and the utilities not paid by the landlord, the matrix allowed the eligibility technician to quickly figure the amount that should be added to the check to cover heat, electricity, and water.

The heaviest training was received by the counselors. Since they were often the first agency contact for the participant, they, too, had to be familiar with the eligibility requirements. Again, Barr and Simonson used fictitious examples so that the new hires could learn "those crucial definitions."

The AAE was bound by rules. Many of these concerned what could and could not be done by the counselors. Interpreting the guidelines literally, the managerial staff decided that three contacts with each particpant would be necessary. The first session was to enroll the person in the program. Next, after a required seven-day waiting period, program information would be given out. Finally, the lease and self-inspection form would have to be approved before payments would begin. To avoid confusion, the trainers had fashioned a "Counselor's Handbook." It was a ten-page annotated listing of areas to be covered during each of the three sessions. At the end of the two-week training period, Bob Olsen and Kris Sundberg rewrote the guide. For them, it was the equivalent of writing the plan.

The last two counselors to be hired also attended informal workshops. The difference was that Olsen and Sundberg assumed a teaching role. Since the enrollment process was already underway when Siri

Ellisen came on board, she was able to observe the actual sessions.

At the end of the one month "start-up" period, the evaluation contractor sent two people out to show the agency how to allot their time charges to the fourteen administrative categories. It was of little relevance for an actual program, but crucial to the experiment. HUD also held a two-day workshop on Equal Opportunity in Bismarck. It was knowledge that was never used: there were no EO cases at the North Dakota site.

COMMUNICATION

The most formal vehicle for inter-staff communication was the staff meeting. Originally, these were to be held on a weekly basis on Friday afternoons so that everyone "would have the weekend free." Kuhn considered the traditional Monday morning meetings to be something which was done out of force of habit. Somewhere, some time ago, someone had gotten the idea that Monday was when staff meetings were supposed to be held.

There were other, practical reasons for holding the meetings at the end of the week: it was the easiest way for the satellite center counselors to attend. The branch offices would close at noon, and the full staff could meet in the Bismarck office by two in the afternoon. It gave the director the chance to meet with these staff members individually to review the week's work. After the meeting was over, the two "out-state" counselors would have the option of returning to their homes or spending the weekend in the capital city.

The original idea for the staff meetings was to have a rotating chairmanship, with a single person responsible for the content of the meeting. Kuhn had hoped that this would provide training to the younger staff he had hired. He envisioned the experiment as a place where new workers could acquire parliamentary skills that would be of use in their careers. In practice, things did not work this way. Instead, Kuhn settled for somewhat less. He informally chaired the meeting and would ask, round-robin, if there was anything which should be discussed or contributed.

The frequency of staff meetings varied, too. At first, the Friday afternoon pattern was adhered to. This was the opportunity to "get everybody thinking together." In the early stages, the program definitions were still troublesome, and the staff was still unsure of procedures.

Thus, the first meeting held after applications were being taken was used to reassure the housing counselors. Two of them had home visits scheduled for the following Monday. This was the first client contact for the agency; both Olsen and Sundberg were nervous. The families to be approached were described, and justifications for the home visits were given. Time charge categories were discussed.

As the experiment wore on, different types of staff meetings could be observed. At first, the main purpose was to reassure new staff and to help them learn the requirements of the experiment. In the middle of the enrollment period, they served to chronicle the progress of the experiment. Later, the meetings were used to discuss philosophical aspects of the program; Kuhn was often uneasy about the definitions of the administrative functions. The issues were discussed and the time charges revised.

As the project began to run smoothly, the Friday afternoon meetings became more sporadic, averaging once or twice a month. Often a particular problem would be discussed in the middle of the week by the local staff. Final decisions would be deferred until a full meeting could be organized. After the enrollment period was over, a new kind of staff meeting was invented. The agency had to prepare for the annual redetermination of eligibility and quality control procedures. New forms had to be devised and new guidebooks created. Individual staff members were given assignments. Betty made recertification forms and explanatory brochures. Barr developed a quality control handbook and adapted the state's quality control forms for AAE use. Olsen studied inspection codes until he felt confident enough to produce forms which would assess the absolute quality of participant housing. Each of these efforts were critiqued during staff meetings that were really workshops.

NOTES

1. North Dakota Experimental Housing Allowance Project, <u>Detailed Plan</u>, (xerox, 1973), p. 4.

2. Abt Associates Inc., <u>Agency Program Manual</u>, (Abt Associates Inc., Cambridge, 1972), p. I-35.

An Agency Staff Meeting/Workshop

5. The Agencies and the Community: It Ain't Gonna Be That Way

A Low Profile Approach with Landlords

"Relations with Suppliers and Others" was the unwieldy analytic name given to agency contacts with landlords, community groups, and governmental organizations. Although this meant anyone who was not an applicant, enrollee, or participant in the AAE, the North Dakota group was most concerned about landlords. The first version of the plan had taken care of this category of relationships with two words: "Not Applicable." The same section in the final Detailed Plan had been expanded to three short paragraphs which indicated that the agency did not intend to pursue any systematic program of contacts with housing suppliers.

This hard line is not the one that would be taken if the AAE were to develop into a full-scale program with broad entitlement: "I would vigorously promote housing allowances through the services staff, individually through the households, and would deal with the people who owned property," the director later said. "That's the only element that we didn't have that needs to be in a real program."

Since the AAE was a limited effort, restraint was called for if the agency was to operate successfully. Just as the director did not want a wild stampede of applicants, he did not want a crush of landlords, either. The latter would want to know how they could benefit from the new idea, and might be disappointed if they did not get any tenants. This was a much more optimistic view of the program's acceptability than many of the other agency directors had. Durham and Jacksonville were having difficulty in getting supplier cooperation. Tulsa had planned and implemented a $50,000 advertising campaign that was, in part, directed toward landlords.

---

* All quotes are from agency personnel or program participants.

To Kuhn, the best approach seemed to be to keep a low profile. If landlords found out about the program the same way participants did, that was fine. He wasn't going to try to sell the project in the communities. There was not enough to sell. Then, in a curious twist of logic, he noted that government programs were touchy things in North Dakota, anyway. Food stamps and welfare were still unpopular in many parts of the state. Once a program got a bad name, for whatever reason, it was hard to rescue it.

Kuhn also felt that his outreach program was adequate and realistic. If the one-third response figure proved to be an accurate estimation, the staff would have plenty to do. Inquiries would come as a matter of course. A participant would approach a prospective landlord, and the landlord would want to call the agency for more information about the project. Maybe he would even want a character reference. The staff felt that actually seeking out landlords would run against the tenets of the experiment. The APM indicated that agencies could not make prior arrangements with housing suppliers. This would have been "steering," and would have limited participant choice. Kuhn and the rest of the agency took the restrictions one step further.

The idea was to test how independently the participants could handle their own housing affairs. If the experiment was supposed to duplicate what went on in a free market, then a "free market" it would be.

The tenant would also be the one who would negotiate any repairs required to bring a unit up to agency standards. Theoretically, a landlord could make the necessary improvements and then recoup the costs by charging higher rent. It could be an attractive program for a property owner, but Kuhn didn't want to be the one to push this possibly inflationary aspect of the AAE.

Instead, he wanted to observe just how many cases of rehabilitation there actually were. The allowances were usually under $100, and he felt that it was a realistic position they had taken: for that sort of money there was a limit to how much fixing could be expected. He felt that the eventual quality of participant housing was intimately tied to the dollar amount of the allowance. Later, when the "stayed with rehabilitation" figure stood at 5 percent, he was satisfied. North Dakota ranked fifth out of the sites in this regard, but the percentage was only one-half of the aggregate mean.

One could also look at the agency's "locational maps" and reach the same conclusions about the modest improvement that had occurred in housing quality. The maps of each city showed that participants tended to cluster in the somewhat older neighborhoods. In Bismarck, for example, no one had rented a house in exclusive Highland Acres, near the country club. Undoubtedly, the allowance relieved rent burden; most of the people had elected to stay in their original units.

Kuhn also felt that the lease requirement alone would insure that the program was advertised. Most housing was owned by private landlords who rented by verbal agreements only. Even the largest property management firm in Bismarck handled things this way. When the prospective tenant produced the Model Lease Agreement with its four special classes, anonymity would be over, anyway. It spoiled the purity of the experiment, and that fact irked him. He retreated even further into the experimental constraints: information given out by the agency would be only about the project. He wouldn't give character references, or divulge the amount of the tenant's monthly housing allowance payment.

There was no middle ground in their approach. If landlords were to be outreached, all property owners would have to get an equal chance. The market in the four-county area was unorganized and fragmented. No landlord associations existed. Trying to reach all of the individual owners would have been time-consuming. Such a step was never seriously considered.

Unlike many other AAE sites, the potentially eligible in Bismarck were also unorganized. Tenants' unions did not exist. Militant welfare rights organizations still lay somewhere in the future.

Indeed, free legal services were not made available to the North Dakota poor until mid-1974; however, only the elderly were eligible for the new program. Relations with renters would be individualized, too.

For a while, the director thought about speaking directly to community organizations and clubs so that the public-at-large would come to know about housing allowances. This was planned for after the enrollment period, when the experiment could no longer be affected. He decided to wait for either HUD or the evaluation contractor to indicate what they wanted him to do. No word came, and he contented himself with a newspaper interview in September, 1974. Even then, he simply outlined the new concept in housing and explained how the experiment was working in North Dakota.

The article was dry and factual. He gave cost figures for the experiment and quickly explained that the program's approach was not intended as a replacement for other housing programs. He also stressed the fact that all dealings were between the tenant and the landlord. "We're moving out of the paternalistic approach in housing," Kuhn told the reporter.

Privately, Kuhn later allowed that his approach might actually have been the opposite of what would have been required for a full-scale program. Landlords would have to be educated. The task was envisioned as an easy one: "You can experience success in selling something when you have a price tag on it, but I wasn't interested in that as far as our plan was concerned. If somebody's testing this elsewhere, good."

Even after what had been a slow enrollment period, Kuhn still felt that the techniques could be simple and direct. One would go to a real estate agency and say, "Look, if you did these things to your property, and you brought these up to standard, here's a group of potential lessees who can rent this, and can afford to pay the rent if you rehab this." But again, the AAE was an experiment and not a program.

DISCOURAGING WELFARE REFERRALS

Kuhn still had another group of suppliers to contend with: the caseworkers within the welfare system. Kuhn had strived to break away from the welfare system by setting up an autonomous agency. As it was, his only local reporting was done directly to the Executive Director of the Department of Social Services. He wanted to take this independence one step further by not having to depend solely upon the clientele of the contracting agency. "That would prove nothing," he later observed. Welfare recipients were captive audiences, anyway. He already knew that he could reach them: the department had been doing that for almost forty years.

Because of these considerations, many of the early "relations with suppliers" took the form of "negative outreach." He used his ties within the welfare system to free the EHAP agency from the system.

The first of these occurred in early July of 1973. Kuhn was in Jamestown to distribute the first news releases about the AAE to the local papers. After he had done this, he stopped by the Stutsman County Welfare Office and visited with the director, Chuck Norton:

It is the first that Norton has heard about the project. His assistant, Mr. Hertz, breaks in and says tht he had seen something about it in the latest issue of *Case and Counsel*, the house organ of the Social Services Board.

"Yes, I didn't mean for *Case and Counsel* to scoop the local papers, but the timetable was delayed," Kuhn tells them. There are four of us sitting in the office. I feel like the outsider I am. Nobody I know talks about "scoops" any more. Lois Lane, Clark Kent and little Jimmy Olsen of the *Daily Planet* used to, every Wednesday evening on television.

Kuhn explains that they had waited for Senator Young to announce the award in Washington. Norton nods; he knows protocol.

Kuhn outlines his low-key outreach approach and pointedly refers to the experiment as a *project*, to emphasize its limited nature. "Originally, we wanted Kidder County. That's as rural as they make them, only they didn't have a housing authority. They were so small that we couldn't include them."

Kuhn wants to leave some brochures, since there are going to be seventy households selected from Stutsman County.

Norton leans forward in his chair and asks if there is anything that he can do to help out. Then he leans back again to wait for the answer. His head is outlined against a background of books on mental hygiene.

Kuhn says that the AAE isn't like other programs. Selection isn't going to be done on the basis of need, *per se*. Instead, there will be a stratified random sample by which households will be chosen. If a given family type is fully represented in the experiment, and a needy family of the same type comes alone, it doesn't matter. "They aren't going to be taken on," he says simply.

Norton asks if he should tell his clients about the project. Kuhn tells him that the project shouldn't be oversold, that not everybody will get on due to the design of the plan, and that this could create a "real public relations problem" for all concerned. It could even backfire on the welfare office, Kuhn offers. People might get angry if they are sent over and aren't selected for particiation.

The suggestion is made that the clients should have to ask about the project themselves. Then, they can be told to send a letter to Bismarck. He wants it all handled through the central office, even though there will be a housing counselor in Jamestown. "What about the elderly?" Norton asks.

Kuhn informs him that they're eligible, too, but they have to be willing to move if they're living with the housing authority. He then explains the method for determing the amounts of the payment. Norton replies that it is "an interesting formula."

The meeting seems to have a time of its own. I am not used to the slow speech and the pauses. My watch tells me that only fifteen minutes have elapsed. Hertz has not said a word and sits stiffly in his chair next to Norton's desk.

The low outreach profile is again discussed. The welfare director's concern is that only people from Jamestown proper will hear about the program in time. It will take longer for the news to get out to the countryside.

Kuhn tells him that the low profile is necessary, at least for now. In fact, he is worried that the news release may generate more response than can be handled. "If that's the case, a second newspaper article will have to turn things off." The hard thing will be to get people to understand the limited scope of the program. He names a social service agency and says that they've already contacted him, wanting to know if one of their clients could be assured of getting in. "They wanted to know if it could be fixed. Well, it ain't gonna be that way."

Norton agrees that the best approach is through newspaper ads instead of through "an agency like this." He is frankly glad that he doesn't have to participate in the project, a turnabout from his early optimism less than a half-hour before....

We have coffee in the next room and meet the rest of the staff. One of the caseworkers is reading aloud an article about North Dakota in some national magazine. The piece makes it sound as if the state is located near the Arctic Circle, with the natives making mad dashes between buildings before their lungs are seared by the cold.

In the next month, Kuhn visited with the welfare directors in the other participating counties and delivered this same message. The technique was successful. If the personalized approach could be used to turn things on, it could also be used to shut them off, at least within the system. At the Bismarck site, welfare recipients made up 11 percent of the eligible population, and 49 percent of the eligible applicants. This disparity is about average for the 8 AAE sites; however, for the only other welfare agency in the experiment, the percentages were 8 percent and 58 percent respectively.

HANDLING THE LHAS

The directors of the four local housing authorities were similarly discouraged from making wholesale referrals, and it was only at the very end of the enrollment period that the directors of one lagging county was asked to send people over.

Joe Queenan took care of many of the early contacts with the LHAs. He had each of them secure approving resolutions from the cities and towns within their respective jurisdictions. He also met with them in regard to other HUD programs and used these visits to brief the directors on the progress of the experiment, thereby reducing their contact with the agency.

While interactions between the agency and the LHAs eventually became cordial, close working relationships were avoided during the enrollment phase of the North Dakota effort. This was apparently done to insure the integrity of the experiment:

> "There is no way of knowing who the people are that we have in there," Kuhn said. "In the early beginnings, let's say the first five or six months, the directors had asked me whether I could give them a list of the HUD people we had in our project, but we never did."

All four of the LHA directors felt ambivalent about housing allowances. They welcomed the additional funds that these Section 23 units would bring to their operations when the experiment ended and the participating households were transferred to them. They also felt that dispersed, private leased housing was an ideal way to serve the varying needs of low-income families. At the same time, they had reservations about the suitability of cash assistance for the elderly. To varying degrees, the directors felt that senior citizens needed services which could most readily be provided by congregate housing with an attached social center.

The directors with comprehensive recreational programs felt the most strongly that the elderly could be best served by other, more conventional housing programs. In an interview, one of them noted: "All of a sudden they're retired, their interests become more common. They can't discuss work anymore, and the question for them becomes, 'What do we do now?'" In contrast, he felt that low-income families had no such common needs and interest. If nothing else, he said, the age span was too great: from less than twenty years old to around sixty-two years.

Another director thought that, if funds later allowed, his organization would purchase a van that would be used to provide transportation to the social center for the elderly who did not live in the housing project. He, too, had developed an extensive social program at the local senior citizens' center, and believed that the elderly were most happy when living together.

However, a different view was expressed to the observer by a senior citizens' coordinator in another county:

When I arrive at the center a rummage sale is going on. Ten or so grey-headed women are poring over piles of clothing that are heaped up on some of the long dining tables. Two groups of men are playing poker, and off at another table a man plays cribbage with his son.

Two women come in carrying heavy bunches of gladiolas. I know there is only one place they could have gotten the flowers, and the thought makes me give an involuntary shudder. The senior citizens' coordinator notices, and laughs: "Yeah, isn't that something? To them it doesn't matter that they're from a funeral. They don't associate it with anything bad. For them, death is like having a meal. It's something they have just come to accept."

She anticipates my first question: "But they're not all alike. Sometimes people are ostracized from the group--like Mr. Sims. He's very clean, but not very tidy about his dress."

She also notices that there are severe class differences among the senior citizens. The ones who own their own homes and have a little money put away are often looked up to. "Even the ones who live in the residence don't feel the same about living there. Some of them like it, and some of them hate it. A lot of them have never had any better. There was this retired worker..."

The two women have put the flowers into vases. I lose my train of thought, as one of them walks over to our table and places the container in front of us. "Thank you, Ella," the coordinator smiles.

"They're so pretty," the woman says, and then she walks away.

I ask the coordinator how she feels about the elderly project. "Well, the rooms are tiny, but what's worse is that we've congregated the senior citizens into a group. Now they're talking about having church services here. It'll be all self-contained. I don't know if it's a good idea to have them separate from everybody else.

"With EHAP, it's different. They live in their own house, they have pride, they get their checks sent to them. Mr. Sims just got on the program, and he bought lunch for somebody here the other day; I was amazed."

"Is EHAP the best answer for them?" I ask.

"Not necessarily. There should be a choice, it's just like with this center. Some people come by every night, but plenty of others avoid the place. That's the way it should be."

None of the directors was actually opposed to cash assistance. They realized that there was a shortage of subsidized housing in the area and saw the experiment as a way of securing more units. Many of these officials later modified their views in the acceptability of this type of help for the elderly: "I don't want to be one of these guys who say, 'Goddammit, you need it.' It has to be something they want. Sometimes the hassle starts when one of their grown kids wants their parents to get into one of our units."

RELATIONS WITH THE FEDERAL GOVERNMENT

One final area of external relationships where there could be potential friction was with HUD itself. As did the evaluation contractor, the sponsoring federal agency had an official "hands-off" policy toward the AAE agencies. There was one important difference, however. HUD was in some sense responsible for the conduct of the experiment. While they wanted to a test of the housing allowance concept, they were unwilling to allow an agency to fail due to sheer incompetence. One of the jobs of the GTRs, or in the case of North Dakota, the assistant GTR, was to monitor the experiment. Financial troubles were a sure way of bringing in HUD intervention. There was no cause for concern in the case of North Dakota.

In addition to official intervention, the GTR was also in a position to influence the experiment in an informal way. At least some of the sites had difficulties in their relationship with the GTR. Commonly, these frictions came when the HUD representative felt that the local agency was violating the spirit of the experiment. One agency, for example, was chastized for doing too much "handholding." That is, for giving the recipients too much help in locating housing.

In the case of North Dakota, agency/HUD relationships remained warm. The planning period had brought the core staff and the GTR together. Kuhn and Queenan had the same outlook, which the latter expressed in governmentese: "Cost minimization and cost elimination." Anyway, he had helped with the plan; he was part of the team.

6. Participant Flow

MRS. FEIST: "ANYTHING YOU WANT TO ASK, ASK..."

An agency that administers a social program may be seen as a piece of machinery that secures and processes applicants, and turns them into participants. The program guidelines and requirements, set forth in the Agency Program Manual, gave a superficial air of sameness to these operations at all AAE sites.

Each agency was required to plan around a core of fourteen administrative "functions" that all had Newspeak names. Thus, advertising the program became "Outreach," while monitoring the demographic characteristics of present and future participants became "Phase-in." By "compartmentalizing interactive activity" at an agency, cost analysis could be performed and complicated office procedures reduced to "flow charts." Abstraction by functions thus allowed for systematic comparisons to be made between agencies.

By living with these constructs throughout the course of the experiment, the North Dakota staff members began to think of these functions as something very real. Workers allotted their time among the categories and wrote monthly narratives to the project director with these in mind.

After a while, the staff began to converse easily in the new language of the experiment. Metaphysical discussions would often ensue during meetings. They took the form of "When is Maintenance of Records really Management Support?" Like a Talmudic scholar, the director would pore over the definitions offered in the APM, and the office personnel would discuss the meanings of The Word. They felt that in order for the findings to be true, their time charges had to be "right." Within the limits of the program guidelines, every agency performed the necessary functions its own way. The relative emphasis on any given area varied greatly. As a result, analytical process documentation and the flow charts for each agency would look somewhat different.

But a flow chart does not represent the everyday reality of agency life. Rather, it is like the diagrammed sentences of the English composition teacher. Flow charts remove human elements from the agency process just as surely as sentence diagrams remove tone and inflection from speech. Participants become anonymous tokens on a game board or a maze. The agency takes on the look of a mass of bureaucratic plumbing, with administrative valves and shunts located at strategic points.

Another limitation to such documentation is that the products do not really touch on what is important to the participant: Were the people at the agency friendly and helpful? Was there a long wait to get to talk to a counselor? More basically, was he or she selected to participate? Agency staff members are like gatekeepers, but the term can cover both friendly concierges and scowling jailers.

Another way of showing how the agency operates is to walk a typical participant through the entire administrative process, from application to the receipt of the first payment:

ABOUT MRS. FEIST

Erna Feist is a widow in her middle sixties. For the eleven years since her husband passed away, she has lived in the downstairs of an owner-occupied duplex. Long ago, she became friendly with the landlady, who herself has been a widow for eight years. Until recently, the two of them have exchanged services: Mrs. Feist would keep the sidewalk swept from snow, and Mrs. Buck would drive her tenant to the Red Owl once a week to shop. Last year, however, Mrs. Feist suffered a heart attack, and now the exchange is more lopsided.

The two woman attend the same church and go to early Mass together every Sunday. Mrs. Buck always drives. Mrs. Feist can offer nothing in return except companionship. Her life is a very quiet one. She can no longer get around like she used to. Her older daughter also lives in Bismarck, and is very attentive. The two of them visit once or twice a week. When she can afford it, she gives her mother quiet gifts of five or ten dollars. Erna managed to just get by on her social security benefits. Although she would be eligible for assistance from welfare, she is too proud to take it: "I've never asked for anything."

HEARING ABOUT THE PROGRAM

It was her daughter who first heard about the Experimental Housing Allowance Project. In the early fall, Dialing for Dollars had a young fellow on the show, and he had talked about it. Later, she also heard a radio spot. For two months, Elisabeth tried to talk her mother into applying for the program. In late October, Mrs. Feist agreed.

Elisabeth called the agency the same day. This was the most common way of finding out more about the project. Only occasionally did people drop by one of the offices or write a letter. Betty Throndset, the eligibility technician, took the call and explained that the program was for both low and moderate income renters. "I can send you a brochure, and an application form that you can fill out at home. If you have any questions, you can call again, or come in and talk to us. We're in the basement of the Vogel Building."

Elisabeth said it was for her mother and asked that an application be sent to her mother's address.

As soon as the conversation was over, Betty handed the information she had written on a pad to Delores, the secretary. She, in turn, wrote down Erna's name and address in a ledger book, and stamped in the day's date beside it. The application form and brochure were enclosed in a large envelope along with a stamped return envelope.* The package went out in the evening's mail.

APPLYING

The application arrives the next day, the first of November. However, there is a delay in filling it out. The four page form looks too complicated to Mrs. Feist, and she wants Elisabeth to help. This week, though, Elisabeth is visiting her sister, who lives on a farm in Wishek.

---

* A copy of the application form is included in Appendix B.

When they actually do fill it out, Elisabeth finds that the form is much simpler than it appears: "Ma, what's your social security number?"

The first part of the application elicits personal information such as name, address, sex, and age. Another section is for recording present living arrangements and amount of rent paid. The part on income, Section D, often gives seasonal workers problems, since their income fluctuates. In Mrs. Feist's case, it is easy: there is only her social security payment, plus a small annuity that is paid yearly.

As the two of them work, the daughter reads each question out loud. Erna finds the triplicate of her hospital bill for last year: $2,978.96. This figure is entered as her medical expenses. She remembers.

Listing assets is the easiest part of all: she has none, except for $15 cash on hand. For "Other Personal Property," Elisabeth checks Yes, and dutifully writes "some furniture."

She has her mother sign the certification statement, which warns that anyone who knowingly makes false statements "shall be subject to fine, imprisonment, or both." The words are on all applications from the Department of Social Services, in spite of the fact that fraud is almost impossible to prove.

Elisabeth signs below, as she has helped prepare the application.

SCREENING AND CERTIFICATION

As soon as the return envelope is received at the office, Delores makes a tally in the ledger book. The day's date is stamped opposite Erna's name, and the way she first heard about the project is recorded by making a check in the appropriate column.

She is officially made an applicant when a prenumbered application form from the evaluation contractor is filled out on top. From now on, she will be 053347 to the evaluation contractor's computer, and all the operating forms that concern her will be so identified. At the agency she will still be Erna Feist.

Betty receives the new file and scans the agency application form to see that all the blanks have been filled in. She checks to see if "technical eligibility" is present. The income is small enough; even the gross figure is more than $2,000 below the upper limit. Mrs. Feist is single. In order to be eligible, she must either be disabled or over sixty-two years old. She easily qualifies on that score.

This is called "Screening" in Newspeak. It is rapid and somewhat intuitive. Eligible applicants are "screened in," but for those who do not meet the criteria, the logical Newspeak construct is not applied. They are not "screened out," for the term is too harsh. Instead they become "ineligibles," but later. Screening at the North Dakota agency was intimately tied to the verification of statements, or "Certification." Unlike many other agencies, Bismarck uses "self-certification." As much as possible, the applicants' statements are taken at face value. Using the "prudent person principle," the eligibility technician is assumed to have enough sense to question any statements which appear suspicious. For example, if someone states that he pays $100 a month for rent, and yet claims to have an income less than this figure, a further inquiry should be made. It also works the other way: a working mother should probably have child care expenses. If she lists none on her application, then perhaps she should be asked about it. Otherwise, she may receive a smaller payment than she is entitled to.

In Mrs. Feist's case, everything is in order, except that Betty wants to know more about the $3,000 in medical expenses. She circles this amount with a red pen, a standard procedure of the Department of Social Services. The question is one which can be answered over the telephone. Did Mrs. Feist pay these expenses herself, or were they only actually incurred by her and paid by Medicare?

The telephone call makes Erna a little nervous, and she answers truthfully that the government paid the bulk of the expenses.

"You paid only the deductible, then?"

"Yes."

"How about medications? How much do they cost you a month?"

Betty jots down the new figures, notes the date of the telephone call and signs her initials. The case is routine. Almost one-third of the applicants have to be recontacted.

COMPUTING THE ALLOWANCE

On a mimeographed worksheet, Betty computes Mrs. Feist's housing allowance. Gross income is figured on a monthly basis. Then the deductions are allowed. Since Mrs. Feist is elderly, 10 percent of her gross monthly income is subtracted from the total. Her average monthly medical expenses are also taken from the total. This gives the "adjusted gross income."

Participants are expected to contribute one fourth of this figure towards housing. The project pays the difference between this and the average cost of a standard unit for a household of a given size.

The estimated cost of such a rental dwelling for Erna is $90 per month including utilities. Assuming she can find a unit that rents for that exact amount, she will be expected to contribute $27, since her net monthly income is only $108. The agency will pay the $63 difference.

In reality, she may pay more or less than $90, but the agency contribution will remain constant.*

AWAITING SELECTION

Mrs. Feist is now a "Certified Eligible." Before her file is handed to the secretary for typing, the assistant director checks the calculations.

At this point, Erna's file grows thicker as Delores adds several forms which will be used if she is chosen to participate in the experiment. All of these are solely for the use of the evaluation contractor: the agency has developed its own way of doing things and its own forms are drawn off those of the parent agency. As required, the second copies of the completed application and certification forms are sent back to the evaluation contractor, where the information will be keypunched. Meeting a more immediate human need, a form letter is sent to Mrs. Feist telling her that she is eligible. However, she is cautioned that not everybody will be chosen, and that her name has been placed in a "pool" with the names of other eligibles.

BEING SELECTED

Like most of the others who applied for the project, Mrs. Feist waits patiently. Due to the experience of the staff and to the smaller-than-anticipated number of applicants, it takes less than a week to bring a person to the stage where he or she becomes a "potential enrollee."

---

*However, the amount of the housing allowance cannot exceed the amount of the rent plus utilities.

At this point, the director of research and fiscal management transfers the name of the "certified eligible" into a <u>potential enrollees log</u> that is kept separately for each county. Name, sex, and age of the household head are noted, as are the family income and the size of the housing allowance. From a program point of view, she would be a very desirable participant. At the time she applied, there was room for more elderly people in the demographic profile, and her comparatively low payment of $63 would help keep the size of the average housing allowance payment at slightly below planned levels. As a result, she is only in the "pool" for a week when she is chosen for enrollment and her name is entered in an <u>enrollees log</u>.

THE FIRST SESSION

Her assigned counselor is Bob Olsen, and he immediately sends out another form letter informing her that she has been picked out for the program. A suggested meeting time is included.

All enrollees are required to attend three sessions at the North Dakota agency. The first is probably the most artificial from a non-experimental point of view. This is the "Enrollment Session," and its purpose is to acquaint future participants with their rights and responsibilities as project participants.

From an individual's outlook, little information of personal relevance can be communicated during the introductory meeting. The agency staff has interpreted the experimental constraints correctly, and no housing information is given out until a seven-day waiting period has elapsed. This gives the evaluation contractor an opportunity to conduct the initial interviews with a sample of new enrollees. It is also during this time that the occupied unit may be inspected to provide a baseline against which any future improvements in housing quality can be measured.

When Mrs. Feist leaves the half-hour session, she knows that the project is a federally-funded experiment, that she will receive payments for a minimum of twenty-four months, and that she might be interviewed by someone from a research company. She also knows that she will have to sign a lease, and that she will have ninety days in which to find a standard unit that she herself will inspect. She has no idea of how large her payment will be. On the other hand, Mr. Olsen has assured her that her social security will not be reduced because of the money.

Mrs. Feist thought that Mr. Olsen looked like a nice boy, well-groomed and clean-cut. And he had carefully answered all her questions.

THE SECOND SESSION

Mrs. Feist arrives ten minutes early for her second appointment with the agency--a "Counseling Session," in the parlance of the experiment. In truth, the North Dakota agency does little actual counseling. Most sessions last only a half-hour and are geared toward advising the enrollee of the program requirements so that he or she can meet them and become a participant. Few need any more help than that; the staff members think it is insulting to offer unwanted aid.

This meeting is the most important one for Mrs. Feist, as she will find out exactly how much money she will be getting. Optimistically, she hopes that it might be as much as $25. She will also receive the necessary lease and self-inspection forms which must be completed and approved before payments begin. Finally, she will have to sign more legal documents that are a requirement of the experiment.

It is the day before Thanksgiving. Even at 11 o'clock, the temperature is still five degrees below zero. Two days ago, fourteen inches of snow fell on Bismarck. The city has recovered now. The plows have heaped snow into mounds in the middle of the main avenues. The streets look as though they are walled.

Mrs. Feist has a problem getting to the agency. Her landlady is visiting her son in the hospital, and so Mrs. Feist prevails upon her son-in-law to drive her. He is a trucker, and this is one of his rare days off. He tells her that he would pick her up in an hour, and that she should wait in the foyer of the building so she can be seen.

As she waits in the reception room, she unbuttons her coat, revealing a heavy woolen sweater underneath. She then removes the babushka from her head, and unwinds the long scarf from around her neck. These she places in an oilcloth shopping bag that she often carries. Her face begins to lose some of its flush.

Bob Barr, the assistant director, comes out from behind the participation that is one of the walls of his "office." "Mrs. Feist?"

She follows him and sits down on the side chair next to his desk. She is barely five feet tall, and her feet, even in thick-soled rubber boots, only graze the floor.

Ordinarily, Bob Olsen would have continued with her, but at the beginning of the week the project director had Barr take half of the Bismarck caseload. Olsen had been doing the work of two people since Kris Sundberg quit in September. His reporting had gotten a little behind because of it.

There is no privacy in the cubicle. Actually, it is more like a stall with a desk in it. The front is completely open, and the temporary walls are merely paneling which does not reach to the ceiling. The noise level is high, and Bob is aware of Delores' Selectric typewriter. Since it is the end of the month, she is preparing the Department of Social Services payment forms that will go to the Capitol this afternoon for processing.

The phone rings in the cubicle next to his. Barr can hear the on-site observer talking to someone. Jokingly, he thinks that Mike didn't have to ask him to tape this session--the company could have issued him a long-stemmed wine glass to listen with. Just put it up against the panel and you're in business, for all the good the "walls" do.

Mrs. Feist gives permission to have the tape recorder on, and he flips the switch on the microphone.

"...thank you, Mrs. Feist..."

"Anything you want to ask me, ask me. Anything I can answer, I will answer."

"Okay..."

"If I can't answer, I'll ask the question."

"Fine," *he says goodnaturedly, with a half-laugh ....*

"And here's the thing, but I'm not able to do a darn thing, anymore. I've got heart trouble, and I don't know if it's going to get any better. And it's bad, my doctor told me. Yeah." *The statement serves as an explanation of why she finally decided to apply.*

"Well, the most important thing I can tell you today is that the amount of help you can get from our agency is $63."

She only nods. Barr is a little worried that she did not hear him, but the log sheet from the previous session says that she is alert and gets things the first time they're said. Actually, she is surprised that the payment is so much, but is intent on getting all the details so that she doesn't have to ask questions.

Bob extracts the worksheet from her file and explains how her payment was computed. This involves showing how a net income figure was arrived at, and how one-fourth of this is subtracted from $90, the estimated cost of standard housing for her.

"Uh-huh. That's fine. I'd be willing and satisfied. I'd be willing and satisfied." Mrs. Feist often repeats things twice when she wishes to stress them. Her "W's" sound more like "V's." "I tell you that for eleven years I made my own living, and never thought of going to places and asking for help." Her voice is unsteady. "I can't help myself anymore. For eleven years I made my own living."

"Well, look at it this way, Mrs. Feist. This is an experiment for the U. S. Government, and they're hoping to learn whether or not this can work as a national program." It is an argument he often uses when an individual is sensitive about accepting assistance.

"You're actually helping the government."

"Uh-huh. Like I say, anything you want to ask, ask me. Anything I can't answer, I'll ask the question..." It is her part of the exchange--honesty.

The session continues, and Barr follows the outline in the Counselor's Handbook. This ten-page xeroxed guide highlights the points that he must cover at each session. He has committed the whole thing to memory: he helped write it in the first place and has processed many enrollees. Each time, he varies the format, as do the other counselors. In Mrs. Feist's case, nothing will be said about what to look for in an apartment or in a neighborhood. She is planning on staying, and such information is superfluous. Similarly, in her first session with Mr. Olsen, he said very little about her rights against discrimination. Again, he knew that she wanted to stay, and also, she is white.

In practice, almost all of the elderly who participated in the program did not move. They had usually been living in basement apartments for several years. They had gotten to know their landlords and relationships were familiar and smooth.

"Now, we have a self inspection form here.* You have to use this to make sure that your place complies with the requirements for the program." He hands her a copy of the form. The noise of the typewriter continues, and now, the ancient xerox machine begins to click as someone feeds a sheet of paper through the slot.

---

*A copy of the inspection form is included in Appendix B.

In most cases, he would walk her through the thirty or so questions that must be answered with a yes or a no. However, Bob Olsen has noted in the log sheet that her married daughter visits her frequently. He makes a decision:

"Can your daughter or son-in-law help you out with filling in his inspection form if it gets to be too much for you ?"

"Well, neither of them have had high school. My son-in-law's had the eighth grade. Maybe you can fill it out," Mrs. Feist suggests hopefully. She is bent over the desk and perches on the edge of the chair so that her toe-tips are on the floor.

"Well, I can't. You see, it has to be filled out by you or a relative."

"I tell you, I'll try my son-in-law. If he can't do it, then I'll get my landlady. She's had experience with leasing and things like that..." Mrs. Feist lapses into what is really a soliloquy: Mrs. Buck was always nice about fixing things and painting the apartment. About how she hadn't raised the rent in five years....

"When I told her about the program, and there would be some papers to sign, she said, 'Anything you want, Erna. I'll be upstairs to sign the papers.'"

The Model Lease Agreement is next, and Mrs. Feist is shown a sample that is already filled in. The minimum and maximum lengths of coverage are explained, and he tells her that she can take the form with her. In addition, she is given two blank copies.

"Now, if you want to use another lease, it has to have these four provisions added to it," he says, giving her yet another sheet of paper.

She decides that she will use the agency lease, since Mrs. Buck rents to her by verbal agreement only. "Would you maybe put a a little x in the corner so I know which one it is?"

"Sure, and if you have any trouble, just call us here, or have your landlady do it. We'll be happy to explain things to her if she doesn't understand." He hands her an appointment slip that has his name and agency telephone number on it.

Finally, Mrs. Feist is instructed that she should report any change in her financial condition to the agency, as any change in income could affect the size of her allowance. "But the only way you would become ineligible for our project is if you net income went above $4,400 a year."

She allows that this is unlikely. "I don't know if I'll ever get back to work. I tell you, my doctor says it's bad. I keep on waiting to get better, but maybe I think that I'm not going to get better no more."

"Well, of course you never know, but you can't let it get you down." Her talk about her health is a little unsettling to him.

"I tried to sweep the snow off the porch this morning, but I got this pain right _here_," she explains, running her finger beneath her breast. "It just feels like it _holds_ on my heart. Like that."

"You're getting a little older now, and maybe you shouldn't be doing all that work."

"But you can't let the snow pile up and drag it through the house like that. You have to be clean, you know." Mrs. Feist had taken on the task herself years ago. Now, she says, Mrs. Buck will have to get somebody.

"Now, there's one more form that you have to sign, and I'll get you a copy of it. It's called the 'Certificate of Eligibility.' You should read this carefully."

She reaches down into her shopping bag and extracts a pair of glasses that are in a worn leather case. Even with these, she still has to hold the paper at arm's length.

"Maybe I should read it for you," he suggests.

He does, simplifying the language as he goes along. "HUD has designed an experiment, and..." The reading gives him an opportunity to make sure that she understands everything that has gone on in the session.

The language in the document is terse, and even as he softens it, the words still seem harsh to him. "Now the only reason we'd stop making payments to you is if the house got into, uh, a condition that it was no longer decent, safe, and sanitary. Or if you didn't put the amount of the allowance toward the rent."

"Oh, I'd never do that. In all my years here, I never..."

"I know, Mrs. Feist, but I have to tell you that so you know what this says."

She signs, and he excuses himself to make a copy.

"Now, probably the soonest we can get a payment to you is January 1." He thinks for a moment: "Do you think that you could get this filled out today?"

No, she says, her landlady will be down at the hospital when she gets her car started. Her son suffered a stroke that weekend.

"Was he a young man?"

"He's only fifty years old, but he has high blood pressure and sugar diabetes, so there's nothing they can do for him..."

Again, the kindly remarks are made. Then, "You actually have ninety days to find housing, but in your case, it'll only be a few days or a few weeks before

these forms are filled out. If you can have these
back to use before the twentieth, we can get you a
payment by January first."

The conversation is warm. Her words are melo-
dramatic because they are truthful: "You know, Robert,
I've had a lot of trouble and heartaches in my life.
But I always figure I've got enough money for one more
month."

He remembers her condition and says, "You give
me a call when those papers are done, and I'll stop
by your house and pick them up so you won't have to
come down here again in the cold..." If things hadn't
been so hectic here, he would have held this visit at
her house. When Olsen had the double caseload, there
wasn't much time for that.

"All right, Robert, I am ready to go." The
manners are now more formal. She rises and shakes
his hand.

THE THIRD SESSION

Two weeks later, he gets a call from Mrs. Feist
and drives to her house for another "counseling
session." This is normally the shortest of the three
meetings, as it takes only a few minutes to examine
the lease and inspection form.

Everything is in order, and he tells her that
he'll send her copies in the mail. She offers him a
cup of coffee and a piece of stollen. In spite of the
fact that he is on a diet, he accepts.

The apartment is tidy, and overheated for anyone
with a normal circulatory system. The couch he sits
on is a piece from the 'forties , but is spotless.
It dawns on him that she probably took the slip cover
off because he was coming over, and he is company.

ISSUING A PAYMENT

When he gets back, Bob still has to fill out a
"payments initiation" form for the evaluation contractor. A copy of each piece of paperwork is kept in
her file. Then, too, he has to write up another log
sheet on this session. Near the end of the month the
agency secretary will type up a Form 600 that will
tell the computer to print out a $63 check for her.

It will arrive in a plain white envelope a few
days after the first of the year. The system is
reliable.

COMMENTARY

Mrs. Feist is really a composite of several different people. During his stay, the observer sat in on several participant sessions, and taped many more. Permission was always asked, and always granted. The people in North Dakota were accomodating that way.

In spite of the fact that she is not a "real" person, the treatment she, Mrs. Feist, received was typical of that which the agency people gave participants. If the personnel did not adopt an advocacy stance, they were always ready to extend quiet, personalized help. Because of this, each session varied according to the individual.

Much of the interaction with participants was conventional and not related to participation in the project, per se. If the person was a farm worker, much of the talk might have been about this year's crop. It is important to the individual, and the counselors were interested and concerned. In a larger sense, they, too, were affected by the agricultural economy of the state. Many of them have relatives who are farmers. The tone was always genuine. Because she was elderly, and ill, Mrs. Feist received more direct help from the agency than was ordinarily necessary. The home visit is an example of this.

Other enrollees and eventual participants received more help. Some had additional follow-up contacts.

The vast majority of people in the program, however, made only the three required visits, completed the necessary forms and began receiving their monthly payments. In such cases the counselor acted only as a guide to lead them through the red tape that marked the program. Many of them marveled at the "simplicity" of it all, unaware of all the processing that went on.

7. Program History

<u>INTRODUCTION</u>

　　　The North Dakota agency was quiet and intimate. Management was firm and benevolent. Interactions often had an air of thoughtfulness that was marked by geniality. At least it seemed that way to an outsider such as myself. There were no crises during the course of the experiment. Panic was alien to the director's management style. He believed in a "sense of orderliness," and communicated this to his staff.

　　　Corrections were made slowly, and constantly. The administrative mechanisms were used to control the experimental environments. Yet the demands on the agency were substantial, when one looked at things objectively. Four hundred people would have to be receiving payments on April 1, 1974, if the experiment was going to reach its planned size. Since the agency began its operations during July, 1973, this meant that the last enrollee would have to be processed by January 31 of the coming year.

　　　During the planning period, the core staff had made timetables to represent what they wanted to happen in an ideal world. This was one of many such requirements placed upon them by HUD. The first month of payments would be August, and the staff wanted to have twenty households receiving payments by then. This would be a test of the administrative apparatus they had devised.

　　　Forty more families would receive their first checks in September, then 160 in November. This would be before the onset of cold weather. The planners thought that house-hunting efforts would be hampered once the winter began. Still, they figured on an additional forty households in December. Then, things would tail off even more. For the last three winter months, the aggregate total was aimed at forty.

In equally optimistic fashion, the planning staff had anticipated that no one would drop out during the enrollment period. They could not think of reasons why people would leave the AAE, and indeed, estimated that only twelve families would terminate during the course of the experiment. As each household received its twentieth payment, it would be transferred to the appropriate LHA in the program area. The four LHAs would have a total of 388 new households by the end of the thirty-third month of program operations. The last ninety days would be used for writing up the final reports. Then, the records would be stored in the basement of the Capitol and the work of the North Dakota Experimental Housing Allowance Project would be finished.

HUD had also required that the agencies set demographic profiles for enrollees that would match the characteristics of the population at large. Thus, the plan was to enroll 102 single-person households, 81 two-person households, and 145 three- or four-person households, each consisting of five or more people, would also participate in the program. Similar profiles for age, sex, and race of head of household were also devised.

The average annual C^* had been figured at around $1,700, or $142 per month. For the "typical" family participating in the experiment, the mean net income was projected to be $3,129. This meant that the experiment would pay $77 per month towards the rent—if everything worked out as the planning staff imagined.

The North Dakota group was confident that they could fill the demographic profiles. They had envisioned an immediate response to the program. The 2,000 applicants they had projected would mean that they could pick and choose the participants by a "stratified random selection procedure." Simonson would judiciously pick the families so that all types of people would be represented. This meant that 1,600 households would have to be turned down. Eighty percent of the applicants would not have a chance to participate, which was why the agency didn't want to overdo outreach. Disappointed people would be angry people.

Things did not work out this way. The multitude of applicants did not materialize, and the agency was forced to make trade-offs in an imperfect world. The trick was to maintain a level head and to sort out what was crucial for a successful experiment. They began to realize that planning tables could become imprisoning sorts of things.

The director decided that sticking to the timetables was not important, as long as there were the full 400 participants at the end of the housing search period the following April. They had to be the "right" participants, however. The two key variables were the amount of payment and the size of the household receiving it. These would have to be controlled in the aggregate.

According to the Annual Contributions Contract (ACC)* they had signed, each specific household size generated a certain amount of funding. Thus, a single-person household would earn ninety-five dollars from HUD for every month it was in the program. At the other extreme of size, HUD would contribute $190 per month for a nine-person household. By meeting their household size profiles exactly, the 400 participating households would generate the full amount of money from the contract. If there were too many small households, the agency would wind up being underfunded, since no more than 400 families were allowed to participate under the terms of the agreement. Too many large households, and the financial limits of the contract would be exceeded before the full complement of participants had been achieved. Either alternative was unacceptable.

Since the agencies were not given separate administrative funds to run the program, these would have to come directly from the ACC money. Because of this, it would prove necessary to keep the average housing allowance within bounds. If to many low-income people were in the program, an agency could be faced with a situation whereby it would not have enough operating reserve to pay office expenses and salaries.

For Kuhn, this was a new way of looking at things. With the Social Service Board, you went before the state legislature every two years with your appropriation request. The budget committee looked it over and made cuts. Then you went back and managed on the money until the next biennium. To the neediest first.

The AAE was a little different, since it required that a broad spectrum of people be served, but everything was still tied up with money. Money was the key. The ACC set the outer limits of the effort. You

---

*The Annual Contributions Contract (ACC) was the funding mechanism for each agency.

143

couldn't go over the stipulated amount without amending the contract. An amended contract was a sign of failure to Kuhn. It meant that you couldn't live within the rules, that you couldn't manage.

The North Dakota strategy solidified: Keep payments reasonable, watch family sizes, and cut administrative costs. If that was done, you could still run the experiment your own way. At least during the enrollment period, all this was something that <u>kept</u> having to be done. Once this realization was made, what followed was a series of minute adjustments in agency outlook and behavior. Because corrections occurred on an almost daily basis, the temptation is to report on them, to give a chronology, to give the reader fieldnotes taken during a thirteen month stay in Bismarck.

Stepping back, however, one can see an evolving design to agency activities. The experiment had a time clock inside it, but the stream of events can be broken up. A grid can be overlaid which shows that a series of strategies was used to achieve the central goals of full participation and financial feasibility.

At first, the staff was optimistic, and concentrated on outreach in an inductive fashion. If one technique did not bring in the desired response, another approach would be used. The pool of applicants grew, but never to the proportions originally envisioned.

Next, heavy monitoring was used to correct the "mistakes" of the outreach effort. If people weren't applying in direct proportion to their numbers in the population, then phase-in would have to make whatever adjustments were possible. Sex, age, and income categories became secondary to straight feasibility concerns.

Toward the end of the seven-month period, a slight rush occurred. The AAE was not an on-going, open-ended program. It had a definite beginning, middle, and end. Outreach efforts were intensified and more enrollees selected. Enough people had to get to this stage before the deadline fell, so that the drop-outs could be replaced. This was the only way that the full complement of participants could be insured.

In March, the agency became more active in helping those enrollees who were still searching for housing. Again, this is an artifact of the experiment and its time clock. Those last few people had to be brought to the payments stage. "I want a strong 400," Simonson remarked.

Finally, there was a slide, or a lull. The agency had to move into a steady-state mode. The *assistant GTR had to develop a transition plan to be approved by HUD. New forms had to be advised for the upcoming annual redetermination of payments that was required by program regulations. An optional Quality Control field review of selected cases meant additional work for the North Dakota staff.*

The payoff was to be that they could do their own analyses of their efforts. This was something that was not in the contract, but they wanted to do it. They ran the AAE as an experiment, and now that the program was in steady-state, the agency staff wanted to become the analysts of their own efforts.

Each one of these periods meant that agency activity was different. From an analytical point of view, one or two "functions" or areas of activity would become important, and then would recede into the background.

THE ISSUE OF OUTREACH: THE EARLY OPTIMISM

The distinct period in the North Dakota agency history runs from July to September, 1973. Many of the activities of the first month were centered on "start-up," or those things which were necessary for the agency to "get operational."

The core staff had moved into the basement of the Vogel Building the week of June twenty-fifth. The following two weeks was a period of training and waiting. The desks for the new counselors had not arrived yet. This was one of the minor irritations Kuhn had experienced many time in the past. "We're waiting patiently," he told the observer when asked what he was going to do about the situation.

"We don't need much office furniture until the applications start coming in," Mrs. Ovre had added.

The quarters were grim. Windowless and lighted by flourescent tubes, the offices resembled a concrete block bunker. The walls had been painted a flat white, while the floors were covered by a mottled brown tile.

On the positive side, the rent was a low $350 per month and Kuhn was able to pay a year in advance, as he had planned. The office equipment was also paid for.

Kuhn felt lucky to have gotten the space in such a convenient location. There was no room at the Capitol for the new agency, and there was almost nothing for rent in Bismarck. For a while, he had thought about locating the main office six miles away, in Mandan, but the present arrangement was more convenient for all concerned. The Vogel building was downtown, right off the main drag. Almost half of the recipients would be coming from Burleigh County, and everyone in Bismarck knew where the building was located. The separate office would also help to mentally separate the agency from the welfare system.

The Agency Offices were Spartan

Another advantage was that the Capitol was only twelve blocks away. The agency was still tied to the contracting agency for certain services. Even the office supplies were going to be coming from there, and Kuhn anticipated that there was going to be a lot of running back and forth, at least until things got underway.

In the midst of last-minute administrative details, outreach seemed to be the least of their worries. They had to wait to begin that, too. Senator Young had not yet made the announcement in Washington. "We don't want to jump the gun," Kuhn said. Protocol had to be followed, otherwise people would feel that their toes had been stepped on.

That their efforts would be successful was something that was expected. Already, there had been indications that word was spreading through the grapevine. The latest issue of Case and Counsel had a feature story about the experiment. Every employee in the welfare system had received a copy of it by now. If anything, Kuhn felt that the feature article had been released a bit prematurely. He had planned on having his first newspaper articles out by the time it appeared. Some calls were already coming in; Barr had handled several callers who wanted to know when the new housing was going to be built. He assumed these were from welfare recipients who had heard about the project from their caseworkers. One woman was being evicted from a mobile home, and needed immediate help. The agency director had observed that there would probably be many such cases, and that there was little that could be done for them. The required selection procedures and the seven-day waiting period had to be followed.

Only Simonson seemed a little less sure about the ease of outreach: "Do you think we'll be operational?" he would ask the observer periodically once he was settled in.

In the end, Simonson sided with the others and offered that there would probably be a lot of uncompensated overtime worked in the first few months. Two thousand applications would mean that as many as twenty-five per day would have to be processed, he figured. The staff hoped that maybe only half that would apply. In the Case and Counsel article, Barr had made a stab at 800.

While they waited, the three managers wrote an introductory brochure that could be mailed with each application or left with various agencies. Barr ran the copy up to the Graphics Department at the Capitol. They were quick, and using them represented a cost savings over the commercial shops in town. The press run was 2,500 copies, small enough so that the job would not have to go out on competitive bidding.

On Monday, July tenth, Kuhn announced to the staff that Senator Young's office had made it official, and outreach could begin. The director spent the following two days in the outlying counties.

Kuhn had prepared a dry news release. The intended article mentioned HUD and the Social Services Board, and explained who was eligible:

> As estimated by HUD, income limits for admission range from $4,400 for a one-person household to $9,000 for a nine- or more person household.

The piece also gave the formula for figuring out payments. At the bottom was the address of the agency and a request that inquiries be made by mail to the Bismarck office.

The effort seemed typical of the Social Service Board. In North Dakota, welfare programs are not advertised. The department has no media budget and disseminates information by the wire services. The releases seem to appear in the large daily newspaper first, and then the small-town weeklies pick up on these and inform residents in less populous areas of the state. Even as it was, legislators sometimes accused department officials of trying to push welfare programs, especially food stamps.

Kuhn's visit to Stark County was an involved one. As in his trip to Jamestown, he stopped by the welfare office to obtain the director's cooperation with the program. He again discouraged wholesale referrals from caseloads. It was a form of negative outreach in itself, since Kuhn wanted to draw applicants from other sources which would not be so easily tapped.

Then he met with the building owner at the new Dickinson site office. The two of them signed a ten-month lease and laughed about the thirty day termination clause. Like the participants' Model Lease Agreement, it seemed to be a contradiction in terms. The owner had rented to government agencies before, so there was no problem.

The space consisted of a single room above a bar and steak house. Since it was on the second floor, elderly participants would have to negotiate a steep flight of stairs. The office itself was cramped, stuffy and depressing. There was no waiting area. During the winter, the steam heat would rage, and a window had to be kept open. But the price was right: thirty-five dollars a month. It was all that was available.

After lunch, Kuhn visited with a reporter on the Dickinson Press, and said that he would appreciate it if the article were run as is. "No live wire stuff," Kuhn explained. They might have to turn things off pretty quick if the response got out of hand, he added. The image of outreach was one of a high-pressure faucet, or maybe one of those tricky drinking fountains in grade school--you had to twiddle with the valve gingerly to avoid getting drenched.

On the way back, he stopped by the weekly newspapers in Morton County. The Hebron Herald was in the middle of printing. He again quickly explained the experiment, and again said that he would appreciate it if the article could be published as written, since he didn't want people to get "too excited."

He drove to Glen Ullin, another town of about 500 people. The Times was closed. He decided to pass by New Salem, too. They'd probably be trying to get the next edition out, and he didn't want to bother them. Instead, he'd mail the material to the two weekly newspapers.

Roadside Slough

He still had to talk with the dailies in Bismarck and Mandan. That would finish the first, and with luck, last round of outreach.

Another period of waiting followed. It would take at least another week for all the articles to appear. More administrative details were handled in the meantime. Kuhn arranged for a meeting with the people at Central Data Processing (CDP) up at the Capitol. He wanted to set a payments system. The three managers attended, and brought along one of the secretaries, since she would have to be familiar with this aspect of the questions.

Kuhn does most of the talking as they sit around the conference table in the Blue Room. He wants to use the Form 600 already in existence. That way, they can tie into the state payments system instead of having to invent their own. He wants to know if CDP can do it, and if so, are they willing?

The CDP men tell him that they think everything can be arranged, but they have to know the volume, since there are several options open to them.

Kuhn explains that the most there will be is 400 checks.

One of the men smiles and says that most of the work can be done manually, and the computer used only to print the check itself. The cost will be slight. "About $100," one of them says. Keypunching will take less than a half-hour per month.

There is only one slight drawback: the agency will have to keep close watch over terminations. There will be no special checking done by the CDP, and the machine will write whatever it is told to write.

Kuhn says that this is fine, and then tells them that their first payment will probably be September first.

The system will be set up in time. The CDP people feel that they will need only five days' notice to print the checks. In an emergency, two days will be sufficient. They'll come down next month to show the EHAP staff how to fill out the Form 600 properly. That's the most important thing: if they make mistakes, the program won't run.

The meeting ends with Kuhn offering to buy everybody coffee down in the cafeteria. Walking to the parking lot, Simonson tells me that it's a good deal, knowing people like that. "Otherwise, somebody could really rip you off."

By July twentieth, the agency had received forty or fifty inquiries. A few walk-ins already had been given application forms, too. Apparently, no one was having trouble finding the office. Eleven applications had been returned. Of these, seven were immediately processed. Four needed follow-up telephone contacts, but Betty felt the success ratio was OK. The form was long and complicated, but manageable. It was still cheaper than having to interview everybody, or having to check third-party sources. The first enrollment session would be held the following Monday. Kuhn was confident and pleased.

Problems began to appear in the next few days, however. Although ten more applications were returned, new inquiries had stopped.

Something else was wrong, too: the average housing allowance payment was up around eighty-five dollars. The planned target was seventy-seven dollars. Simonson felt that C^* had been set too low by HUD.

Kuhn was concerned, too. Either fewer households would have to be enrolled, or payments would have to be brought into line.

Everything else seemed to be going fine. Peggy Mickels had arrived in Bismarck and was being trained by the other counselors. Greg's assistant still had to be hired, but it wasn't vital yet. The only trouble spot was the Dickinson counselor's position. Kuhn had talked to his friend, Joe Heiser, and thought he might get him to take the position, at least temporarily. It was crucial that someone be out there, since a few people had already applied from Stark County.

The last two days of the start-up period, HUD sends an EO* training team to the North Dakota agency. The EHAP staff is shown how to handle discrimination cases. Role playing is heavily used as a pedagogical technique. Kuhn is disappointed that they will have to handle all discrimination cases themselves. His attitude has always been that "HUD has the experts."

No, the trainer explains, HUD has no enforcement powers, and there is a backlog of cases at the federal level. Using local sources is "the quickest way to justice."

The thought of using agency people as checkers worries Kuhn. It's a small town, and word gets around fast.

The HUD people suggest using the general counsel at United Tribes Employment Training Center. If they want to go outside the staff for checkers, volunteers could be used. The League of Women Voters is a possibility.

Privately, Kuhn isn't taken with the idea of using volunteers. He later decides that he will hire somebody if any cases of discrimination come up. In point of fact, the league is a tiny organization in Bismarck. They have no set meeting place and get together in each other's homes. The suggestion to use the United Tribes' lawyer is a sound one, in his opinion. The only minority population in the area is Amerindian, and UTECT is a vocational training center for Indians all around the country.

In the next few days, the payments situation worsened. Greg calculated the average payments of those who had been certified. The amount was up to eighty-nine dollars. "The experiment is predicated on an average payment of seventy-seven dollars," Simonson remarked. It was also clear that outreach would have to be stepped up, too. The inquiries hovered around sixty, and the last week in July had brought only ten calls.

Kuhn wanted to begin a more personalized outreach effort, but before anything was done, they had to figure out a way of attracting higher-income families. He had rejected the idea of enrolling fewer families. That move would put the project under.

Technically, the second round of outreach had already started. The Mandan <u>Morning Pioneer</u> had run

---

*EO is an acronym for Equal Opportunity (anti-discrimination) laws and training.

a human interest article in their Sunday edition: "Burleigh, Morton People Letting a Golden Opportunity Slip Away." In it, Kuhn admitted that enrollment had been slow: "So far, only those in the lowest income bracket have shown any interest."

There had to be some sort of qualitative change, he thought. The Mandan article was just a more human version of the first outreach attempts. The danger was that it would just bring that many more of the "wrong" type of applicants.

For the time being, they were all right. Around twenty-five families had been enrolled in the program and were looking for housing. The processing had gone without a hitch and the high payment level was no immediate threat. "If we're going to get into trouble with twenty-five people, we'd get into trouble no matter what," Kuhn observed. He agreed with Greg that the trouble lay in the $77 dollar figure, but there was nothing that could be done about that.

Over coffee, Kuhn told the assistant director that he thought he knew what the problem was: People were taking the income limits as gross figures, instead of the net figures they really were. In reality, a person could be making over $12,000 and still be eligible for payments if the household was large enough. But people didn't know that.

Still, he was leery of publishing the higher gross income figures and feared that there would be a major scandal if he did so. The EHAP project was run by a welfare agency, and hence was vulnerable to public criticism. More, wages in North Dakota were low. Many professionals made less than $10,000 a year. "A substitute teacher gets $20 a day," he noted.

The following day, he discussed his predicament with Les Ovre over breakfast at the Red Owl. Les had been the department's executive director and had been taking flak for years. He knew about adverse public opinion. His advice was to load up on one- and two-person households who would tend to have lower payments. Large families, he felt, were deadly. They would tend to have extremely high payments.

Kuhn finally calls a staff meeting to discuss the "analytical aspects of income limits." He has already talked to Joe Queenan in Denver about what he wants to do. Joe told him that there was no restriction on advertising gross rather than net income. Now that he has the go-ahead, Kuhn wants the staff to participate in the decision. It is part of his "open management" philosophy. In past conversations with me, he has admitted that perhaps he does swing a little heavier vote, but he also insists he's never found himself in a four to one situation.

Kuhn repeats much of his earlier discussion with Barr. The thought of publishing the $12,000 figures makes the staff visibly nervous, and they repeat the same arguments Kuhn has used on himself the day before.

Betty suggests leaving the $9,000 figure and calling it "net income" in all future releases. "Would that do it?" she asks hopefully.

Kuhn says nothing, and the rest of the staff begins to talk back and forth. "Would the readers see the 'net' before the income?" somebody asks.

Barr seems to feel yes, and then adds a fragmented sentence that has its beginnings somewhere else: "... if they're making that kind of money...."

Kuhn asks another question: "Why do we want to talk about <u>net income?</u>"

"Because $12,000 is more than ninety percent of the people in North Dakota make?" Barr suggests awkwardly.

"But <u>net</u> income is also deceiving," Greg offers. He gives an example of how a farmer can invest most of his profits and become a very rich "poor person."

The discussion has to be put on the right track: "We have to either change the tables or live with it," Kuhn says quietly. "We've all got to speak the same language externally and internally. We have a language problem." The problem has to be resolved before any more outreach occurs.

And then, the point of it all: "One hundred dollar payments can't be tolerated. The program won't stand it. We'll run out of money."

Barr says that the upper gross income limits might actually be something like $14,000, if the agency were allowed to yield a true zero payment to a nine-person household. As the regulations applied the minimum payment allowed for a family that size was forty-three dollars. With normal deductions, this meant an income of about $11,800.

Once Barr has actually mouthed the unthinkable higher income figure, $12,000 doesn't seem so horrible. "Maybe there won't be an uprising," he says.

Simonson still wants to hold off on any decision. Kuhn tells him with a quiet firmness, "We will not hold off. We have to make a decision and transmit it to HUD."

Barr becomes more confident: "Maybe if we make it <u>ever</u> so clear that the $12,000 limit is for a family with seven children, maybe there won't be a problem."

The meeting is over and the tension dissolves. Barr jokes that the $14,000 figure "will never see the papers." Paula is told to type the new limits into the brochures.

Kuhn calls me into his office. He wants to talk about the decision just made. EHAP in North Dakota was faced with a dilemma, he says. They could either go on recruiting the wrong sample, or else they could change outreach and risk an adverse reaction. He still does not reel that the income limits are tailored to the area. "We're a poor state." He only hopes that the press won't jump on and kill an embryonic idea he is quite taken with.

The agency staff had reached their most important decision thus far. What remained was to try various methods to reach this broader spectrum of the population. Outreach had to be directed beyond getting raw numbers of people applying.

The staff realized the change that had occurred and labeled their new efforts "Phase II." The title was kind of a joke. The President of the United States had instituted programs of wage and price controls that were similarly titled in serial fashion.

The entire staff participated in devising new outreach methods and trying them out one by one. The methods employed were unremarkable, and at no time was an all-out effort made. Kuhn still feared the deluge that would never actually materialize; the rest of the staff was still leery of publicizing the new income limits. The intensity of the activities cannot be envisioned as a smooth incremental curve. Instead, outreach was sporadic and seemed to stutter-step. The agency would raise its metaphorical head above the terrain, and then draw it back. Then, after the results had been evaluated, the agency would be visible again for a short period of time.

On August fifteenth, Bob Barr appeared on the TT&O Show. "This, That and (the) Other" was a morning wake-up program with a talk format. Bob Olsen also taped a short TV blurb for the local television news programs. The previous day, he had appeared on "Dialing for Dollars." He stressed the fact that EHAP was for low and moderate income families. "We'd like the working man or woman," Olsen had told his host.

Appearing on "Dialing for Dollars" had been Olsen's own idea. "A lot of housewives watch that to win their $100," he had told the director during a coffee break at the Red Owl.

There seemed to have been some truth in Olsen's statement. Two women came by the agency for applications the following day. After Barr had given the necessary introductory information about the AAE, one of them began to talk about the show: "They haven't had a winner for weeks now." The jackpot was at $140, less than two month's worth of average housing allowance payments.

The radio and television outreach seemed to bring a brief flurry of calls that would taper off in about a week. Barr concluded that they would need a lot of such activity to be effective. This carried the danger the director feared: A response that couldn't be "turned off" at will.

After these initial media appearances had been made, the agency tried other, quieter advertising methods. Bob Olsen suggested printing an "apartment stuffer" that could be slipped under doors. It would be postcard size, and printed on stiff card stock. By using a Chamber of Commerce list, they could cover the rental units in Bismarck. For Jamestown and Mandan, the assessor would be willing to supply addresses from the tax rolls. Dickinson's Chamber of Commerce was in the process of creating an apartment listing similar to the one used in the capital city. The apartment stuffer could also be left at restaurants, clinics, and other public places.

Although the idea seemed sound, the response was negligible, and the method was abandoned. The failure was a source of bewilderment to the staff, since the flyer was put into the hands of those who were eligible: the renters.

During this early period, the director also contacted the heads of a few community organizations personally. He visited with the head of the North Dakota AFL-CIO in an attempt to recruit working people. Kuhn doubted that this would bring much response. North Dakota is a nonunion state and the organized workers are scattered. Many of them would not be eligible unless they relocated within the program jurisdiction.

The AFL-CIO had no house organ, and the president agreed to inform the heads of the member locals by personal letter. The eventual success of this effort is not known; however, the working poor made up 33 percent of the total applicants, while they represented 63 percent of the eligible population. This would prove to be an average disparity among the eight sites.

Kuhn was also disturbed by the existence of racial profiles and felt that they could be too easily used as limiting quotas. He would rather have kept enrollment unrestricted and treated Indians simply as "eligible families." Without waiting to see what the response from this minority group would be, he decided to actively encourage Indians to participate in the AAE.

After he had talked to the leaders of two Amerindian organizations, he was hopeful that as many as "thirty or forty families" might surface and that "the profiles would be ruptured beyond anyone's dreams." Once the visits were made, the requests and the suggestions were out of Kuhn's hands. He believed in the community organizations and felt that they would have the most ready access to the people they served.

However, as he monitored the applications over the next few weeks, it became obvious that Indians were applying only in proportion to their representation in the census. He visited again with the senior staff at United Tribes Employment Training Center. Although he was well received, there were still no applications forthcoming, a fact which mystified all concerned. Kuhn knew that the trainees at United Tribes were housed on the grounds of the facility itself. It was also possible that some of the staff, who were almost all Indians, were living in Community Homes. This was a moderate-income development in Bismarck which was federally subsidized. The director finally satisfied himself by saying that "maybe they've had enough of welfare programs."

The staff felt that newspapers were the best form of active outreach. Much later in the program, they tried to target portions of the program area where enrollment was lagging. This was done by printing news articles only in certain newspapers. This strategy was amplified further when, at the very end of the enrollment period, they decided to take out paid ads.

The two westernmost counties were troublesome from the start. Many conjectures were made as to why this might be so. The most likely hypothesis seemed to be that Morton and Stark counties were more conservative, and suspicious of government programs. "The only thing they like is the USDA," one of the staff members said. Another agreed, and offered that poor people out there were intimidated.

As a result of this slowness, Joe Heiser was given complete freedom in his activities in Stark County. He talked to the heads of various community organizations, and even spoke once to the president of the German-Hungarian Club. Like Kuhn, he seemed to favor going to the leaders in an organization, and then letting them carry the message.

Heiser was confident that the program would eventually catch on, even though it had not done so by the time he left in the fall. "Dickinson is like a melting pot," he said. With such an odd mix, he felt that word of mouth was the only effective approach. He had seen the same thing happen with food stamps.

Another thing: "We told the truth. We told them that this is an experiment, and that we can't guarantee anything." He still felt that all that was necessary was for a few of the large "clans" to hear about it--families like the Kovachs, or the Kubeks, or the Kosteleckys. "All it will take is a few checks coming in."

He also pointed out that media outreach in Stark County had been delayed until August when Siri was hired.

The agency tapped some of the more usual scores of applicants during the first two months of the program. In August, Kuhn decided to try to reach food stamps recipients. Many of these people were working, but had moderate incomes. Posters were made up, and each counselor appeared at the place where stamps were sold. The week that this was tried, seventy-five applications from all sources came in. Kuhn felt that it was a one-time thing, since food stamps recipients were also a captive audience. The rush of applications seemed to prove that outreach would have been a simple matter were it not for the financial constraints of the program.

In the end, Kuhn was puzzled by the overall low response rate. Even given the low profile the agency had assumed, he had never seen anything like it in his forty years of public service. "I would have lost a lot of money, if I had wagered." At the end, a total of 569 eligibles had applied, about one-third of what they had expected. The agency had not misunderstood outreach so much as it had controlled it timorously. Some things worked and others did not. Moreover, different approaches seemed to work better in different counties, but they had no firm idea of why this was so.

Finally, a substantial number of those applying heard by word of mouth. The question that remained was "How did the people who told the applicants about the AAE first hear about it?"

It can be argued that the agency may have been too concerned about community reaction to outreach. It is true that there was only one instance in which the public did not receive the project well. Yet, the incident is illustrative and shows that there was a reservoir of ill feeling toward government programs. The reaction occurred when Bob Barr and Kris Sundberg appeared on the TT&O program again in September:

The program begins after the Bismarck chief of police has given his public service announcement: "Today, among other locations, traffic radar will be posted on Thirteenth Street. Please drive carefully."

Bob and Kris take turns answering the host's questions. The two of them had prepared a list of questions to be asked. Their replies would give the necessary information about the project. They feel they are prepared for "a lot of off-the-wall questions" about the Experimental Housing Allowance Project.

"Let's go to line one." It is almost a relief to begin to receive the calls. The introductory portion of the show has been slow and repetitious.

"Good morning, I'd like to know how many people are working, the salaries, how much rental fees, and the administrative costs to the taxpayers of this country for those 400 people."

Barr stumbles, and then suggests that she call the project director, Gottfried Kuhn....

"I think everybody would like to know, and you're on the radio for the purpose of informing people. This would be a good thing to tell them." She hangs up and the air goes dead.

It's a ten-second knock-out. Barr is lying on the canvas. His eyes are open, and his pupils are dilated. His leg is twitching spasmodically.

Finally, the moderator asks, "Yes, Bob?" Verbal smelling salts. Barr pulls himself together, gives a nervous laugh, and explains that "the lady wanted to know the total administrative costs of the project." He offers that there are eleven people, including four counselors, but that he doesn't have the cost figures.

The talk show moderator stresses that this is an experimental project. Another call is on the line.

Kris handles it: "Say, the other lady that was on the line was just right. It just seems that it hits the taxpayers, the ones that own their own home. It seems like the other people can do the way they want, and the taxpayers have to be the ones to pay. I thank you." It is the politest hostility I have ever heard in my life.

Kris repeats the message, and Bob takes over. He explains that HUD has homeownership programs, including Section 235. "There's a Mr. Akers in town who handles these."

The news rescues them for five minutes.

Bob gives the progress of the experiment to date. On September first, they had made twenty-four payments, he says.

The next caller is a woman who explains that a lot of people feel that government programs go for administrative costs. "A lot of these experiments aren't equipped to take care of what they advertise; they only have room for their own, and most of this goes to take care of their building. I don't think it helps the public." She rambles on.

Barr agrees that there is distrust of governmental programs. "You say there's 400 families in four counties?"

"That's right."

"Bismarck alone could use that many."

There is time for one more call. This one is friendly, too. "Say, I was real interested in your project there, and I wanted to know how long I'd have to find housing."

"You'd have sixty days to find standard housing. You could either stay where you are, or else move."

"In other words, I could move out of my unit?"

"Sure."

It dawns on me that the voice belongs to Greg Simonson.

Perhaps the important thing was that they were able to operate a potentially controversial program quietly. As the applicant pool began to grow, Simonson could choose people for enrollment more carefully.

By the time the September checks went out, the average payment had been reduced to seventy-five dollars. The planned maximum seventy-seven dollar figure was never exceeded again.

Other Activities and Events

The staff had settled into a routine. Applicants were being processed smoothly. Betty found that only a few cases required third-party verification of income and assets. Usually, this was when the applicant was just getting on assistance or unemployment compensation and did not know what the amount of the check would be. Once Betty had received permission from the person involved, she would make the required telephone call to the proper agency. Public organizations seemed to be cooperating with the new housing agency.

Enrollment sessions were underway. There were all individual ones. The staff had toyed with the possibility of having group sessions, but rejected the idea. At best, the applicants were neutral about public meetings. Kuhn felt that the reluctance was grounded in the issue of confidentiality: "They probably felt that it was an invasion of their privacy to reveal in a group their reasons for applying for a housing allowance, and to some people the need would have had to be unusually great before they would have incurred the indignity of the group process."

The director admitted, however, that had the full complement of applications surfaced, there would have been no choice: group sessions would have been held as a matter of course. Because of the low volume of applications, peoples' wishes could be respected. The director felt that there was no need to push the issue.

In order to keep careful records of agency contacts, several new forms were devised by the staff. "Case Control Cards" were adapted from those used by the Department of Social Services. These were kept both by the eligibility technicians and by the housing counselors. Each card had the name of a participant on it and provided a one-line summary of each contact, whether agency or participant initiated.

More detailed accounts of interactions between the agency and participants or landlords were kept on special, color-coded log sheets placed with each enrollee's file. In the beginning days, at least, few housing suppliers had called about the project. One of those who did was also KXMB-TV's Ombudsman, and he gave the project a favorable report on his five-minute show, which followed the local evening news.

Simonson had set up a multi-drawered filing system which followed participant flow as the applicant moved through various processings which culminated either in recipient or termination status. The records of any AAE household could be found in this central file, regardless of county of residence. The counselors in the satellite centers had duplicate files of only those individuals in their caseloads.

Staff members were required to submit monthly narratives to assist the production of the required monthly report to HUD. These were lengthy and occupied much of Kuhn's and Simonson's time during the beginning of each month. Each staff meeting was also recorded, and the tapes transcribed, "so that we know we've got it all down," the director said. The resultant pages were filed away in a black looseleaf notebook that Kuhn kept in his desk.

The assistant GTR had returned to Denver at the end of July. In the next few months he would appear only occasionally:

"It's like he helped get us going, and now it's our baby. He wants to see if we can run it," Bob Barr said.

THE RISE OF PHASE-IN MONITORING
SEPTEMBER 15 - DECEMBER 1, 1973

While the agency staff had realized that they would have to recruit higher-income people to participate in the project, the critical variable was still the average housing allowance payment. Higher-income people were simply those who would be more likely to have a housing allowance payment below the planned level of $77. The trick was to match the low payments against those with high payments so that the average would be acceptable in terms of the final estimate made in the Detailed Plan.

Bob Barr had implicitly come to this conclusion at the very beginning of the experiment. An elderly woman had gone through the first enrollment session and then had balked about signing the papers which would make her an official enrollee. A housing counselor had mistakenly informed her that her social security payments might be affected, and she was worried. Barr was told about the woman, and that her payment was only going to be around $14. "I hope she changes her mind," he said. "We need that one bad. God, do we need that one bad."

As more and more people applied, this informal reckoning became unsatisfactory. Simonson devised a new set of forms to keep track of things. These were a <u>potential enrollees log</u> and an <u>enrollees log</u>. They were identical except that the former kept track of eligible applicants, and the latter followed those who were either participants or looking for housing. Since there were four counties in the project area, this meant that the director of research and fiscal management had to keep eight separate logs. When the experiment was over and the remaining families transferred to the LHAs, the ACC would be split into four parts. When this occurred, Kuhn wanted to be sure that the LHA director received a financially feasible operation.

In tabular form, each log page listed the name of the household head, I.D. number, age group, family size, sex, income, C*, and housing allowance payment. By scanning the potential enrollees log, Simonson could pick a "desirable" family for enrollment. After he had done this, he would draw a line through the name and assign the case to a counselor. After he received the enrollment form back, he would make the necessary entries into the enrollees log.

By using the enrollees log, Simonson was able to keep track of the housing allowance payments and the demographic characteristics of the enrollees. In mid-September, he began to circulate a weekly fact sheet of the critical information. This was a way of keeping the staff informed about the progress of the experimental effort. The assistant GTR would also send computer printouts that were similar to this inter-office communication, but Simonson found it quicker to make his own calculations. He focused upon enrollees rather than actual recipients, since a high percentage of those reaching this stage went on to receive payments. Enrollees represented which way the experiment would be going on in the future. The average housing allowance entitlement of the _enrollees_ would eventually become the average housing allowance payment of the _participants_.

Since the project emphasized financial feasibility, Simonson's role assumed greater importance as more and more people entered the program. At first, almost anyone could be chosen. Then more care would have to be exercised as different categories began to be filled.

It seemed to the observer that Kuhn and Simonson were more comfortable with phase-in than outreach. Advertising the program was chancy, while the former activity was a tool of administration. Moreover, it could "correct" the mistakes of the outreach effort. Kuhn recalls:

> Greg kept reporting to me not the name, but the kind of household it was, and where in the enrollment process they were. So I was informed whether we were enrolling all single-person households, or if they were all households of five or six.

Some of the households would be held back and "saved" for a more opportune moment:

> Instead of taking all the two-person households right now and filling that to our enrollment plan, I would suggest to him to hold off and we will wait. The same thing would happen if all the households of a certain size were in the lower income levels. I would caution that we not select too many of these at once. We would have to keep them in balance with our enrollment plans, so that the experiment all the time ended pointed in the direction of financial feasibility.

Given the low outreach profile, there were some problems inherent in this approach. The advertising of the project brought only 665 applicants, of which 569 were eligible. Over 85 percent of these actually became recipients of at least one payment. This high ratio meant that the agency was not able to meet their planned profiles.

The sex profile was the first to show variance between the planned and the actual. From the very beginning, female-headed households applied in greater porportions than male-headed ones. During the second planning period, the agency had estimated that only ten percent of the eventual 400 households would be of the former type. As their reviewers had suggested, the original staff had made their final estimates on the basis of figures that reflected the proportion of female-headed households in the population at large. In the Strategic Plan, the number of this type of family had been set at double the final figures, since Simonson had counted as eligible only those who were inadequately housed.

Kuhn and Simonson Go Over the Books

At first, agency staff felt that it was only a matter of time before the situation would correct itself. They thought that by reaching the working families, male-headed households would come forth. By mid-August, however, it was obvious that the sex profile could not possibly be met. Out of a total of 121 enrolled households, over half had a woman as the head. This was beyond the 25 percent variance allowed by the contract.

Kuhn apparently told Simonson to ignore this and continue selecting households on the basis of housing payments and family size alone. The disparity between planned and actual profiles was duly noted in their lengthy monthly reports to HUD.

On September twenty-first, Kuhn announced that he was going to ask HUD to change the profiles for female-headed households so that they could enroll enough of them to make up 65 percent to 70 percent of the total recipients. For the past three weeks he had been scanning every application that came in and had found that this was the approximate ratio of eligible applicants. He would argue to HUD that although only ten percent of North Dakota's households were female-headed, this family type made up the majority of eligible households. He said that he would discuss it with Queenan the next time he was in town.

By October, Kuhn had done the necessary research. Using the Social Service Board's statistics, he found that less than 30 percent of the state's AABD* and AFDC recipients were male-headed households. Apparently, he relayed the figures and his arguments to the assistant GTR. On November nineteenth, a letter was sent to Kuhn approving the requested change in the sex profile. The communication was signed by Arnold Nelson, the Governmental Technical Representative for the North Dakota Experiment. He had used the same statistics that Kuhn had. Also included was additional information on unemployment for females in the work force. These statistics had been obtained from Denver University's Center for Social Research and Development.

The final paragraph repeated the arguments that Kuhn had used around the agency staff:

> To summarize, it is apparent that the raw census data continue to overstate the number of male-headed households and simultaneously underestimate the number of female-headed households which might apply for and be enrolled in the North Dakota Experimental Housing Allowance Project. It is equally apparent that data previously unavailable to us, i.e., data supplied by the Social Service Board of North Dakota (on the relationship between various types of assistance program and the sex of recipients), more accurately reflect the population which may potentially apply for and receive housing allowance. Given these new data, I would approve an enrollment ratio of thirty (male): seventy (female).

During this second two-month period, other variations occurred and were verbally approved by the assistant GTR. They had no effect on the financial feasibility of the project and hence were not "serious" deviations.

---

*Aid to the Aged, Blind and Disabled

By the end of November, it was apparent that the distribution of family sizes was also skewed. The number of two-person households selected was over the 81 called for in the Detailed Plan. In contrast, there were only 78 single-person households, although there was room for 102.

Kuhn had discussed the matter in mid-November with Queenan when he was on-site. The director felt that the large families just weren't there and that they should over-enroll two-person households. He then said that they had miscalculated during planning, anyway. He felt that they had planned on too many one-person households, and argued that few of this type of family would be eligible since, according to the regulations, the household head or the spouse would have to be over sixty-two or disabled.

On the last day of November, Kuhn sent a four-page letter to Arnold Nelson, the GTR, and suggested that they simply switch the number of one- and two-person households participating in the AAE. Thus, there would be only 81 of the former and 102 of the latter. He noted that this would require an amendment to the ACC.

Joe Queenan called Kuhn in early December and suggested an alternate plan. They could enroll fewer one-person households and fewer large families, since both these categories were not applying, anyway. Instead, they could carefully balance the number of two-, three-, and four-person households so that the same ACC income could be generated, and no change in the contract would be required. An amended ACC was something that both of them wanted to avoid.

As a result of this decision, the agency would eventually miss the planned profiles in almost every category. Yet, the goal of 400 participating families would be attained, and the project would remain financially feasible. "Household size and income can skew the ACC and run the project awry," Kuhn later said.

Simonson's careful monitoring assured that whatever the final profiles looked like, the finances would be all right.

Other Activities and Events

In September, HUD held an EO workshop for agency attorneys. The counsel for United Tribes Employment Training Center accompanied a lawyer from the Social Services Board to the Chicago meeting. Upon their return a staff meeting was held, and the conference was discussed. Both lawyers felt that the training was useful, but felt that the session was aimed at discrimination problems in urban areas. "Landlords aren't that sophisticated out here," one of them offered. "They just come right out and say, 'I won't rent to Indians'."

Several staff changes also occurred during this two and a half month period. At the end of September, Kris Sundberg announced that she was going to be leaving. Her husband had secured a job elsewhere in the state. This seemed to leave Bob Olsen directly in line for the job of director of housing services for the second year of the experiment.

Barr privately thought that her position would be easy to fill, since the job was in Bismarck and not in one of the outlying counties. Kuhn, however, felt that she should not be replaced, since he wanted to cut staff. Instead, he said that he might later bring Peggy Mickels or Siri Ellisen in for a few days at a time. The latter seemed to be a more logical choice, since enrollment was lagging in her county.

No action was taken for a month. Olsen was worried about his growing caseload. He felt that he could handle fifteen or twenty cases a week, given the amount of documentation that was required. "And that's the maximum," he added. "By the time I write all the reports, and maybe meet with Gottfried..." He thought that eventually he might not be able to keep up.

The matter was resolved gradually. Barr began holding enrollment sessions, and the entire Bismarck caseload was formally split between the two men in November.

Paula Ovre also left the agency during the middle of November. This was a preplanned termination, and again, administrative costs were reduced. Joe Heiser left the Dickinson post at approximately the same time. This made no difference in finances, since he was a volunteer.

Almost all of the contacts with landlords were still supplier-initiated. None of the callers had ever used a lease agreement before. Most commonly, they wanted to know just how binding the document was. Could they evict if the tenant didn't pay the rent or damaged the premises? What if they decided to sell the place?

The callers were assured that the lease could be broken by thirty days' written notice by either party. The only thing that the agency asked was that the landlord inform them if they planned on evicting one of their EHAP tenants.

Not everyone was convinced: one owner in Jamestown insisted that the lease was binding for a whole year, and the thirty-day notice clause was just a lot of "legal double-talk." The counselor then told the man that he could use his own lease just as long as the four required clauses were added. At this point, the prospective landlord told her that he didn't believe in leases, and the hell with it, anyway.

In two or three cases, participants brought in rental agreements that had objectionable provisions in them. These were documents in which the renter had signed away certain rights in any legal disputes that might arise. In such instances, the director contacted both the HUD and the Social Services Board counsels and obtained opinions regarding the acceptability of the agreement. Then the director would call the management company and explain the situation:

> I told them that it didn't make any difference to me personally, but that for purposes of the experiment we couldn't approve the lease agreement if those clauses weren't stricken. Otherwise, the participant couldn't rent the unit from them.

In all cases, the property managers agreed to modify the lease for any prospective tenant that was in the project.

The counselors continued to conduct their sessions and found that most people were able to participate with only the minimal services called for in the design of the plan.

"What kind of housing information do you give them?" I asked one of the counselors. I knew that Kuhn had discouraged them from showing any housing lists to the enrollees, since he felt that this would be "steering them" to certain units.

"If they're going to move, I go into the selection of an area. Like close to medical care, if they're elderly. Or close to a school, if they've got children." But usually most of the people knew what they wanted. Many of the elderly just wanted to be within walking distance of their children or to be close to the downtown area, the counselor felt. Admittedly, they had already stretched the inspection rules in such cases. If an elderly woman was living in an apartment that was in a good location, but did not have a bathroom fan, they would usually approve the unit. They felt that this deficiency was a minor one and did not justify the rejection of the unit.

They also found that almost all of the participants were able to complete the self-inspection form without help, although each counselor could recall a few cases where he or she helped to complete the form, either in person or over the telephone.

It all seemed to be working. The independent approach was a viable one. Almost no one required any post-payment counseling. Those referrals that were made usually wound up sending the individual back to his or her own caseworker, who had made the referral to EHAP in the first place.

Kuhn had drawn the boundaries of agency involvement, and the housing counselors were free to operate within these restrictions. Differing viewpoints found their expression in the number of home visits made. The two counselors at the satellite centers held almost 40 percent of their sessions in the participants' home*. Their workloads were much tighter than at the central office, and both of them felt that the elderly would have a particularly hard time getting around in the cold weather. Barr concurred, and said that he would go whenever the participant asked, "but I reserve the right to get 'hacked off' sometimes." Almost 30 percent of his sessions were held outside the office. Olsen, who had the heaviest caseload, tried to hold his sessions in the office, unless there was no alternative. "I used to go out all the time. Most people will try to get you to come to their house. This week, I'm only going out twice."

Kuhn's attitude was closest to Olsen's, although the reasons behind it were different. He felt that dropping in on someone could be sort of an imposition, whether there was an advance appointment or not. If a family requested such service, there would have to be a justification. The disabled, the elderly and those with children all merited having a home visit during working hours.

Similarly, if a spouse worked, and the family felt that both should be present, this would be reason enough to make a visit after work. "It's too cold," would be no excuse, as far as Kuhn was concerned.

Escort services, he felt, should be similarly handled. Only after the client had exhausted other

---

*This figure includes all counselor-participant contacts, and was calculated after reviewing the records of each housing counselor.

resources should the counselor step in. The goal of the experiment was to preserve self-reliance. "People have a right to do for themselves," he said.

Peggy Mickels disagreed somewhat with this outlook, but accepted it for purposes of the experiment. Privately, she argued that the AAE had heavy reporting requirements, and that the time used filling out log sheets could have been better spent actively helping the participants. She felt this was especially true in her area where the onset of the cold weather had cut the supply of available housing. Kuhn observed that this was a common pattern in rural areas. People who worked on farms often spent their winters in town.

The concern with the amount of actual counseling done became the topic of several philosophical staff discussions.

A short staff meeting, with only Simonson, Kuhn and the two Bismarck counselors attending. Kuhn says that the time sheets do not have enough time charged to the enrollment function. He feels that the agency does little actual counseling, although the second and third sessions are called "counseling sessions," in the language of the experiment.

"Even the third session, when it's the examination of the leases and self-inspection forms, that's enrollment."

He shows them the previous month's time sheets. In October, Olsen had 68 hours of counseling, and only 34 in enrollment. For Peggy, the ratio was 42 to 63. Siri has the correct ratio of 109 hours charged to enrollment and only 9 to counseling. "There is really 10 or 20 times more enrollment than counseling," he says.

The others nod, and he continues. If they continue to charge time this way, there will be an inconsistency between the hours charged and what they are trying to say in the monthly reports. Time has been allotted incorrectly, and does not support their contention that counseling is of minimal importance in the North Dakota effort. Originally, when they were doing only first sessions, the time charges were correct. Later, as the second and third sessions began to take up staff time, they had slipped up and been fooled by the language of the experiment.

He instructs the staff to read over the definitions in the APM. When the next full staff meeting is held, he wants to bring up the issue again and get the opinions of the whole staff. Things have to be right, for the experiment.

Kuhn was highly committed to the experimental aspects of the AAE. In late October, everyone but three clerical workers attended a conference in Oklahoma. It was the first time that the staff of the various agencies would get together for the purposes of exchanging their experience in running the AAE. Kuhn chose Simonson to chair one of the sessions, feeling that it would be a good experience for him. "Don't let anyone intimidate you. You're the chairman," he told him in a private meeting.

For the rest of the staff he had a caution: not to get carried away with enthusiasm, and to realize the limits of the data. He said that they should stick to what they had done without trying to evaluate the results of it yet. They were to remember that the AAE was an experiment.

When they returned, Kuhn was somewhat disappointed. Many of the other agencies were willing to talk about policy making even at this early date. He would have preferred to talk about the philosophical aspects of housing allowances, he said.

November also brought the realization that the two western counties might not reach full enrollment. Outreach had virtually ceased in Burleigh and Stutsman counties as of the end of October. The director had given the word to continue grass roots outreach in the Dickinson area. "There's no way of overdoing it here, at least not now." A month later, the westernmost county still needed twenty more enrollees to reach its quota of seventy. Morton County was even worse off; it needed twice that many to fill out at ninety. A special effort would have to be made in December, the director decided. If that failed, then the extra slots would either have to be left open, or else filled with residents of the other two participating counties. He preferred the latter course, if worst came to worst. This was somewhat of a turnabout from his feelings of a month before. Kuhn had addressed a meeting of urban renewal and housing authority personnel in mid-October. He said that he still feared "a groundswell" of applicants who would have to be turned away.

Daily administration continued: they had their first case of rent skipping. The Chuck Decotah family had left in the middle of the night without paying the rent. Their landlady, a woman on social security, had called the agency at the end of the month to find out if the checks had been mailed. Simonson told her that these went out on the first. The family was probably gone for good, then, she said. They had borrowed money from her and taken some of the bedding she had let them use.

The agency stopped any further checks to the family. It was all according to the plan. If the landlord wasn't getting paid, he would call and complain to the agency. No policing actions were necessary. Any special arrangements between the landlord and tenant that involved rent forgiveness were between the two of them. The agency had no part in this. They simply investigated complaints as they occurred.

As a rule, landlords were patient with the few EHAP tenants that were troublesome. Sometimes, this patience was laced with benevolent paternalism:

Ten-fifteen: a middle-aged man walks into the office and tells the secretary that he is Lucille Sherwood's landlord. He wants to talk to a counselor. She tells him that he'll have to wait for a minute until Bob Barr gets back from coffee.

As he waits, he makes small talk with me and Delores. The bromides dribble from his lips. It all has to do with self-reliance, and the energy crisis. He remembers during the war when he was a farmer and could get all the gasoline he wanted. "Of course, you were supposed to use it for the tractor." Now, he's taken to riding a bicycle. His eyesight has been going bad.

Finally, Bob Barr returns from coffee, and the two of them talk about the problem. "Let's face it, Lucille needs help," he begins.

The tenant is a divorcee with three children. She uses foul language with the kids and that bothers him. His other tenants are also beginning to complain. "She denies it, but I went down in the basement a couple of times, and listened.

"I don't know what it is, I can't reason with her. When I walk in she's the most politest person in the world, but when I shut the door...." He says he doesn't want to kick her out, but is tired of <u>lecturing</u> her. Maybe somebody from the office can talk to her, he suggests.

It is Olsen's case, and the task falls on him. In the end, she will be evicted, anyway. Olsen will tell her to warn the new landlord in advance that she has children and cannot keep the kids in straightjackets. He says nothing about the language, however.

The program wore on. It was the period of fairly normal functioning. There were no real rushes. People entered the program, and a few dropped out and were replaced. The staff thought they might be having their first discrimination case, and Kuhn alerted the United Tribes Lawyer. Elsie Snowball was approaching the ninety day limit for finding housing. The question was whether she was actually looking or not. Nothing materialized.

By the end of November, there were 331 enrollments. Seventy to go, but something had to be done about Dickinson and Mandan....

THE RISE OF THE ENROLLMENT SESSION (DECEMBER 1 TO JANUARY 31, 1974)

On November twenty-seventh, Kuhn held an important staff meeting. He announced that Betty and the counselors should start pushing the applications through, so that there would be as many enrollees as possible by the end of the year. The agency still needed another 100 participants if they were going to reach their goal of 400.

In future sessions, people were no longer to be told that there would be an automatic one-month extension for those who were approaching the sixty day mark in their search for housing. Further, those who were already nearing this point would be contacted and asked why they had not returned their lease and inspection forms.

That same day, the director drove to Mandan to speak with a reporter on the <u>Morning Pioneer</u>. The reporter listened as Kuhn explained that both Morton and Stark Counties were "quite far behind." The pool in Morton County was almost exhausted, and he was particularly puzzled by the fact that very few of the elderly had applied from that part of the project area. He then dropped a subtle hint about what else the article should say: Two-person households were no longer needed in the profile.

The reporter agreed that it was puzzling that enrollment was lagging in Morton County. She had been interested in following the progress of the experiment, and said that more programs of that type were needed. "I'd like to see something for home buying in the urban areas." By "urban," she meant Mandan. She agreed to run an article that would appear on December fifth.

Then, Kuhn asked to talk to someone about taking out a paid ad for a week or so. He wanted a two-column insert, and said he would bring back the copy as soon as he had it written.

This would be the last outreach that the agency attempted, and was the only time that paid advertisements were used. The style employed was straight-forward and unembellished. For each day during the week-long run, the ad would appear in a different section of the paper. The same approach was taken in Stark County where the director purchased space in the Dickinson <u>Press</u>.

Kuhn also held a meeting for the housing authorities on the last day of November. It had been several months since they had been briefed on the progress of the experiment. The directors from Morton, Burleigh, and Stutsman counties were present. The last brought along one of the LHA board members. Also attending was the assistant GTR and an employee of the North Dakota State Planning Division:

Kuhn opens the meeting by passing out the data sheets which Greg has prepared. He explains that Burleigh County has had the least concentrated outreach effort, and that Morton has had as much as the other counties. "Morton County will be hit with newspaper articles and a paid ad. If this doesn't bring results, then the slots will be filled from Stutsman and Burleigh counties." He adds that the Dickinson area will receive the same treatment.

Frank Freezon, the director of the Morton County LHA, asks why enrollment is down for his county, and Kuhn explains that the agency has had few inquiries from the Mandan area. All but two of the eligible applicants from there have been enrolled. The pool has been exhausted; there is simply nobody to choose from.

Gene Sandwick, from Burleigh County, offers that it is perhaps because Bismarck has three times the population of Mandan, and yet

---

Sunday, December 9, 1973 THE Dickinson Press 13

APPLY NOW
FOR RENT SUPPLEMENT PAYMENTS

If you are a renter household residing in Morton, Burleigh, Stark, or Stutsman counties, you may be eligible for a rent supplement payment through the "Experimental Housing Allowance Project." This is a federally funded project designed to assist low and modest income renter households. If your income is within the following limits you are invited to complete an application form.

No. of Persons In Households	Maximum Gross Income Limits
1	$ 4,400
2	5,790
3-4	8,157
5-6	9,628
7-8	10,995
9	12,000

On December 1, 203 renter households received $14,627 in rent supplement payments. Enrollment is limited to 400 families. For application forms and information:

CALL—227-2557
WRITE — Siri Ellisen, Housing Counselor
43½ Sims
Dickinson, N.D. 58601

both have the same amount of public housing. The argument is rejected by the EHAP staff. They point out that almost all of Morton County's units are for the elderly, and besides, Bismarck has Community Homes, a private development for moderate income families.

Finally, Freezon says that if he's given the word, he will go out with Bob Barr and pull people off the waiting list who will fit the profile. He also wants to contact churches for the names of people on their "poor lists."

This will be done, Kuhn answers, if the last try at outreach doesn't produce results.

The apartment stuffer is passed out, and Kuhn comments that the method was a failure. It was only successful in Stutsman County, which had been the quickest to respond, anyway.

Queenan mentions that they are considering trying to get the evaluation contractor to waive the seven-day waiting period, since this would speed up enrollments. Freezon replies that perhaps the trouble in Morton County is that nobody understands the project. Out of the forty-two families whose social worker referred them to the project, only seven have responded. He has been in contact with the welfare agency, and knows.

The ACC is discussed. Each LHA wants its allotted units. They can use the extra money that each family will bring when it is transferred to the LHA at the end of two years--or sooner, if a family terminates after the end of the project's enrollment period. Each slot brings with it a monthly sum for administration purposes.*

Privately, the directors hope that the reimbursement will be more than the nine dollars to eleven dollars per month they receive for each unit in their projects. They feel that using housing stock in the private market will be time-consuming, since each LHA will have to negotiate leases with individual landlords. For Burleigh County, this could mean as many as 170 separate contacts with housing suppliers.

Freezon again states that he wants to work with Barr for awhile, and that Morton's allotment will be filled within a week. The families are there, he says.

As the meeting breaks up, a lively discussion starts between the EHAP staff and the LHA directors. Freezon and the fellow from the State Planning Division

---

*For vacated program openings transferred to the LHA, HUD intended to reimburse the housing organizations in this more traditional manner.

are saying that while it is not a good thing for families to live in housing projects, the new high rises are <u>ideal</u> for the elderly.

Ken Erdhal, the Stutsman County board member and a retiree, disagrees violently: "I'm not ready to live with a bunch of old people and weave baskets."

The planner tells him not to knock it unless he's tried it, and Freezon adds that all his elderly tenants love the housing project. Sandwick tries to mediate the debate, but Barr breaks in and loudly says that there "should be a choice."

In spite of the renewed outreach effort, Morton County continued to be troublesome. The average housing allowance remained a bit too high--just over eighty dollars. There was still no one to pick from. Freezon's efforts were bringing no results. "We ought to pull the string on that one," Kuhn said. The ad in the Mandan <u>Morning Pioneer</u> was bringing more requests for information, but the new applicants were mostly from Burleigh County. Apparently, Bismarck and Mandan, being only six miles apart, were too close to each other for the agency to effectively control the response. Burleigh County would receive the additional openings.

Stark County had reached its quota of seventy households. Apparently, the last round of outreach had had its desired effect. Referrals, if any were made, did not come from the housing authority list as far as families were concerned. The Stark County housing authority had few nonelderly units, and the waiting list was short.

The evaluation contractor turned down the waiver of the seven-day waiting period until the last of the interview sample was drawn. This slowed the push a little, but the agency was able to prepare eighty new payments by December twentieth. This helped to make up for the fact that they did not reach their November planned goal of 160 new enrollees. Bob Barr proudly announced that he had pushed through thirty-four payments himself.

The pace was hectic. Barr admitted that he had gotten a little sloppy, with all the sessions he had to hold. He had OK'd an unsigned lease and had to make a home visit to get the participant's signature. In another case, a file clerk revealed that an enrollment statement had not been signed. He drove over to the participant's house and had her read the statement. It was then he found out she was illiterate.

Barr also assigned two VISTA volunteers to help a pair of elderly women who were approaching the ninety-day limit. In one case, the landlord had refused to sign the lease; she had been a troublesome tenant as far as he was concerned, and he wanted her out. The second woman was living in a tenement on Sweet Avenue. She didn't want to move since it was close to church, and her landlady would take her shopping once a week. The services were more important to her than having her own bathroom.

Olsen mentioned the use of the volunteers to the director. Kuhn was irritated. It was fine to help the enrollees, but he wanted to know about it. It would have to go into their documentation. He reminded Barr and the rest of the staff that the AAE was an experiment and they had to keep track of things. Also, he alone would be responsible for program decisions.

The VISTA workers located several units, but neither of the women wanted to look at them. The woman whose landlord wouldn't sign the lease was worried about other things, too. She feared that she couldn't afford the new places that the VISTA volunteers were locating for her. She worried that the housing allowance would affect her social security payments and her welfare check.

Eventually, the woman's landlord talked to one of the counselors about the program and agreed to sign the lease. The other woman was terminated from the project. This was the last time the agency initiated contacts with the outside agencies for the purpose of assisting enrollees.

Barr was more successful getting people into the program on his own. At the very end of the enrollment period he was able to convince an elderly couple living in a shack on the river flats that the project was for them. Since outreach had ended on December twenty-first, every enrollee was important. In January, the numbers grew by bits and pieces, and it seemed that the counselors worked harder for each case.

Simonson wanted the books cleaned. The list of applicants was static, and he wanted to know the status of those who had been selected but didn't show for their sessions. He wanted letters sent out to each of the no-shows. If the people didn't surface within a short time, they would be sent a letter of termination.

Kuhn seemed confident now. They would definitely reach their enrollment goal. Around the first of the year, he said he didn't care if anybody else applied. They had enough for the experiment and hadn't made any serious waves in the community. He worried about the word getting out, though. The recent "employment crisis" across the country might have serious ramifications, he said. Even the least bit of informal outreach might have a "mushrooming effect." Kuhn would say these things calmly. He was in control of things in the office. Still, he seemed to be remembering the depression 'thirties when he first started working for the Public Welfare Board.

Something about the quality of the agency had changed. In their pursuit of the final few enrollments, the staff had operated more like a traditional welfare organization. It was most apparent in Barr, the only counselor with previous welfare experience:

Riverflats Shack

    Barr drives out to the Haefle's "house" on the river flats. It must be the third or fourth time he's been out there. The last time, nobody would answer the door, and he had heard them running into the back room of the shack. "Mrs. Haefle? Can I come in?"

    He's been through it all before with them, and he still wants to try it one more time. Goddamn, there's a mountain of wood ash in the backyard that is cluttered by the junk of rusting automobiles and construction materials that Mr. Haefle collects and hoards. Barr steps over an ice-cutting machine that is next to the back door.

    He has decided that he's going to be more quiet about the project. Once before he had talked to Mrs. Haefle about the "Golden Opportunity." He had felt a little like Willy Loman that time. She had answered that the only lucky people were dead people--they *didn't have to worry about anything. The old man had been in the back room, and when he finally came out, he told Barr that they weren't going to sign any papers, that they had this place here, and the county wasn't going to take it away from him yet. There was a lien on the property, and this would prevent the seizure for back taxes. He had it all figured out.*

This visit, he is nowhere to be seen, and Barr talks to Mrs. Haefle. Both of them have their coats on because of the cold. The woodburning stove over in the corner barely takes the chill away. The room is dark. There's only one light and it seems to be bulging out like some sort of growth on the end of an extension cord that is wound around the nails hammered into the fiberboard ceiling--or what's left of it.

She says she'll sign, and he can hardly believe it, or understand why.

Each of the counselors seemed to have one special case that required more extensive help than the others. If these few people didn't need special encouragement to enroll in the program, then they needed help to <u>participate</u>. Peggy Mickels had just completed a series of contacts which would culminate in the program's only extensive rehabilitation of a dwelling. Siri Ellisen was heavily involved with an elderly Ukrainian woman in Dickinson.

To act as an organizer or catalyst, the counselor first had to clear it with Kuhn. Peggy Mickel's case involved a mentally retarded family who lived outside of the city limits in rundown farmhouse. They had been there for the past seven years and the social services they had received from other agencies came to nothing.

Kuhn gave permission for Peggy to take a more active role. It was she who got the family's social workers, homemaker, and landlord together. The property owner agreed to put in hot water and a heating system and refurbish the kitchen. A church group came and painted and paneled the interior. The same volunteers cleaned up the huge yard and hauled away a tarpaper chicken coop. The landlord had a new small building moved on the premises for this purpose. When it was finished, the agency had a showcase example of what a housing counselor could accomplish, but it remained unique--a special case.

Two weeks before the end of the enrollment period, the evaluation contractor agreed to waive the seven-day waiting period, and the final push began. The last few people serviced would be "provisional enrollees." A special clause would be attached to the document signed at the first session. It would state that they would be accepted into the program only if somebody dropped out and a slot opened up.

The "provisional enrollees" would attend a different kind of enrollment session. The first and second meetings would be telescoped, and each counselor would go as far as possible with the new enrollee.

The feelings were mixed after the staff had done a few of these. The sessions ran as long as two hours each. The counselors said that they wished they'd redesigned the client contact sessions. Cramming two sessions into one wasn't working. If they knew about the program and were sometimes confused, there was no telling what the participants felt like. Siri was sure that one elderly woman believed she would only get in if someone in the project died.

The enrollment scramble and the subsequent departure from the standard enrollment sessions marked the first departure away from close control and careful orchestration. The scene was hardly one of wild abandonment, however. Paper flow still ran smoothly, and financial feasibility was assured. The agency kept its low profile. The necessary goundwork with the LHAs had been done. Perhaps the reason that so much can be made of the enrollment push is because the edges of complete tightness, of complete control, unravelled for a moment. During this time, the agency resembled a program that was going full-bore and trying to meet some sort of participation quota.

Other Events

A mixed team from HUD and from the evaluation contractor made the first site review during the last days of January. Four large maps were prepared, one for each of the major cities in the project area. Map pins were used to represent where each participant family was living. Different colored pins were used to show whether the unit was an apartment, private home or trailer house. Less than a dozen families were living outside of the four cities.

With the help of the assistant GTR, a presentation was given, and the visitors were taken on the standard tour of the Bismarck-Mandan area.

"Did they have their fill of Bismarck-Mandan housing?" Bob Barr asked a day or so later.

"Yes, they were quite pleased by what they saw."

"I imagine they didn't find much substandard," Barr commented.

Kuhn nodded in agreement. By this time, the entire staff was aware that the condition of the housing stock may have contributed more than anything to the success of the project. Most applicants already lived in housing that would pass agency standards. No matter what the vacancy rate, the project could still function. Only 24 percent of the recipients had moved out of their original units by the time they received their first check. This was by far the lowest percentage in the AAE. Later the evaluation contractor's surveys would show that a very large number of North Dakotans in the experiment were happy with their original places and neighborhoods, regardless of the condition. Still, the tightness or looseness of the local housing market was used as an explanatory device when activity lagged at certain times and locations. If things were slow in Dickinson, it was because housing was "kinda tight" there-- even though the latest studies of the vacancy rate seemed to show that, relatively speaking, the market was "kinda loose." At any rate, such explanations helped the staff make sense of their world.

Things went on. There was another case of rent skipping. The landlord called and said that Nancy Mickels (no relation to the Jamestown counselor) had left town without paying the rent. He offered that she had been recently involved with a divorce action.

Barr investigated the matter, pulled the check, and put the case on suspension status. As soon as it was clear that she had left the area, Barr terminated her: she didn't answer his letters, and the Form 600 was filled out and sent to the Capitol.

Staff meetings were held and became more philosophical. The agency decided that they would not automatically recertify those who had gotten the automatic 5 percent AFDC grant increases. It would be a good test to see who called in the change of income. Not that it would make much difference in the payments, anyway. It would just be something they could check for during their Quality Control*, which would begin in the fall.

GETTING THE LAST ONES IN (FEBRUARY-APRIL, 1974)

When the agency stopped enrolling new people on January 31, there were forty-six "provisional enrollees" in a special pool. Each of these households was in a state of limbo. Most were technically involved

---

*Quality Control (QC) is an auditing technique employed by welfare agencies to check the accuracy of an agency's income certification methods. It involves interviewing a random sample of recipients and checking their declarations of income with third parties.

in "housing search." This was a misnomer, however, since most of the project participants remained in their original units. More accurately, there were getting their leases signed and inspecting their units.

Once the paperwork was done, these cases were classified as "completed provisionals" and could then be chosen to replace those who were terminated. There were no guarantees, and each provisional enrollee had signed a waiver which stated that he or she would become a participant only if there was enough room in the program. For those of the forty-six who completed the necessary paperwork, there would be a wait of up to three months. A participant would either have to terminate, or the ninety-day housing search period would have to expire for some earlier enrollee.

It was now obvious that Morton County still would not fill out. Most of the provisionals came from Burleigh County. It was the most populous portion of the project area, and next to Stutsman County,* had been the most responsive.

The director had planned on having a drawing during the latter part of each of the three months that remained for housing search. It became apparent, however, that not all of the "provisionals" would complete the necessary paperwork at the same time. It made more sense to make substitutions on an "as needed" basis. Greg still wanted to be careful about filling the vacated slots, though the financial feasibility of the contract was now insured.

The project director was satisfied with the way the seven-month enrollment period had gone. Early difficulties faded into the background, and he was even pleased with the response that the outreach effort had generated. In the case of Morton County, he felt that the ninety openings were too many to fill. They had miscalculated. Burleigh County was the only jurisdiction that varied much in population from the others, and because of this had been allotted 170 slots. The seventy household quota for Stark and Stutsman counties would have been appropriate for the Mandan area, too.

Kuhn also felt that the entire enrollment process had been "very orderly." The words seemed to be his stamp of approval on the whole operation. Their procedures were administratively simple, and there had been no untoward incidents.

Even the final enrollment push had given him a certain satisfaction. He had relaxed office procedures

---

*Outreach had ceased early in the Jamestown area and there were few from this county in the enrollee pool.

and people were allowed to drop in without making a prior appointment. During the last few days, he had called Peggy and Siri back into the Bismarck office "so people won't have to wait so long."

Kuhn recognized that the next few months would be different. "A period of transition," he said. "A new outlook." The agency would have to shift to a planning mode once again. There were the Section 23 transfers that would inevitably occur after the end of April. At that time, people who dropped out of the project could no longer be replaced. The vacancies would be transferred to the local housing authorities and would no longer be the responsibility of the agency. Queenan would devise a plan to insure that the transfer would be a smooth one.

In September, the agency would begin the required annual income recertifications. The Detailed Plan also called for a quality control review of a selected sample of 100 families. Agency inspections and full verification of participant income and assets were going to be used. The quality control review would provide the staff with the first information about participants' housing quality, and would also allow them to make a judgement as to whether self-certification was really working. Having their own analysis was important. None of the agencies had any access to the data that the evaluation contractor had collected from the participants. This was done to preserve the integrity of the experiment, but left the agency without any idea of how they were actually doing. "Your company never shares anything," Kuhn had often joked.

Kuhn started the staff on their "special projects" in February. Betty was assigned the task of creating a new recertification form. Bob Barr was given the responsibility for developing quality control mechanisms. Olsen was told to familiarize himself with the local housing codes; Kuhn wanted to create a new inspection form that would be used in the field visits. It would have to test the participants' ability to do self-inspection, and there would have to be a section which would objectively determine the quality of the units selected by the participants. Finally, Simonson was told to talk to the computer people at the state capitol. If they were going to be doing their own research, they could need help. If the Social Services Board didn't have the right computer program, they would use the facilities at one of the universities in the eastern part of the state.

---
* Outreach had ceased early in the Jamestown area and there were few from this county in the enrollee pool.

The special projects meant an increased workload for the staff, especially for the housing counselors. For the first time, reporting fell behind schedule. Olsen and Barr found that there was little time to write the monthly narratives that the director had required to be submitted at the beginning of each month. Contacts with enrollees had become fewer but were more intensive, while those with landlords had increased greatly. The latter were still calling with questions about the leases. In contrast, prospective applicants seldom called anymore, and there were only a few provisional enrollees who would need services.

In most cases, the agency had met only three times with a participant family, once for each of the required sessions. The first two sessions were the longest, and now everybody who would ever be in the program had attended these two meetings.

Another reason to expect more landlord contacts was that there were more participants in the program now, and the likelihood of tenant/landlord friction became greater.

The agency's eighth report to HUD, which covered the month of March, noted the new quality of these relationships:

> Relationships with suppliers in the housing market are changing somewhat. During this reporting period, there were fifteen contacts with suppliers covering a range of subjects such as: late payment of rent, non-payment of rent, lease agreements, and rehabilitation of housing unit.

The next month's report repeated the same short paragraph, except that the number of contacts was not specified.

The cases involving withholding of rent were relatively easy to handle. The landlord would call the agency, and the counselor would investigate the complaint. If the participant admitted that he or she had withheld the housing allowance, the counselor would remind the person that people in the AAE were required to put the amount of the check toward the rent and utilities. Failure to do so, he would tell them, would jeopardize their participation in the project.

If the participant agreed to pay the rent, the landlord was called back and informed. This was as much policing as Kuhn wanted to do. If the landlord didn't receive his money from the tenant, he would be expected to inform the agency so that action could be taken. If he decided to let things go, then that was his decision; the agency had no part in that. Similarly, the agency would tolerate any private arrangements made to repay any back rent. This again was considered to be a private matter.

On the whole, landlords seemed to be understanding in those few cases where rent-skipping was involved. The director would explain that the agency would not issue another check to the landlord, since the contract was between the participant and the property owner. The agency would be obligated to terminate the recipient only if he or she had not applied the housing allowance toward the rent. One landlord who had been faced with such a problem said that there should be a two-party check so that this couldn't occur. "Some of these people need an education about how to live," he said. Yet, in a later interview, he claimed not to bear any ill will towards the program or the agency. People needed help, he felt.

In cases where the conflict involved personalities, there was little a counselor could do except encourage the two parties to talk. The results were sometimes unspectacular:

Bob Olsen has been servicing the Dickinson office since Siri left in February. Every Wednesday, he makes the trip in, stops by the post office to pick up his mail and then sits in a stuffy little room for several hours and watches the flag wave on top of the building across the street.

Today, Old Man Gallo is waiting for him. Olsen has his doubts about the man's sanity. He's a kind of a bully, and had Siri in a state of barely controlled terror whenever he visited the office. Gallo had tried that number on him, too. But he had told him to sit down and calm down.

Gallo has an eviction notice with him. Olsen looks the paper over and then calls the landlord as his client has requested. The fellow says that he wants Gallo out next month because he borrowed thirty bucks from him to buy food stamps and never paid him back. Anyway, Gallo was always bugging him to use the telephone. He doesn't want to talk about it; he wants him out.

Olsen hangs up, and explains why he's being evicted.

Gallo wants to know if his landlord can do that, and Olsen explains that yes he can as long as he gives thirty days' notice.

"All right! I'm not paying him back, now that he's evicting me!" His voice is skrieking now.

Olsen tells him to lower his voice, and then says. "It's up to you."

"I borrowed cash, and he can't prove nothin'," Gallo chortles. He turns and leaves. Olsen shakes his head. The same trouble cases keep cropping up, the same four or five that you have to handle over and over again. He's got to talk to Ferber's landlord again, too. Mrs. Ferber had sent a cryptic note.

Last week, the owner had called about a pile of rags that was growing larger and larger each time he stopped by to check the place out. "They're for a quilt," Mrs. Ferber had told Olsen. "If he wants the place spotless, then he should call the welfare board because I'm disabled now, too."

Olsen had agreed to talk to him and to relay the message.

"Another thing: I'm not taking any more shit." Then the line had gone dead, and Olsen had been left holding the receiver.

Now, she wants me to call again. Okay, Olsen laughs to himself. How come they all have to be from Dickinson?

It's ten o'clock now, and time for a third session. He'll call them both later.

Sometimes, word about a participant would come from another agency. In February, for example, a probation officer called and said that Dave Johnson had jumped his parole. If he shows up, the official said, tell us. The parole officer had referred Johnson to the agency, and now he was simply calling all of the people and agencies with whom Johnson had known contact. Even if they had not been notified, the EHAP agency would have known that something was amiss: the check envelopes were non-forwardable.

As it was, Barr terminated Johnson routinely. The evaluation contractor's termination form was checked, appropriately enough, "Cannot be located," and another household was chosen to take his place.

"They'll catch up with him," Barr tells me.

"Why?"

"Ah, hell. If I remember, he was supposed to be a con-man. But his glasses are like the bottoms of Coke bottles. It must hurt your style, you know."

"I don't think they'll get him."

"They'll catch up with him."

"No, it will be like trying to catch the wind."

A few incidents occurred during the February to April period which again indicated that the agency was willing to assist participants actively if they did not seem to be able to manage for themselves. In one instance, the agency investigated a complaint that a couple in the program had not paid the rent.

Bob Barr met separately with Mrs. Silbernagel, the landlady, and with the EHAP participant, Sam Yellowhorse. The two of them agreed about one fact only: the rent was $100.

Mrs. Silbernagel claimed that Sam Yellowhorse owed her a total of $170 for the last two months. She also remembered that on two occasions, he paid her an "odd figure," something like $83. Then, she claimed that the $170 owed went back to October, which was before the Yellowhorses got on the program. "Sam knows what he owes me," she said.

Barr had already talked to Sam Yellowhorse and his wife. He claimed that she had cashed the checks at the Red Owl, and had given Mrs. Silbernagel the $83. Neither of them had a receipt, which complicated matters. He claimed that he owed her only $34--$17 for each of the two months in question.

Barr returned to the office, and talked the matter over with Kuhn. The director felt that Yellowhorse wasn't much better off than before, except that the $170 was not for the months that he was on the program.

Barr argued that the landlady's case was weak, too, and that Sam's contention seemed to make more sense. The numbers added up right, at least. If he had used his EHAP check to pay the rent, he was also in the clear with the agency, he said.

Kuhn agreed to let Barr fill out an answer to the summons which would state the tenant's side of the story. Both Barr and Olsen would be allowed to accompany the couple to small claims court.

Mr. and Mrs. Yellowhorse came in that afternoon, and Barr advised them to respond to the charges. Then, he turned them over to Olsen. They were in his caseload, anyway, and Barr had broken an admininstrative rule in handling the case: whenever possible, a participant kept the same counselor. In that way, one person would be responsible for being familiar with a set number of cases. The same person would also be required to do the record keeping for the people in his caseload.

Olsen looked over the lease to the Yellowhorse's new apartment. Mrs. Silbernagel had told them to move immediately. Olsen asked the couple if the new landlord had done the exterminating job they had requested. He had. Sam Yellowhorse then said that he didn't want to seek any damages, even though their food stamps had been suspended because the landlady had called the welfare office with her complaint.

The case was heard in small claims court at the end of March. The two counselors and a social worker attended. Olsen testified that the couple was on the project and had been receiving $83 a month from the agency.

"Do you know if he paid the money to Mrs. Everett?"
"No," Olsen said.

Less than a week later, a copy of the judgement is sent to Yellowhorse. He brings a copy to the agency for xeroxing:

> Neither party has kept any record of the rental payments. Essentially, the dispute is whether the December rent was paid. The burden of proof rests with the Claimant. I do not feel this burden has been met.
> Defendant admits owing thirty-four dollars rent for January and February, having paid eighty-three dollars in each of those months. Claimant says $100 was paid on one of those months. In view of this, the claim will be allowed for the sum of seventeen dollars, together with three dollar costs, making a total judgement of twenty dollars.

Below was the judge's signature. Sam Yellowhorse and his family could remain in the program.

In another case, a counselor tried to nudge a landlord into renting a house out to a provisional enrollee engaged in housing search. They had several children and were living in a four-room apartment. The wife had just returned from a stay at a mental hospital. The counselor had been working closely with the family. The prospective landlord had called the counselor at home on a Sunday afternoon. They talked for fifteen minutes about the program.

In April, the director curtailed all staff meetings. These had lately become workshop sessions for the special projects. More time was freed, and the final humane push began. The last people were being inched into the program. Barr again visited the Haefle family, the ones living down on the river flats. A Senior Citizens' coordinator had been working with them, but they had refused to take the unit she had located for the couple. Barr met twice with them and also had extensive contacts with the county welfare office. Finally, an acceptable place was located through a church group. The Haefles were the last people to get into the program.

Other Events and Activities

In February, Kuhn had made inquiries in the social services system and found an opening for the Dickinson counselor. She left in mid-February. Less than a month later, Peggy Mickels found a position as a social worker in Barnes County. This allowed Kuhn to close the Jamestown office, and represented a savings of almost $100 a month in rent.

Ironically, this was the only office that was located in an ASSC.

Since the lease was not up for the Stark County office, Kuhn decided to retain this space until June. Each satellite center would be served once a week by Barr and Olsen respectively. Notices of the new arrangement were sent out with the checks.

Delores Hummel also announced that she would be going on half time in April. This was a satisfactory arrangement with Kuhn. There was less clerical work that needed to be done now that enrollment was over.

Kuhn also began to think about rearranging the office structure. Barr would be made director of housing services when the time came, he told the observer. There was no justification for having an assistant director when the level of activity was so low. Indeed, he offered, if he had known how few applications there would be, he would have not hired one in the first place. Barr would have been brought aboard as a counseling supervisor, and some of the redundancy in the organization table would have been eliminated.

In February, the first report of the experiment's progress was made to the Social Service Board of North Dakota. The actual meeting had been postponed a few times, but the officials were aware that the project was running smoothly. Kuhn had had many informal meetings with the department's executive director, and used the opportunity to keep him abreast of new developments.

The presentation is given by Joe Queenan, and it lasts for over an hour. Kuhn has told the board that the assistant GTR from HUD is "a neutral and more unbiased person," and for that reason will do the talking. Queenan focuses upon the financial aspects of the project, and the board seems pleased that the admininstrative costs are running at about 65 percent of what had been anticipated. As Queenan outlines the experiment, he uses--perhaps significantly --the net income limits employed during the first months of the experiment. An overhead projector is used to display the elaborate charts and graphs he has made for the occasion.

*There are few questions from the period. One
member asks about the small number of Amerindians in
the project. Kuhn quickly explains that they had been
working with an American Indian organization but that
few applicants surfaced.*

*Another person asks about how non-payment of rent
was handled. Kuhn tells him that the landlord would
inform the agency and the check could be stopped.*

*The board is satisfied with the way the program
was being carried out. "But we expected that from
you," the chairman laughs.*

*In the back of the room, the department's infor-
mation specialist is making notes. A story about the
Experimental Housing Allowance Project will appear in
the next edition of <u>Case and Counsel</u>.*

A BROADER VISION: TOWARDS REGIONALIZED HOUSING AUTHORITIES (MAY - JUNE, 1974)

May first marked a very real change that occurred
in agency operations. As of this date, no more people
could be accepted into the project. The agency had
achieved their goal of 400 participant households.
From now on, if someone terminated from the experiment,
the slot would remain empty until it was transferred
to the appropriate LHA. Alternatively, Kuhn considered
retaining control over the vacancies, reopening outreach and beginning agency operations once again. The
newcomers would not be a part of the experiment, and
paperwork concerning them would be kept separate for
analytical purposes.

The central issue was one of control. Terminations were occurring at a much higher rate than expected. In the first two months of "steady-state"
operations, they would exceed the number planned for
the whole experiment.

The ACC committed two years of housing allowances
to be paid to each of the 400 "units" in the experimental caseload. Thus, if a family received its first
check in May, and then decided to leave the project
the next day, that "unit" or slot would still have
twenty-three more monthly payments coming to it. The
agency was still held financially accountable for these.
The juggling act between household size and average
payment had to continue if the project was to remain
financially feasible.

There was a certain irony to all this: the agency
no longer had any experimental interest in the new
households, and yet the choice of the type of family
remained critical as before. The right mix of house-

hold types had to be maintained if continued financial feasibility was to be assured.

The reasons for the terminations were varied. During the planning period, the core staff had not been able to think of reasons why anyone would become ineligible for the program. As soon as there was a substantial number of people in the program, it became clear that they had miscalculated. Younger people moved out of the program area, family income sometimes increased, a few people bought homes or terminated voluntarily. Finally, a number of single women with children "married out of the program." Simonson estimated that as many as eighty might terminate in the first year of steady-state operation. The true figure would be closer to 100.

With such a large number of terminations, the financial feasibility of the contract could be jeopardized if the agency did not have final say over what sorts of families were selected to fill the openings that would inevitably occur.

Kuhn and Queenan considered two different possibilities for the actual transfer. The units could be handed directly to the LHAs, or else the agency could retain the units. If the latter option were chosen, this would mean that the agency would have to renew its outreach efforts, and start to enroll people just as before. This time, though, they would have just a single enrollment session. They would redesign the Counselor's Handbook so that the necessary information could be transmitted smoothly to the new participants. There would be no "cram sessions" like those which had marked the last few days of the enrollment period.

By keeping the units themselves, the agency would retain total control of the ACC. The agency would have to become active again, however. "It would have required an effort, but we could have done it," Kuhn later remarked. The other alternative--that of transferring the vacancies immediately to the housing authorities--would be admininstratively simple, but more reliance would have to be placed on each LHA. Also, if just a few units trickled in, at first, it would give the four directors a chance to get used to handling the Section 23 units before the wholesale transfers began to occur. The agency director and the assistant GTR decided, for the moment, to let the housing authorities handle the early terminations. Back in March, an attorney from HUD had met with Queenan and Kuhn to discuss the transfer mechanisms. The lawyer appeared a day early so that the two of them could brief him before the matter was discussed with the LHA directors.

Kuhn had privately expressed concern that the housing agencies might not be able to provide the correct type of replacement families. His worry was that a director might take a slot that was formerly occupied by a household receiving a very low payment, and replace it with one that was eligible for a much higher one. Thus, the conversation with the HUD official was about "concurrent responsibility."

Kuhn said that he didn't care which way matters were handled, except that the EHAP agency had to have the final approval of any new families. The actual payments could be handled any number of ways. Either the housing authorities could write the checks, or else this function could be performed by the agency. In either case, he wanted "a clear audit trail."

The following day, three of the four LHA directors attended the meeting held at the Bismarck office. The presentation centered around the transfer of early terminations, and the housing officials were given the option of receiving the units as they became vacant, or else having the transfer made on a quarterly basis.

Queenan stated that either method would involve a fair amount of paperwork, since the LHAs and the EHAP agency would essentially be sharing the original ACC. Only when each unit "matured"* would the LHAs receive payment directly from HUD under a new contract. Until that time, the EHAP agency would continue to issue the checks to the new recipients. Kuhn then explained to the LHA directors that it was necessary to watch both the household size and the amount of payment. He again stressed that no violations of the present ACC could occur.

Finally, each LHA would have to provide counseling and inspection services. Since this would involve some administrative costs, HUD would authorize the EHAP agency to reimburse the LHAs on a per-unit basis. The actual amount each LHA received for their present units would be used as a starting point. Queenan allowed that there would probably be more contact with the landlords than there had been in the experimental effort.

The meeting adjourned with Queenan saying that he would write a preliminary plan for their approval. The issue of who was going to handle the vacated slots was not yet settled, however. In late spring, a revised set of Section 23 regulations came out. Instead

---

*i.e., had received twenty-four payments under the ACC.

of using the experiment's C* figures, a set of "Fair Market Rents" (FMRs) was substituted in their place. These were substantially lower than the rental rates in force for other housing programs, and Kuhn began to doubt that the LHAs would be interested in the units until the termination phase of the experiment. The assistant GTR agreed with the decision, and informed the four directors of the change.

Kuhn used his financial feasibility arguments to explain the new plan to the EHAP staff. Under the new arrangement, the units would be transferred <u>en masse</u> when it came time for a new ACC to be written. Keeping the units would "protect the agency," he explained. If a family had an $8 payment and then quit, they would be the ones to find another $8 payment to fit the slot.

In June, the assistant GTR returned to the site for a month's stay. Much of his time would be spent working on a transition plan. Now, Kuhn and Queenan were again unsure of how to handle the transfers. The FMRs had not been revised to more realistic levels. At the lower end of the scale, things were all right. C* was $90 for a one-person household, while the FMR was $81 for an appropriate efficiency or "zero-bedroom" unit. However, things got steadily worse, until the disparity between the C* and the FMR for a four-bedroom unit was $100 per month. What made it worse was that administrative costs were included in the FMRs; this was not the case with C*.

There was another issue which had to be resolved: Could the EHAP agency legally continue to run a housing <u>program</u>? The original approval from the Social Services Board had been for an <u>experiment</u>, a special case. Kuhn and Queenan talked with an attorney from the Social Services Board. He checked the North Dakota Century Code* and found that the contracting agency was empowered to administer welfare funds on all governmental levels. By construing "welfare" to include housing, he thought that the EHAP agency could retain the slots that were freed prematurely.

Queenan brightened upon hearing this and requested that the attorney write HUD a letter to that effect.

---

*The North Dakota legal code book, adopted in the 1930s. It is generally regarded as a progressive work and it remains unrevised to this day.

At this stage, he wanted to keep all possible options open. If the LHAs refused to participate, the outreach activities would be resumed by the agency.

Another meeting is held with the local housing authorities:

Queenan has prepared a series of flow charts which are pasted along the walls of the room.

The first transfers will be scheduled for August, Queenan explains, so that the new recipients would have their checks by September first. The experiment is now in "Phase II*", and early attritions are of immediate concern. There have been nine so far.

The transfer mechanism is then outlined. "ND-EHAP notifies the LHA, and then ND-EHAP terminates the households."

The Stark County director says that he is concerned that they won't be able to meet the profiles.

Queenan answers that the LHA will have to provide public information to the effect that the slots are open. They cannot simply cull the waiting list. An interested party would then be required to submit a new application. These would be screened and certified and put into a pool of eligibles. Again, he refers to the charts: "This will take the household from a point of interest to a point of eligibility."

The explanation goes on and on. Finally, he gives them the FMR figures.

"Why are we even talking about it?" one of the directors jokes, but the humor has an edge to it. All agree that the figures are unworkable. "Gottfried, you can keep them for another eight years."

Queenan says that these figures will be challenged, and that the original C* figures can be used instead. In the meantime, he wants each LHA director to be sure that their local governing boards will approve the early transfers, and that each housing authority has a general depository with the Bank of North Dakota.**

---

*The first ten months of enrollment and housing search were called "Phase I" by the assistant GTR. Phase II covered the period between the end of this latter period (April 30, 1974) and the transfers of families that had received twenty-four monthly payments.

**In North Dakota, the state-owned bank also acts as the State Treasury.

Separate sets of books will have to be kept, too, he says. He will develop costs for them.

The LHAs are still concerned. The Dickinson LHA director says that he's director of a consolidated LHA and is already spread pretty thin. The Bismarck director is concerned about the 189 leases he'll have to renegotiate. The meeting ends at lunch time, and another is set for the next day.

This time, the HUD attorney is there to give an opinion about the FMRs. He thinks that the FMRs won't apply, since the transfer would be covered under rules of the old ACC. The contract is still binding, as far as he's concerned. The only difference is a change in management. "The important thing is not to touch the ACC for several months until the Fair Market Rents are adjusted upwards."

They have a few other questions. The new regulations say that all maintenance must be taken care of by the landlord. "Even grass cutting and putting in new light bulbs."

The attorney says that this can all be adjusted to conform with local practice.

This seems to satisfy the agency staff and the LHA directors. The latter agree to take the units, and all that remain are the final negotiations.

In the month preceding the final negotiations, Kuhn considered another possible innovation for the transfer: the new participants could keep their eligibility as long as they moved within the four-county project area. In all previous housing authority programs, a move outside the jurisdiction meant that a low-income family would have to start all over again at the bottom of the waiting list.

Queenan was also intrigued with the idea, although he considered it too controversial to put in the transfer plan which was now in rough draft. Both of them felt that the broadening of the residency requirement would be a precursor to a state housing authority with regional offices in each of the eight governmental planning districts.

The parallels with the welfare system were obvious. Prior to the mid-1960s, welfare had been administered on a strictly local basis. Then, with the creation of the Area Social Services Centers, those in sparsely populated counties could receive the benefit of more extensive services. Then, too, there was the fact that many of the truly rural counties did not have enough people to justify the existence of a housing authority.

Kuhn and Queenan wanted to bring the new idea up to see what the reaction of the four LHA directors would be:

"I see that Bismarck's the biggest, so I might as well go home," an LHA director jokes. The figures have been passed out, and it is a time for easy humor.

Queenan is chairing the meeting and states that "Phase II" will be a mixed operation that involves both the agency and the LHAs. There will be no real trouble with finances, Queenan says; there is a large surplus in EHAP's budget.

An administrator from HUD-Central speaks. The only thing is that he wants a uniform set of procedures, and that's what the transition plan is for.

Queenan notes that everybody can relax about finances: the FMRs aren't going to be used. C* is acceptable to HUD. Then, he passes out a series of forms that all of them will have to use. Essentially, they are the same ones the agency has been employing throughout the experiment. Queenan tells them that there will be a workshop in August for the four of them.

The issue of the p.u.m.* reimbursements is brought up. The fellow from HUD-Central suggests that a single standard payment be used for all of the LHAs. "This is not a fat operation, but we want it done well. How does fifteen dollars a month sound?"

The director from Burleigh County says that it's generous. The Morton County official plays a little closer to the vest; he says that there should be flexibility, and that each LHA should have its own figure if necessary. In his county, the bookkeeping is farmed out to a local firm, while Burleigh does its own.

Queenan suggests that there will be cost analysis so that nothing gets out of line. The Morton County director then agrees that fifteen dollars per month would be a good starting point.

One of the other directors complains about the moving allowances that are provided for the ACC. He thinks these should be kept to a minimum. In truth, the surplus in the budget is large enough so that no one can get into trouble no matter how many moving allowances are paid. But it is something that hasn't been done before.

Finally, the issue of eligibility is discussed. Queenan says that he is enthusiastic about the EHAP project because it was the first time participants were able to move without losing their subsidy.

---

*"Per unit month"--for each of the occupied units under its control, an LHA is given a fixed sum each month by HUD to defray administrative costs.

Kuhn suggests that this freedom of movement could be extended to Phase II of the experiment. Silence. Then, one of the directors says that the idea sounds good. "But we have to take care of our own first."
Only the Burleigh County director is in favor. The HUD members are split over the issue. One of them thinks that the only way this can be handled is by having a "consolidated ACC," and anyway, he is worried about mass migrations and "moving a demand market."
He continues: The freedom movement might mean that an area would have to be redeveloped by HUD five years later.
Kuhn counters that movement would probably be slight, and balanced. The issue is left undecided. Someone makes a suggestion that perhaps the gains or losses would be limited to 10 percent of the total units in any one county.
Nobody picks up on it, and the idea seems to die. No one wants to risk losing units.

Other Activities and Events

In May, Kuhn made the staffing changes official. They were retroactive to April first. His justification was that he didn't want to run an "unrealistic program even though the money's there."

By having Barr "demoted" to the director of housing services, Bob Olsen was cut off from advancement within the office structure. Barr spoke to Kuhn in Olsen's behalf. He suggested that the housing counselor be given a two-step pay increase since he had been hired at a salary that was $300 a month below that of the remaining professionals.

Outside the agency hierarchy, two other staffing changes occurred. Queenan was made the Government Technical Representative for the experiment, and the evaluation contractor's on-site observer left the North Dakota site as specified in the experimental design.

Now that the agency activity had lessened, the director instructed Barr and Olsen to bring their reports and participant files up to date. Although one of the counselors had suggested it, Kuhn rejected the idea of hiring more secretarial help. He felt that this would be costly and a duplication of effort. The log sheets could be handwritten just as before, he said, and the agency could thereby avoid putting an intermediary between the counselors and the case records. This would mean the first substantial amounts of overtime to be worked by the counselors. In contrast, Kuhn and Simonson had frequently stayed after work or come in Saturdays to do the fiscal planning which seemed so central to the question of the North Dakota agency.

Financial policies were also tightened during this period. A few families had terminated while still owing the agency portions of the damage deposits which had been advanced to them. The staff decided that they had not made it clear enough that these were really loans which were automatically repaid by issuing smaller checks to the particular recipient for the first year of the experiment. It was decided that letters would be sent to all those who had been given deposits to inform them of this fact.

This still left the problem of what to do about those few who had already left the experiment and taken their deposits with them. Most staff members were in favor of writing these bad debts off, since prosecution would be costly and most of the people wouldn't have the money anyway. Kuhn privately agreed that this was the most sensible course; however, he stressed that the decision was not theirs to make. Information about each case would be forwarded to the state's attorney, and he would make the decision. "We are not a collection agency," he stressed. Nevertheless, clear records would have to be kept. "The GAO* will want to know what happened to the money."

Further administrative changes were made. From mid-summer onwards, Jamestown and Dickinson would only be served twice a month. Notices were sent in the check envelopes to participants advising them of the changes. The files from the satellite centers were duplicated and integrated with those at the Bismarck office. The convenience was two-fold. The staff expected that participants in the outlying counties might be calling about their status. It made sense to have the case records in Bismarck, where all the staff were located. Also, having a central file would help in the agency's own research effort. In order to make the individual's files more easy to scan, a <u>supplemental information log</u> was designed. This form gave a short synopsis of the information contained within each participant's records.

The staff members also completed the forms and handbooks necessary for the annual recertification and for the quality control review. The entire process

---

*The Government Accounting Office (GAO) performs an auditing (watchdog) function for the legislative branch of the federal government.

had taken five months, and was the subject of numerous staff meetings. Each draft of each document was given a sentence-by-sentence reading until the entire staff was satisfied with the end product.

Finally, for much of June and July, most of the male staff members were on the road, helping Queenan with an inspection tour of Section 23 housing throughout the state. Kuhn felt that it would be a good experience for those who were going to be doing the quality control inspections in the fall.

The agency had planned, operated a full-blown project, and then had planned again. All that really remained was the analysis of the results, and the servicing of those who were already in standard housing.

They wanted to get on with it.

STEADY STATE OPERATIONS (AUGUST-MAY, 1974)

Quality Control (QC) began in the fall. Using a random numbers table, Simonson selected a sample of 100 participating families for a full field review. Due to the large number of terminations, this meant that approximately one-third of the families in the project would be required to have a home interview by one of the housing counselors. Those households selected were notified by a letter telling them that their financial records should be ready, and advising them of the date and time of the home visit. If the time of the interview was inconvenient, the letter explained, the participant could call the agency and arrange for another appointment.

The quality control review was conducted independent of the HUD-required annual redetermination of eligibility. This latter task was essentially a duplication of the original application and certification process. Trust and heavy reliance upon the "prudent person principle" were again employed in determining the correct housing allowance to be paid to the households. Betty Throndset and the rest of the staff had designed a new form and instructional brochure, but these were primarily refinements of the original application materials. As soon as a household had received its eleventh monthly payment, the redetermination process would begin with the mailing of a cover letter, the redetermination form and a set of instructions.

In contrast, the quality control review could be instituted at any point during a family's participation and thus had no relation to the date of the latest recertification, whether agency or participant initiated.

The field review was a time-consuming process. Even before the home visit was made, the housing counselor had to go through several administrative steps which began when Simonson assigned the case and the initial contact letter was written. Since the names were randomly assigned, a counselor did not necessarily quality control those in his usual caseload, except at the outlying satellite centers.

The first task for the housing counselor was to obtain all pertinent data from the individual participant file. The most recent information available was used in all cases, and this was especially important where income and assets were concerned. The file information would provide the baseline against which payment errors would be determined.

Letters were sent to Unemployment Compensation, Social Security, and the Social Service Board as necessary or appropriate. The counselors found that the turnaround for welfare and unemployment cases was quick, averaging less than a week. However, to get information from Social Security took longer, sometimes as much as two or three weeks. No release was required from the participant, since the Social Services Board had the right to make such inquiries about anyone receiving assistance from state programs.

A copy of the latest payment worksheet was made and placed in the individual's QC file. Similarly, a copy of the self-inspection form was xeroxed, so the counselor could reinspect the dwelling during the visit.

The actual home visit took anywhere from forty-five minutes to an hour and a half. The thirty-page Quality Control Handbook was used as an interviewing guide. Not all items on the review sheet required documentatary proof. For example, family size was believed to be as stated by the participant, unless there was evidence to the contrary. On the other hand, earned income required verification in the form of pay stubs or income tax forms. Medical expenses claimed by the participant also had to be backed by receipts. Rent receipts were requested so that the amount of rent would be known. If a rent receipt or cancelled check could not be produced, the counselor would contact the landlord for the information. Finally, the participant had to sign a release which would allow the agency to receive information from banks regarding accounts that a participant might have. All members in the household over eighteen years of age had to sign this authorization, which was good for a thirty-day period. If one of the adult members of the family was not present, the release form would be left with a self-addressed, stamped envelope.

Each variation in income, assets, or special expenses which might affect the payment was noted, and columns were checked to indicate whether the error was that of the agency or of the recipient. When the interview was completed, the unit was inspected by the housing counselor. The inspection came in two parts. First, the original self-inspection report was validated. Any discrepancies found were discussed with the participant. Then, a more comprehensive evaluation was made. Each room was measured, and components were rated on a five-point scale.

This ended the home visit portion of quality control. Once the outstanding letters had been returned from the banks and social service agencies, the counselors would calculate the amount of the payment based upon the verified information supplied during the review. The completed forms would then be sent to the agency director for approval. In cases where an error was found, the eligibility control technician would be notified. She would then recontact the family if no recent change in payment level had taken place.

However, quality control was a lengthy, involved procedure and it was often found that the new, supposedly "correct" payment level was not, in fact, the most current one. In some cases, a new redetermination of eligibility had already been made. In others, the participant had called the agency to inform them of a more recent change in income. Fluctuations in payment levels were common, especially among the seasonally employed recipients.

Kuhn later commented upon the working poor in the project: "They lose their jobs first. Seasonal labor affects their jobs first." He felt that the time of year that the quality control review or the annual redetermination was done affected the size of the payment change, especially where men who worked sporadically in the construction trades were concerned. He cited a case where, for a period of one month, a recipient had received an income of almost $1,000 a month. If he had reported the change immediately, the agency would have been forced to declare the family ineligible. As it was, the man was laid off and went back to collecting unemployment.

As the quality control review continued, certain patterns appeared. As early as January, it became apparent that decreases in payment size were more common than increases. This seemed to indicate that prosperity in North Dakota was continuing to rise, in spite of the usual seasonal variations. The staff knew that the state unemployment rate was low, less than 5 percent.

The director joked that North Dakota only looks better than other states during the bad times: "We've been living on a shoestring for years and have already made all the adjustments."

Whatever the reason for the general decrease in the amount of housing allowances, it was also apparent that not everyone was reporting changes in income:

It is January, 1975--four months into the QC review. I walk into the middle of a conversation between Kuhn and Olsen. "I think we kinda missed the boat on that a little by not asking them why they didn't report changes," Olsen says. "I didn't think of it then."

Kuhn agrees and says that the agency should have gotten some sort of <u>reason</u> for their own records. "I'm not interested in the payment differential. I want to know whether self-declaration is a valid program technique." He then adds that QC is not supposed to be some sort of policing device. Instead, it is to be a management technique "to find out where the problems lie, so you can change your program regulations."

"I don't think that self-declaration works for the elderly," Olsen offers.

"Why?"

"I haven't had one that reported an increase in social security."

The director asks if anyone lied on their self-declaration form. Olsen answers no. Kuhn smiles and says, "Don't get this mixed up with <u>continuous reporting</u>." It is an important point with him: if recipients deliberately falsify their applications, then self-certification really doesn't work. On the other hand, if payment errors result because participants don't know they are supposed to report any economic changes, then the responsibility is not with the method, but with the administration.

Olsen nods his head, and then Kuhn offers another reason why the difference should be kept clear: "If you get the two confused, the observer'll put it in his notes, write a report, and then we'll all be in trouble."

The scene dissolves in laughter.

By May, all but the last few quality control reviews had been completed. The counselors found that, in 25 percent of the cases, there was no change in payment. For the remainder, decreases were twice as common as increases. The staff still believed in the basic honesty of the participants. They observed that when the annual redetermination of eligibility closely preceded the QC review, there were few errors. The director felt that in other cases, "They would

have reported accurately if they had been invited to
do so." The housing counselors noted that, in many
cases, the elderly and AFDC recipients had not reported
blanket increases in grant income because they had
assumed the agency was already aware of the changes
and would make the adjustments accordingly. Then, too,
there was still the confronting fact that twenty to
thirty calls were received from participants every
month, and that changes which would result in reduced
housing allowances were reported more frequently than
in reverse cases.

As more reviews were completed, the staff members
formed opinions as to which aspects of the process were
useless. Checking bank accounts often took a long time.
Sometimes it took as long as a month to receive the
requested information. "There doesn't seem to be any
pattern to it," Olsen noted. "One time it'll be the
Bank of North Dakota that's slow, and another time
it'll be some other bank." Barr felt that it was a
waste of time to check savings institutions. People
at low income levels never had any money to begin with,
he said. None of his investigations had uncoverd disqualifying amounts of cash assets.

All of the staff felt that certain groups of
people did not need recertification at less than yearly
intervals. The elderly were the best example of this.
"The only way they can have a major income change is
through inheritance," Kuhn said.

AFDC grants also tended to remain constant. This
suggested that perhaps different categories of people
could be recertified at different intervals. The
working poor might have to have this done as often as
four times a year, the staff decided.

Barr found the verification of medical expenses
to be difficult, but necessary. He remembered one
case in which a family had over $700 in medical bills.
This meant that he had to review almost fifty check
stubs during the home visit. The counselor's tabula-
tions came to within twenty dollars of what had been
claimed on the redetermination form. "You know, I
think the only reason that it didn't check out per-
fectly is because he couldn't find a couple of cancelled checks."

The results of the inspection portion of the
quality control review were more even than was the
case with payment error determinations. The housing
counselors found only one case where extensive damage
to the dwelling had been done by the tenants. Olsen
found a few cases in Stark County where ventilation
fans had not been installed in the bathroom as promised. He suspended payments in these instances
until the rehabilitations had been completed. Barr

had one case where a woman was living as a boarder in someone's house. When informed that this violated the regulations of the project, she promptly found an apartment elsewhere in town.

The participants seemed to be satisfied with the program. Bob Olsen had designed a series of questionnaires, with the GTR's help, which were designed to measure tenant satisfaction with their EHAP units. A different form was used, depending upon whether the participant had moved, stayed without rehabilitation, or stayed with rehabilitation. In cases of multiple moves, a questionnaire was sent for each program residence. These were mailed in January by the evaluation contractor, who insisted on pulling those families who had already been interviewed for their own evaluation efforts. The agency estimated that over 90 percent of the forms had been returned. Most of these came back to the agency within three weeks.

One of the open-ended questions read, "In what ways do you feel the Experimental Housing Allowance Project helped your household?" The responses were typed by Delores and copies were made and circulated among agency staff. Many of the respondents indicated that the allowance had helped them make food and appliance purchases. There were no negative comments. A few said that they hoped the allowance would be adjusted to account for the inflation that had taken place over the last year.

It has given me the opportunity to have a home, instead of a two-by-four apartment. When one is alone, as I am, it is very important to have your own furnishings and things you love around. Your project has helped me to be able to buy more food and clothing. I'm much happier and may God bless you and all those who are involved, for taking me in on this project. Please accept my sincere thanks.

The transfer of vacant slots to the four local housing authorities also occurred during the steady state period. The transition plan had gone through several revisions, and final approval by HUD was delayed. As a result, it was December before the LHAs could begin to select families for participation in the non-experimental portion of the AAE.

The evaluation contractor's forms were adapted for use by the LHAs. Unlike the EHAP agency, the housing authorities required verification of income and assets. In theory, agency inspection was substituted for self-inspection. In practice, units were approved by self-inspection if the personnel at the housing authority were familiar with the neighborhood and the units selected.

The housing authorities also seemed to get more involved in agency-landlord negotiations. In many cases, in LHA staff member would take the potential recipient to an arranged meeting with the prospective landlord.

Because Kuhn has insisted on retaining control over the financial aspects of the transfer, the LHAs at first had to get verbal permission to select any households which could have a larger payment than the previous recipient who had terminated from the AAE. "It's not hard work," one of the housing authority clerks explained. "But you got to find time to fill it." One of the disappointments was that you could go through the trouble of calculating a payment and then find that the amount would not fit the slots available.

Later, in February, Kuhn relaxed these restrictions. There was no possible way that the feasibility of the contract would be endangered. After this time, the only restriction was on household size. The match had to be perfect there. Kuhn cautioned the LHAs exceeding an average payment figure by too much more than the originally planned seventy-seven dollars: when the experiment was over, the ACC would be split into four parts, and each operation would have to be financially feasible.

By the end of April, the LHAs had filled almost ninety slots. There were less than 300 active cases in the AAE. The housing authority directors were enthusiastic about the program. The negotiation of leases was proving to be no problem. The payments under Section 23 were more generous than under the new Section 8 regulations.* "I'm glad we went to bat to get the project," one of the directors said. "I don't know if Section 8 will fly. You can't get financing for new construction, and the Fair Market Rents are too low for existing stock."

The directors were also relieved that the Brooke Amendment requirement that recipients contribute no more than twenty-five percent of their income for rent would not be applicable. All of them felt that inflation had caused rents to rise drastically in the past several months. C*, however, had remained at its original levels. The agency had been concerned about the Brooke Amendment restrictions, too. Almost one-third of the EHAP families were paying more of their income for rent than would normally be allowed. They had been concerned that this would cause problems when

---

*Section 8 is that part of the Housing Act of 1975 which supercedes Section 23 of the Housing Act of 1937.

these families were transferred to the local housing agencies after the experiment was over.

It was apparent that the LHAs had quickly mastered the intricacies of maintaining financial feasibility. Most of them were watching the levels of payment closely: "The minute I feel that we're in trouble I'll be more selective in choosing people."

The Stutsman County director, Clair Christensen, had become fascinated by the possibilities of direct cash assistance. His housing project did not have family units, and the empty EHAP slots gave him his first chance to deal with the non-elderly. The EHAP staff were bemused by Christensen's interest. "He's become a social worker in the best sense of the word," Barr commented.

At the Stutsman County Housing Authority offices. One of the women there fixes me a lunch from some of the leftovers from the noon lunch program.

"We're EHAPing a little," the director jokes. Stutsman County now has sixteen people in payments. There are a lot of referrals from the welfare office. "A lot of people call and say, 'The welfare board says that you're supposed to help me pay my rent.' We have them come down and apply. We get 'em by word of mouth type of thing." Like the other LHA directors, Christensen has done almost no formal outreach.

"It's a gratifying program." he continues. "We've done a lot of good." He then relates a story of how he got a woman and her children into a new home. "It was at the end of the month when she came in. Geez, there was worry all over her face.

"I took down the information and got on the horn to the EHAP office. I worked with that young fellow, Simonson. They took my word about the amount of the payment. It was a big one, too--$131." He pauses to take another sip of coffee. Both of his hands are wrapped around the mug. Then he continues:

"They pushed it right through, and she went out and got a new first floor apartment. It was a heck of a thing before. She was living with her mother in a mobile home. One of her kids had to go to a special school way over on the other side of town. She used to have to drive him. Now she can watch him walk right into the school. She's just across the street.

"We gotta think about people," he says. "Not just dollars."

Other Activities and Events

In January, a HUD team arrived at the agency and performed an audit. The report was issued on the last

Mobile Home Court-Bismarck

day of March. The auditors found the fiscal controls to be adequate. There were a few questions, however. The purchase of office equipment and the payment of a year's rent out of the planning grant were questioned. The auditors felt that these should have been charged against the ACC. The argument stated that the equipment and the office space were utilized primarily during the ACC period, and not during the planning stages.

The report also noted that the agency had drawn funds on the basis of 400 units during the entire enrollment period and had accumulated a large surplus. This was acceptable practice; however, the interest had not been credited to HUD. The funds had been deposited in the state-owned Bank of North Dakota. There, the ACC funds had been comingled with other state and federal funds. The 6 percent interest had accrued to the state's general fund. Although Kuhn explained that this was the usual practice followed in North Dakota, the auditors felt that the interest--over $9,000 by the end of 1974--should have been returned to HUD. "I don't care one way or the other," Kuhn later commented. "We have enough money to pay the bills."

As planned, the agency did not request HUD funds for the spring quarter of 1975. Kuhn and Queenan felt that there might actually be enough surplus--paper and actual--to run the agency for five months without making an additional request for more ACC money.

As at many other sites, North Dakota had requested funds on the basis of their full ACC authorization. Nevertheless, the various economies the agency had practiced had also given them a substantial surplus of earned funds.

In February, Kuhn met the Social Service Board to discuss the possibility of having a Section 8 housing program under their administration. The month before, a HUD representative had broached the idea to the agency director. Such a program would be statewide, with as many as 1,000 units of existing housing to eventually come under lease.

In order for the board to run a housing program on a permanent basis, the organization would have to become a public housing agency. The board members thought that the idea deserved further study and suggested that one of their staff attorneys consult the North Dakota Century Code to see if a public welfare agency could be empowered to run such a program. The attorney general would also have to rule on the legality of such a step. In many ways, Kuhn's activities resembled those used in getting the original EHAP contract. For example, after the attorney general opined that the Social Service Board could become a PHA*, Kuhn met with the Legislative Research Council in mid-spring. They voted in favor of the proposal. The final approval of the Social Service board was still needed. Kuhn felt that the board would probably want to consult with the LHAs in the state to see how they felt about the new turn of events. Even assuming that the board did eventually give the go-ahead, the governor and the Emergency Commission would still have to approve the program before any funds--state or federal-- could be spent. The legislature had already had its biennial session, and the legislators had gone home until 1977.

Kuhn himself intended to retire as soon as he reached sixty-five. If a Section 8 housing program were run by the Social Service Board, he would help set up the administrative machinery before stepping down. Privately, he felt that EHAP had been a more desirable program than the proposed Section 8 offering; the payment levels were higher, and complete self-inspection and self-certification was permitted. This was not the case with the new regulations. Also, the check had gone directly to the participant in the AAE.

---

*A public housing agency (PHA) is an agency, regardless of the size of its jurisdiction, which administers housing programs.

The rules were different for Section 8. Still, the use of cash assistance allowed for freedom of choice, and for this reason alone it was desirable that North Dakota participate. Besides, regulations were always being amended and changed. He knew that from almost forty years of public service.

In the meantime, the director prepared for the eventual transfer of families who has received twenty-four monthly payments. The first of these would occur in June, since the transition plan called for a ninety day notice for all parties concerned. The secretaries prepared mock-up informational files for a meeting to be held with the four participating LHAs in May. Contained in each folder were the participant's redetermination of eligibility form, the most recent payment worksheet, and the approved lease and inspection forms for the current residence. A cover letter was also prepared to be sent to the participant informing him or her of the forthcoming transfer. As was usual at the North Dakota agency, various versions were critiqued by the staff until one was selected for use. Kuhn wanted to have the LHAs approve the letter at the forthcoming meeting, since it committed them to caring for the families:

The four directors are present, along with the GTR and the EHAP staff. The directors feel that the mock-up of the case files contain all the information necessary to bring a family to continued payments. The sample letter, addressed--aptly enough--to John Q. Citizen, is also approved with only minor changes.

Kuhn stresses that once the LHA director receives the file, he should immediately contact the participant.

"They've got ninety days. If you wait for them to contact you, they might not contact you until the eighty-nineth day," he says. The LHA directors nod. "This way, if you contact them, you retain control rather than leaving it up in the air and having to back into it."

Kuhn then passes out a HUD brochure about lead-paint poisoning and asks that the housing authorities mail a copy to each of their recipients who are occupying existing housing.

Joe Queenan says that terminations from the EHAP program are slowing down now. This is something that should be expected, he says, since the number of EHAP participants active in the program has gotten smaller.

Eddy Hoff from Stark County asks, "Is there any set range we should be striving for now?"

Kuhn looks at a sheet of figures and says, "The average payment is $75.90." He explains that this is *under planned estimates of $77. Furthermore, the average payment in his own program has been steadily decreasing and is now around $67 per family per month.*

"Burleigh is $71.23, Morton is $80.24, Stark is $72.58 and Stutsman is $86.31," Kuhn says.

"I'm getting to the people," Christensen jokes.

Kuhn nods and then says that he has to start watching the average payment soon. "As soon as the ACC is split, you'll no longer have enough money, if this continues.

"You're not in any trouble now, but if you continue that way, it's pointing to it."

The director of the Morton County Housing Authority notes that his average payments are a little high, too. "Social Services have been referring a lot. That's why ours is up there." He says that a lot of the applicants are two- and three-person households: "Divorcee and child." The other directors indicate that their experience is similar.

The meeting ends, and the men step into the next room for coffee. Christensen is talking with Kuhn, "You know, we've got to think about people, not just dollars." It is his slogan now.

The same week, Kuhn, Simonsen, and Queenan prepared a new budget for year three of the experiment. The agency would soon be moved to a new building that the Social Service Board had leased. The EHAP agency would be co-located with the ASSC. The new quarters would be more expensive, but there was money for this.

More money was put into the data processing budget, although the agency had underspent their estimates for the second year of operations. Kuhn was also planning on reducing staff further, assuming that Section 8 did not come into effect: "One housing counselor less on January 1, 1976. And another housing counselor or eligibility technician the following March." He stressed that this was an internal budget. The agency was already financially in the clear.

A final note: In May, Joe Queenan, the young GTR, informed the staff that he would be stepping down as of June 2, 1975. Although he would retain his ties with HUD, he would be working with the Social Services Board of North Dakota for a period of one year. His position: Director of Public Assistance.

NOTES

1. In June, 1974, 2.2 percent of the state's population was on AFDC, the second lowest in the country (DHEW Publication, No. SRS 74-03100). The situation was similar with food stamps. However, there had been a lawsuit in neighboring Minnesota charging that low participating rates were due to lack of outreach. In the spring of 1975, the Social Services Board began an outreach effort for this USDA program.

James River Valley

8. Participant Case Studies

INTRODUCTION

This section contains the individual case studies of seven participants in the North Dakota experiment. The households were chosen so that a variety of household types would be represented. Included are a working mother, an AFDC family, a middle-aged couple, a large family with a working male as the head, and a young, middle-class couple obviously on their way up. Two elderly people are also included for these longitudinal, in-depth studies. The first of these is a male retiree. The second is a female ethnic American. She was chosen as a "minority" household; there were few blacks and few Amerindians in the program area. While these seven households in no way resemble a statistically significant sample of people in the North Dakota project, none is especially unusual or aberrant.

In order to insure confidentiality, I did not use the participants' real names. In some cases, I made changes in the characteristics of the interviewed households. Most commonly, I changed the area of residence. In all cases, I attempted to make changes that would not destroy the sense of any individual's story as he or she related it to me. At the same time, I wanted to reduce the chance of identification by outsiders. I have no doubts that an astute person with access to the case files might be able to make an educated guess as to who the individuals involved might be; I only wanted to prevent identification by possible readers of this case study in the community at large. In actual practice, most of the participants I knew were open about their participation in the AAE. That was their decision. For my part, visiting with people in the program gave me the opportunity to see--at least in part--how the experiment looked from the other side.

"MY HISTORY IS VERY POOR." -- MRS. ERKO

Oksana Erko is Ukrainian, eighty-one years old, and frail. Writing about her is confusing. One can point and say, yes, she is definitely better housed than she was when she applied. At the same time, it cannot honestly be said that she is any happier than before. Subjectively, her narrative is a series of disappointments punctuated by remembrance of happier times. Her memory is excellent, although the dates and order sometimes get lost.

I do not think she would have been any better off in one of those cubicles that housing authority directors always seem to be pushing as <u>the</u> answer for everyone over sixty-five. In truth, she would not live there if she had any say in the matter. If she is physically weak, she is also passively tenacious. She had to be in order to survive a long life that was spent mostly in small-farm poverty.

Oksana came to western North Dakota in 1897, at the age of five. A year before, her sixteen-year-old brother had come to the United States and gotten his own homestead plot near the town of Gorham. Then he sent for the rest of the family--Oksana, her sister and their parents. These were good times. There were a lot of Ukrainians in the vicinity, and they had built their own small, Ukrainian Catholic church. She met her husband there. "We go to the same church, and he started to see <u>us</u> sometimes," she recalls.

In those days, things happened quickly for a young girl: "I didn't have fifteen years when I married." The photograph she often shows was taken one week before their marriage. It was at someone else's ceremony, and the two of them had ridden eighty miles on horseback to get there.

They were married four years, and then the accident. Her husband was driving a team of horses across a frozen stream bed when they got away from him. He was thrown off the sleigh. A long splinter was driven into his skull.

John lay in a coma for three months, and when he came out of it, he had changed: "He couldn't think good...he was no good for nothing." He had also turned mean.

John Erko was hard on her, but they eventually had six children, including a daughter who died as an infant. It was pneumonia, she thinks.

She worked on the farm mostly by herself until the two boys were old enough to help out. The real problem, however, was lack of land. A quarter section homestead plot is 160 acres--enough in some parts of

the country. Out here, farms are often ten times
that. Worse, theirs was rocky land, good only for
raising a few head of cattle.

Her oldest boy was killed in the war. "On Christmas Eve the body came, and on Christmas we had the
funeral." When she talks about it, the tone she uses
is flat, almost matter-of-fact. The U. S. Army didn't
know that the coffin would arrive just in time for
Ukrainian Christmas. Better they should have sent it
on December 25th, instead of in January like they did.

Her husband had already died of cancer earlier
that same year: "October 7, 1944." He and her son
are buried in the church cemetery.

Middle-aged Ukrainian widows seldom remarry, and
Mrs. Erko was no exception. When asked, she says
simply that kids don't like stepfathers. She hung on
alone, then, for almost another ten years. Finally,
it became apparent that she could no longer run the
farm and pay the taxes, too.

She turned the farm deed over to her surviving
son, Stephen, and left for Dickinson. Almost sixty
years old, she took odd jobs--cleaning homes, taking
down people's storm windows and washing them, mowing
lawns: "I didn't have a penny. I look for work...
thirty-five cents an hour...after, fifty cents, then
one dollar. It was hard."

When her health gave out, she wound up on welfare:
"My history is very poor. I never had any luck in my
life. Something always happens. Worry and worry and
sickness." Now, her children are in middle age and
their health is gone, too: "Operation, operation...
Luba, four times."

Before she went to the program, Mrs. Erko's income was less than $130 a month. The bulk of this
came from Social Security, and the rest was from the
Stark County Welfare Office. Somewhere along the line,
one of her employers had paid the Social Security tax
on her, so she now qualifies for the minimum amount.

The place in which she was originally living did
not have a complete bathroom, and she had to haul pails
of water from the basement. The rent, not including
lights, was only $65. However, in the past year, the
landlady had begun to complain that her tenant was
using too much water. Also, she suspected that Mrs.
Erko used the oven to help heat the apartment. She
said she could tell because the utility bills shot up
during the fall and winter months. Her charges were
probably true--one of Mrs. Erko's complaints was that
the apartment was drafty.

Besides being inexpensive, the place had other
advantages. There were several large, sunny windows

in the living room, and her plants thrived. More importantly, the apartment was near downtown, the center of Mrs. Erko's activities. Every afternoon that the weather was good, she would look at the displays in the store windows. The clinic was also close by.

Once or twice a week, she would walk the three blocks to the post office to purchase stamps. Occasionally, she would mail a package to one of her grandchildren.

Her daughter Luba had named her first baby after her mother. They lived in Albuquerque, New Mexico. Except for Stephen, all of the children had moved away. They had all married Ukrainians, and still they left. Their husbands had found jobs elsewhere. Katia, the second girl, was living in Idaho. She was married to a retired brakeman. Ukrainians often found work on the railroad lines that had brought settlement to the Great Plains. Lesha married a salesman, and now they lived in Florida, where he sold real estate.

The mails are Mrs. Erko's means of communication with her kin. They seldom come back to North Dakota anymore, except for occasions like weddings. Even her grandniece had moved away. She was living in Detroit. Mrs. Erko felt a special bond with her, because she was <u>kresny mama</u> (godmother) to the child. Before, it wouldn't have been like that, living all over the United States.

Besides being close to downtown, Mrs. Erko's apartment was also near St. Matthew's Church. For twelve years, she had attended the early morning Mass. She had never actually joined the parish, however. Instead, she kept her membership to St. Demetrius' Ukrainian Catholic Church where she had been married. St. Matthew's was a Latin Rite* Church. It wasn't the same, even though a Mass was a Mass.

In many respects, her daily routine substituted for the close family ties she had previously enjoyed. Stephen was the one she saw the least. He was only sixty miles away, trying to make a living off the farm. Recently, the deep well had given out, and the shallow one gave black water that only the cows could drink. He had moved his family into a trailer in Belfield and now lived on the farm alone.

Mrs. Green, a Stark County caseworker, brought Mrs. Erko to the satellite center in Dickinson. It

---

*Roman Catholic as opposed to Greek (Ukrainian) Catholic.

was in August, during the first month of enrollment. Word travels fast through the welfare system, and Mrs. Green felt that Mrs. Erko would make a good candidate for the program.

Since Mrs. Erko could not read English very well, the housing counselor, Siri Ellisen, helped her fill out the application form. The informal session went more quickly than it might have, had the caseworker not been there. She was familiar with the economic facts of Mrs. Erko's case, and Siri acted as a recording secretary.

Agency records indicate that the application was certified almost immediately. In less than a week, she was chosen for enrollment, and the enrollment session was held on September 11. At the time, none of the demographic quotas had been filled, and the agency was in need of participants. Outreach methods were bringing only spotty results, especially in Stark County.

By coincidence, Katia was visiting from Idaho. She drove her mother to the session and acted as interpreter. Even with this help, the session lasted an hour, about twice the usual length. Because of the lack of a bathroom, Mrs. Erko's apartment was unacceptable by agency standards. It was explained that she would have to move, and Mrs. Erko was agreeable.

She was looking for a place that was on the first floor, so she wouldn't have to climb stairs. Also, there had to be a hot water heating system. Wood heat was good, too. They used to have that on the farm, but it was "a lot of work." Forced air furnaces, she felt, provided "bad heat," were dangerous and caused headaches. Her son had once almost been asphyxiated by one.

During the second session, held a week later at home, Mrs. Erko said that she had been looking for a new place, but hadn't found anything yet. Siri suggested that Mrs. Green could help, since Mrs. Erko had no way of getting around. Taxicabs were too expensive. Siri also offered to explain the project and the lease to her prospective landlord, when the time came. After the meeting, Siri called the Stark County Welfare Office to tell them about the aid Mrs. Erko would need.

Although she had ninety days in which to find housing, Mrs. Erko barely got into the program. Her insistence on steam heat automatically eliminated most of the available units from consideration.

Siri was drawn to the Ukrainian lady. As she later explained, "Mrs. Erko is one of the <u>sweet</u> people." At first, the counselor's assistance consisted of scanning the want ads and telephoning her suggestions to Mrs. Erko.

The early attempts brought no results. Many of the advertised units were already rented, or so the voices at the other end of the line said. Yet, some of the ads remained in the paper for another week or more. Apparently, Mrs. Erko would also require a translator.

It became more obvious that she would need more help with the housing search than Mrs. Green alone could provide. The caseworker had many other people whom she visited on a rotating basis. In contrast, the workload at the Stark County satellite center was light. Gradually, Siri Ellisen was drawn into the search process.

The Dickinson counselor estimated that she had driven the enrollee to a dozen or more places by the time a suitable unit was found. Although the $61 payment would increase Mrs. Erko's income by 50 percent, many of the units were still out of her reach.

They would have left her in the same financial situation as before. Then, too, she wanted a place near downtown.

It was Mrs. Green who finally located an acceptable unit on the west side of the city. Mrs. Erko's private standards had to be lowered because the ninety day housing search period was about to run out. The rent was higher than expected, and she would only be about $15 more ahead by moving into the new place. It was a basement apartment, almost a mile away from downtown. Mrs. Green and Siri both felt that she should rent it so she could stay in the program. When a more convenient place became available, she could move. Anyway, it was almost winter, and the landlady had begun to complain about the utility bill again.

The third session was held at the new landlady's house. Siri witnessed the lease and also helped with the inspection. She sent in the necessary forms to the Bismarck office and recommended that a check for two months' rent be written so Mrs. Erko could move in as soon as possible. Then she began to think of what help Mrs. Green could provide with the moving.

I was interested in following Mrs. Erko's progress in the program for several reasons. For one thing, the North Dakota project area had few non-white minorities. Mrs. Erko, as a ukrainian-American, would provide the chance to study someone who was not in the "mainstream" culture and yet was still representative of the population within the four participating counties.

Another reason for my interest was that Mrs. Erko was an exception to the agency's contention that most of the eligible people were capable of participating in the program without receiving extensive supporting services. That the staff was able to provide these was an illustration of their flexibility in this regard.

I had also done field research among Ukrainian-Americans and had some familiarity with the ethnography. I felt that I could overcome the language barrier and could interpret her experience in light of what I already knew about this ethnic group.

Finally, I am myself of Ukrainian descent. Mrs. Erko's story could just as easily have been that of my paternal grandmother, had my ancestors decided to settle in the Great Plains instead of heading for the city to find employment in Henry Ford's auto factory.

Finding the right address was easy: the streets in Dickinson are consecutively numbered. Locating the correct apartment was more difficult. From the outside, the new shingled house looked like a single family dwelling. I crunched around in the snow trying to find the basement entrance. Baffled, I rang the landlady's doorbell, and she instructed me that the stairway was inside the garage.

As I entered, I felt as though I was doing something vaguely illegal, and that the neighbors would be calling and saying that they had just seen a stranger sneaking into the garage. Even after I had made four more visits, I always had this uneasiness.

Then there were the stairs. They were long and steep; I wondered how she managed them.

Mrs. Erko opened the door. She seemed very happy to see me. I had phoned her earlier in the week, and she was pleased to learn that I was also a Ukrainian. The first question she asked was, "You speak Ukrainian?" Not very well, I told her honestly, and I could feel that she was a little disappointed.

When I entered the apartment, I had a feeling of deja vu. There was a crucifix on the wall, and behind it were the traditional two palms and a length of pussy willow. On Palm Sunday, Ukrainians gather outside the church and strike each other on the shoulders and back: "It is not I who hits you, it is the palm. Easter is one week away."

She had me sit down while she fixed the inevitable meal for her guest. I glanced around a little more. Her glass-fronted china cabinet had a bowl of pysanky (Ukrainian Easter eggs) that she had collected over the years. I could see the stacks of white, glass plates, and without even looking knew that they had wheat lemmas on them.

The water for the dumplings she was making boiled over, and I swear I heard her say "Sonofabitch." Her tone was almost emotionless. I doubt she knew what it meant.

The pot she used for cooking was Graniteware, the type that has become chic to buy in antique stores. Hers was brought with her from the farm. The same was true of the radio on the shelf above the sink. The case was battered and held together by pieces of tape.

The apartment was impressive. It was new and all the rooms had been recently panelled. Mrs. Erko did not consider this an advantage, I later found out. It was stained a dark color, and she worried about the light bill.

As we talked, I found that she was happy to be on the program. It was a "big help," and her worry was that EHAP would be cancelled, or that she would be dropped. If that happened, she didn't know what she would do. This place then would be too expensive for her.

I wrote between bites, until she finally said, "Mike, you write too much. You should just eat. You're too skinny."

These 3,000 calorie brunches became a routine. Sometimes, in addition to the Ukrainian fare, she would fry a small steak, or a skinny chicken leg. "Eat all meat," she would say. "I too sick for meat." She also thought that it was too expensive for herself, in spite of the fact that her doctor had recommended more protein. Instead, she ate potatoes.

Her freezer wasn't plugged in, I noticed during my first visit. The cord had been neatly coiled and was lying on top of the appliance. She had just moved in, and was short of money. On subsequent visits, the freezer would be operating, but she filled it with pyrohy (dumplings) instead of with meat. Once, I felt guilty and brought her a package of hamburger, although I knew she wouldn't eat it. She served it to Siri when they returned from one of their trips to town that the counselor would make on her own time: "You know, just once I'd like to take her out to dinner, but she never lets me." Siri, a tall, large-framed woman, was also too thin for Mrs. Erko's tastes.

From the beginning, Mrs. Erko expressed displeasure with the new apartment. It was too far out of town, it was too dark, it was a basement, it bothered her arthritis. She also felt that the place was too expensive, although she continued to look at places that were slightly higher-priced. After she had been on the program for a few months, what she hoped for was a "little raise."

The only thing she really liked about the apartment was that it had the hot water heat upon which she had insisted. She not only disliked forced air heat, she was terrified by it: "It makes me dizzy, and I shake in the nighttime."

During the first interview, it appeared that she was resigned to staying there: "I have to like it... but it's a basement... I've got arthritis and rheumatism and (trouble with) my blood pressure. Maybe in summer I can look for a new place. The doctor says I need lots of sun. I can do that, I hope?"

I looked up at the window. The sun was behind the winter haze. She was right about the darkness of the apartment; the electric bill would probably be higher here.

She began to talk about her life in Dickinson. "I am lost here," she said. "Lots of people are Ukrainian here, but I can't see them." She felt that no one was interested in seeing an old widow. "You and your wife, that's _people_. But if there's just you, that's not people."

Sometimes Mr. and Mrs. Danyluk would stop by after church, but they didn't do that much anymore. The same was true with Mrs. Dowhan. Her grandson used to bring her over. "Now the style is different. Young people don't like old people. Everybody busy."

Stephen's son John often visited, though. He moved her furniture into the new place. Stephen had sent him over from the farm; his own health no longer permitted heavy lifting.

The phone rang. It was her sister-in-law. Mrs. Erko switched to a mixture of Ukrainian and a sprinkling of English. Yes, she had been to the doctor yesterday. He had told her that the medicine for her blood pressure was too strong, and that's what was making her feel faint.

When she was through, we talked about the new church that had been built in Minneapolis. It had cost over a million dollars, and only 800 souls were in the parish. She already knew about that, she said. Swoboda* had lots of articles about it. "You know about Swoboda?"

"Yes."

She walked into the other room and started rummaging through a pile of papers. Finally, she had what she wanted--the thin, English language section of the paper. She handed it to me, and told me I could read it at home.

---

*A nationally-distributed Ukrainian newspaper.

There used to be more Ukrainian things here, she said. Once, a young man had come to school here from the east. He had organized a dance group. Then he married a local girl and moved to Cleveland. The dance group fell apart.

"I miss church very bad." She had always gone to Mass at St. Demetrius. They sometimes had "a nice program" there. Now, she couldn't always go to St. Matthews; sometimes she was too sick.

"How do you go to church now?"

"A lady drives me."

Mrs. Erko began to tire, and I terminated the interview. She had me promise that I would call in advance the next time, too. She didn't want to take the five dollar check I offered her and protested that the food she had fixed didn't cost anything. I explained that it was from the company I worked for, and that they wanted her to have it for talking to me. With that explanation, she accepted the payment.

Driving back to Bismarck, I ran parts of the interview over in my mind. Her isolation probably wasn't as total as she had indicated. She had mentioned a few other people who sometimes came by. One was a nurse who had befriended her during a stay in the hospital.

It could even be, I decided, that Mrs. Erko had more visitors than many elderly people. What she missed was the Ukrainian community life she had had in Gorham. Worse, her children had grown up and moved away. Life in Dickinson was alien to her, and a poor substitute for what she had known before. Her worsening health and the location of the new apartment had curtailed much of her activity. Now, she was dependent on people for rides.

Some months later I asked Siri Ellisen about how well Mrs. Erko got around. She laughed, and said that one Friday, Mrs. Erko had called to ask if Siri could take her downtown. Siri had told her that she couldn't, since she was leaving for Mandan right after work. Her car was already packed, and there was no room.

An hour later, as Siri was driving down Villard Avenue, she spotted Mrs. Erko walking past a lighted store window. The woman had gotten a ride from someone else, or else she had walked.

The search for the ideal apartment continued at a slower pace. At each of my visits in February and March, the theme was the same: she wanted "a little raise." She felt that with just a few more dollars, she could be satisfied. Twice, she had found a better place, but in the end decided that she couldn't afford the extra money.

Siri would soon be leaving for a job in Devil's Lake. The enrollment period was over, and the satellite center would only be serviced once a week by one of the Bismarck counselors. She suggested that Mrs. Erko might want her apartment, since it was close to the center of town.

"Looks to me too tight," she told me. "And it's still a basement, still a basement." She was more concerned that Siri was leaving: "Ellisen, she help me."

Mrs. Green wasn't having any luck with the search, either. Maybe in the spring, she thought, when things opened up a little.

Food prices were rising, and this hurt Mrs. Erko, too. SSI* had come into effect, and her income increased. Because of this, the price of her food stamps had almost doubled. She was now paying $34 for $41 worth of stamps. They were too expensive, she decided, and did not buy any after the first of the year. It was a common enough pattern; almost all of the people I interviewed who were on food stamps did this. One had made the break a permanent one.

I didn't see Mrs. Erko for two months. Indirectly, I heard that she was in the hospital with gall bladder trouble. By the time I visited her in April, she had been out for a few weeks and was already walking around.

Her daughter, Katia, was there. Both she and Luba had flown in just as soon as they heard. Her sister had already gone back to Albuquerque, and she would be leaving in a few days, too. She was anxious to get back. Her own husband had to take it easy since he had had a heart attack two years before. I conjured a mental image of a very muscular but heavy man who was made that way by his work on the railroad and thousands of <u>pyrohy</u> drawn in butter.

Looking at the two women, it was hard to see the family resemblance. Katia was a very tall woman and rather slender. Her hair was still black. In contrast, her mother was short and heavy. Her grey hair was dyed an old lady's shade of blue.

In spite of her recent ordeal, Mrs. Erko looked the same to me. She moved around the apartment as if nothing had happened. Katia and her mother begun to prepare another meal. This time it was sausage and ham served with homemade beet horseradish. I watched them working in the kitchen, and it was obvious that

---

*Supplemental Security Income

they had cooked together many times before. The actions of each complemented those of the other.

Katia told me that the operation had been on March twenty-fifth, and that her mother had remained in the hospital for three weeks. She was out in time for Easter. The doctor claimed that the reason she recoverd so fast was that she was in good physical condition because of her activity.

As Katia talked, I was amazed by the thickness of her accent. She was born in North Dakota, but the first generation communities were tight. She had learned English as a second language.

The last week had been rough. Mrs. Erko was vomiting frequently, and couldn't go anywhere because of her weakness. Katia was still a little worried about leaving her, but explained that a homemaker would purchase groceries for her mother. She was taking food stamps again.

The two of them were a little disappointed. Katia had called the satellite center office on Wednesday, and Bob Olsen told her that Mrs. Erko was already getting as much as she could on the program. There would be no "little raises" forthcoming.

Katia had located another apartment. This one was on the ground floor. The landlord was renting to a couple of college kids and wanted to get rid of them. They made too much noise, and he felt that older people made better tenants. But again, the issue was price. Even with the raise in her Social Security, Mrs. Erko did not have enough left over to rent the place.

Another disappointment was that her original landlady had fixed up her old apartment. Mrs. Erko wanted to rent it, but had gotten sick. Now someone else had it. It went for $100 a month, ten dollars less than her present place. And her old landlord had wanted her back.

I asked Katia if she had ever taken her mother to see the senior citizens' residence.

No, she hadn't, but once she went and looked herself. The model unit seemed too small. Also, her mother was very withdrawn and probably would be even more unhappy there. She did not think that her mother could participate in a Meal on Wheels program if the housing authority ever got one. Her mother is shy and depressed, Katia said.

"I think too much, and maybe I cry too much," Mrs. Erko interjected. "I heard they have fifty people in one room."

In response to my question, she thought that yes, the agency helps her enough. "But I am not finished yet." She still wanted to move to that as yet unlocated apartment that is close-in, cheap, on the ground floor and has steam heat.

The kind of help she needed, as she told me many times before, was with transportation. The kind of aid she had in mind was more than an escort service. "Sometimes I have to go downtown, to cleaners, to hospital, to church."

"Is there any other kind of help you need?"

"I don't think so. I just want another apartment very bad on main floor."

"Do the people upstairs help you?" I knew that the landlady had offered to let her son run errands for Mrs. Erko.

"I don't know...I not ask...maybe if I ask, they help."

I look over at the coffee table. The paper was open to the want ads. What she would really like, Katia allowed, was for her mother to rent from a Ukrainian landlord. But she had asked around, and called some family friends. There was nothing available. Katia and her husband had offered to take Mrs. Erko in several times before. Each time, her mother's excuse had been that she couldn't travel and she was afraid of flying. Mrs. Erko also told me that it would cost money to ship her body back to North Dakota when she dies. She wants to be buried in Gorham.

The last interview with Mrs. Erko is in May. Her grandson, John, has just gotten married the night before. She attended; it was the first time she had been back to her church in over a year.

At her apartment is her grandniece, the one who is named after her. The young woman is fixing her husband, Larry, a breakfast of bacon and eggs.

The two of them are students at the University of New Mexico. He is a political science major, and she is in education. Larry is a heavy-set, round-faced kid. We talk a little about their life there, and he says there was no trouble with the family when the two of them decided to get married. There aren't any Ukrainians in Albuquerque, and her parents had always accepted the possibility that she wouldn't marry a Ukrainian.

They eat, and she tells her grandmother about the reception. "Baba (Grandmother), the dancing didn't bother me, except for Uncle Steve. There were three polkas and I was getting tired."

The conversation shifts. Mrs. Erko has a discoloration on her arm. Her granddaugther is worried that it might be a blood clot. It is puzzling. She cannot remember hitting her arm, and yet the spot hurts to the bone. Yesterday, the mark was bigger, but today, the pain is worse.

Her granddaughter calls the clinic. Mrs. Erko wants Dr. Hamilton, and not Dr. Fisk. "Baba, the soonest you can get in is Monday. Why don't you see Dr. Fisk?" Her hand is cupped over the receiver.

Mrs. Erko still wants Dr. Hamilton. "OK, Monday, at three."

We sit and drink coffee. Oksana says that her grandmother would be much happier if she could only raise her plants again. Growing things was her hobby.

The phone rings. The doctor can squeeze her in, if she comes down immediately. I offer to take her.

There is a small discussion about the key, about the door, about where the kids will be when she gets back.

As we drive, Mrs. Erko points out the various flowers along the road. "Beautiful, beautiful," she says.

She knows her way to the clinic well. "Turn here, on this highway." Her word for street amuses me.

We talk a little. Food stamps were still high this month. She again paid thirty-one dollars, but this time for fourty-four dollars worth of stamps. Katia did manage to take her out looking for a new apartment. "Too far, and too high priced." Katia did not take her to the housing authority.

"How come?"

"I don't know. Katia had two day's car, and I was too sick." No one else offered to take her where she didn't want to go. "No place to move."

At the clinic, she is nervous and quiet. Finally she gets called in. I look around snd see some EHAP flyers near the magazine rack. They must have been there for five months. I read magazine articles: Bobby Kennedy and Marilyn Monroe...A Volkswagen Powered Plane You Can Build Yourself...The French Foreign Legion...The new Toyota Celica GT.

After an hour and a half, she comes out, tired It is a bruise after all.

"IF I CAN JUST KEEP ON LIKE THIS, AT LEAST I'LL BE EVEN..." -- Sally Klein

    I knew Sally Klein before she went on the program. Both of us were regulars at the Wagon Wheel Bar, and as a result had several mutual acquaintances. She sometimes stopped by after her shift at the Blue Horse Inn and had a few beers.
    I always felt that Sally was unusual in that she was one of the few Bismarck women who go there alone. She would also talk with just about anybody who came through the front door. There was a refreshing air of independence about her. It was all relative, of course: "I don't go along with all this women's lib stuff," she later told me. "I still like to be treated like a lady. I like to have the door opened for me, and my cigarette lit."
    Sometimes her emancipation was viewed as forwardness. She would never accept a drink from anyone without buying another one in return. She also had a sharp tongue, especially when she was drinking. It put some people off. The men who came into the Wheel seemed to prefer women who were more docile.
    My friend Cecil, behind the bar, had wanted to ask her out, but was always shy around her. Instead, he contented himself with musings about her social life. He liked to keep track of all the unmarried and divorced women who came into the place. He was the Wagon Wheel's gossip columnist.
    When Sally started dating a friend of his, Cecil seemed almost relieved. He no longer felt that he had to take her out, and he seldom mentioned her any more in our conversations. Anyway, he had recently turned his attention to one of the waitresses. She was a quiet, petite redhead, four years out of Bismarck High School.
    "Whaddya think of her?" Cecil would ask me.
    I could never think of anything to say.
    Sally, was thirty, attractive, and divorced. She managed carefully on her salary, tips, and food stamps. She was determined to avoid going on welfare, if she could help it. Her relatives pitched in and bought clothes for her. Jimmy, her two-year-old son from her second marriage, wore hand-me-downs from a cousin's child. The two of them got by. She also sometimes had custody of another son, Carl, from her first marriage. He was a teenager, and usually spent the summer with his father. During the rest of the year, he lived with Sally and she received child support payments. This augmented the money she brought home from

her hostess job. At the time of her application, however, Carl was still with his father.

Although the Blue Horse is the nicest restaurant in the area, salaries are low. When she was the bartender, she received $2.25 an hour. This was more than the rest of the women were making; Sally had eight years' experience. Working the tables was often better. The hourly rate was sixty cents an hour less, but there was a chance to pick up more than the difference in tips. Usually, she worked half-time, but came in every day to service the rush-hour customers. "I get them started, and then the evening girls have to handle them when they're drunk," she laughed.

Sally was one of those who found out about the program through food stamps sales. Her attitude about both forms of help is practical: "If you need it and can get it, why not?"

Not all of her family feels the same way. None of her relatives has even been on assistance. Her Aunt Florence threw it up to her, in the beginning. She had raised a child alone, too, and had never gone looking for a handout. "I went out and worked."

Sally's retort was that at least she does some work, and wasn't on welfare like a lot of people. It is a form of consolation she uses on herself. Food stamps are from the USDA, the housing allowance is an experiment, and welfare is from the county.

If Aunt Florence didn't think much of the program, the people at the Wagon Wheel saw it as a good deal. As soon as she had her second session, Sally had told everybody about the project and how much she was getting: $95 a month. Louise, the barmaid, started thinking about getting on it, too. She made less than $300 a month, and the drinkers at the Wheel aren't tippers.

Later, Louise was disappointed. The people at the agency had told her that single people under sixty-two weren't eligible unless they were disabled. The barmaid gave me a lecture about how hard it was to keep an apartment on the money she was getting. I kept on repeating, "I know, I know..." And she reiterated that it wasn't fair.

One reason Sally's allowance was larger than average was that she had child care expenses. Jimmy needed a babysitter every weekday, and these costs were deductible. Her net income was calculated to be around $1,500 a year. This is at best a rough estimate: Sally's hours are irregular, and tips made up a major part of her income. Also, her mother sporadically contributed food and clothing, the actual cash value of which would be almost impossible to determine.

Sally had decided to stay in hour four-room Mandan apartment. She had been living there for two years, and it was a convenient spot. The Blue Horse is located on the Strip, between Bismarck and Mandan. It took her only about ten minutes to drive there.

The landlord is a pain. Even the amount of the rent he charges is a kind of joke to her. Eighty dollars was for the actual apartment. Five dollars was added to this for the water bill. Then, when her mother gave her an old washer, the owner had wanted to tack on still another five, arguing that she would be using even more water. Sally wouldn't stand for the raise, and told him so. Finally, he agreed to split the difference. It all came to $87.50.*
One of the added benefits, she says, is that the landlord prays for her soul. She is divorced, and he is concerned. Sally is a backsliding Baptist, and the owner's efforts tickle her. He did the same for another of his tenants who was separated. She got back with her husband, and now Sally gets more attention. "Maybe it works," Sally jokes.

Our first interview is in December. Sally has just quit her job the day before. The bar manager cut her hours with no explanation, and she thinks that he was trying to ease her out to cut costs. She feels there is no other explanation: the holidays are coming up, and this is the busiest time of the year. Sally was suspicious when they brought a new girl in, and she had to train her. It is a common enough pattern at the Blue Horse. New help will work for lower wages.

She wants to talk to the assistant manager, Grant, about the whole thing. "Nick went to bartender school, and doesn't think he can do anything wrong. But then, why did he ask me how to make a drink?"

She is embarrassed: "Maybe I shouldna said that."

With the loss of the job, Sally's income has been cut drastically. Now there will be only unemployment compensation and the check from the Experimental Housing Allowance Project. For the past few months, since the divorce was granted. She had been receiving thirty dollars a month from her second husband. Now that she has final custody of Jimmy, she is supposed to be getting $100 a month. She hasn't seen any of this yet. Having the allowance means that she is able to get by for another month.

Her food stamps will be high this month, over three times as much as before. Because of her fluc-

---

Sally received her full allowance of $95 because C includes utilities, which she had to pay herself.

tuating income, the county eligibility worker makes her recertify her income before the stamps go on sale. As a result, the price of an order varies. It was the allowance that made the cost rise, as she still had a job then.

The stamps themselves are something of a necessary annoyance. She doesn't care for the attitude of the people down there. Last time, they had asked her, "Well, why isn't your husband paying you the support money that he's supposed to?"

"I told her, I don't know. Why don't you <u>ask</u> him?"

It also bothers her that you can't buy toilet paper or Tampax with the stamps, only food.

Sally's apartment is cozy, and she is proud of the way she keeps it up. The decorations are from the Blue Horse. On one wall is a Hamm's Beer Clock. One of the table lamps is a Michelob lava light. The heat of the bulb causes bubbles to float up through some viscous liquid that is in the base. A large blow-up plastic whiskey bottle is one of Jimmy's favorite playthings. It was really meant to be hung from a lamp fixture. The advertising items are too gauche for a place like the Blue Horse and would have been discarded, anyway.

The knick-knack shelves show more evidence of her last job. They are filled with minature liqueur bottles. The inevitable Galliano is there, but the rest are more exotic.

Jimmy wanders into the living room. He is a tall, slight child, and blonde like his mother. His uniform is a standard one--a polo shirt, jeans and an orange-ade mustache on his upper lip. He tugs on Sally's arm and motions toward the back of the house. The phongraph is stuck. Elvis Presley keeps repeating the same half-phrase over and over again. She excuses herself.

I look around the apartment for something that pleases me. All I can find is an impressive leather and wood chair that looks completely out of place. The rest of the furniture is well-kept, squarish stuff that was popular ten years earlier. The charcoal and sick greens clash with the bright new shag rug. Most of it is probably from her mother, I decide.

The only thing bad about the apartment itself is the layout. Everything is built around a central kitchen. The house was obviously converted to multi-family use, but for a basement apartment it is fairly bright, at least in the living room. There are two tiny bedrooms in back.

"Jimmy, no!" Sally jumps off the chair and runs over to the corner. She had been trying to toilet train him for the last two weeks, but he was still sneaking off to fill his pants.

After she changes Jimmy, I start to take a personal history, and get lost in the complexities. Her father had been an engineer in the Merchant Marine, and the family had wandered all over the country. When he was killed, her mother moved back to Bismarck. The relatives were there, and it would be easier to start over again. She never remarried.

Sally feels that her own first mistake was getting married right after high school. She was four months pregnant, and the minister married them in his study.

Tom moved her out to a rented farm in Flasher, and they stayed there for almost four years. It was primitive living. She had to fetch water from a well. Tom was never around to help her. He was either working in the fields or else doing some carpentry job.

They finally split up after they made the big move to South Dakota. "It had been coming for a long time," she says. She had to get residency before she could file for divorce. That was where she met Jim. She was working in a bar to support herself and her first son. They got married just as soon as the papers were final. There is no waiting period in South Dakota.

The second marriage lasted only five years, too. Now, she doubts that she will every remarry, but it is a doubt tempered with the realization that she said the same thing when she separated from her first husband. Right now, she is going out with a guy. "We have a good relationship. We see each other about three or four times a week. A person doesn't always want to be alone."

Sally insists that I know him, too, because he sometimes drinks at the Wagon Wheel, although he usually prefers the Buffalo Bar. She produces a picture, and Jimmy shouts out, "Ron!"

Jim Klein was still balking about the support payments. Recently, he had said to her, "A hundred dollar payment? Do you realize that over eighteen years that adds up to $21,000? It's like paying for a Cadillac that you'll never be able to drive." The imagery, she thinks, is apt enough. That's what Jim cares about: big, heavy cars. He was driving them all over South Dakota. She snickers about this and tells me that the one good thing he did for her when they split up was to let her keep the little Chevy Bel Aire that is parked out in back. It was easy on gas and nothing ever went wrong with it. The Lincoln he insisted on keeping had already blown its engine, and was probably junk by now.

I didn't visit Sally again until January. She now had a new job as a clerk at The Yarn Shop. The pay was only $1.65 an hour, and there were no tips. But the hours were regular, and she got a 15 percent discount on whatever the store sold. She had taken up knitting and was working on a scarf for her oldest son, Carl.

He lived in Billings, where his father was a maintenance man at the courthouse. The arrangement she and Tom had worked ut was a loose one. Part of the year, Carl would stay with her, and part of the year, he would live in Montana. Last summer, Carl had decided that he would stay the whole year in Montana, and return to Mandan the following June. Now, even though it was January, she was beginning to think of the arrangements she would have to make for him. Maybe, she said, she could buy a used bunk bed, and he could room with Jimmy.

Last month, she didn't buy food stamps. She had decided that she couldn't afford the sixty-four dollars they were going to cost her. Also, there was Christmas that she had been thinking about. This month, Sally had taken the food stamps again; the price had finally gone down. The woman at the welfare office had recertified her on the basis of her reduced income. It irritated Sally when the woman told her that she would still have to come back every month to declare her financial status. The reason was that she didn't work <u>exactly</u> the same number of hours each month.

I ask her what changes the program had made in her life, and she answers that she is now going to the dentist for the first time in six years. "I shouldn't do that. My mother spent $500 on braces." She always thought it was more important to take Jimmy to the doctor than it was to take care of her own teeth.

The new job has more fringe benefits. When she's there for ninety days, she'll be getting hospitalization. In all, Sally feels lucky. She was actually only out of work for two weeks. "It's gotten me out of the bar. It's a different clientele." Near the end, it had been a chore even showing up at the Blue Horse. "Maybe I like being on the other side of the bar," she jokes.

The lady who owns The Yarn Shop is easy enough to work for. "You probably know her husband, Leo. He's with Northwestern Bell."

When I tell her that I didn't think so, she says, inevitably, that he comes into the Wagon Wheel a couple of times a week. What else?

Christmas was good this year. Ron brought Jimmy a tricycle, and had gotten her a hairdryer and some slippers, fluffy red things that are very popular in the area because they are so warm.

New Year's Eve, they went to a house party and took Jimmy along. It was better than last year. She spent that one alone: I got out a bottle of Cold Duck, watched Guy Lombardo and said, 'Happy New Year, Sally,'"

Things weren't so bad, now that she was working again. She allows that it was the EHAP check that kept things going after she got fired. Unemployment compensation wasn't enough. In truth, then, the EHAP money was not really "extra" yet.

Once she found the job at The Yarn Shop, she called the agency to tell them of the change. Though she would be making less money than at the Blue Horse, the amount of her next check would be increased by only $5 a month. Sally was receiving close to the maximum amount, anyway.

The March visit. Her hairstyle has changed. She no longer has a shag. Instead, she has a more severe cut with bangs. It was her Valentine's present from her mother. Everybody likes it except a male cousin who thinks it makes her look too young.

Sally is nervous during the visit. Her ex-husband has left only forty-five minutes before. He gave her forty dollars, but she still figures she has over $300 coming.

He brought Jimmy an Easter basket and then ignored him for the rest of the visit. He only stayed an hour and a half, and then said he had to get back on the road so he could work.

Sally had optimistically told the agency that her ex-husband was sending her $50 a month. Now, she doubted that he'd keep the payments up. Her last check from work was only $70, and most of it went to Jimmy's babysitter. She pays her on a monthly basis.

She still thinks that she is better off than when she was at the Blue Horse. By working some evenings, she has more time for Jimmy.

Recently, she took a big step and applied for credit for the first time in her life. Last week, she received a Sears card, but was turned down by Woolworth's. It surprised her that Sears gave it to her, and she wants to be cautious with it. When Carl comes this summer, she might buy him a new bed.

Her trips to the dentist are over with, and she only owes him $20. She feels pleased with herself.

She tells me that a friend of hers is on EHAP and just started the WIN* program. She herself is thinking of going on when Jimmy gets older. It would help her learn "a profession;" it doesn't matter what. The fact that it is a welfare program doesn't bother her. She would just be bettering herself, she explains.

The only other thing she thinks she might want is a day care center, since babysitting costs are so high. There was really nothing more that the agency could do for her. Maybe, she says, if she ever decides to move closer to work, she might want to look at a housing list, or something like that.

Right now, "It helps me pay the rent. They don't hassle me like food stamps." Everything was easy about the program. The inspection form provided her with the most amusement, she recalls: "Do you have running water?"

Her food stamps are still down, and she is satisfied. The job is going well, too: "I would be working at the Town House, or the Gayety. Or when the Legion called for a party." One of her girlfriends at the Blue Horse had recommended her for the position. "But I turned them down because I didn't need the money," she says. "If I can just keep on going like this, at least I'll be even."

In June, Sally moves to a new apartment in Bismarck. It is closer to work, and there is a yard for Jimmy to play in. A friend of her mother had told her about the place. The landlord had rented the apartment to hippies. After they moved out, he had to refurbish the whole place. Sally's mother helped paint the inside. The owner did the outside and put in new carpeting and kitchen cabinets.

The new landlord seems like a nice guy. He's letting her keep the stray cat she found a few months before. It was a point of contention for her old landlord at the Mandan apartment. One of the other tenants knew about it and demanded the right to have a dog, since pets were now apparently allowed. It got so bad that she kept the animal at her Aunt Florence's the month before she moved.

Carl has also come back from Montana. He is a short, thin kid, and very quiet. As his mother and I talk, he listens in, and then wanders off.

---

*The Work Incentive (WIN) program is a vocational training program for which all adults receiving AFDC must register if they are able-bodied and do not have to care for a child under six years of age.

Sally explains that the agency had let her recertify the household at three people. Thus, even though she had received a small raise at work, the payment was now $125. The apartment itself rents for $110, plus heat and lights: "I figured I couldn't refuse it." Sally had to make a fifty dollar damage deposit. The agency would have advanced her the money, but she wasn't aware of this. "I had the money saved up, anyway."

She takes me on a tour of the place. It is about the same size as her previous apartment, but the layout is much better. The living room is in the center of the house, and the kitchen is off to the side.

"I don't know what I'll do with all the freezer space. The stove is smaller, but all four burners work."

Although the apartment is also a semi-basement, it is fairly light and airy, more so than her old place. The windows are new combinations; "I can yell out the window at Jimmy." I look out at the large back yard and notice that there is a tractor tire laying on its side--a North Dakota sandbox.

Things are good now, she feels. She is making two dollars an hour at The Yarn Shop, and has been made the night manager. Right now, all that meant was balancing the cash register out at the end of the evening and locking the joint up.

She lost her old babysitter, but felt it was all right. "It's my old neighborhood, and I know lots of people. I'll find somebody."

Her mother was going to watch Jimmy, but they had a fight, and it was just as well. Being close to the woman had its good points and bad points. She tended to be overly protective of her only daughter.

"The only thing that's sad is his babysitter back in Mandan is just _sick_, now that he's moved." Perhaps that was just as well, too: Jimmy and the babysitter were getting "too attached" for non-relatives, as far as she was concerned. Anyway, she could drive over whenever she wanted to see the child. Right now, Carl takes care of his little brother when Sally is working. He doesn't mind at all.

The move was traumatic for Jimmy. Whenever Carl leaves the house, Jimmy asks if he is coming back. Jimmy was more insecure now: he also pounds on the door when Carl is in the bathroom. Carl is trying to decide whether to stay or go back to Montana. He misses his friends. Sally avoids pressing him.

"The only reason I didn't move back to Bismarck before is that I couldn't find anything," Sally offers. She wants to change the subject.

Lately, she has been going to a reducing salon which isn't too far away. It costs her $12.50 a month. Ron paid for the first month's dues. She claims to have lost three inches on her hips, one-quarter inch on her thighs, and has added one-half an inch to her bust.

I tell her that sounds like the best of all possible worlds....

"IF I COULD JUST GET THOSE NUMBERS STRAIGHT..."
-- Edward and Roxanne Kunst

Talking about the impact that the AAE had on Edward and Roxanne Kunst is easy enough: the Experiment Housing Allowance Project means that every month they receive a check for seventy dollars. With help from food stamps and the $262.80 Edward gets as disability payment from Social Security, they are able to buy medications and the lean meat he needs for his special diet. They can also remain in the modern, two bedroom apartment that costs them $150 a month plus lights. This figure is $30 above what HUD has estimated a modest unit for two people rents for in the area. Because they don't get around much these days, they can manage.

Before he had a stroke two years ago, Mr. Kunst worked as a layout man in an iron works. He was almost forty when he took up the trade. That was nineteen years ago. "When he started, he couldn't even hold a decent hammer," Mrs. Kunst explains. Over the years, he had worked his way up until he was in the front office with the boss and hardly ever worked out in the shop any more.

The stroke had been a major one; it left him paralyzed for three months. Then, he had a heart attack, and it interfered with his therapy. He is just now learning how to write again.

Mr. Kunst's memory was also affected, and there are times when he cannot find the right words. The effect is eerie: during our first interview, he could recall the name of the road construction company for which he once worked, but he could not remember that he drove a Caterpillar tractor for them.

"It's funny," Mrs. Kunst says, "the work he did he doesn't remember." Numbers give him special trouble. He sometimes reverses the digits. Once he told his barber that he had just turned ninety-five. Apparently, the man understood and had only said that he sure didn't look his age.

"If I could get those numbers straight, I think I could go to work," he tells me.

I nod.

"It could happen," Mrs. Kunst agrees. Right now, though, his vision is still blurred.

The illness changed their lives. Before, they had lived well. For many years, there were two salaries coming into the house. Mrs. Kunst worked in a meat packing plant. Then she got arthritis and had to quit. Unlike many of the program participants, their furniture is relatively new and expensive. The couch is a gold brocaded piece. They also have a 1970 Buick Riviera that he bought a year before he got sick. It's all paid for; they had the cash then.

The savings didn't last long, she explains. They had to wait six months before Social Security gave them any money, and even then it wasn't enough. By the time they got on the program, there was only $300 left.

They found out about the program in November, the first time they tried to get food stamps. For some reason, the welfare office had turned them down, but the eligibility worker suggested that they might be able to get help from the agency.

"We told them we'd take anything there was," she says. "By golly, we were broke." The application form was confusing, though, and Mrs. Kunst had to return to ask several questions. Paperwork is something which scares her. Edward used to do it all: "He's smarter than I am."

After they were chosen, Bob Olsen drove over to their home and helped her do the inspection. He also told them to apply for food stamps again. "It was lucky that Olsen fellow could help us out." The two of them have nothing but good thoughts for the people at the agency, and claim that they would go there if they ever needed any help. "If we had to move or something, that's where we'd go," she says.

"Well, maybe I can go back to work."

"It could happen," I say.

"Yeah, I sure would like to..."

In the meantime, they aren't telling anybody about the food stamps or the housing allowance. Their son in Montana doesn't even know. "Nobody says anything, and we don't say anything," Mrs. Kunst says. "We wouldn't be able to make ends meet without help." She singles out his special diet as an especially costly item in the budget.

She still feels that she would be ashamed if they had to go on relief, but Mr. Kunst says that it's foolish to think that way. And anyway, he adds, feelings have little to do with it. That was how he decided to apply for food stamps: "I got hungry." Both of them say that they were desperate enough to have applied even if EHAP were a welfare program.

In point of fact, Mr. Kunst still doesn't care for the idea of stamps: "I worked for years, and I don't like something for nothing. I like to <u>pay</u> for food." EHAP is easier because it comes in the form of a check. Nobody has to know that you're on it.

"If I could only go back to work and forget it... but my numbers, I just can't..." Any kind of job would be all right with Mr. Kunst, even janitor's work: "I'm not fussy."

Every Friday morning, he goes back to the shop and talks to the fellows on their break. Mostly, he stays home. At 10:30 every morning they drive down to the Husky Truck Stop and have a cup of coffee. He has Sanka and she has the real thing.

They have a routine. First they watch a little T.V. while they have breakfast. Then he helps clean the house. Mr. Kunst usually washes the dishes. It makes his stiffened hands feel better and is something he never did when he was working. The house was always her job.

As he talks, I get the feeling of extreme mellowness. When the weather is nice, he sits on the little balcony and watches the cars go by. When he turns sixty, he wants to join the Golden Age Club so he can shoot pool at the Senior Citizens' Residence. "Once I got started, it would probably be all right."

Mrs. Kunst thinks that they'll move there as soon as they're old enough. "They keep pretty active, those old people. They have bingo parties."

The EHAP project is for now. It keeps them from having to move to a cheaper, basement apartment, which would be damp and bother her arthritis. They are well satisfied with the payment: "We get along. We can make it. We don't spend on anything foolish."

Their old friends sometimes drop by their place in the evening. Mr. Kunst is just beginning to drive again. He doesn't feel that he can see well enough to go anywhere in the nighttime.

Life goes on and on for them. Twice a month, a worker from Vocational Rehabilitation comes by to see how Mr. Kunst is progressing with his handicrafts. At first, she had him making fishing lures. Now it is flower pot hangers.

She gives him squares of lucite. His task is to drill a small hole in each corner, and then to attach nylon monofilament to form a suspension device. It is arduous work for him because of his eyesight: the plastic is colorless, and so is the fishing line. He can finish six in a month.

Recently, their son lent them $100. They haven't reported this to the food stamp people. "I think that maybe they should know," she tells me. They have to recertify every three months. Last time, she was going to say something, but she got nervous and confused. There was nothing on the form about loans. "Maybe Mrs. Anderson would have asked, but she died. The new lady never asked and I never...I think I should, don't you?"

Life goes on: once a week they drive down to Kirkwood Plaza and window shop. Mr. Kunst likes to stop and have a _real_ cup of coffee instead of the Sanka the doctor makes him drink.

Life goes on: now she buys fabric and patterns to make her clothes. Before, she used to buy ready-made dresses.

Life goes on: during Lent, they went to Mass and took communion every day. St. Matthew's doesn't even have the stations of the cross anymore. They did them by themselves at home.

Life goes on: during Easter, they went out to Montana to visit their son and their grandchildren. The son paid for the plane tickets. They were supposed to stay here for three weeks, but Mr. Kunst got a little nervous sitting around the house once the kids went back to school.

"Sitting around...you go nuts..." She mentions a friend at the iron works who had a similar health problem. But he didn't keep his diet and ate pork because it was cheaper than beef. He died recently, and they think of it as an object lesson.

Life goes on. Quietly.

"IF YOU CAN GET IT, TAKE IT." -- The Maddings

Steve and Mavis Madding are in their mid-twenties. They are solidly middle-class, and their dreams reflect this. However, talk about this sort of thing disturbs them: they would rather be thought of as individuals. Still, most of their friends are from work, or else from Gwinner, the small town in eastern North Dakota from which they both came. They sometimes attend the activities at the Moose Lodge and meet the same people there. The Elks Club, they feel, is too expensive, and only for people who want to put on airs.

There is a lot of the frontier ethic in both of them. They are presently living outside of Bismarck in a double-wide mobile home. The landlord is a friend of theirs, and he rents to them at a reduced rate in exchange for Steve's help with the horses.

The land is flat and almost treeless. The owner has over twenty acres and so it qualifies as a farm. Livestock can be kept there. The work isn't really too much for Steve: there is only a single Hereford in addition to the five horses. He feeds them in the morning and chases them into the barn at night.

Someday, Steve wants land of his own. "I've never seen Montana, or Wyoming. I liked Washington, but it was always rainy..."Anywhere, then, just so the spaces are open.

He doesn't mind living in North Dakota where the wages are low: "All I've got to see is the looks on the faces of guys who've gone away and come back."

"Gone away" means to Minneapolis or Chicago. The Big Apple is moveable and relative. Many of their friends think that Bismarck is bustling. Mavis remembers moving to Fargo after high school. "Anything to get out of dinky Gwinner."

Once, she went to graduation ceremonies at Jamestown High School. She thought the line would never end. Over 100 people received their diplomas that night.

She laughs about it now. When Steve was in the Army, they lived in Columbia, Missouri. Nearby St. Louis was very large and very confusing. Life at the Army post was little better. Steve found that everybody was concerned about rank. Officers associated only with officers, sergeants with sergeants, and the lower grades kept to themselves.

Even Bismarck sometimes got to Steve. When he was first out of the service they had lived in a

239

series of basement apartments. Kitty was just a baby then and the dampness bothered her. She was always coming down with colds. "After a while those basements even started getting to me." That was all they could find until they rented this place.

"Nobody bothers me here. If I want to holler in the pasture, there's nobody gonna bother me. If I want to shoot my rifle, nobody's gonna say something."

The only drawback they can see to the mobile home is that there isn't enough room for the washer and dryer. When he gets *his* land, he's going to build a foundation and basement and then put the trailer over it. Of course, he would prefer a regular house, "but when you consider the savings, a mobile home is good."

Steve and Mavis first heard about EHAP on the radio when they were eating breakfast. It was on the TT&O Show, and somebody from the agency was on. A few days later, their landlord also heard about the project and encouraged them to apply.

Steve was working days, and Mavis took care of all the paperwork. "I heard about it, and did it," she says, a little proudly. She was eight months pregnant when she went to the sessions. Steve wrote down all the things he wanted her to ask: Was it tax free? Was the check sent to them or to the landlord? What happened if the landlord decided to raise the rent--would the payment go up, too? This last worried Steve. The cost of propane had recently doubled and was now over thirty cents a gallon. He anticipated that the coldest months would bring bills of over $100. Their fuel allotment had also been cut back 15 percent on the basis of the previous year's use. It had been the mildest winter in history, and he didn't think they'd be lucky two years in a row. If he had to pay more rent in addition....

The agency certified them on the basis of Steve's salary alone. Mavis was working as a practical nurse at the Baptist Home but was scheduled to quit within a week. After the baby was born, she planned on going back to work. They didn't think they could get by on one salary.

She found out during the second session that their payment was going to be $71. This would pay over half of the $125 rent. Bob Olsen sat down with her, and they drew up a budget. They figured that she would be only about $40 a month ahead after she paid the babysitter for watching the two children. They wouldn't be living quite as well as before, but she decided that she could stay home after the baby came.

Since they were living in a mobile home, the agency had sent the state building inspector to look at their place. The unit was fairly new, but did not have the state inspection sticker. The trailer was located outside the city limits, and the sticker was not required by law in unincorporated areas.

This was all fine with the Maddings. Steve was enthusiastic and pragmatic about the program: "If you can get it, take it."

Mavis agrees: "It didn't faze him in the least." She was more uneasy. It was connected with welfare, somehow. "I sort of thought that welfare is for people who couldn't make it in life." She is embarrassed, but continues, "I shouldn't really say this, but...or are too lazy to work." She cites a former co-worker as an example of this.

There is a softer line, however. Mavis thinks that most people really deserve the help they get, and the cases she knows are all unwed mothers. She felt a little better about the housing allowance when she reasoned that they didn't really <u>need</u> it, that it was just something extra.

When Dolph was born, Mavis reported this to the agency, and the payment was raised $6 a month. Steve figured that they were taking home less than when Mavis was working, but it was worth having her not work. She could spend time with the kids. Kitty was enrolled in a Lutheran nursery school, and both of them felt good about it. Every day, Mavis would bundle the baby up and drive her five year old to the church over on Divide Avenue. "Every day she learns something. Like a prayer or a song."

"It'll give her that much more of a head start when she goes to first grade," Steve says. Bismarck has no public kindergarten. That fall, the option was voted down. People thought it would be too costly. There weren't any busses for the older children, either. This would mean more driving. Already, Steve was worried about what he was spending for gasoline. It was the one disadvantage to living outside of town. They had a $96 propane bill, too.

Mavis isn't quite as enthusiastic about living out in the sticks. Sometimes, it gets lonely with just the kids. "Oh, I don't know," Steve says, "it seems like someone comes out here almost every day. Monday, it was the landlord. Yesterday, it was the minister. And tonight, you're here."

"Well, last week the car wouldn't start, and I thought about moving back to Bismarck."

He shushes her with sibilant laughter.

In February, their financial situation changes. Steve's company is bought by an outside firm, and the employees go union. His hourly wage increases substantially. He calls the information into the agency, and his next check is only for $25.

He says he's glad he was honest about the whole thing. He's rather have the raise than the housing allowance check, anyway. They have just purchased a new Ford Bronco* and financed it for four years through the new company credit union.

She says that their old car was getting too small. "This one's not any bigger," Mavis offers. "He wants it for his outdoor work." He is thinking of buying a new Weatherby rifle, too.

They are considering buying a house in one of the new developments outside Mandan. These are springing up all around the town limits so that FmHA** can fund them for low and moderate income people. They have changed their minds--or rather, Steve has changed his. He would rather own in the city than rent in the country. It'll be a few more months, even if they do decide to go through with it.

They still like the project. "There isn't any third degree when you apply," he says. One of the reasons he never asked for food stamps is that his father was on the program, and they hassled him all the time.

"I guess I like the whole set-up," he says. "I don't know if I would have gone on it if we were only going to get twenty five dollars from the start."

"Was there anything that could have made it better?"

Steve thinks a little before answering. "No, I can't think of anything."

"Except more money," Mavis says, breaking into a self-conscious giggle.

---

* A jeep-like vehicle with four-wheel drive.
**The rural version of the FHA.

"I DON'T WANT TO BE ON THIS THING FOR MY WHOLE LIFE..."
-- THE WEBBERS

For Carl and Christine Webber, there are two kinds of people in the world: the "big guys" and the "little guys." They put themselves in the latter category and say that without the housing allowance they wouldn't have been able to get by. The $106 they have been receiving since the first of the year makes up for the raise that Carl was supposed to get before wage and price controls came into effect.

They insist that their troubles are caused by big money interests. That, and corruption in government. They feel that North Dakota is the most backward of all the states, with its right-to-work laws: "The big money comes in, and the big money takes it out," Christine explains.

Montana-Dakota Utilities personifies corporate interests to her. A few years ago, the company installed heating elements in the concrete sidewalks to melt the snow instead of hiring someone to do the shoveling. The latest outrage is the intended rise in utility rates. The energy crisis forced everybody to cut back, and now she feels MDU wants to make the same profits while supplying less electricity.

"Things are getting tougher every day. Every time you go down to the store, you almost faint." Store prices are Christine's economic indicator. Last year, ten pounds of sugar cost $1.49, and now it is over double that. North Dakota is a wheat producing state, and yet a loaf of bread is fifty-six cents. "It's getting so you leave more and more of your paycheck at the grocery store."

They figure it takes $50 a week to feed their large family. They have six children. The only relief they can see is that beef is going down in price because farmers are sending their cattle off to market sooner. The price of feed is so high that it doesn't pay to fatten them.

For Carl, gasoline prices are what hurts. Standard Oil is behind it all, he says. In retaliation, he buys only off-brand gasoline, and mentally exaggerates the savings at the M&H station. Government and big business are "in cahoots." He offers me proof: "If they aren't, then why did this happen all of a sudden? Nothing was ever said about it."

The Maddings are in their mid-thirties. Christine is a tall, heavy woman who wears cats-eye glasses that are held together at the bridge with electrician's tape. Carl is blonde and burly. He looks like the truck driver he is. His job is well paying by North Dakota standards: Carl gets almost $3.50 an hour delivering packages to Grand Forks for a private mailing service. However, he gets very little overtime; the eight or nine hour layover he has before he starts the return trip doesn't count as work time. The hours are lousy: "It's really nothing for me to go to bed at midnight and be up at 3:00 AM."

A change of jobs is out of the question. This is the most money that Carl has ever made in his life. Last year, he grossed over $8,000. Before this job, he used to drive a bread truck and get less than $2 an hour: "My Twinkie route," he jokes.

Still, the contract rankles him. The company gets more money if costs go up, while the drivers haven't had a raise in almost two years.

"There's really nothing here. I had a younger brother that went out to Washington to work for Boeing. If we wouldn't have been under this program, I would have really been stuck." The squeeze started a year ago last December, when prices started to take off.

Christine first heard about the program on a daytime television show. She didn't do anything about it until her mother came by with a pamphlet some months later. They decided to apply because they figured they had nothing to lose. Christine is more specific, "It covered rent and utilities, that's what caught my eye."

They were worried about red tape. Several years before, they had been on food stamps when Carl's brother and his children had lived with them for a while. As soon as he moved back to the coast, the Webbers had gone off the program.

The Experimental Housing Allowance Project was a pleasant surprise. "This is the best program they've come up with," Carl says.

"You didn't have to bring up your great-grandfather's existence," Christine adds. She was the one who dealt with the agency. When they were chosen, Mr. Olsen called her up and asked if it would be easier for him to come by for the session. Carl was at work; the only thing he had to do was sign the lease. Christine repeats her feelings about the program: "No hassle. You apply, they interview you, and that's it. They don't want to know how many pairs of shoes you've got."

"Would you have applied if it was welfare?" I ask them.

"No, my heavens, no!" Carl's gestures are extravagent. "We don't even want to be on this program forever." He would sooner have Christine go back to work than accept welfare. In truth, having her work wouldn't pay; she quit her job when the third baby came along. Now they have three more. "We'd like to get ahead."

Carl feels that most of the people on welfare really need it, "but it can get to be a crutch, too." Christine is angered by the stories she hears about women on AFDC who get pregnant every year. Their husbands haven't really deserted them at all, she says. Those guys come home on weekends, like boarders.

Another irritation is that some groups get more than others. Christine reads the school lunch menu for the kids on White Shield Reservation. The Mandan Pioneer prints this once a week for all the schools in the area. "Those kids really eat," she says, and then reads for comparison what the kids in Mandan are having.

Still, they feel that they are farther ahead than people on public assistance. "We have our own money that we can manage. Welfare doesn't really give you a chance to get out of the hole. They deduct what you make from your check." This last statement is erroneous, and their knowledge of the welfare system seems to be third or fourth hand. None of their relatives has ever been on welfare.

Christine's aunt rents them the house they're living in. It is a massive ten-room affair that sits on a small hill. The thing they like about it is that there aren't any neighbors around. The land surrounding the house is actually about the size of four normal city-sized lots. Yet, it is in the middle of Mandan: "We're only a couple of blocks away from two different schools, and three blocks from the grocery store."

Carl has plans for the place. He would like to build a smaller home, using the material from their present dwelling. He would first pour a basement and then build over that. Some time ago he tried to get some financing for the deal. "HUD wouldn't go for it," Christine recalls. "You had to use their sites." They also wanted all the materials to be new.

This spring, they had looked into self-help housing. They liked the idea that you could use your own labor to help defray some of the construction costs. In the end, they decided against it because of Carl's irregular hours.

Another problem is that Carl isn't all that handy. Christine likes to tease him about how it took him nine months to put up a new cupboard for her.

"Well, then you try to find a stud between plaster," Carl retorts. She laughs and explains that for most of the time the cupboard just sat there on the back porch.

The two of them can see advantages both in renting and owning. Owning gives you more freedom. You can pound a nail in the wall without asking anyone's permission. There are also the investment possibilities which are especially attractive to Christine. At the same time, there's the taxes, interest and insurance. Then, too, there's no landlord to call when something goes wrong.

Anyway, Carl says, if he owned a place it would be even better if it were out in the country. That way he could keep a cow for milk and a horse for the kids. Even here in the city, they always plant a large garden. This year, they had eighty hills of corn. Her father buys the seed and they do the planting. The vegetables manage to get them through the summer months. The apples last longer, through mid-winter, if they're careful. She doesn't think they'll do much canning--the price of sugar won't allow it.

It's hard to find a place that will take both pets and children, especially when you have six of the latter. When they first came to Mandan, they lived in a three-room shack, and it was tough. The houses were close together in that neighborhood, and the next door neighbor was a gossip. They wanted privacy, and that's what they got when they moved here, two years ago.

Even the convenience doesn't matter, they had long ago decided. The important thing is the kind of neighborhood. It has to be a place that's clean, where you can raise a family, Carl insists. It helps if there's not too much traffic, so any of the places near Collins Avenue are out.

It's harder to raise kids today, Carl points out. They're smarter than their parents were at the same age, and they won't listen like when he was a boy. In those times, everybody lived in <u>fear</u> of the old man.

The four oldest go to a Catholic grade school. The Webbers pay a nominal tuition fee, but figure that they save on clothes. St. Matthew's requires uniforms, so the poorest kids don't have to compete with those that come from the better-off families.

This way, they can wear the same thing day after day. "My boy is just as style conscious as the girls, too."

The two of them feel that their children get a better education in parochial school. They learn religion, and they get more personalized attention because the classes are smaller. In a few years, the oldest will have to go to public school. St. Matthew's only goes to the eighth grade.

Carl likes the idea of them getting a little discipline there, too. On all my visits, the children were herded into the living room, where they watched television. I never saw them all at one time. Once in a while, one of the older ones would get brave enough to come into the kitchen where we were talking. Bedtime would bring in a steady procession for good-nights and final glasses of water.

On each of my three visits, I asked the Webbers if the project had changed any of their recreational habits. Each time, the answer was that they were still basically stay-at-homes. A sitter for six children would cost too much for them to go anywhere, and the last time they went out was at Christmas. The two of them went to dinner and saw a show afterwards. It was Slaughterhouse Five, and Carl was disappointed.

"I don't know why the hell they make movies like that," he says. "I'd just as soon go to something comical."

The way they figured it, they were staying even, and that was about it. "We are getting behind," Christine admits. They couldn't afford the $90 each month for the rent. It was owed to her aunt, but they felt it was still an obligation, a debt to be paid.

Instead of getting ahead, there were the little economies designed to help them to stay solvent. The year before they got on the program, Carl bought a used Vespa motorscooter to save on gasoline. Then, he started doing all his own repairs to their two used cars. Little things. "I used to fill up the Dodge with a $5 bill. You can't do that anymore.

My last visit with them. Their worry is that the program will be cut off. "We'd be sunk," Carl states flatly.

I assure them that they will be receiving payments for a full two years. The only question, I tell them, is whether or not it will become a national program. Some people in Congress have criticized the concept of housing allowances.

"I bet the criticism is from big people who don't have more days at the end of the month than at the end of the paycheck," Christine asserts. She believes that the subsidy guarantees that the little guy will get the money, and not the banks or the contractors.

The discussion turns to me, about what I'm going to do. They know I'm not going to be around for a while. When I tell them I'm moving to Massachusetts, Carl has me write down my new address on the back of my card. "You never know. We might get out there. We'll look you up."

He walks me back to my car. I get in, start to close the door, and then notice his hands are still on the window ledge. He pushes the door shut for me, but his hands stay put.

We talk for a while, and he rambles about how he wants to get by, how he wants to make it. "I don't want to be on this thing for my whole life. I've got some ideas. Hell, a lot of things I want to try...."

"IF THEY'RE OUT TALKING ABOUT ME, THEY'RE LEAVING OTHER PEOPLE ALONE." -- Alice Sadowski

Richardton is twenty-two miles east of Dickinson and lies off one of the exits on I-24. According to the state highway map, it has 799 people. Assumption Abbey is located there. The locals say that the name was sold to a California wine maker many years ago. Although you can buy a bottle of this inexpensive white wine anywhere in the area, it will never compete with Christian Brothers.

Alice prefers to live in a small town. She associates larger cities with violence. Once, she went to Chicago to help her sister drive a car back from Gary, Indiana. That was enough for her. Then, too, her relatives are nearby. Alice's mother works in a bakery in Dickinson. The two of them are very close, and often visit each other. Alice's father is employed by the charcoal briquette factory. The two of them do not get along, for reasons she will not discuss.

Richardton has its drawbacks, however. She feels she is an object of conversation. People like to talk, and she is both divorced and an unwed mother. The man next door used to try to come over when he was drunk. She threatened to tell his wife, and now he doesn't bother her any more.

She feels that being a single woman is rough. For example, she can't go into a bar and have a drink alone. Guys used to call her up. They were married and thought she was easy. People here get married young, "and then mess around." But not everybody: her sister was only seventeen, and she has a "perfect marriage."

She feels the trouble is that the sexes are kept separate. The women go into the kitchen when it's time to do the dishes. "I don't have to play that role. I like to mix with people. Johnny wanted me to stay home."

They got married when she was eighteen and pregnant with Robbie. They were divorced in 1971 when he was four. She went on welfare right after that, and has been receiving assistance ever since. John is somewhere in Ohio working as a welder. He never did pay any of the child support that the court ordered. Welfare is trying to locate him, and she hopes they'll be successful. It's been two years since he's been around. Three months ago he called her long distance to brag that they'd never catch up with <u>him</u>. If they do find him, it won't make any difference in her financial situation--

welfare will just subtract the child support from her check.

Alice was on the WIN program when she found out that she was pregnant again. In a way, she was glad to be able to quit. The job they were "training" her for was one that she feels anyone could do: filing. The people at work were nice to her, though, and she liked the WIN counselor.

Now that she has Jason, she feels held back. It will be five years before she can try to work again. "It's not so easy when you've had one six years ago, and now you have to start over."

Giving the baby up was something she never seriously considered. "Once I knew he was coming, I knew I was keeping him," she says firmly. "It's part of my upbringing. I would have been able to give him up, maybe..." But then she would have felt guilty.

She never tried to get child support from Jason's father: "The lawyers, going to court, having to fight for every penny..."

Because she was having trouble getting by, she decided to take food stamps. That was how she first found out about the project. The Dickinson counselor was handing out information at the place where the stamps were sold. It was one of the more successful outreach techniques that the agency had used.

Alice didn't think that the program was for her, but she took the brochures home and read them. After talking it over with her mother, Alice decided to apply. She was afraid that the allowance would count as income. The counselor cautioned, however, that her food stamps would be affected.

Agency records indicate that her three sessions with the Dickinson counselor were short. The first two lasted a half hour, while the third took only fifteen minutes. Each time, Alice borrowed her girlfriend's car and drove to the satellite center. She even returned the application in person, figuring that it would be quicker than by mail. Richardton does not have home delivery. Residents rent mail boxes at the post office and have to walk down there whenever they want to send a letter.

The yearly income limit for a family of three was $7,000.* Alice's AFDC grant came to $2,200. Because of this, her payment was larger than average:

---

* after deductions

$100 a month. She was actually entitled to ten dollars more than this; however, her rent and the utilities estimates came to this lower figure. Program regulations would not allow the allowance to be more than actual housing costs.

One of Alice's former in-laws had already rented a small, five-room home to her. After she moved in, he made repairs and repainted the outside. For a while, there was a large pile of wood in the front yard, but someone hauled it away for salvage.

The inside of the house was very sparsely furnished with second-hand furniture provided by her mother. Once, I noticed that the overstuffed chair in the living room was gone, and I asked her about it.

"Oh, the springs broke, and I had it taken away. I've got to get another one."

But she never did.

Alice wants to leave Richardton. She is afraid that Robbie will be taunted, now that he's in school. "I'd like to find a place and stay there. I don't think that Ricardton's the place. People would punish the kids for my mistakes."

She knows about that: "When I had Jason, everybody was nice to my face, and then...I just made up my mind that it would never bother me." That's the way it is when everybody knows you, she says. Alice can even be philosophical about this: "If they're out talking about me, they're leaving other people alone."

During the first interviews, Bismarck was the place she had in mind to move to. It was within the program area, and she could still receive her housing allowance. Her plan was to just disappear there and start all over again. She would tell everybody she was divorced. No one would ever have to know about the unwed mother part.

Dickinson was another possibility, although she felt that the town was too small and that her reputation would follow her. "It takes longer for the good things to get around," she joked.

There was another reason behind her planned move: Alice had been dating a prosperous middle-aged rancher. He had never been married before, and in March told Alice that he didn't plan on doing so. In May, however, they were back together, although he still didn't feel ready for marriage. Moving to Dickinson seemed a more likely possibility. "Maybe George will miss us," she said to me as she snuggled Jason.

Her mother had also advised against living so far away, pointing out that she didn't have a car and wouldn't be able to get around during the wintertime. Alice also realized that she would be totally alone out there.

"I've never been on my own as a career girl," she tells me. She is twenty-four years old now, and will be almost thirty when she gets a chance to be one. Off and on, she has worked as a waitress and barmaid. People drinking make her nervous, and she doesn't know if she could ever go back to it. "I think the fanciest place to work around here is The Esquire Club in Dickinson, and I wouldn't ever want to work there."

She reconsiders. "I might work downstairs where they eat. As a waitress."

This is a time for waiting. Looking at her, I feel that time may have stopped earlier. She wears new white bobby sox and her hair is set in a bouffant style. Perhaps it's only cultural lag, I thought; they don't get Sesame Street out here, either, for that matter.

If she is only waiting, as she says she is, then EHAP helps her wait. Alice is quietly enthusiastic about the program and doesn't feel embarrassed about being on it: "It's not a hand-out job. I don't really need it for living, like welfare."

To her, the program is having money for little extras. She can crochet more and does a lot of baking. In January, two months after she had received her first check, Alice bought a used washer from Frank's Appliance Store. It cost $80, and she paid for it in cash. Then, a girlfriend lent her an old dryer. She no longer has to go to the laundromat three times a week.

She also joined a bowling league. It was something she wouldn't have been able to do otherwise.

During Easter vacation, she took Robbie and Jason to visit relatives in Michigan. She and her mother split the driving and Alice paid for half the gas.

Finally, she bought Robbie a new bicycle for his birthday. She had thought a lot about this purchase, and at first felt that a used one would be all she could afford. Even these were $20, and she figured that for just a few dollars more he could have a brand new balloon tire one from the Simpson's Catalog Store.

Being on the program also affected her food stamps. Originally, $94 worth of stamps cost her only about $50. She voluntarily recertified with the eligibility technician, and the cost of a monthly order was recalculated.

When Alice found out that the coupons would cost over $90, she decided not to take them. She had been aware that the housing allowance would raise the cost, but didn't think it would be that much. Another thing which irritated her was that the amount of her monthly stamp allotment had been raised to $112 to cover inflation.

"It all depends on whether or not it's to my advantage. I never used them, but when Jason came, I took them," she explains. She figures that she still spends less than a $100 a month for all household items, including detergent, which she cannot buy with the stamps. "I'm better off on EHAP."

She found the counselor at the satellite center to be friendlier than the people at the welfare office, and says that she would go to her if she ever needed help. Right now, she doesn't want any: "I've always gotten along without other people."

But maybe Robbie could use a Big Brother. She feels that boys need a man around. Still, "They need a mother more. A mother can teach them manners and respect for themselves. I think men are more sloppy, or more careless."

In short, she has no complaints about the program and thinks that she gets more than enough money: "Just because you have somebody helping you doesn't mean you have to go hog wild."

She even likes the lease. This is the first time she has ever used one, and she feels that it gives both parties security: "They just can't tell you you have to be out in a week. Plus, they're protected, too."

So, she waits for Robbie's school to be out. Then, she can move to Dickinson. Alice accepts the fact that she may not ever marry George: "If it was up to me, I'd be married. I don't know, sometimes I think we will, and sometimes...

"Oh, I'm happy, but I could be happier."

"YOU'D SEE THEM WITH THE GRAVY RUNNING DOWN THEIR CHINS...." -- Peter Barnes

Peter Barnes does not like to think of himself as old. He belongs to a senior citizens' club, but finds that members of his generation have "closed minds." And so, he prides himself on being active and looking less than his seventy-five years. He likes to believe that he could pass for fifty-five. Sixty-five would be closer to the mark.

Unlike many of the elderly who applied for the program, Peter has a fair cash reserve. Thirty years ago, he sold his farm to his son for $30 an acre and banked the money. He still has over $6000* of this left. Until last year, it was $10,000, or so he claims. Then, he married a widow and laid out $3,000 to furnish their new home. The union lasted only two months when she threw him out. Now, he is both angry and embarrassed. He feels that he was taken financially and worries that people are talking behind his back.

A housing authority director told Peter about the program and referred him to the agency. At that time, he was on the authority's waiting list; Peter kept pestering the director about getting in. The director was fond of Peter, but also thought he was a little bit of a troublemaker with his swaggering and bragging that was topped off by a short temper. Peter had been one of his tenants before he had gotten married and moved out.

The way Peter tells it, he hadn't been all that happy living there. It was cheap, and that was about it. The rooms were too small, and he did not get along well with the other residents. Everybody wanted to be a Big Chief up there. Besides, it was better not to live with old people, if you could help it: "You'd see them with gravy running down their chins. Or they'd eat ice cream, and it would be all over their mouths.

"When they play cards, they'd cough like this, 'Arrrkkk! Arraugh! Ark! Ark!' It made me sick. I'm not some sort of nurse, you know." His rendition is accompanied with gestures, and his face turns a beet red.

So, he drove down in his 1971 Pontiac and applied for EHAP. There was nothing to it. He found the agency people to be "gentle, conscientious, and intelligent." They, in turn, were charmed by him.

---

*The asset limits for senior citizens was $12,000.

The counselors' reports say that he is an active, well-preserved, and engaging man. Sometimes he would drop by the agency just to chat. He often shopped at the Red Owl, and the agency was located only a half-block away.

Peter was pleased when he was chosen and found out that he would be getting $40 a month. His meticulous financial records showed that every year, he was short almost $300. With the housing allowance, he figured that he wouldn't have to dip into his bank account. By carefully planning his food purchases, he could manage on the $165 he got each month for Social Security plus the $50 or so he got from writing occasional insurance policies.

This was the remnant of his last business before he retired, and he no longer did cold canvassing.* Instead, he serviced those customers who remained after all those years. His worry was that the company might decide to drop him. It was hard to get a job at his age, "Not even a part-time one. It's almost a federal criteria to eliminate older people from jobs."

Peter Barnes' first program residence was the Pioneer Hotel. He liked its convenient downtown location, but didn't care for the management. As soon as he came by with the EHAP lease, they raised his rent $10. He didn't feel the place was worth $105. There were only the two rooms, and he had to pull his bed out of the wall every night. Another thing which irked him was that they once charged him 80¢ at the cafeteria to fill a small thermos bottle with milk. He resolved to move as soon as possible, and located a nice apartment by looking in the paper and driving around in his car.

There were several possibilities. For a while he considered moving into a place that cost $165 a month. He could stay there until something else came along, even if he did have to pay a transfer company $50 to help with the heavy stuff. Peter rejected two other apartments that he considered to be too run down and dirty. He didn't want to dust every day.

After two weeks of looking, he found a one-bedroom apartment in the lower part of a four-plex. It was owned by the son of one of his friends. "We used to raise cattle together," he explains.

The rent was $125, but he liked the spaciousness. "If someone comes by to stay for a while, I can

---

*going door to door

accommodate them a little." This wasn't possible at the Pioneer, or at the housing authority, for that matter.

The people at the hotel were glad to get rid of the contentious old man and did not require him to give a thirty days' notice. He inspected the new place and got the landlord to sign the lease, all in a single day.

Peter views the program requirements as just that: "something you have to do in order to qualify." Besides, the inspection form "wasn't very severe," and the agency struck him as being pretty tolerant. "They wouldn't put you down to the last mark to make you eligible."

Because the apartment is centrally located, Peter finds that he has to use his car less. When he was living in the senior citizens' residence, he had a gasoline bill that ran up to $20 a month. Now, church is within walking distance, as is the Knights of Columbus Hall where he spends a lot of his time. He made me promise that at least once I would come on a Saturday, so we could have dinner there together.

There is also free off-street parking in back. When it gets cold, he runs an extension cord out his back door and plugs the block heater into it. "But now, I don't even use my car," he says with a satisfied grin on his face.

He was also able to purchase a spring coat that was on sale for $49. Clothes are one thing which interests him. He still dresses Western style. Once I met him on the street, and he was wearing a ranch coat, a Stetson hat, and hand-tooled leather boots that made him at least 5'4" tall. "The World's Shortest Cowboy," I thought to myself.

Program participation was an easy matter for him. He thinks that housing allowances are good for older people if they are active like he is. "You couldn't get me into the high rise; it's all too small. I've got a cousin who lives there."

"I'm right near a grocery store. I don't have to use my car. I'm two blocks from the church and a block from the KC. I don't have to use my car for nothing." His words have a certain stridency to them.

"I've got plenty of closets, too," he adds. He stops to light his pipe. "Oh, I lied to you—you asked me how my health was. I have a little cold, but I never cough. Why? I don't know!" He says that he hasn't been sick for forty years. The only medication he takes is an aspirin twice a week to "stimulate the blood," and some antacids to "strengthen the stomach." He draws on his pipe, and then tells me emphatically, "Try it. You'll never have a heart attack."

Talking to him, I can sense his pride in his independence. He is ineligible for food stamps because of his assets.* He says he doesn't want them: "It's a discredit to your integrity to go into a store like that." He feels that if somebody needs help, he should get money, and not stamps that identify you as someone on assistance of some sort.

His days are filled with battles over slights he feels he has received. His recent divorce still fills him with bitterness, and he shows me a letter he sent to the Bishop. It is a long tirade against the priest that introduced him and his former wife. The closing line reads, "Your Excellency, why don't you exercise your ability if you think you're so smart."

He doesn't want to be involved with women anymore. "That wedding cost me $3,000." This includes a freezer which he stocked with meat. "But I never got to taste any of it!"

No, better to steer clear of romance for now. "I'm fed up with them. But I still love one woman. I wrote her a letter, but I'm not going to date her."

Peter reaches over to his bookcase and picks out an astrology book. He is a Libra. "Proud, pretentious, a brilliant talker...."

---

*Asset limits for food stamps are substantially lower than for the AAE.

THE PARTICIPANTS REVISITED

January, 1975: I return to North Dakota for a two-week field visit. It has been almost six months since I left the site, and I am interested in two things: catching up on agency operations and re-interviewing the people who had been the subjects of my participant case studies. Before contacting any of them, I check through the agency records to see if they are all still in the program.

Only the Maddings have dropped out. In mid-June, Steve had received another raise. An entry in the Supplemental Information Log indicates that their housing allowance was reduced to four dollars due to increased income. Then, less than three months later, another notation was made: Mavis had called to inform the agency that they were no longer eligible for the program. They had purchased a home at the Tumbleweed Estates, one of the new, federally subsidized developments near Mandan.

The development is located outside the city limits because FmHA funds are available only to those areas which have less than 10,000 people. Mandan is somewhat larger than this.

The houses themselves are on average-sized lots and do not fit Steve's dream of having a place where he could "holler in the pasture" if he wanted to or fire his Weatherby rifle without anyone telling him about it. During my last visit, he had said that he would rather own in the city than rent in the country. Mavis had long felt this way, and Steve had gradually come around to her point of view.

Since they are out of the project, I decide not to call them.

The first participants I do visit are those in western Stark County: Oksana Erko and Alice Sadowski. It is a few days after one of the worst blizzards in the century, and everyone is still talking about it. The temperatures had dropped to -20°, and the wind started to blow, picking up topsoil and mixing it with what little snow there was. Some of the drifts are actually black.

Heading west on I-94, it is cold and overcast. Around Richardton, it suddenly brightens up, and things don't look quite so depressing. Near Denton, I see a herd of antelope grazing inside the fence of some farmer's field.

Outside of Dickinson, a familiar sign reminds me that the area is Beef Country, and implores me to enjoy a beef dinner today. Just before the exit ramp, Bob Olsen passes, honks, and waves. He probably left a half hour before I did, but the roads aren't heavily patrolled out here. I speed up a little and follow him into town.

Bob drives west on Main Street, and I get a little nervous. He turns down the same street that Mrs. Erko lives on, and I assume the worst, that he has an appointment with her. Instead, he passes her house and continues toward the Dickinson State College campus. Then I remember that the Badlands Human Resources Center has rented new office space there.

I get out of the car and enter the garage that is over Mrs. Erko's apartment. The steps, and again I wonder how she manages them. Downstairs, something is different: one of the many doors is open, and I can see a college kid sitting on a sofa. He is drinking a beer and nods to me as I walk by. I had always assumed that there was only one apartment in the basement and that the extra doors led to storage areas.

I knock, and Mrs. Erko lets me in. "Mike, I thought I never _see_ you again!" The intonations are familiar. An American would have also stressed the word "never." We shake hands, and I close the door behind me.

Mrs. Erko looks good, but has obviously put on weight. She takes my coat, and then motions for me to sit down at the kitchen table. "You put everything down, and you _yeat_ something."

I obey after I jot down that things still look the same inside the apartment. I can see only two changes: on one of the walls is a picture of the Ukranian Cardinal Slipyj. It is in full color and looks as though it was cut from a magazine. The other difference is a 1975 calendar from St. Matthew's Church in Dickinson. Apparently, she didn't go to the Ukranian Church for the Christmas Mass.

My meal is already prepared--some kind of hamburger patties. I begin to eat, and she returns to the stove where she fixes some fried eggs.

She apologizes as she sets down another plate in front of me: "I am not very good cook. I forget everything."

I tell her that she should have something, too.
"No, I'm gain too much. No exercise."
I show her a picture of my new son. "That's baby. So _cute_." I look at the china cabinet behind me. She keeps her sugar in a cup on the bottom shelf. For some reason, it makes me sad.

"Yeah, I look after another place. Too high priced...is basement."

"This is a nice apartment," I offer.

"I don't know. Not handy. Too far to everywhere, and it's a basement. All the time I have to use lights."

"You tried to move, though?"

"I try to move, but nothing."

"How?"

"How try? I check the paper, and call somebody." She says that there are few apartments in the winter, but even during the summer months she couldn't find anything that she could afford. "Lots of places I find be all right, but too high priced." Now, she says, nobody helps her look. Mrs. Green no longer works for the welfare office. "Nobody calls me." Her new caseworker is a man and is not as friendly.

She had hoped that somebody could find her a new place. Siri and Mrs. Green had both been good about taking her around: "That's very nice help for me, that's good help. Except I make a mistake, I move too far. The girl says 'No time.' Three days and I miss that program. She says to move in, and we steady-look for something better. After, that one moves here, the other moves there..." She remembers the promises vividly.

Since my last visit, she has gotten involved with the Senior Citizens' Club. They have a bus service that she uses to go downtown. "Because I can't walk, or nothing. That's all I have." She calls up ahead of time, and they stop by her house. She waits inside the garage for it to come. But there's only one bus: "They have about 200 people. Cab is very high-priced now." She likes the driver: "He's so handy. Good to people. A lot of time he taking people in wheel chair."

Once, the bus went to the senior citizens' residence. The driver had to stop there to pick up more passengers. It was the first time she saw the place. "It's too far. That's so sad. It's like on the prairie. No garden, no flower, no nothing..."

Apparently, it had been in the summer. "I hoped that woman would help me find another place."

The Senior Citizens' Club has contacted her frequently. "Yesterday, somebody call and said. 'We're having a birthday party. We'd like to have you'."

"Are you going?"

"No, I not go. I not feel good." The feeling is a general one: "I think it's because I am too old."

I ask her what she did for Christmas, and she tells me that she didn't do anything special. She had the flu, and the next day she went to the clinic.

Mrs. Erko thinks for a while, and then says that Mr. and Mrs. Schmidt took her to midnight Mass at St. Matthew's: "Father calls these people. It was very nice. But it's not Ukrainian, not Ukrainian. I like Ukrainian better. I bet you was in the church on Christmas." I tell her yes, and she asks me if it was a Ukrainian church or a Latin rite church. She is disappointed when I tell her it was neither.

"You know, I got cut from this check."

"Why?"

"I don't know. I need more. Everything higher and higher." She shows me a letter from the agency. It says that her housing allowance will be reduced $7 due to the increase in her social security as reported for the annual eligibility redetermination. I make some calculations and find that she is still $36 further ahead than she was before the increase in her grant.

"Do you still get food stamps?"

She nods and says, "Little bit of help, little bit of help, but not much. A little bit."

She wants to talk about the apartment. Recently, the landlady rented the other downstairs apartment to some college boys. This upsets her: "Too much drink, too much fight...too much company...too much dirt. I have scrub steps every day. This not help. This not help...I like to move to some better place."

The only thing which pleases her is that the apartment is warm. During the blizzard, she turned the heat up.

"You're lucky you weren't living in the old place."

"Yeah, yeah. That's pretty bad cold." Then: "The wintertime is very sad to me. Lots of people died in that storm."

I have lunch at the Esquire Club, below the former location of the Dickinson satellite office. I talk to a cattle rancher, and he tells me that he was lucky, he didn't have any storm losses. His herd is small and a lot of his cattle were sheltered.

Western Edge of Stark County

    Finding Alice Sadowski's place is a little difficult. According to her case records, she had moved to a mobile home in August. The previous evening, we had talked over the phone, and she had given me directions. But the trailer court is small and easy to miss from the highway. There are only about thirty-five units there, and the name, Queen City Villa, seems pretentious.
    I drive up and down the narrow "streets" for ten minutes trying to locate the right one. The house numbers aren't sequentially ordered, and the recent storm had blown some of the plaques away. Finally, I ask somebody, and he points out the correct place.
    The trailer is a brand-new twelve-wide. The platform stairs in front are polished aluminum and slippery. Alice looks the same to me, except that she has changed her hair style. It is combed out, and doesn't look so old-fashioned.
    "Jason's really grown," I tell her. She nods. He is walking around the living room and working furiously on a red sucker. In his other hand is a small tattered piece of blanket.

She tells me that she's been living here since the summer. Her boyfriend, George, bought the place for her. She pays him $100 a month for rent, plus another $35 for the park. Then, he writes the check to the bank. The sale price of the mobile home is almost $6000. Before she agreed to the arrangement, she made it clear that moving in implied no commitment on her part. She had long ago decided that George would never be ready for marriage: "I've given up on that, I think."

At the same time, she recognizes that it was generous of George to offer to help her out: "He's real good about material things." She points out the wind-up swing that George had bought Jason for Christmas. "But there's more to life than that. He just can't seem to make that final step."

The location of the trailer court is convenient. Robbie still walks over a block to school, and there's a grocery store on the other side of the highway. "We've been real lucky," she says.

Alice began looking for a new place in June, after Robbie's school let out. The apartments were high priced, and many of them didn't allow children. It was something that always bewildered her: a two or three bedroom place for couples only. What would anybody do with all that extra room?

"I didn't want it to be ritzy, but I didn't want to live in a dump, either."

Although it was fruitless, the search process was easy enough; she could always borrow a car. Sometimes, her mother would volunteer to take her.

At the end of July, Alice accelerated the pace. The landlord said that he wanted her out. He said he could rent the place out to someone else for $125 a month, $50 more than she was paying him. "I didn't figure it was worth that much."

Alice insists that she prefers mobile home living, although she was skeptical at first. "I don't know if there's any advantage, but it's a lot nicer than that house was." Now that Robbie is going to school, she wants to quit moving around. That's why she insisted that there be no obligation on her part when she moved: even if they break up for good, she wants to be able to stay there.

The only disappointing thing about the trailer is the furniture. She sold her old stuff when she moved. The things which came with the unit aren't of as high a quality. "It doesn't hold up as well as the other."

August was the month that Alice started working at the Esquire parttime. She waits on tables three or four nights a week, and they pay her $2 an hour plus tips. "I didn't want anything steady. When I started I told them three or four nights a week, and they had me working five or six. It was too much."

The sitter lives across the street. She charges Alice 50¢ an hour. Alice goes to work at 6:00, Jason goes to bed at 7:00, and Robbie at 8:30. "They're only with the sitter a little while before they have to go to bed."

The extra income has made a difference in her life. Welfare won't let her accumulate too much in savings, so she spends any leftover money at the end of each month. Since July, she's bought a new dryer, a youth bed for Jason, and a winter coat for herself. "Little things that you don't get otherwise. This is all since I moved into the trailer house. One thing at a time, but it mounts up, too."

Recently, she opened a savings account for Jason. Again, because of the welfare office, she tries not to keep too much in there: "I can understand. If you've got enough money to save away, then there's no reason to be on welfare."

Another thing she's done recently is to open a checking account--her first. That way she can show the welfare office her expenditures if they have any questions.

Because she works irregular hours, and the tips vary, Alice recertifies with the welfare office and with EHAP every month. This month, her AFDC is down to just over $200, and her housing allowance payment was $72. According to her records, she earns an additional $250 per month. Her total net income is almost $4,000 per year, almost double what it was when she started the program.

"The extra money is real nice," she says. The only disadvantage is that it leaves her with less free time. Neither she nor George has driven down to Bismarck for sports events at the Civic Center. "Since I've been working, I haven't had the time. We'll probably miss the basketball tournament, too." She also quit the bowling team because it was at night.

I ask her how she likes being out of Richardton. "I've enjoyed every minute of it."

"Do you tell people you're divorced? I ask. It had been part of her plan.

"I don't tell people anything. 'Course, nobody asks. I guess they just assume."

"And nobody talks about you any more?"

"Not that I know of, and I don't care if they do."

On my way back to Bismarck, I spot a herd of white tails around the same spot that I saw the antelope earlier this morning. Near Mandan, Bob Olsen passes me again, driving to beat hell.

I visit the Kunsts the next day. Their records show that the amount of their housing allowance had been reduced to $59 per month, a decrease of $11. The reasons cited were increased social security benefits and fewer medical expenses.

When I knock on the door, Mr. Kunst answers. The is the first time this has happened. Usually, Mrs. Kunst would let me in and we would go into the bright living room where he would be sitting in his chair.

Both of them want to talk about the blizzard. They set the thermostat at eighty degrees, but the living room never got any warmer than sixty-two degrees. "It was the wind," she says. "Once that died down, it was wonderful." The two of them simply waited it out. She was just getting over the flu, anyway. Mr. Kunst had tried to take out the garbage during the second day of the storm: "I couldn't hardly make it."

"It took his breath away."

I ask them if there's been any changes in their lives since the last time I talked to them. "It's still the same," Mrs. Kunst answers. "All we do is go for coffee, or a little drive. We visit relatives and friends. For Christmas we drove down to the farm and visited his sister."

They had thought about visiting their son over the holidays, but he had been transferred to Jacksonville. "We were gonna fly, then all of a sudden he backed out: 'I don't know, I don't feel so good. My place is home.' That's what he said."

Mr. Kunst nods in agreement. The two of them actually prefer bus travel, but that would have taken too long. "Florida is a long ways. I just couldn't take it."

They talk about their payment. "They cut us down. We had a letter. We were getting $70, and now we're getting $59." Their medical expenses had been reduced, and this was one of the reasons for the decrease--that and increased social security income. Mrs. Kunst had gone off her high blood pressure pills, Mr. Kunst was cut back to one diabetic pill a day. "Those damn pills," he says, with mock ruefulness.

"Yeah, that's what really costs." She was also taking Valium for her nerves. The doctor thought that it was hard for her to adjust to the new life they had been forced to lead.

"I was gonna get rid of my pills all the way," Mr. Kunst jokes, "but the doctor won't help me."

The increase in social security had also raised the price of food stamps for them, but they had decided to continue to purchase their monthly allotment. "We'd go off them if it wasn't for his special diet," Mrs. Kunst reiterates. Recently, they had discovered the Wholesale Market, a store which specializes in goods that have been slightly damaged in shipping. "Canned goods are cheaper there," she says. "But we can't use much of them. He has to watch his salt, and we still have to go to the K-Mart to buy meat. That's what costs." Mr. Kunst nods.

The two of them haven't gone over to the Senior Citizens' Center yet. We're *going* over, though!" she says, more to him than to me.

"Yes, we are! We made up our minds. I'm kinda shy around people." Actually, he had been there twice, but his speech wasn't very good at the time. He couldn't talk, got embarrassed, and then left. Now, his condition was improving. He had started to read again: "I'm getting better. My speech is better. My eyes are getting better--double vision." Still, he couldn't read too long.

"His stomach gets quite upset if he does," she explains.

"You have to keep going, I guess."

Mr. Kunst also plays gin and solitaire. Again, he can only do it until he begins to feel woozy. "The doctor said last time that it's just gonna take time." His memory is also coming back. He can watch a TV show and understand what it's about before it's over with.

One of the things he wanted to try was leatherwork. "But my eyes. I should try it once. It's getting better, but everything's so high-priced now." The rise in social security was only $18.

"But we're getting by," she says.

"We have to," he says.

The Webber family, with their six children, have been hit the hardest by inflation in the six months since I left the site. Still, they are optimistic about the downturn in the economy. They see the decline as an eventual cure for rising prices. "I think it's probably good for the country to have this," Carl says. "Things have been going clear out of the sky. We've got to get back to the fundamentals, and get it back to accountability again. You can't go downtown to buy groceries without having the First

National Bank bail you out."

Carl is talking between mouthfuls. It is 8:30 at night and he has just gotten in. This is the first time I've seen him dressed in something besides coveralls. He is wearing a red cowboy shirt and faded Levis.

A few of the prices have already started to go down. "Two weeks ago, Super Valu had hamburger at 49¢ a pound." It was lean meat, Chris says, and there was hardly any grease to pour off. Sugar is still up; it can even be seen in things that have sugar in them, like cookies and canned goods. The new lettuce crop is in, and produce prices have begun to drop.

"Do you think you're any better off?"

"No, Mike, we didn't make any gain. I figure we lost from $2500 to $3000 with the economy going up." Carl gets up from the table and walks over to the stove to get himself another helping of stew. "I've got a job. We've got a roof over our heads. Not much of one, but we've got a roof...."

The other day, Carl stopped by an auto showroom for kicks and looked at two cars, a Chevy and a Buick. "They were both $6,000. There's nothing there. These big companies, they take it from the little guy."

Chris shows me a utility bill from December. It totals almost $75. Of this, $16 is for lights, and the rest is for heat. She thumbs back through her checkbook until she finds the entry for January, 1973: the bill was for $55 then. Garbage and sewer charges have also gone up, she says. "Now they want to up the telephone."

Carl snorts: "These big companies, they sit on their money. They don't spend a damn cent. It's a real rat race." Carl wishes that the place was heated by oil. Then, he could shop around. "With natural gas, you don't have a choice."

They've begun to blame the unions now, too: "They've gotten out of hand. They've gotten too much power." But not in North Dakota, he cautions: "They're big money, and the big money men are all in the East."

Chris feels that the area hasn't been hit by the recession, just inflation: "Back here, it's different. Like car sales. They're selling cars. And, you look in the paper, and there's still jobs." She stops and looks at me humorously, "But don't go telling anybody back there."

I agree to keep North Dakota's secret between us.

Chris tells me that there was a TV special on

North Dakota a few weeks ago. The program compared a family living in Harvey to one living in India. "The program tried to make you feel guilty about living here," she says. "Feel guilty about what? They don't believe in birth control. The'll have a kid every nine months if they want...." I suppress a smile. The Webbers have six children, and most of them a year apart.

She worries about coal gassification, and what that will bring. "There's air pollution, and riff-raff from the outside. They say that North Dakota could become another Appalachia."

"This coal is a one-shot deal," Carl adds. "That's some of the best farmland in the United States."

Chris says what makes it worse is that North Dakotans won't benefit from the mining operation, and the "big money" will be the only ones who profit.

Carl tells me that his EHAP check has been cut: "We were getting $106 a month. Now they tell us we're only gonna get $90. I was hoping it would reverse itself." The letter they recieved had confused them. It cited "increased income" as the reason for change, and yet, Carl hasn't had a raise in almost two years. Then Chris remembered that she had used the previous year's W-2 form to declare their income. For this year's redetermination she had used a pay stub.

Even with the decrease, they are still enthusiastic about the program, and feel that it has made up for all the raises that Carl didn't and won't get: "The new contracts are up, and I heard we're only going to get a 5 percent cost of living adjustment." Next July will make it three years since he's had his last raise.

They still feel the squeeze, however. They applied for food stamps at the end of the year. It was something they swore they'd never do. They pay $103.50 for $133 worth of stamps every two weeks.

It was Chris's idea. "She wouldn't let me sleep. She'd pound me on the back and say, 'Get on food stamps. Get on food stamps.'" Chris laughs. "You use more and more of your income to buy groceries." Carl still feels bad about taking them, and makes Chris do the shopping now. When he has to run down to the store at night for a quart of milk, he always pays cash.

"One thing, I found it's who the hell you see. There's one old witch that acts put out any time you ask a question. I kept thinking, what the hell do they do with somebody without an education?"

Still, they feel they are always one month behind: "They want you to anticipate all your expenses. How can you do that?"

I ask again how they feel about the downturn of the economy, and the answer is still the same. "We've got to get back to the basics where things are more liveable. They're pushing it to the limit right now. People have got to quit buying. That's the only way they'll get prices down."

In the meantime, they have their dreams. Carl would like to haul a trailer up to where he has his layover. Right now, the owner of one of the town buildings lets him nap in the basement. It used to be an old bank vault, and it's musty down there. They'd both like to take some sort of Big Vacation once things get a little better. "You know, Mike, I'd like to drive to Alabama, or clear down to the tip of Florida, just to say I've been...."

I visit Sally Klein Friday evening of the first evening of the first week I was back. She has recently begun working day shifts at The Yarn Shop, and she no longer has her afternoons free for interviews. The holiday rush has just ended, and things are getting back to normal. Actually, things are slow there, and her hours have been cut. The latest worksheet in her file showed that she was now making little more money than a year ago, even though her hourly rate had been increased to $2 an hour.

I ask her about the change, and she tells me that the manager had to cut back because business is slow. "She got a letter from Minneapolis saying to cut hours to the minimum." The Yarn Shop is a syndicated operation with outlets all over the country.

As a result of her decrease in income, the amount of her housing allowance was raised again to $100. Over the course of a year, the amounts had varied from as little to $79 to as much as $126. The lower figure was after her oldest son, Carl, had returned to live with his father. The higher figure was when he was living with her during the summer.

She is still hurt about his decision to return to Montana. "I don't know how to explain it. I think his Dad just promised him everything. He's quiet and withdrawn like I was at his age..." Her voice trails off. "I don't blame him. It hurt when he went back." Sally thinks that he missed his friends out there, too, and that it might have been different if he had stayed for the opening of school.

Jimmy took it hard, too. He didn't say anything about his brother leaving, but just suddenly began to wet the bed at night.

She offers me a drink.

On the table is a new family picture: Sally, Carl, and Jimmy. It was taken in the fall, just before he left, she says.

Jimmy walks in from the bedroom where he has been playing. "Do you remember Mike?"

He nods and scratches his ear.

"He's been sick," she tells me. Last week she finally had to take him to the doctor for a shot of penicillin. December had been an expensive month for her. First, she had gotten bronchitis, and then Jimmy had the ear infection. The medical bills came to $112 with all the X-rays.

Jimmy spots my jacket on the chair and begins to rummage through the pockets: "No! That doesn't belong to you or me!" He laughs and runs back into his bedroom. She apologizes to me and says that he's at that age now where he gets into everything.

We talk about the blizzard. The apartment was warm enough. She set the thermostat at 80° for Jimmy's sake, and the termperature stayed at 76° or 78°. So much snow was blown into the basement entrance that Ron had to come by the second day and shovel them out.

I tell her that I still miss North Dakota, even with the blizzards. She laughs and says, "I think that anywhere from here west the people are pretty friendly. The people in Billings are nice, too."

She tells me that her rent was raised $10 in August. The landlord found out that the two apartments were on a single meter. Now, he pays for the gas, and she only has to pay the lights. With the rent at $130 and the housing allowance at $100, she has to make up the difference. "This is the first time I've had to kick in."

Her food stamp situation is straightening out now that she's in Burleigh County. She only has to recertify every three months. The eligibility clerk doesn't make her prove anything. "She says, 'Oh, I believe you.' It's a lot nicer. That Mr. Simle in Morton County...well, it's like he's degrading you."

Her food stamp cost is now $26 for $84 worth of - stamps. "I usually have a couple of dollars left over. I don't think I ever ran out before the end of the month."

Now that Carl has gone back, she had to get a new baby sitter for Jimmy. She's a divorcee who lives near work. The woman only charges her 55¢ an hour. Sally found out about her through the paper.

I ask Sally if she's bought anything new recently. The only thing she can think of is a sewing machine: "I pay $5 a month on it. I got it on sale for $113." She is still cautious about using her credit card. She had already bought a new double bed. Together with the sewing machine, it sends her bill to $11 a month. She says she likes the *idea* of having credit. "If I want to charge on that for something, I can do it."

Sally has been having trouble with her ex. He still calls. The last time, he said: "You've got one more chance. If you don't come and see me right now, I'm gonna get married again."

"I told him, 'Go ahead. I hope she has money. Then maybe you'll keep up your support payments.'" He's $300 behind, she says, with a touch of sarcasm.

Sally still has the same relationship with Ron. They go out a couple of times a week, and he's nice to Jimmy. Her ex never even asks about his own child, and Ron's attitude is a pleasant change.

"I like it the way I've got it, really." She likes to feel independent. "I don't know, I like to be able to go into a bar without feeling I'm a saloon girl. I like to be able to go to bed with somebody without feeling I'm a whore or a bad girl."

"But I still like to be courted. Ron's kinda old fashioned. I don't know. I like to have the door opened for me--unless he's got his arms full of packages. Then I'll open it for him."

Still, her liberation isn't complete: "I still have in my mind a prim and proper type."

She feels lucky: "I have a job. A lot of people don't have them at all. Then, you can't even draw unemployment."

Then, I reminded her that the last time I saw her, we had talked about her joining or forming a women's group. "You know, I don't think I want it now. I'm at peace with myself."

Like Mrs. Erko, Peter Barnes has also gained weight. Thirteen pounds, he says. With his short frame, it looks like a lot more. He claims that quitting smoking is the cause of it. "I've had tongue trouble with my pipe." It scared him. He thought he was developing cancer, and it's one of the things he fears. Recently, his eyes have begun to water in the morning. This he blames on sitting too close to his color TV.

He wants to know why I'm in town. "Did you come to straighten the boys out?"

"No, I'm just getting some information on the project."

"Well, they raised my rent the first of the month," he offers. "It was $125, and now it's $135, plus utilities. He shoulda given us thirty days' notice, but he didn't."

Peter has some other complaints. The gutters in the front are leaking. The goosenecks had clogged, filled with water, and then frozen during a cold snap. "It's so slippery out there, I can't go out there with my good clothes on. I fell twice already. The icicles are ten pounds and ten or fifteen feet up."

He says that he called the landlord about it. "He won't do a thing. I called the city, and they won't do anything." The gutters are his only major complaint. "I like my apartment. It's got enough room. It's not too hot or too cold. Now I won't do nothing for him." Previously, Peter had fixed the faucets and made a few other minor repairs.

"I'm trying to get up to Liberty Heights, if I can," he confides. "I think it's more permanent than the other place." The "other place" is the EHAP program.

"I thought you didn't like it there."

"I don't, but they've got some new apartments. I can get it for $32 on my income." His worry is that this project will end in a year, and then he won't have any help at all. He is being phased out of his insurance job and this makes things even more uncertain for him financially. He had a fight with the agent they hired to supervise him: "He made a liar out of me. Called me a crook! And everything else!" Peter's face flushes as he speaks.

I switch the conversation to the storm last week and hope that it will calm him down. "I just stayed in. I couldn't get out. I just stayed put for two days."

He wants to talk about Liberty Heights, the Morton County Housing Authority's Senior Citizens' residence. "I've got my name in. There are too many ahead. It will take a year or maybe two years."

The state of the economy depresses him. He says, vaguely: "It doesn't look like we'll be here much longer." As evidence, he cites an astrologer who predicts a catastrophe in 1975. "Right now, everybody's happy. They've got money. They're living high off the hog. But eight months from now, everybody'll feel the pangs of 1974. You can put that in your book."

I tell him that I will.

He thinks a bit and then begins a diatribe against Kissinger*: "He sold us down the river!!! He sold us down the river with our own money!" Peter says that he's going to write Governor Link about the economy. "I've always got to use my own money. I"m short about $300 to $400 a year."

In October, he had completed the redetermination of eligibility form. Due to increased costs for prescription drugs, his housing allowance had gone up one dollar to forty dollars per month. "She said she forgot to give me deductions on one item."

I ask him if the check is enough, and he says yes. "You know, you can always use more money, but I wouldn't bother anybody."

We watch a quiz show on TV, and it rankles him. "They're begging people to contribute to the starving people all over the world. Here they're throwing away $20,000 or $30,000 just for one person."

I nod.

"Or that prizefighter. What's his name? Muhammed? He gets five million for the next fight. Who needs that kind of money?"

We talk again about his intended move to the senior citizens' residence. He applied with the LHA two months ago. "Maybe it will never materialize."

I ask him if he'd move there tomorrow if a slot opened up. He says that he would because of the security involved with the housing authority. "But I'm not going to take just anything they've got. I'll tell you that. In case this E.P.H. (sic) would drop out, that would be pretty tough on me." It's obvious that he doesn't know he will be transferred to the housing authority at the end of the experiment. I tell him, and he says, "If you give me the right information, and that guy calls tomorrow, I'd turn him down."

He still likes the convenience of his own apartment. "I don't have to start my car for a whole month if I don't want to. I can walk to church; it's only three blocks. The K.C. is only a block and a half."

I ask him if he still eats there, and he says yes, every Saturday, like clockwork.

---

*The U.S. Secretary of State at the time.

Peter wants to talk about the disaster he feels is lying ahead. It will be something unforseen, he thinks. Like the blizzard that hit North Dakota. Then, after the natural disaster, something spiritual must happen among the people. Finally, there will be a moral revolution, and everybody will have to change their way of life. Somewhat immodestly, he adds: If everybody was like me, they wouldn't need no states' attorney, courts or jails, nothing like that."

He reads me a list of eleven questions he has prepared for the governor. They touch on Watergate, the Middle East and "pessimism." "I tell you, I'm a white man, and I believe in live and let live. I believe everybody should do the same thing." The statement seems incongruous when I think of what he has just said before.

I tell him I have to go. He wants me to take one of his pipes, since he won't be smoking them anymore. He brings out his pipe rack and asks me to pick one.

"I can't. The company won't let me."

"Well, you wouldn't have to tell."

I make a joke that he doesn't pick up on: "But that would be a lie."

"Sometimes a white lie don't hurt."

And so on. Just as I am putting on my coat, he says: "I'm glad somebody came by to see if I'm alive. I'm alone. You know how it is in town. My family don't come here. They've got other places to go."

It is death that is on his mind, I decide. He talks about how he still likes to play Penochle with his buddies. One of them, Colstad, insisted on playing, even though he was very sick with cancer. "I asked him, 'Gus, are you physically able for us to come out?'"

The friend had said yes, and three of them came out of the farm and played until late in the night. "Four days later, he was dead."

COMMENTARY

The case histories show that the housing allowances were not everything in the recipients' lives, as a reading of the participant flow chapter with "Mrs. Feist" might lead one to believe. The extra money helped, but it wasn't a panacea.

In some cases, the interviewed participants seemed to use the money directly to improve their housing situation, usually some time after their entry into the program. In other cases, the cash payments were viewed strictly as additional income for the household. This was probably a more frequent use of the allowances at the North Dakota site. Almost three-quarters of the recipients initially remained in their original units.

Invariably, the rent supplements were fitted in with an array of other devices that made up the individual households' survival strategies. Since direct cash assistance was originally envisioned as a way of improving the housing situation of recipients, it is safe to say that treating the money as an income transfer is something that was unexpected, at least by HUD. The North Dakota AAE acted like a progressive welfare program.

The program rules were liberal in regard to the types of families that could participate in the AAE. Communes, and single-person households where the individual was under sixty-two and not disabled were about the only exclusions. In the sample presented in this chapter, the households seem to represent fairly common living arrangements. The North Dakota residents do not seem to have developed the patterns of co-residence and three generation households that blacks have.[1] Nevertheless, they are involved in a complicated set of exchange networks that are a response to poverty. Most commonly, the respondents are dependent upon relatives to help them get by. This is a de facto form of subsidy.

While all of the households depicted in the case histories received payments from the North Dakota Experimental Housing Allowance, their experiences were different ones. The analysis which follows highlights the participants' experience with the program, the agency, and the impact of the program upon their lives.

<u>The Elderly</u>

The case of Mrs. Erko probably represents both a programmatic triumph and a humanitarian failure for the North Dakota agency. Since the intent of the AAE was to improve housing quality, there can be no doubt that the Ukrainian woman will contribute to the statistical success of the local program, and the AAE as a whole. She now has hot and cold running water, a full bathroom, and objectively pleasant surroundings. Spiritually and emotionally, she is worse off than before.

Mrs. Erko is also paying too much rent, even with the subsidy. Before entering the program, her monthly income was about $125. The original, substandard unit rented for $65 per month. This meant that almost one-half of her net income went for housing. The $61 housing allowance increased Mrs. Erko's net income to about $185 per month. However, the basement apartment which was her program residence cost $110 per month. This drove her rent burden to almost 60 percent of her net monthly income, or more than twice the proportion she should have been paying. Nevertheless, she still had a few more dollars left over than before the program. Subsequent increases in her Social Security payment also helped, especially since participants were penalized only 25 cents on every additional dollar earned.

It could be said that many of Mrs. Erko's difficulties are of her own making. She did, afterall, insist on steam heat. This is a cruel assessment. She has never had any money and has been hit by inflation that increases faster than grants do. C* for a single person household was set at $90. Her apartment is $20 above this without even figuring in the cost of lights. The unit itself is modest enough.

Mrs. Erko represents a certain kind of poor person that has been described in The Other America:

> Many of them are those who have been poor before. Their misery of their old age is simply a conclusion of a life of misery. They are the ones who have grown up, lived, and will die under conditions of poverty.[2]

Ill health will insure that the scenario will come to its conclusion. Her medical expenses will be paid by the government and she will die a ward of the state. Her offsprings' lack of good fortune, at least that of her son still living in North Dakota, means that she will receive little economic help from family. The new life styles and distance of those who have moved away dictate that she will remain alone.

It is doubtful that services provided by the agency could have made things different. Mrs. Erko barely got into the program because of a ninety day time limit for housing search. Her stringent housing requirements, self-imposed, would probably exhaust any agency which tried to locate new quarters for her.

Mrs. Erko's most pressing need is not more money, however. In the interviews, she indicates that she is willing to pay even more of her income for rent if she can be in some place that is more convenient. Barring an experimental taxi-cab allowance project, a downtown location would seem to be the best thing. The local housing authority might also seem to be a good bet, if she would only agree to live there. She seems to fit the stereotype of the dependent elderly that the directors of housing authorities seem to hold. However, the elderly project is still located far from downtown, and transportation services are poor. If Mrs. Erko moved into the senior citizens' residence, she would probably be lonely in the midst of company. As with her present apartment, the housing project is not the same as the Ukrainian town of Gorham. An encouraging sign, however, is that Mrs. Erko has begun to avail herself of certain senior citizens' services--the free bus, in particular.

Peter Barnes is a much happier story. Although somewhat of an eccentric, Peter is still independent and mobile. His income is much higher than Mrs. Erko's and he was able to afford an apartment in downtown Mandan. He did not require extensive agency help. Unlike most of the elderly in the AAE, he moved, and moved voluntarily. It is instructive to note that, even though he has a car, he still wanted to live within walking distance of the institutions that were important to him. In this case, it was the K. of C. club.

Barnes also has a fair amount of assets upon which he can draw if necessary. The housing allowance means that he does not have to touch his capital. The $40 payment each month more than negates the $300 annual shortfall he had before he became a participant. Subsidized housing is important to an elderly person. As the final visit with Peter Barnes shows, he was worried that the AAE would end. In forward-looking style, he put in an application with the Morton County housing authority, even though his previous stay there had been a stormy one.

Basement apartments were the eventual choice of both of the elderly households studied, and for one other family as well. This is a common pattern in North Dakota. Basement units were constructed after World War II to meet a severe housing shortage.[3] The rents are cheaper than for other types of apartments, although they do not provide an optimal level of housing services. Economic factors often win out over personal preferences. Perhaps Peter Barnes' complaints to his landlord, all about conditions undetectable to the observer, are expressions of discontent.

Being Disabled

The Kunsts used their subsidy purely as added income and they recognize this. Before Mr. Kunst's stroke, the couple was moving along toward a secure old age. The AAE, then, picks up the tab for a catastrophic illness insurance program that does not yet exist in the United States. The AAE is a stop-gap measure until they are old enough to qualify for senior citizens' housing.

The Kunsts, like Mrs. Erko, are also paying high rent, about $30 too much. This works out to about 45 percent of their total net income; however, they are not living quite as close to the line as she is, and the rent payments do not hurt quite as much. Further, they have consciously chosen to live in a place they like and to cut corners elsewhere so they can manage. This is a flexibility that other housing programs do not allow. The Brooke Amendment stipulates that a household can pay no more than one-fourth of its income to a housing authority. If they were accepted to live in Liberty Heights, they would pay only $65 for an apartment, though it would be a smaller one than they are in now. A savings of about $25 would be realized.

The Kunst's contact with the public assistance system came late in life. It is obvious that they are intimidated by it. Mrs. Kunst, suddenly saddled by what were her husband's (male) responsibilities, is befuddled by the income certification procedures employed by the local welfare office. Her fear of the eligibility worker is shown by the fact that she does not want to report a $100 "loan" from her son but knows that she should. In the end, she resorts to procrastination and rationalization to avoid having to declare the gift as income.

While the husband's illness obviously caused stress, their potential mobility and being near church and friends helped to mitigate this.

The Male-Headed Households: The "Working Poor."

The participation of the Maddings is a curiosity in any poverty program. They used the AAE as a temporary way station. Their small family size and his job makes it likely that the family will not become ensnared in poverty. Ironically, their economic situation improved because of outsiders who are often thought of as exploiters by North Dakotans. The firm which purchased the plant at which Steve works is based in the Midwest.

The Maddings were also confident that his earnings would continue to increase. The purchase of a new vehicle, financed by a long-term loan, attests to this. As long as the firm prospers, the Maddings will, too. The union wage scale will remain high and Steve will be able to make more money there than if he worked for a local firm.

The past history of the Maddings points to a steady progression from basement apartments to a rented mobile home, and finally, to a conventional house of their own. When they were in the program, the housing allowance payment was used solely as an income supplement, allowing Mavis to quit her job.

The original consideration of a mobile home, actually purchasing one, bears comment. This type of housing, while initially inexpensive, is not durable and depreciates quickly. Within two years, a mobile home is usually worth about one-half of its purchase price.[4] This loss in value is comparable to that of an automobile. Worse, the financing is bad. The notes are shorter-term than a mortgage and the interest rates are higher. Nevertheless, they continue to have an appeal to low-income families, especially in rural areas. While inflation affects conventional home purchase, it also affects trailers. In 1967, about a third of the mobile homes bought in the United States sold for more than $8000.[5] The higher-priced models are usually owned by families. This is a high price to pay for housing that lasts less than twenty years. The Maddings choice of buying a regular home was probably a wise one.

The future of the Webbers looks less bright than the Madding's. Their many children are still young. His income will probably remain steady. It is doubtful that Christine can go to work for several more years, if then.

The Webbers are really receiving two housing subsidies. The first is the EHAP check, which seems to defray a high utilities bill. The second is from a relative who lets them rent a three bedroom house, whatever the condition, for only $90. C* for a family of six or more was set at $230. Assuming that the house meets modest standards, this means that relatives are, in effect, paying almost half the rent, if one makes adjustment for gas and lights.

This family was, as noted, the hardest hit by

inflation. Food stamps offered a way out. It supplemented a strategy which involved not only careful shopping, but also, growing a substantial amount of food in their garden. Entertainment for this family remains minimal. Like all of the other families, the Webbers had a color TV. Unlike the others, they had two sets. Welfare critics to the contrary, this was no "luxury." After the initial costs of this appliance, the rest was gravy. As Carl noted, it was much cheaper than paying for a sitter and going to the movies.

Carl's view of the world as being composed of "little guys" and "big guys" would make solid material for a community organizer. It is doubtful that they could ever be radicalized, however. The Webbers scrape by and still seem to have hope. Carl has plans for the future and they both have their good humor. The housing subsidy helps them subsist, but it does not really change things.

The Female-Headed Households

Both Sally Klein and Alice Sadowski initially used their housing allowances as income supplements. Both were also dependent upon relatives and friends for assistance--usually not in a cash form. Both eventually moved to new places and upgraded their housing.

In Alice's case, a fair amount of manipulation of the program was involved. In order to start again in a new city, she had her boyfriend purchase a mobile home "for" her. Program regulations would have required that she be terminated had he put the title in her name. By having George listed as the owner, she was able to keep her subsidy. With George's generosity, it is possible, even likely, that ownership will eventually be transferred to her. The exchange relationship was designed to get by the requirements of social programs.

With Sally, the effect of the allowance was more dramatic. She quit bartending, a job she did not particularly enjoy. At this stage in her participation, she was using her checks like an assistance grant. The money tided her through a financially tight period. Later, faced with the prospect of having her older son living with her, she rented a larger apartment more suited to her needs. Although Carl did not stay, Sally's gain was a definite improvement in housing quality. More, she was closer to friends and relatives. This was probably not quite as important as it might have been had she not owned a car or had relations who did.

Alice seems much more cynical than Sally when it comes to her prospects of getting off assistance. The WIN program did little to train her for a place in the working world. In contrast, Sally is hopeful about what the program can do for her. Thus far, she had been able to stay off AFDC because she could work.

The two women's relationships with men are instructive. Both have established informal alliances with locals who give some small amount of fathering to their children. The men give the women companionship and, at least in Alice's case, economic assistance. This is a common pattern in impoverished, female-headed households, which again leads to criticism from anti-welfare people.

In terms of the program, both would be labeled success stories. They used their allowances to secure decent housing.

Views of the Program

All of the interviewed participants thought positively about the AAE. For those who had been on other assistance programs, especially food stamps, the AAE seemed a welcome and dignified contrast. The agency's attempts to keep the income certification procedures as simple and private as possible were cited by most of the households in the case histories. The rules of the USDA food stamps program are stricter. Recipients must bring documents verifying their economic situation and are also required to report any changes at specified intervals.

The fact that many of the recipients had been on other programs seems to indicate that stringent regulations do not necessarily prevent people from submitting to indignities associated with loss of privacy. Nevertheless, few of the participants liked being on the program. The exception were the elderly, who felt less stigmatized receiving public aid. This age group is often thought of as the deserving poor. That is, it is no fault of their own that they have no money.

Work is highly valued in conservative North Dakota. Most of household heads wanted better jobs and felt degraded--to some degree-- by having to take any public assistance. As Piven and Cloward have noted the stigma that accrues to welfare recipients is real and calculated:

What has to be understood, however, is that the loathing of "reliefers" is not an accidental feature of American culture. It has its roots in the two main tenets of market ideology: the economic system is open, and economic success is a matter of individual merit (and sometimes luck); those who fail--the very poor--are therefore morally or personally defective.[6]

In work ethic, but cooperative-minded North Dakota, the dualistic "credo" quoted in Chapter Two comes to the fore: One should take help if one needs it, but those who need help somehow do not deserve it.

The North Dakota strategy was congruent with the mentality of at least these seven participants. The agency tried to make the taking of assistance as painless as possible. Self-certification and self-inspection are used to protect privacy and communicate trust. Since the need is purely an economic one, services aren't usually necessary. The participants are economically disadvantaged, not psychologically defective. The participants use the program as an income supplement. At the same time, the connections with the usual source of such assistance, the county welfare departments, is downplayed. It isn't welfare, it's from the state--an experiment. It all works easier when both sides play by the same mental rules: *"If I can just keep on like this, at least I'll be even... I don't want to be on this thing my whole life...."*

A dissenting voice: *"My history very poor...."*

NOTES

1. See, Carol B. Stack, All Our Kin, (Harper and Row, New York, 1974).

2. Michael Harrington, The Other America, (Penguin Books, London, 1964), p. 105.

3. U. S. Department of Housing and Urban Development, Analysis of the Bismarck-Mandan, North Dakota Housing Market (HUD, 1971), p. 6.

4. Richard J. Margolis, Mobile Homes and the Rural Poor, (Rural Housing Alliance, Washington, D. C., 1972, p. 14.

5. *Ibid*, p. 9.

6. Frances Fox Piven and Richard A. Cloward, *Regulating the Poor*, (Vintage Books, New York, 1971), p. 149.

9. Analysis and Commentary

PROGRAM GOALS

The previous seven chapters of this book have focused upon the North Dakota experiment in isolation from the other sites in the AAE. This gave a "ground-level" view of the local agency, beginning with the planning stage, continuing through the enrollment phase, and concluding with the preparations for ending the project. However, the North Dakota agency was not alone. It was only one of eight that created and implemented a housing allowance project under a uniform set of rules. One of the features of the AAE research design is that it allows one to make cross-site comparisons. Once the relative performance of each agency has been ascertained along certain dimensions, the reasons for the outcomes at any one site can be examined. In this case, the concern is still with the North Dakota, or "Bismarck" agency.

The introductory chapter lists six goals that all agencies attempted to achieve. These include: (1) reach full participation; (2) serve a representative cross-section of the eligible population; (3) attain financial feasibility; (4) improve the housing conditions of the participants; (5) maintain the dignity of the participants; and (6) have the program accepted by the local community. Not all of these goals can be readily quantified, nor is the list exhaustive. Each agency had its own goals, too; however, for purposes of comparison and discussion, the six goals are used as an organizing device in the examination of program outcomes.

Participation

The most central goal of the experiment was to maximize participation. Because of the experimental nature of the AAE, each agency could serve only a limited number of families. For six of the sites, the target figure was 900 households. Durham and Bismarck were exceptions, with 500 and 400 program openings, respectively. Failing to serve the full complement of people could be due to two causes. An outreach program could be badly designed so that it would not attract enough applicants, or the enrollees could have difficulties meeting program requirements, thereby causing a high attrition rate. Either of these can be viewed as a programmatic failure. It meant that the agency, even with a very small program, could not aid the numbers HUD had authorized.

On a long-term basis, a shortfall of participants meant that local prospects for low-income housing relief had been damaged, however slightly. Each program opening was a potential ten-year financial commitment from HUD. However, in order for the full funding to be activated, an agency had to reach its participation goals at least once during the enrollment phase of the experiment. Only when this had been done was the long-term funding assured. At the end of the experiment, the local housing authorities would administer these program openings, or "units", for an additional eight years.

Five of the agencies met their participation goals. As Table 9-1 shows, Jacksonville, San Bernardino, and Springfield did not reach the 900 household level. The deficits in Springfield and San Bernardino were minor. In Jacksonville, they were serious. Had HUD not agreed to allow the agency to redesign its approach and try again, almost two-thirds of that site's program openings would have been lost to the local area.

Implicitly, Table 9-1 also indicates that the North Dakota agency adopted a different enrollee selection strategy from the other agencies. All of the sites overestimated the number of applications they would receive. North Dakota did a particularly inaccurate job in this respect. While most of the other sites enrolled only about one-half of their total planned applicants, North Dakota was forced to enroll three-quarters of them. This is a direct function of the small size of their applicant pool.

Once the applicants had been selected, full participation at the North Dakota agency depended upon an inordinately large proportion of enrollees becoming recipients. Since the director specified that few social services were to be given or needed,

Table 9-1

ENROLLMENT PROCESS: PLANNED VS. ACTUAL

Agency		Applicants	% of Applicants Becoming Enrollees	Enrollees	% of Enrollees Becoming Recipients	Recipients
Salem	Planned	3000	33%	1000	90%	900
	Actual	2529	44%	1108	85%	947
	% Difference	-16%		+11%		+5%
Springfield	Planned	5600	18%	1000	90%	900
	Actual	2479	49%	1209	70%	852
	% Difference	-56%		+21%		-5%
Peoria	Planned	3600	38%	1350	67%	900
	Actual	2241	64%	1445	65%	934
	% Difference	-38%		+7%		+4%
San Bernardino	Planned	6000	19%	1125	80%	900
	Actual	2050	49%	1004	82%	822
	% Difference	-66%		-11%		-9%
Bismarck	Planned	2000	22%	444	90%	400
	Actual	665	75%	499	86%	429
	% Difference	-67%		+12%		+7%
Jacksonville	Planned	3617	39%	1424	63%	900
	Actual	1806	57%	1035	33%	338
	% Difference	-50%		-27%		-62%
Durham	Planned	2500	22%	555	90%	500
	Actual	1337	55%	732	71%	517
	% Difference	-47%		+32%		+3%
Tulsa	Planned	2500	48%	1200	75%	900
	Actual	2292	47%	1068	85%	913
	% Difference	-8%		-11%		+1%
Aggregate	Planned	28,817	28%	8098	78%	6300
	Actual	15,399	53%	8100	71%	5752
	% Difference	-47%		—		-9%

Note: "Recipients" is the total number of recipients who received at least one payment. The number of recipients receiving payments at any one time was smaller, due to recipient terminations during the enrollment period.

Figures on planned number of applicants are taken from the agency Detailed Plans completed prior to the start of the enrollment period.

287

the burden of meeting program requirements fell squarely on each individual household. The planners' estimate of just how successful the potential recipients would be in this task was a fairly accurate one. The Detailed Plan projected a 90 percent success rate for enrollees, while the actual figure was 86 percent, the highest in the AAE experiment.

Not every AAE organization used this strategy of high selection rates coupled with enrollee self-reliance. Durham, for instance, gave enrollee households extensive assistance in locating new housing, as did the Tulsa agency. Peoria, in contrast, did little to help families in housing search. Instead, it enrolled relatively large numbers of households and let the market decide who would become a participant and who would not. The comparatively low (65 percent) enrollee success rate at the Peoria site shows that an agency could tolerate large numbers of dropouts and still reach full participation.

Had the North Dakota enrollees experienced difficulty in reaching the recipient stage, the agency would have had two alterntives. First, the director could have authorized the counselor to give the families more assistance in finding housing. This would have run against his belief that most in the program were ordinary, independent people who were economically, not socially or psychologically, disadvantaged. Alternatively, the director could have ordered a more intensive outreach effort that would have surfaced additional applicants who could have replaced the pre-payment terminees. This cold, bureaucratic approach was one that the director probably would have abhorred. Further, he was worried about adverse publicity, and having disappointed enrollees would have carried with it this risk. It is also questionable whether the inexperienced staff could have mounted an advertising campaign successfully. Peoria, Salem, and Tulsa were three agencies which hired public relations firms to conduct their outreach after initial efforts did not bring in the desired numbers of applicants.

Things worked out well for the North Dakota agency. The applicant pool was large enough to provide the necessary enrollees. All but a few of the enrolled households were able to meet program requirements. Landlords were receptive to the idea of signing a lease, even though few had ever used one before. Thus, there seems to have been a congruence between agency expectations and enrollee performance. Undoubtedly, a high percentage of stayers contributed to the low pre-payment termination rate. This, more than anything else, made the selection and enrollment strategy a workable one.

While the response of the eligible population to the North Dakota agency's low-key outreach program is factual, the reasons why the planners were expecting more applications are much more open to conjecture. The most reasonable explanation for the miscalculated outreach response seems to lie in a planning error that was made by the core staff of the North Dakota Experimental Housing Allowance Project. The tables in the Detailed Plan indicated that there were 6725 "income-eligible" households in the program area,[1] or so the planners thought. At best, this figure was only a rough approximation of the number of "program-eligible" households within the jurisdiction. In 1973, only the first count census data was available to any of the agencies. These raw figures give vital information in aggregate form. North Dakota was further hampered by the lack of an SMSA, which forced the staff to work with less detailed statewide figures. Because of this, the estimate of the eligible population includes both homeowners and renters, a factor which helped make the North Dakota estimates especially high. Further, there is no easy way to get household income by family size if the census area is untracted, as was the case with North Dakota. This contributed to further inaccuracy.

Working with the agency figures, had the 2000 applications materialized, the gross response rate would have been 30 percent. Since it was thought that only 1600 of the total applications would come from eligible families, the net response rate would have been 24 percent, a fairly modest figure and one that was congruent with other social programs operating in the state.

Only after data from the Census Fourth Count Population and the Public Use Sample became available in 1974 was it possible for the evaluation contractor to calculate the eligible families at a more accurate and modest 2673 households. Assuming this figure is correct, the 665 applications the North Dakota agency received, with 569 of them from eligible households, means that the gross response rate was 25 percent, and the net response rate, 21 percent. The 499 enrollees thus represent 19 percent of the total eligible households in the North Dakota program area. This is the second highest percentage in the experiment.[2] This all seems to suggest that low-key outreach can be an effective way of inducing families to apply for, and enroll in, a program of this type. However, it is questionable whether grass-roots advertising would have produced too many more applicants. The North Dakota agency spent no money on radio or television spots. Nevertheless, they were still forced to take out paid advertisements in the local papers at the end of the enrollment period, an admission that more powerful techniques were required.

The small number of eligible families in the area makes the director's fears of over-subscription by the local populace seem too cautious. This is with the benefit of hindsight. It is likely that, had the planners had access to more accurate statistics, outreach would have been approached less timidly and with more imagination. This would have provided good experience for the younger staff, many of whom could be expected to be running social programs in the future.

As it was, the North Dakota agency seemed to cut a fine line between coming up short and running an agency with wasteless efficiency. Most of the eligibles who applied were selected. Most who were selected became participants. There were few disappointed unchosen households.

Unknown to the staff, then, who thought the program advertising was recruiting only a small proportion of the eligible population, the outreach effort produced results. The "trouble," if there was any, lay in the fact that the number of program openings was almost too large for the area. Had the size of the experiment been much larger, it is doubtful that North Dakota could have achieved maximum participation without paying for a media outreach campaign.

Serving A Cross-Section of People

A central tenet of the AAE was that the experiment was not intended to be "just another poverty program" serving a welfare clientele. Housing allowances were designed for the elderly and the working poor as well. At all sites, it was crucial to attract people from all parts of the eligible population, since applicants became enrollees, and enrollees became recipients.

In North Dakota, recipients were demographically identical to the program applicants. That is, no group seemed to be disadvantaged in attaining payment status.[3] The other sites usually had minority populations who tended to terminate before receiving payments to a much greater degree than did whites. Assuming that the North Dakota outreach attracted a representative sample of people, it can be said that the agency ran an equitable program. Table 9-2 examines the characteristics of the eligible applicants to see if this is true.

The most serious shortcoming of the North Dakota AAE seems to be that it did a mediocre job of recruiting the working poor. This sector of the population was under-represented at all sites. Only Tulsa, which directed a media campaign toward the white, lower-middle class, seems to have had adequate non-welfare, non-elderly applicants. At the North Dakota site, the disparity between the proportion of working poor in the eligible population and their proportion in the applicant pool is thirty percentage points, which ranks the site fifth in this regard.

The reasons for this disparity are many. Certainly, the work ethic had something to do with the low response. While hourly wages are low in the state, so is participation in assistance programs for which the employed are eligible. In fiscal 1973, the national average for food stamps participation was 39 percent of those who were eligible for the program. In North Dakota, the participation rate was 23 percent, the fourth lowest in the nation after Wyoming, Nevada, and Kansas.[4] These states have two distinguishing characteristics: they are rural, and the work ethic predominates.[5]

Low application rates may also be due to inadequate outreach. The few efforts that were aimed at lower-paid workers, such as those at hospitals and nursing homes, seemed to produce little response, however. It remains an open question whether additional attempts to reach workers would have represented a wise use of limited staff time and resources.

The elderly, though also under-represented at the North Dakota site, were less so when compared to the AAE as a whole. This is in spite of the fact that North Dakota made only one attempt to reach senior citizens. In the middle of the enrollment period, the assistant director addressed the Mandan Golden Age Club. Although fifty people attended, no applications resulted from this effort. The individual who had invited the assistant director to speak before the group felt that he had come at

Table 9-2

COMPARISON OF THE DEMOGRAPHIC CHARACTERISTICS OF THE ELIGIBLE AND APPLICANT POPULATIONS AT EACH AGENCY

	SALEM				SPRINGFIELD				PEORIA				SAN BERNARDINO			
	A	B			A	B			A	B			A	B		
Percentage who are:	Eligible Population 6,993	Eligible Applicants 2,432[a]	A − B	Rank	Eligible Population 21,054	Eligible Applicants 2,333[a]	A − B	Rank	Eligible Population 6,049	Eligible Applicants 2,063[a]	A − B	Rank	Eligible Population 22,369	Eligible Applicants 1,921[a]	A − B	Rank
Elderly	26%	11%	15*	3rd	41%	10%	31	8th	32%	16%	16	4th	28%	11%	17	6th
Working Poor	61	46	15	2nd	41	24	17	3rd	56	35	21	4th	54	21	33	6th
Welfare	13	43	−30	2nd	18	66	−48	6th	11	49	−38	5th	19	68	−49	4th
Male	42	46	4	1st	41	32	9	3rd	42	32	10	4th	46	31	15	6th
Female	58	54			59	68			58	68			54	69		
Non-Minority	96	91	5	2nd	89	63	26	6th	77	72	5	3rd	78	49	29	8th
Minority	4	9			11	37			23	28			22	51		
Income																
$0-1999	44	31	13	4th	33	7	26	8th	34	20	14	5th	30	7	23	7th
$2-3999	35	42	−7	6th	41	54	−13	7th	40	44	−4	3rd	44	59	−15	8th
$4-5999	17	21	−4	3rd	20	26	−6	5th	15	22	−7	6th	24	25	−1	1st
$6,000+	5	6	−1	2nd	7	13	−6	7th	10	13	−3	5th	2	9	−7	8th
Number of Applicants Reporting No Income		11				45				7				29		

Source: AAE Application Forms, Census Public Use and Census Second Count.

[a] Applicants reporting no income are excluded from the elderly/working poor/welfare and income distribution

* positive sign = under-application, negative sign = over-application.

Table 9-2 (continued)

	BISMARCK				JACKSONVILLE				DURHAM				TULSA			
	A Eligible Population 2,673	B Eligible Applicants 569[a]	A - B	Rank	A Eligible Population 21,177	B Eligible Applicants 1,694[a]	A - B	Rank	A Eligible Population 6,764	B Eligible Applicants 1,230[a]	A - B	Rank	A Eligible Population 10,702	B Eligible Applicants 1,849[a]	A - B	Rank
Percentage who are:																
Elderly	26%	18%	8	2nd	22%	7%	23	7th	14%	14%	0	1st	29%	13%	16	5th
Working Poor	63	33	30	5th	68	29	39	7th	78	28	50	8th	54	48	6	1st
Welfare	11	49	-37	3rd	10	64	-54	8th	8	58	-50	7th	17	39	-22	8th
Male	48	43	5	2nd	42	21	21	8th	48	28	20	7th	43	33	10	5th
Female	52	57			58	79			52	72			57	67		
Non-Minority	98	98	0	1st	61	33	28	7th	47	31	16	5th	72	63	9	4th
Minority	2	2			39	67			53	69			28	37		
Income																
$0-1999	26	18	8	3rd	37	42	-5	1st	32	37	-5	2nd	49	27	22	6th
$2-3999	44	45	-1	1st	34	31	3	2nd	36	31	5	4th	40	45	-5	5th
$4-5999	20	27	-7	7th	27	22	5	4th	25	23	2	2nd	11	25	-14	8th
$6,000+	10	10	0	1st	1	5	-4	6th	6	8	-2	3rd	1	3	-2	4th
Number of Applicants Reporting No. income		6				13				11				6		

Source: AAE Application Forms, Census Public Use and Census Second Count.

[a] Applicants reporting no income are excluded from the elderly/working poor/welfare and income distribution

* positive sign = under-application, negative sign = over-application.

the end of an already long meeting.

The comparatively brisk response of the elderly, as opposed to the working poor, is perhaps a result of the lack of stigma which accrues to senior citizens who receive assistance in North Dakota. The elderly are the "deserving poor." Government assistance, whether in the form of a housing allowance or in a special grant from the welfare office, is more likely to be viewed as something which is due them, rather than as a hand-out. The elderly are not expected to work, and hence are not constrained by the work ethic. Their response to the program therefore lies between that of the low-paid worker and that of the welfare recipient, the latter being used to take assistance from public agencies.

The North Dakota agency seems to have done a good job of attracting male-headed households to the program. The Salem agency shows a similar outcome. This is probably due to the fact that both of these sites had low numbers of welfare recipients in their application pool. Females are far more likely to be AFDC recipients than are males. Thus, oversubscription by public assistance beneficiaries is likely to skew the sex ratio in favor of females. One can see this pattern emerge in the two southern sites, Jacksonville and Durham. The pattern at these agencies is over-application by blacks, females, welfare recipients, and those whose incomes are in the lower income categories-- at about the level of an AFDC grant. As is common knowledge by now, minority families are more likely to be poor, female-headed, and receiving assistance than are majority families.[6]

The lack of minorities at the North Dakota site also made it easy for the agency to achieve balanced racial demographics. Here, the site ranks first, but the statistic is relatively meaningless. As the text of this book points out, the director's outreach attempts for Amerindians were ineffectual. If it is true that this group is under-enumerated in the census, then the representativeness of the race profile is probably overstated.

Finally, North Dakota seems to have been able to reach higher-income households fairly well. Indeed, this family type is somewhat oversubscribed. This suggests that the attempt to get higher-income people into the program by advertising the gross, rather than the net, income limits achieved its stated purpose. Having this type of household among the recipients also had a salutary effect upon the financial aspects of the program, which is the next topic of discussion.

Financial Feasibility

A program becomes financially feasible when it has a positive cumulative funding balance. That is, the initial start-up deficit must be eliminated and the program must continue to run in such a way that total agency expenditures are less than the money it "earns" from the funding agency. In Section 23 programs, it is expected that the break-even point will be reached no later than eighteen months after the beginning of a new program.

In the AAE, financial feasibility could be achieved when an agency did three things. First, it had to control its administrative expenditures. This the North Dakota agency did with its austere approach to program administration. Second, it had to control the size of the average housing allowance payment. This was also accomplished by the North Dakota agency. Last, it had to control the distribution of family sizes so that the full amount of the ACC money would be earned.

Table 9-3 below shows the average housing allowance at each of the agencies. North Dakota shows the second lowest average payment, $72 per month or $5 below their planned level. This means that for a program serving 400 households, a monthly surplus of $2000 could be achieved, if all other expenditures were held constant. This totals $24,000 per year--a potential, but never-realized figure, since the agency did not operate at full capacity for the life of the program. Of the seven remaining sites, only Salem, San Bernardino, and Tulsa had payment levels below their planned ones. These were also the same sites that reached the break-even point the soonest.

Table 9-4 shows the initial operating deficits incurred by each AAE agency, and the quarter in which a positive funding balance occurred for the first time. Two of the sites, Springfield and Jacksonville, did not achieve financial feasibility. A large staff, which was needed for an ambitious counseling program, seems to be one of the primary reasons for Springfield's continuing shortfall of money. In the case of Jacksonville, the reasons lie in the high dropout rates among enrollees.

From a balance sheet point of view, the AAE was a mixed success. While the six remaining agencies became feasible, only four did so within

Table 9-3

MEAN INITIAL PAYMENT TO RECIPIENTS
(IN MEAN DOLLARS PER MONTH)

	Mean Payment	Standard Deviation	Number of Recipients	Missing Cases
TOTAL	81	35	5755	1
Site				
Salem	82	40	948	
Springfield	89	33	851	
Peoria	85	36	934	
San Bernardino	82	33	822	
Bismarck	72	30	430	
Jacksonville	91	36	339	
Durham	74	26	516	
Tulsa	71	33	915	

Source: AAE Payment Initiation Forms
Data Base: Recipients (N = 5,756)

Table 9-4

ACHIEVING FINANCIAL FEASIBILITY

Agency	Initial Deficit	Program Quarter in Which a Positive Cumulative Balance is Achieved
Salem	$ 91,476	Fifth
Springfield	179,086	----*
Peoria	94,661	Ninth
San Bernardino	121,867	Sixth
Bismarck	23,844	Third
Jacksonville	-------	----**
Durham	75,533	Eighth
Tulsa	158,098	Sixth

*Springfield will never eliminate its initial deficit
**Jacksonville, because of its small numbers of beneficiaries, continued to be in deficit throughout its operation.

Source: Agency Financial Reporting Forms

the recommended eighteen month period. These agencies were North Dakota, Salem, Tulsa, and Springfield. Two of them, Salem and Tulsa, were housing authorities which had a history of living within their budgets. Both North Dakota and San Bernardino had directors who were also concerned with fiscal responsibility. In the case of North Dakota, the small initial deficit was instrumental in bringing the agency to feasibility more quickly than at any other site.

Due to the complicated nature of the ACC funding mechanism, an examination of how North Dakota secured all of its promised money is instructive. As explained earlier in the text, funding was tied to the distribution of household sizes of the families participating in the AAE. Each agency was required to project this distribution in their planning documents. Table 9-5 shows the intended distribution at the North Dakota site:

Table 9-5

PLANNED DISTRIBUTION OF HOUSEHOLDS--NORTH DAKOTA

Size (persons)	Number	Annual Contributions Per Unit ($)	Total Earnings Per Year ($)
1	102	1145	$116,790
2	81	1374	111,294
3-4	145	1690	245,050
5-6	27	2030	54,810
7-8	30	2445	73,350
9+	15	2711	40,665
			$641,959

Source: Agency ACC Contracts

As the program history outlines, this exact distribution was impossible for the agency to achieve. Fewer single-person households applied than expected, as did extremely large families. By substituting a different distribution of household sizes, the director was able to generate 96 percent of the projected ACC earnings with the allotted 400 households: Table 9-6 below shows how the North Dakota agency achieved its level of funding.

It was at this sort of financial management that the North Dakota agency director seemed to excel. In his words, "Money is the only thing that gets programs into trouble."

Table 9-6

ACTUAL DISTRIBUTION OF HOUSEHOLDS--NORTH DAKOTA

Size (persons)	Number	Annual Contributions Per Unit ($)	Total Earnings Per Year ($)
1	95	1145	$108,775
2	119	1374	163,506
3-4	122	1690	206,180
5-6	40	2030	81,200
7-8	18	2445	44,010
9+	6	2711	16,266
			$619,937

Source: ACC Contract, Agency Reports

Improving Housing Quality

Since the AAE allowed participants to select their own housing on the free market, a reasonable test of program effectiveness would be whether or not the living situation of those on the program improved. Improvement in one's housing situation could occur in one of two ways. An enrollee could secure a better unit, or he could stay in his original dwelling and thereby pay less out of his own pocket for shelter.

At the North Dakota site, most of the enrollees planned to stay in their original unit, and did so. According to the enrollment forms, 25 percent of the 499 enrollees told the housing counselor that they wanted to move, while 61 percent expressed a desire to stay. Fourteen percent were undecided. The total for all the enrollees in the experiment was 52 percent, 39 percent, and 9 percent respectively.[7] Initially, at least, the North Dakotans planned to use their housing allowances as extra family income.

As Table 9-7 indicates, most of the North Dakota recipients did as they intended:

Table 9-7

PERCENTAGE OF MOVERS AND NON-MOVERS BY SITE

Site	Moved	Stayed with Rehabilitation	Stayed without Rehabilitation	Number of Responses
Salem	58%	2%	45%	947
Springfield	45	17	38	852
Peoria	40	4	56	934
San Bernardino	46	18	35	822
Bismarck	24	6	70	429
Jacksonville	61	21	18	338
Durham	47	9	45	517
Tulsa	44	21	35	913
AGGREGATE	45%	12%	43%	5752

Source: AAE Payment Initiation Forms

It was not until the second year of the experiment that moving approached a rate comparable to the rest of the AAE sites. Approximately 20 percent of the North Dakota recipients moved within one year of the receipt of their first payment. This is slightly higher than the mean of 17 percent for the AAE as a whole.

One reason for the initial lack of moving behavior at the North Dakota site may be because the enrollment period fell mostly in the winter, a time when few people change residences. However, an interviewed sample of North Dakota enrollees expressed much higher levels of satisfaction with their original units than was true at any other site. Of those contacted, 51 percent at the site were "very satisfied" with their units, as opposed to an average of only 36 percent for the AAE as a whole. At the opposite side of the satisfaction scale, only 10 percent were "very dissatisfied" with their original dwelling, while 23 percent of the respondents for the entire AAE had similar negative feelings about their housing.[8]

Change in living situation for North Dakota recipients came in the form of reduced rent burden. Table 9-8 shows that, at enrollment, the typical AAE household was paying over 40 percent of its income for rent, almost twice the advisable maximum.

The pre-payment rent burden of recipients across sites is nearly uniform, although it is true that those at the North Dakota site were below the mean. However, because of the low percentage of movers at this site, the post-payment rent burden falls dramatically. In fact, North Dakota is one of only two places where recipients are paying less than the recommended 25 percent of household income for rent at the time of payment initiation. Table 9-9 illustrates this decrease.

Physical quality of housing has proven to be difficult to measure.[9] Deciding what a reasonable standard would be is open to conflicting interpretations. If one requires only basic structural soundness, hot running water, a full bath, and a kitchen with a stove and a refrigerator, then the housing of most of the North Dakota enrollees was already standard before they applied for the program. A sample of 141 enrollees at the site showed that fully 80 percent were already living in units that met or exceeded this minimal quality measure. This is the second highest percentage in the AAE.[10]

If one employs a stricter standard which specifies such things as minimal ceiling height, windows that equal 10 percent of the floor area for each room, and cosmetically smooth walls and ceilings, only 17 percent of the enrollees' units in the North Dakota sample could pass this measure, the lowest percentage in the AAE. The remaining enrollees--61 percent of the sample--were thus living in units that could be best described as "modest."

Similar random samples of enrollees were drawn at the other sites and the units were inspected by the evaluation contractor. At most other sites, enrollees were less likely to be in modest quality units. Instead, a bifurcated pattern was more common. In Jacksonville, for example, 59 percent of a sample of 151 enrollees were living in unsound or unsafe dwellings. Twenty-five percent lived in high quality units, while a mere 17 percent were found to occupy modest quality apartments and homes at the time of their enrollment. Unlike any other

Table 9-8

RENT BURDENS AT ENROLLMENT FOR ALL RECIPIENTS

	Percentages of Recipients Within Rent Burden Ranges										Missing
	.00-.10	.11-.20	.21-.30	.31-.40	.41-.50	.51-.60	.61-.70	.71-.80	.81 & Over	Median	N	Cases[a]
TOTAL	0%	8%	20%	20%	18%	13%	8%	5%	7%	.42	5373	383
Site												383
Salem	0	5	20	22	19	12	7	6	8	.42	878	
Springfield	0	6	22	19	16	17	10	5	5	.42	821	
Peoria	0	13	19	16	16	14	9	4	7	.41	880	
San Bernardino	0	8	20	20	22	14	6	4	5	.41	784	
Bismarck	0	10	24	21	15	10	9	5	6	.38	413	
Jacksonville	2	6	18	17	16	10	8	7	17	.45	303	
Durham	1	7	17	15	15	15	11	8	10	.47	461	
Tulsa	0	4	20	24	22	13	6	4	6	.41	833	

Source: AAE Application, Enrollment, Certification and Payment Initiation Forms

Data Base: Recipients (N = 5,756)

[a] Households reporting zero cash rent or zero gross income have been excluded.

Table 9-9

RENT BURDENS AT PAYMENT INITIATION FOR ALL RECIPIENTS

	Percentages of Recipients Within Rent Burden Ranges									Median	N	Missing Cases[a]
	.00-.10	.11-.20	.21-.30	.31-.40	.41-.50	.51-.60	.61-.70	.71-.80	.81 & Over			
TOTAL	12	19	27	19	11	6	3	1	3	.28	5714	42
Site												42
Salem	8	15	30	25	12	5	3	1	1	.30	943	
Springfield	9	16	28	21	12	8	3	2	1	.29	844	
Peoria	24	23	23	13	8	4	2	1	2	.22	930	
San Bernardino	9	18	30	24	11	4	2	1	1	.28	818	
Bismarck	20	25	28	12	9	3	1	1	0	.22	429	
Jacksonville	7	9	12	12	14	9	8	5	24	.47	332	
Durham	10	20	23	19	14	7	3	2	2	.29	514	
Tulsa	7	20	31	21	10	6	2	2	2	.28	904	

Source: AAE Application and Payment Initiation Forms

Data Base: Recipients (N = 5,756)

[a] Households reporting zero gross income have been excluded.

302

agency, the largest single group--40 percent--at the North Dakota site had "pre-program" residences that met the following modest measures in addition to basic soundness:

1. A window present in the living room. Ventilation in the bathroom and kitchen.

2. At least one outlet and wall switch in the living room and kitchen.

3. Adequate exits--at least two for each unit if it is in a multi-family building.

The most frequent cause for a failure to meet an even more stringent quality measure was that window areas in most enrollee homes did not equal the required 10 percent of the floor space. This is an indication that low-income housing in the North Dakota program area was sound, but probably built before 1945.

The high degree of enrollee satisfaction with their initial units, when coupled with the modest surrounding the North Dakotans enjoyed, probably accounts for the large percentage of stayers at the site. Further, if the pre-program units are indicative of the quality of the stock available to people in low- and middle-income categories, one would expect that movers would upgrade their housing only slightly in comparison to stayers.

Assuming there is a relationship between the price of housing and its physical soundness, there is evidence which suggests that the improvement in housing was minimal for North Dakota recipients. Table 9-10 shows the gross rent paid by movers at the time of enrollment as compared with the rent paid at the time they received their first checks, which was after they had found a new place to live.

The eleven dollar rent increase at the North Dakota site is the smallest change in gross rent of any AAE site. It is less than half of the mean rent increase for recipients in the experiment taken as a whole. The use of rent as a proxy for physical quality avoids philosophical discussion of what quality *is*; rather, this measure postulates that quality is something which can be purchased. Rent increases, especially large ones, are thus indicative of increased housing consumption. There is no evidence of such activity at the North Dakota site.

Table 9-10

GROSS RENT AT ENROLLMENT AND FIRST PAYMENT FOR RECIPIENTS
(IN DOLLARS PER MONTH)

	Gross Rent At Enrollment			Gross Rent At Payment Initiation		
	Mean	N	Missing Cases	Mean	N	Missing Cases
TOTAL	$121	5402	354[a]	$147	5755	1
Site						
Salem	122	881		149	947	
Springfield	137	827		164	851	
Peoria	115	881		138	935	
San Bernardino	126	788		151	822	
Bismarck	118	414		129	430	
Jacksonville	112	308		167	339	
Durham	110	462		136	516	
Tulsa	119	841		141	915	

Source: AAE Enrollment and Payment Initiation Forms

Data Base: Recipients (N = 5,756)

[a] Enrollees reported to be homeowner or to be occupying unit without cash rent are excluded from the analysis.

The Plains Just Before a Winter Storm

Dignity

    Those who live in public housing projects are often referred to as "stigmatized." Public assistance, in most instances, has a negative referrent attached to it. Having the poor housed in set-aside areas, living in architecturally distinct apartments or townhouses, assures that this sector of the population will be visible. In the history of public welfare, forced visibility was--and perhaps still is--used to induce a sense of shame. It was felt that this could be used to discourage people from applying for public assistance and to "encourage recipients to get off welfare."[11]

    Housing projects, while engendering negative self-images, have an attendant bureaucratic advantage to them. It is easier to administer a housing program if those receiving the assistance are living in a concentrated area. Maintenance may be performed more efficiently and social services can be given at less cost. A trade-off is involved. In governmental programs, however, cost-efficiency arguments often win out those which center around pride.

The AAE, as an alternative to housing projects, did not deny that there is stigma associated with public aid. Rather, it sought to reduce this by making the recipients less visible. Had there been no lease requirement, it is conceivable that program participants could have rented housing without their landlords knowing where part of the rent came from. The AAE approached the ideal of having a poor person "pass" as an ordinary individual, in Erving Goffman's terms, a "normal."[12]

Similarly, the agencies themselves tried to respect the privacy of the participants as much as possible. While disclosure of income, assets, and family consumption was a requirement, those participating in the AAE were not asked to give personal information about themselves, their relatives, or their friends. The sites which used self-certification of income and assets were also those that especially stressed the need for maintaining recipient independence and dignity.

There are no direct measures of whether the housing allowance concept fostered the desired feelings of dignity and self-worth. In their stead, participant and terminee attitudes about the program and the agencies can be examined. Each agency had approximately 150 randomly-selected enrollees who were interviewed by the evaluation contractor. Allowing the normal attrition, this meant that the First Participant Survey (FPS) was administered to 1199 enrollees during the week following their enrollment. Six months later, those households who became recipients, a total of 878, were given the Second Participant Survey (SPS). Finally, sixteen months after their enrollment in the program, those families still receiving benefits were given the Third Participant Survey (TPS). A Former Participant Survey was also administered to a total of 161 program drop-outs. This was in two forms. If a family terminated before receiving a payment, they were classified as enrollee terminees (ETs). If a family dropped out after receiving program benefits, they were classified as recipient terminees (RTs).

The following questions were asked of households which indicated that they had visited the office of their housing allowance agency. Responses are given in percentage of total answers falling in each category. The data is presented in the aggregate, because site differences are not statistically significant in most cases:

Q.1. How do you feel about your visits to the agency? Do you...

	FPS	SPS	ET	RT	TPS
Like to go	30%	30%	32%	26%	19%
Don't mind going	67	68	65	69	78
Don't like to go	2	3	3	5	3
No opinion	1	0	0	0	0

Q.2. How interested in your housing problems do the people at the agency seem? Are they...

	FPS	SPS	ET	RT	TPS
Very interested	92%	95%	83%	83%	91%
Somewhat interested	8	5	15	9	8
Not interested at all	0	0	2	2	1

Q.3. How often do they try to help you with these problems?

	FPS	SPS	ET	RT	TPS
All the time	89%	90%	67%	80%	87%
Most of the time	10	9	21	10	8
About half the time	1	1	3	2	0
Seldom	0	0	5	4	0
Never	0	0	4	4	4

Q.4. In general, how satisfied are you with the help the agency gives you? Would you say you are...

	FPS	SPS	ET	RT	TPS
Very satisfied	(not asked)	92%	(not asked)	(not asked)	92%
Somewhat satisfied		6			7
Neither satisfied nor dissatisfied		1			1
Somewhat dissatisfied		1			1
Very dissatisfied		0			0

Q.5. How would you describe the kind of people you talked to at the agency? Do you feel they were...

	FPS	SPS	ET	RT	TPS
Concerned about you	98%	98%	97%	96%	97%
or					
Indifferent to you	2	2	3	4	3
Helpful or	99%	99%	95%	96%	97%
Not helpful	1	1	5	4	3
Friendly or	100%	100%	100%	100%	99%
Unfriendly	0	0	0	0	1
Polite and courteous	(not asked)	100%	(not asked)	(not asked)	100%
Not polite and courteous		0			0

Q.6. Once you get to see someone at the agency, do you feel that they spend as much time with you talking about the allowance program or your housing problems as you need?

	FPS	SPS	ET	RT	TPS
Yes	93%	94%	88%	98%	97%
No	6	6	10	2	3
Don't Know	1	0	2	0	0

The following four questions were asked of the FPS and SPS samples only:

Q.7. How do you feel about the amount of checking up the agency does on participants in this program: Do you feel it is...

	FPS	SPS
Too much checking	1%	1%
About right	97	90
Not enough checking	1	3
Agency does not check	1	6

Respondents who reported having contacted the agency on the telephone were asked:

Q.8. How often have your questions been satisfactorily answered over the phone? Would you say...

	FPS	SPS
All the time	91%	90%
Most of the time	7	8
About half the time	1	1
Seldom	1	0
Never	1	1

Q.9. In general, do you think that the agency gives people about as much help as they need, not enough help, or too much help?

	FPS	SPS
Too much help	2%	1%
As much help as they need	94	94
Not enough help	3	5

Q.10. Do you think that everyone gets the same amount of help? [FPS respondents were asked whether everyone got the amount of help they indicated as the norm in the preceding question.]

	FPS	SPS
Yes	77%	71%
No	3	8
Don't know/not sure	20	21

Q.11. The following question was asked of the SPS samples only: Do you or anyone in your household feel you have been discriminated against by the people at the agency because of your or anyone in your household's...responses-age, sex, marital status, race, nationality, source of income, children.

	SPS
No to all responses	99%
Yes to one or more	1

The following questions about the role of housing allowance payments and services in improving participants' housing conditions were asked of respondents in the indicated samples:

Q.12. Do you think that getting housing allowance payments has made it possible for you to live in better housing than you could if you were not receiving these payments?

	FPS	SPS
Yes	92%	92%
No	5	8
Don't Know	3	0

Q.13. In general, do you feel that the people who ran the counseling sessions were very interested, somewhat interested, or not interested at all in your housing problems?

	FPS	SPS
Very interested	(not asked)	94%
Somewhat interested		6
Not interested at all		0

Q.14. Compared with what you knew before, do you think you would be able to make a better choice of house or apartment because of what you learned in the counseling sessions?

	FPS	SPS
Yes	(not asked)	76%
No		17
Don't Know		7

Q.15. In general, do you feel that the agency was fair or unfair in the way it handled your termination from the program?

	ET	RT
Fair	85%	90%
No Opinion	9	1

	ET	RT
Unfair	6	9

Q.16. Would you ever apply again for a housing allowance?

	ET	RT
Yes	84	91
No	16	9

The response to Question 7, concerning the amount of checking done by the agencies, is especially significant in an examination of participant attitudes toward the AAE. Agency checking and "snooping," often thought necessary for the verification of applicants' statements regarding personal need, has long been a bone of contention among welfare reformers. There are those who say that the checking is necessary to prevent abuse and fraud. Others feel that "means testing" or certification requirements insure that assistance applicants come "not as rights-bearing citizens claiming benefits to which they are entitled, but as suppliants."[13] Piven and Cloward note that the loss of privacy is a defining characteristic of welfare programs:

> A central feature of the recipient's degradation is that she must surrender commonly accepted rights in exchange for aid. AFDC mothers, for example, are forced to answer questions about their sexual behavior...(forced to) open their closets to inspection...and (required to) permit their children to be interrogated.[14]

In the AAE, checking was confined to the enrollment session, the initial income certification, and to the required annual recertification. The questions asked did not deal with sex lives or living arrangements. Nor was there any policing of lifestyles as is often the case with project housing for the poor. It is perhaps for this reason that the recipients did not object to certification efforts made by the agencies, though these varied in stringency and intrusiveness from complete self-declaration to mandatory checking with employers and grant sources. The program regulations did not exclude cohabitating couples and this, too, probably was well received by the participants. In contrast, AFDC in many states has had "man-in-the house" rules which could jeopardize a woman's program eligibility.

Little research has been done on what type of questions or checking is annoying to assistance recipients. One study of AFDC recipients in six Wisconsin counties[15] indicates that 81 percent of the respondents were "not at all" or "only slightly" bothered by caseworker questions concerning financial resources, despite the fact that this was the type of question most frequently asked. Questions regarding the whereabouts of an absent husband bothered the respondents more often; however, in no case did the "unconcerned" group fall below 67 percent of the total. It would appear, then, that the apparently innocuous questions required to establish AAE eligibility were responsible for the uniform response to agency probing across sites.

For those who had never been on assistance, there was probably little in the participants' experience that would allow a comparison of the dignity of the AAE approach. For those who had received help before, at least at the North Dakota site, comparisons were easily and bluntly made:

A meeting with elderly participants in a conference room at the Holiday Inn: "...and in Williams County, if you apply for welfare, they make you feel about this tall," the woman says, holding her thumb and index finger close together.

The others agree that the agency's way was more dignified. "That's all we've got left," somebody adds, almost humorously.

Community Acceptance of the AAE

As with participant dignity, there is no direct measure of how the site communities felt about the new concept in housing. There are only the accounts of the site observers. At the North Dakota site, the director's strategy seemed to be to keep a low profile, to avoid letting too many people know about the program. While this was done to prevent overloading the administrative apparatus of the agency, it also had the effect of lessening the likelihood of adverse community reaction. Most landlords first heard about the program when one of their current tenants or a prospective tenant approached them with a lease agreement. The high enrollee success rate seems to indicate that the property owners, at least, were not against the program.

Things did not go quite as smoothly at all of the other sites. Enrollees reported that landlords frequently would refuse to sign a rental agreement with an assistance recipient. The Jacksonville agency director also reported that the major realtors' organization had refused to cooperate with the program. Similarly, the Durham agency, in its monthly reports to HUD, indicated that supplier resistance was a major factor in pre-payment terminations.

Table 9-11 gives the enrollee termination rate at each site, and the major reasons why these pre-payment drop-outs occurred:

Table 9-11
ENROLLEE TERMINATION RATES AND
REASONS FOR TERMINATION

	Percentage of Enrollees Terminating	Time Exceeded	Housing Ineligible or Substandard	Failed to Meet Other Requirements	Attrition or Voluntary Termination	N	Missing Cases
TOTAL	29	76	8	10	7	2335	4
Site							
Salem	14	33	27	27	13	159	
Springfield	30	65	13	12	10	357	
Peoria	35	86	4	6	4	508	
San Bernardino	18	49	17	26	9	181	
Bismarck	14	46	13	22	19	69	
Jacksonville	67	96	2	1	2	695	
Durham	29	88	2	5	5	215	
Tulsa	14	46	20	17	18	149	

Source: AAE Termination Forms
Data Base: Enrollees (N = 8,095), Prepayment Terminees (N = 2,339)

One may assume that those sites which experienced large numbers of drop-outs were those in which participants had difficulty meeting the program requirements. In particular, this analysis suggests that those who exceeded the ninety-day housing search period were either those who could not find an acceptable unit, or those who could but for whom the landlord refused to sign a lease.

Three of the sites which were troubled by prepayment termination, Springfield, Durham, and

Jacksonville, were also the one whose staffs reported a high incidence of landlord refusals. The fourth site, Peoria, made no note of such difficulties and it is likely that the reason for failure lay elsewhere. According to the site observer, the Peoria site had a low vacancy rate and the agency adopted a laissez-faire attitude regarding participants.

Relatively large numbers of families were enrolled, few services were offered to them, and the tight housing market pared down the ranks of the enrollees.

SELF-INSPECTION AND SELF-CERTIFICATION: THE VIEW OF THE NORTH DAKOTA AGENCY

One of the reasons the North Dakota director agreed to run a housing allowance experiment was that it would give him the opportunity to see if a program that stressed participant self-reliance was a viable approach for the administration of housing allowances. While he was confident that the management of an agency would prove to be no problem, the ability of the participants to inspect their own dwellings and to declare their own income accurately was less certain.

In 1974, the agency began a research effort that would test participant abilities on these two points. A sample of 100 households, almost one-third of the remaining participants, was drawn at random. These families were subject to a quality control review that involved verification of household income and agency inspection of program units.

The results of the quality control inspection satisfied the staff that participants were living in housing that met agency standards, regardless of how the quality might measure up to that of other AAE sites. In their final report, the agency wrote that in "only two instances were inadequacies found: (1) substandard housing quality, and (2) non-related household."[16] In the latter case, the participant moved out of a congregate living situation and found private living quarters. In the other instance, the household was unable to locate a suitable unit, and so was terminated from the program.

While the standardness rate in the agency sample seems high, it does nevertheless confirm the patterns that the evaluation contractor found with program enrollees: by and large, those who applied to the program were already living in "decent, safe, and sanitary" housing. The standardness rate also underscores another fact: a 98 percent acceptability rate indicates that the standard the agency adopted was a lenient one which was probably open to adjustment and special dispensations for certain types of participants, such as the elderly.

The workability of self-declaration of income and assets is less clear. According to agency operating forms, 394 recipients volunteered information of income changes during the first year of operations. There was no policing done by the agency, and the staff was heartened by the fact that resultant changes in payments were in both upward and downward directions. No incidents of fraud were uncovered, a fact which is consistent with most welfare programs, critics to the contrary.[17] However, quality control for certification found that there were thirty payment reductions. Only one of these was the result of a payment error. The rest were due to participant failure to report changes in income or family size. In addition, eight payment increases were ordered. These were due to failure to report a decrease in income in seven of the cases. The eighth case of underpayment was due to a failure to report increased medical expenses.

The quality control review found that when the annual self-certification had taken place shortly before the field review, no payment errors were found. This seemed to indicate that the participants were reporting their income, assets, and family composition honestly and accurately. The agency's final report concluded that the fault lay not with the recipients, but with the agency for not making the reporting requirements clear: "The number of payment adjustments resultant from the Quality Control review may indicate agency overexpectations of recipient reporting between certification periods."[18]

Whether the agency's optimistic view, albeit one confirmed by their quality control review, is accurate is something which needs further examination.

One tentative way of determining the effectiveness of certification is to look at the number of income changes that occurred between application and certification at each site. The reasoning here is that accurate and complete certification procedures will catch errors made by the applicant in declaring his or her household income. Table

9-12 shows the incidence of income change between these points in time. As can be seen, North Dakota ranks lowest, an indication--perhaps--of an inadequate certification system.

Table 9-12

INCIDENCE OF CHANGES IN INCOME DATA BY SITE

Site	Changes	No Changes	Total Certification
Tulsa	72%	28%	1,150
Durham	61	39	789
Salem	83	17	1,076
Peoria	57	43	1,440
San Bernardino	26	74	992
Jacksonville	50	50	1,132
Springfield	34	66	1,189
Bismarck	0	100	593
ALL SITES	51%	49%	8,361

Source: AAE Application and Certification Forms

Further examination of other AAE data allows one to rank the relative stringency of each agency's certification. The less stringent sites are those which allowed participants to declare their own financial status: North Dakota, Springfield, Jacksonville, and San Bernardino. The other four sites tended either to use third-party verification or certification on the basis of documents, such as pay stubs, brought in by the enrollee. The more strict agencies are those which depended on outside verification of some sort in a majority of the cases. Figure 9-1 ranks the agencies according to changes in income found by certification and according to the stringency of the methods employed:

	Income Changes	Certification Stringency	
More Changes ↑↓ Fewer Changes	1. Salem 2. Tulsa 3. Durham 4. Peoria 5. Jacksonville 6. Springfield 7. San Bernardino 8. North Dakota	1. Durham 2. Tulsa 3. Salem 4. Peoria 5. Jacksonville 6. San Bernardino 7. Springfield 8. North Dakota	Stringent Certification ↑↓ Lenient Certification

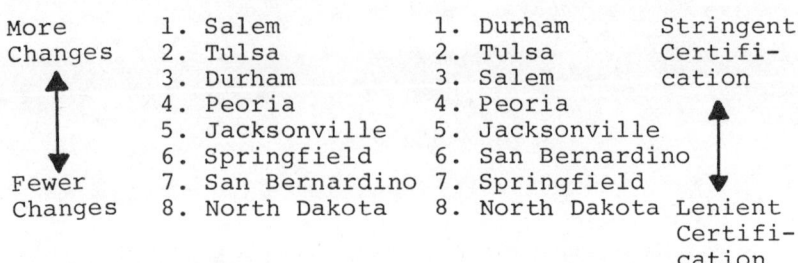

Figure 9-1: Rank Ordering of Sites by Income Changes and Certification Stringency

This would seem to indicate that self-declaration is an inaccurate method of determining income. Indeed, the association appears to be a strong one. Spearman's r_s can be used to illustrate the strength of this relationship. This statistic, used with ordinal data, may be defined by the following formula

$$r_s = 1 - \frac{6 \sum_{i=1}^{N} d_i^2}{N^3 - N}$$

where d_i = the difference between the rankings on each of 2 rank-ordered variables.

The above ranking yields a Spearman coefficient of .9, an extremely high one, which indicates a strong association between the two variables. This is not to imply that the relationship is a causal one, however.

Thoughtful analysis shows that the apparent relationship between certification stringency and income changes between application and certification does not tell the whole story. Checking with outside sources is more time-consuming than self-declaration. Hence, there is an increased likelihood that income changes will occur more frequently at agencies where lengthy investigatory efforts are carried out. Further, at least in the case of North Dakota, certification and application forms would be corrected, with the evaluation contractor's certification form and application forms being essentially copies of each other. These factors provide a partial explanation of the low incidence of income changes for self-declaration agencies, especially North Dakota.

A more detailed and powerful explanation of the relationship illustrated in Figure 9-1 lies in the elicitation of income information at the time of application. As several writers have pointed out, accurate income determination is dependent upon more than verification of applicant statements.[19] It is also important that full and detailed information of financial status be obtained from the person wishing to participate in a program. Most self-certification agencies used supplementary, detailed application forms which asked for income information from specific sources. In contrast, those agencies which used stringent certification methods tended to rely upon the evaluation contractor's form, which was designed for research purposes and asked for only the totals of earned, grant, and other income. The eight agencies thus varied in the amount of specific information that was asked each applicant.

Figure 9-2 ranks the agencies in regard to the number of specific income sources asked by auxiliary, agency-designed forms and also ranks the agencies according to incidence of income change between application and enrollment.

	Elaborateness of Application Forms	Number of Specific Income Sources Asked	Changes in Income	
Less elaborate ↑↓ More elaborate	1. Tulsa 2. Salem 3. Durham 4. Peoria 5. Springfield 6. San Bernardino 7. Jacksonville 8. North Dakota	0* 0 3 3 5 7 10 13	Salem Tulsa Durham Peoria Jacksonville Springfield San Bernardino North Dakota	More Changes ↑↓ Fewer Changes

Figure 9-2: Rank Ordering of Agencies by Elaborateness of Application Forms and by Income Changes

*0 income sources asked means that the agency used only the evaluation contractor's application forms

The Spearman coefficient for the above rankings is also high: .82, indicating that income changes are also very closely associated with application forms that ask only very general questions about income.[20] This analysis thus shows that there were two types of agencies in the AAE as far as income-certification is concerned. The first type uses rather unspecific elicitation techniques and then relies upon stringent certification to set income precisely. The second type, which includes North Dakota, places more responsibility upon the participant and uses elaborate application forms to obtain accurate income information in the first place. This corroborates the North Dakota agency's contention that participants were, by and large, honest and capable in their dealings with the program.

COMMENTARY: THE HOUSING ALLOWANCE APPROACH

Significant federal involvement in housing programs dates from the passage of the Housing Act of 1937. Originally, the legislation was aimed at the creation of low-income housing projects for blue collar or semi-skilled workers and their families.[21]

In the early 1940s, the focus shifted to servicemen and war workers. Then, due to accelerated housing production and the liberalization of mortgage interest rates, concern moved to the elderly and the poor, where it remains today.

Up until the last ten years, the strategy of federal housing policy was to increase the supply of standard units. However, it had become apparent that high-density housing projects did not provide a total solution for the problems of the poor. Indeed, large projects seemed to breed social problems of their own. Section 23, a program which allowed the government to lease existing stock from private landlords, marked a move away from a completely "supply-oriented" housing policy.[22] It was hoped that the poor could still be assisted by local housing authorities without a corresponding requirement that those receiving such help live in designated areas.

The housing allowance experiment continued the trend towards having some "demand-oriented" programs to augment the more traditional, "supply-oriented" approaches. Economic assistance was to provide the means by which the poor could move out of dilapidated houses and apartments in declining neighborhoods. Additionally, the inclusion of the working poor among the eligibles was an attempt to broaden the participation base in federally-sponsored rental programs.

The AAE delegated less responsibility to the administering agencies than was true in traditional Section 23 programs. Up until the beginning of the experiment, the usual pattern was for the LHAs to find and lease acceptable units. Then, the LHAs would "sublet" this housing to their own tenants. The AAE purposefully sought to eliminate contracts between the agency and the landlord. The subsidy would go with the participant rather than with the unit. An implicit ideology of participant independence overlaid and obscured this simple fact: the AAE agencies were not, strictly in the housing business. They were in the business of giving participants services and money.

Housing allowances meant that HUD was acting less as a housing agency and more as a welfare or income maintenance agency. This provided a link between housing policy and broader government programs designed to replace the existing welfare system with one designed around the idea of a guaranteed annual income. One unnamed, high-ranking HUD official acknowledged the shift toward conceptualizing the housing problems of the poor as being primarily economic:

> It seems clear that the lack of housing for low-income families is an income problem. When you solve the income problem, you solve a lot of interrelated problems. You give poor persons the option to seek out the cultural background and amenities that best fit the individual's needs.[23]

Letting the participant, rather than the agency, choose the program dwelling ran a risk that families would use the subsidies for things other than the improvement of housing quality. Even though a standardness requirement was imposed, there was less potential control over the condition of a suitable unit when the participants did most of the deciding. For those agencies which allowed self-inspection, the likelihood was even higher that the families would not use their payments directly for housing expenditures. This would be an acceptable outcome for HUD only if the housing difficulties of low·and moderate-income households were related more closely to rent burden than to low physical quality of the stock. If this was the case, then it could be said that low-income families had already ordered their priorities "correctly." The cash subsidy would make it possible for the poor to be penalized no longer for this judiciousness.

Prior to the beginning of the AAE, there had been some indications that housing allowances improved housing quality in a modest, but significant manner for those who were on this type of program. However, the allowances had little effect upon existing patterns of residential segregation, either individually or in the aggregate.

In late 1970, two Model Cities agencies--one in Kansas City, Missouri, and one in Wilmington, Delaware--administered direct cash assistance programs to a combined total of 360 households. Those in the Kansas City demonstration realized increased quality by a larger percentage of households living in single-family units than was true before the allowances had been received. In the Wilmington experiment, housing improvement was reflected mainly by a reduced incidence of over-crowding. Blacks tended to move out of core ghetto areas and into the fringes of them, following the so-called "black corridor."[24]

Neither program anticipated the income transfer effect of housing allowances in the AAE. Although the average subsidy was around $100, the program rules required that the pilot program recipients move before payments could be initiated. A crude estimate of the "non-housing" benefit of the early program was a low fifteen dollars per month for the typical household.[25]

The publicly available reports on the three experiments which comprise EHAP stress that the effect of the subsidy seems to be a reduction of rent burden first and improved housing quality second.[26]

Pending the development of a workable housing quality measure, it can be said that many recipients felt that they were already living in standard housing, but that the price they were paying for it was too high. Detailed cost analysis will eventually tell the story of whether it would have been easier and cheaper to give pure income supplements without a housing quality requirement attached to them. In particular, the amount of housing quality improvement realized by participants at agencies which had costly counseling components, as opposed to the sites which did not, may be a deciding factor.

If it is found that services and inspection requirements have little effect upon housing quality, it is reasonable to assume that pure income maintenance may supplant subsidies which are "earmarked" for housing.

Housing Allowances in North Dakota

In North Dakota, the low percentage of movers meant that the program there looked like a progressive welfare undertaking. The primary benefit was the increased spending money for participants. However, a minimal housing standard had been imposed, and agency services were available for those who requested or appeared to be in need of them. As this chapter has shown, most enrollees were paying too much of their income for housing. Most were satisfied with their neighborhoods and their units. Few intended to move, and still fewer actually did. Not until the second year of the program did the moving rates approach those of other sites. This is an indication, perhaps, that the North Dakotans were contented, but mobile. Hence, the receipt of the subsidy was not enough, in itself, to spur moving behavior.

Several factors combined to make the use of the payments as income supplements an especially likely possibility at the North Dakota site. First, the program regulations did not require people to move and the agency did not pressure them to do so. Second, the planners believed that most participants were already in modest housing. Accordingly, the quality standard was set at a reasonable level. Third, the individual household was the decider of what kind of unit met their needs. Minimal agency interference during housing search, when combined with self-inspection, insured that participants would operate independently. The decision most of them made was to stay where they were and enjoy the extras that the monthly check would buy.

Housing Allowances as Planned Social Change

The intended impact of housing allowances was very modest. The program promised no new technology, no change in the political structure, and little redistribution of wealth. HUD and the AAE agencies acted as change agents; however, the disruptive consequences of cash allowances, if any can be observed, are far less than when community developers try to impose a new technological system upon the client population. The anthropological literature is replete with studies of programs which succeeded, and programs which failed, in their ambitious missions.[27]

A program's status as being overly-ambitious, ill-suited for the client population, or having trouble in inducing the desired social change or end state seems to be situationally determined. Thus, it may be easy for the county agricultural extension agent to persuade local farmers to try a new strain of hybrid corn. In contrast, inducing peasant farmers in Mexico to adopt a similar innovation may be no mean feat.

At its best, the AAE was an unassuming bit of social welfare aimed at a subpopulation that was relatively similar to the "mainstream" or "donor" society. Except for certain groups, such as American Indians and, to a lesser extent, blacks, it is generally assumed that program beneficiaries are more like the members of the larger society than they are different. Indeed, the philosophy of the AAE, at least in North Dakota, held that the major difference is one of economics. The program aimed at the effects, rather than the causes, of unequal distribution of resources. The AAE, like most social programs, was thus conservative, palliative, and realistic. Comparatively speaking, social programs in the United States look like "milk runs," their many failures aside. This country already has an advanced technology. It is this that is exported to effect rapid social change elsewhere.

The AAE, like other social welfare programs, was not intended to bring profound structural changes "in the system." The concept of housing allowances was a modest bit of social technology that was part of a gradualist strategy to improve housing conditions for the poor within the existing framework of institutions. Each variation of the experiment represented an attempted, significant adaptation to local conditions. It is at this level that the future of a given program is often decided.

George Foster, in his <u>Traditional Cultures</u>, identified seven features which distinguish communities in the United States as compared with those in other parts of the world:

1. Communities have the power to tax themselves.
2. Administrative organizations...(have) the legal powers to take action under community control.

3. Populations are basically literate.
4. Leadership patterns are well developed.
5. Since the time of the frontier there has been a tradition of genuine cooperative work, and formal and informal social devices such as the town meeting and proliferating committees exist to implement this cooperation.
6. However depressed a particular small area, it is a part of a wealthy country which will, in times of need, funnel help from other areas.
7. Technical services in health, agriculture, education and the like are highly developed and available.[28]

The AAE was not a community development program. Yet, some of the seven features outlined above had an impact upon the conduct of the AAE, and upon the North Dakota project in particular. Of special importance at the North Dakota site was the literacy of the recipient population. The only way a large program area could be handled economically was to have applicants certify their own income and enrollees inspect their own units. The forms for this were detailed and complex. By shifting the burden of income declaration and the determination of housing quality away from the staff, the agency was able to function with fewer personnel than would have been otherwise necessary.

The existence of competent bureaucracies at each site meant that the AAE would not have to be "grafted to a foreign body."[29] For most agencies, the AAE was simply another assistance program, though a fairly attractive one. For the recipients, housing allowances were not so alien a concept that program acceptance would prove to be a problem. Even Jacksonville, the only site which failed to meet basic AAE goals, was still able to attract an impressive number of applicants to the program. In the United States, social programs are highly developed. Many individuals and families make use of them or know of their existence.

Since HUD gave the contracting agencies latitude in program design, each organization was free to continue with, or depart from, its institutional traditions. It is safe to say that all of the planners tried to make the AAE a palatable program. In the case of the North Dakota Experimental Housing Project, the director chose to continue in a liberal, welfare-reformist vein, while divorcing the new program from the parent agency.

In emphasizing participant independence, the North Dakota agency was able to seize upon the frontier tradition that still holds sway in the local area. However, instead of stressing the cooperative aspects of the frontier ethic, the focus was upon individualism. Certainly, tapping into the common value system of North Dakotans made it unlikely that the experiment would go awry. The housing eventually occupied by the participants met the agency's expectations. That most participants were able to meet the requirements on their own probably made being on assistance seem less demeaning.

HUD showed a certain amount of wisdom in allowing local people the opportunity to fashion their own approaches to housing allowances. One of the difficulties with planned social change is that the agents of change are often intrusive. They do not share the same values as the client population and this often leads to local resistance.[30] While the "typical" North Dakotan and the "typical" Washington bureaucrat may both be adherents to the "mainstream" culture, by no means are the differences inconsequential. A reading of the participant case histories shows the obvious fact that the dreams and life chances of the participants are different from those of government administrators in the nation's capital. Similarly, the account of the final negotiating session in Washington, D.C. shows that at least some North Dakota bureaucrats have a unique, optimistic view of human nature. This book has argued that the outlook of the recipients and the outlook of the agency staff were congruent.

In the case of North Dakota, independence was achieved at two levels. First, the program was locally controlled. HUD did not interfere. The approach taken by the North Dakota agency thus reflected the philosophy and ideals of the staff. Second, the staff members extended similar freedom to the households in the experiment. All were expected to act as independent but responsible people. Self-determination thus affected two groups of actors at the local site, the administrators and the recipients. As is by now common knowledge, control over one's destiny is conducive to social harmony and enhances a sense of self-worth.[31]

In retrospect, it seems that the key to the North Dakota operations was a set of shared expectations and adequate performance by those on both sides of the agency's desks. The agency's job was to explain the program and to give help only when needed. The participants' task was to meet the requirements and to ask for assistance if difficulties were encountered. While the AAE represented an individualistic and independent approach to subsidized housing, the North Dakota agency pushed this to the limits that the regulations allowed. By and large, the recipients responded by filling the void of lessened agency interference with their own initiative. For the North Dakota staff, this was the way that assistance programs could and should work. The authors of the Final Report said it best:

> The benefits of a direct cash assistance program to eligible households are many. Households enjoy a normal tenant-landlord relationship, uninterrupted by government intervention, households have freedom of mobility, and have the option of choosing a unit size which best fits their needs. Further benefits include allowing a household to make a free choice of neighborhood, price range, and unit size. The household enjoys budget flexibility since the housing allowance payment frees money for other needs. Most importantly, a direct cash payment for rent assures anonymity and preserves the pride and dignity of the individual.[32]

NOTES

1. North Dakota Experimental Housing Allowance Project, Detailed Plan (xerox, 1973), pp. 70-78.

2. See p. 17 of this book, Table 1-3, for the exact figures for each agency.

3. See North Dakota Experimental Housing Allowance Project, Final Report of the North Dakota Experimental Housing Allowance Project (xerox, 1976), pp. 11-14.

4. Abt Associates Inc., Participation in a Direct Cash Assistance Program (Draft working paper, 1974), p. 31.

5. See Donald A Messerschmidt and Marilyn C. Richen, "Federal-Local Relations in Educational Change," (unpublished paper submitted to Human Organization, 1976).

6. See Frances Fox Piven and Richard A. Cloward, *The Politics of Turmoil*, (Vintage Books, New York, 1975).

Also, according to the *Statistical Abstract of the United States* (1974), Table 631, a black family is four times more likely to be below the poverty level than is a similar white family.

7. Abt Associates Inc., *Third Annual Report of the Administrative Agency Experiment Evaluation* (Draft copy, 1976), p. 147.

8. Abt Associates Inc., *Second Annual Report of the Administrative Agency Experiment Evaluation* (Abt Associates Inc., Cambridge, 1974), Table 4-9.

9. Housing quality in the AAE is now the subject of an on-going multi-variate analysis for inclusion in a report on inspection and housing quality.

10. *Second Annual Report*, p. 67

11. Joel F. Handler and Ellen Jane Hollingsworth, *The Deserving Poor* (Markham Publishing Co., Chicago, 1971), p. 164.

12. Erving Goffman, *Stigma* (Prentice Hall, New Jersey, 1963).

13. Handler and Hollingsworth, *The Deserving Poor*, pp. 86-87.

14. Piven and Cloward, *Regulating the Poor*, p. 166

15. Handler and Hollingsworth, *The Deserving Poor*, Table 3.2.

16. North Dakota Experimental Housing Allowance Project, *Final Report*, p. 62.

17. For the New Jersey Income Maintenance Experiment, the incidence of deliberate misreporting was estimated at 3 to 4 percent per year. Source: David N. Kershaw and J. Fair, *Final Report on the New Jersey Graduated Work Incentive Experiment*, (Madison/Princeton, 1973), Vol. IV, p. 264.

18. North Dakota Experimental Housing Allowance Project, *Final Report*, p. 21.

19. See James P. Zais, C. Reid Melton, and Mark Berkaman, A Framework for the Analysis of Income Accounting Systems in EHAP (Urban Institute, Washington D.C., 1975). See also M.G. Trend, "Income Certification: The Importance of Different Administrative Configurations," (unpublished technical paper, forthcoming, 1976).

20. A regression analysis has not been used here since this would require a precise specification of what constitutes a separate, distinct income source and what does not.

21. For those interested in a comprehensive examination of federal housing policies, see: Henry Aaron, Shelter and Subsidies: Who Benefits from Federal Housing Policies? (Brookings Institute, Washington, D.C., 1972).

22. Section 23 also allows LHAs to construct new developments as well as rent existing units on the private market.

23. James G. Phillips, "HUD proposes cash allowance system as link to broad welfare reform," (National Journal Reports, August 25, 1973), p. 1255.

24. John D. Heinberg, Peggy W. Spohn, Grace M. Taher, Housing Allowances in Kansas City and Wilmington: An Appraisal (Urban Institute, Washington, D.C., 1975), p. 36.

25. Ibid, p. 33

26. U.S. Department of Housing and Urban Development, Housing Allowances: The 1976 Report to Congress (U.S. Government Printing Office, Washington, D.C., 1976), p. 29.

27. See, for example, Arthur H. Neihoff, ed., A Casebook of Social Change, (Aldine, Chicago, 1966).

28. George M. Foster, Traditional Cultures, (Harper and Row, New York, 1962), pp. 183-184.

29. Ibid, p. 183

30. See Ward H. Goodenough, Cooperation in Change, (John Wiley & Sons, New York, 1963) for a theoretical discussion of this.

31. See Alexander Leighton, The Governing of Men (Princeton, New Jersey, 1946), passim.

32. North Dakota Experimental Housing Allowance Project, Final Report, p. 63.

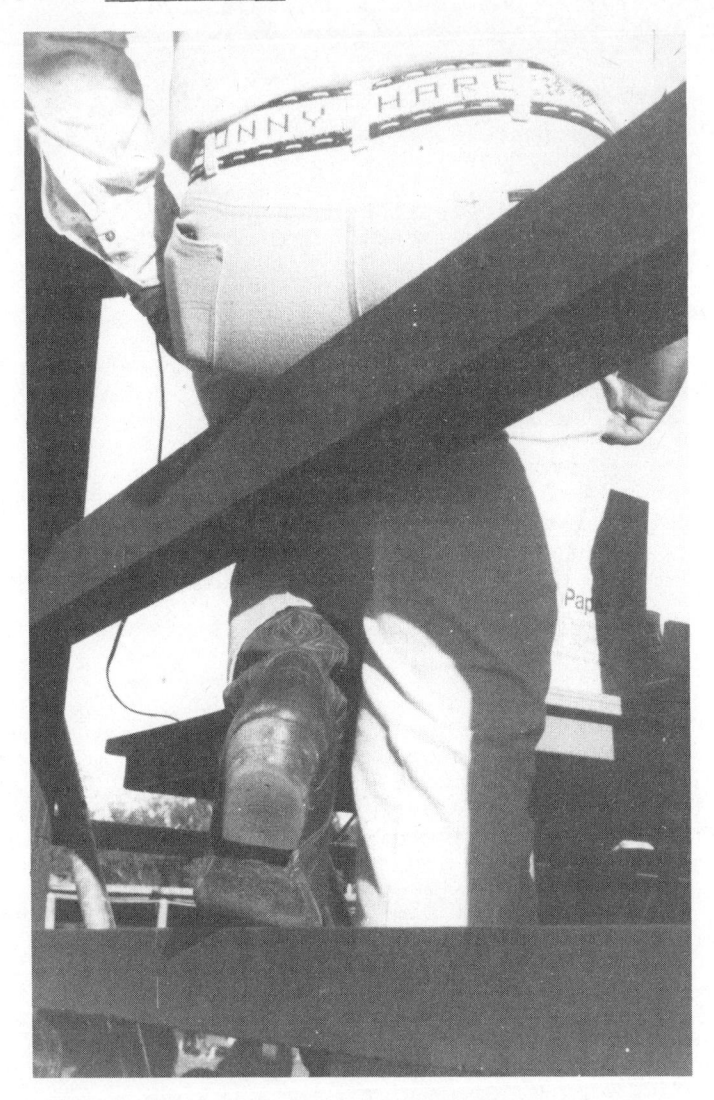

Pow-wow, United Tribes-1974

EPILOGUE

It is almost 11:00 p. m. when I land at the Bismarck airport for another field visit. The young woman at the AVIS counter fills out the forms. Before I left Massachusetts I made arrangements with the Flagship Service to have a compact car waiting for me when I arrived. It is beyond my comprehension how they can do that, across thousands of miles.

She smiles frequently. I look down at the desk and notice that the plastic tag on the key chain says Impala on it.

"I thought I ordered a small car."

"Oh, we don't have any. It's out Basic Rate."

"Ah, a Detroit Toyota," I joke. She smiles again and begins to copy the numbers off my North Dakota driver's license.

I sign the papers, and then she remembers: "There's a message from Bob Barr. He said there was no room at the Inn, and that you're supposed to stay at his house." Then, "You know where he lives, don't you?"

"Yes, I do," I told her.

Appendix A

Chronology of Key Events
Staff Background Information

CHRONOLOGY OF KEY EVENTS - NORTH DAKOTA SITE

Planning (March-June, 1973)

March 7	HUD representative contacts the Social Services Board of North Dakota to ascertain their interest in having an AAE within the State.
March 23	Social Services Board of North Dakota awarded a planning grant.
April	First three members of North Dakota agency are recruited. Work begins on Strategic Plan a few weeks later.
May 10	Review of Strategic Plan held in Washington, D. C. Joe Queenan, assistant GTR from HUD Region VIII assigned.
June 18-19	Review of Detailed Plan held in Washington, D. C. Document given tentative approval.
June 27	Final version of Detailed Plan submitted. ACC is signed.

Key Events During Start-Up Period (June 27-July 27, 1973)

July	Eligibility Control Technician, Clerk-Typist, and two Counselors are hired. Agency located in new Bismarck offices.
	Forms are devised and reviewed. Staff begins training over a two-week period. Outreach pamphlets are required.
July 10	First news release prepared for local papers.
	Outreach begins. Directors of County Welfare offices contacted in an effort to reduce welfare response.
	Satellite center offices rented in Jamestown and Dickinson.

July 10   Check-writing system set up.

                        Jamestown housing counselor hired.

                        Outreach volunteer assigned to
                        Stark County office.

                        Agency revised outreach strategy.
                        More personalized approach to be
                        used.

                        HUD sends EO training team to
                        North Dakota site.

Key Events During Enrollment Phase (August, 1973-
January, 1974

August   Minor payments crisis. Average
                        HAP is too high. Agency decides
                        to advertise gross rather than
                        net income limits for the project.

                        Outreach efforts increase. Radio
                        spots, TV appearances used. Ethnic
                        and union organization contacted.

                        Stark County housing counselor
                        hired and trained.

                        About 100 families enrolled as of
                        August 31. Twenty-four payments
                        made.

September   Agency exceeds sex profiles and
                        elects to concentrate wholly on
                        financial feasibility aspects of
                        profile maintenance.

                        EO workshop held in Chicago for
                        agency attorneys.

                        Bismarck housing counselor re-
                        signs and is not replaced.

                        Food stamps sales outreached.
                        Fliers distributed to apartment
                        buildings in four-county area.

                        HAP is now within limits of con-
                        tract.

October	Request for change is sex profile made to HUD.
	AAE conference held in Checotah, Oklahoma.
	Enrollments lagging in Stark County due to low volume of applications. A total of 214 households have been enrolled, mostly from Burleigh County.
November	Permission granted to exceed female-headed household quota.
	Agency informally granted permission to vary mix of household sizes as long as feasibility is maintained.
	Two westernmost counties have lagging applications. A total of 331 have been enrolled. Burleigh and Stutsman counties highly responsive.
	Assistant director takes over some counseling duties.
	Meeting with LHAs held. Morton County director given permission to make referrals.
	Head secretary and outreach volunteer resign as scheduled.
December	Paid ads taken out in Morton and Stark counties' daily newspapers.
	Outreach ceases.
	A total of 391 people have been enrolled, of which 31 have terminated. Payments are made to 291 families by end of year.
January, 1974	New enrollment session format is developed for last few provisional enrollees. New enrollment statement used.

January, 1974   HUD team makes on-site review.

                       A total of 499 eligible applicants,
                       including 46 "provisional enrollees,"
                       were enrolled in the program. Pay-
                       ments were made to 380 active re-
                       cipients in January.

                       Housing search.

The Transition to Steady-State (February-April, 1974)

February   Staff begins design work on Quality
                       Control and Annual Re-Determination
                       of Eligibility forms. Survey in-
                       struments designed.

                       Stark County housing counselor
                       resigns. Dickinson office serviced
                       weekly by a Bismarck housing coun-
                       selor.

                       First presentation made to Social
                       Services Board by agency staff and
                       assistant GTR.

March   Stutsman County housing counselor
                       resigns. Site office serviced by
                       assistant director on a weekly
                       basis.

April   Director considers the reorganiza-
                       tion of the main office.

                       Housing search period ends April
                       30 with the goal of 400 active
                       beneficiaries having been achieved.

Steady-State (May, 1974--)

May   Office is reorganized. Secretary
                       goes on half-time. Assistant
                       director now made director of
                       housing services. Agency staffing
                       level now six and one-half posi-
                       tions.

                       Satellite center offices serviced
                       once every other week.

May	New forms and documents critiqued.
	Agency informs those who have received security deposits that these advances are loans which are paid back by pro-rating the checks from the first twelve months.
	Case records from satellite centers now duplicated and centralized in main office files.
	Director and assistant GTR discuss alternative methods of handling Section 23 transfers.
June	GTR (formerly assistant GTR) begins work on a Section 23 transition plan.
	New agency forms nearing completion.
	Agency counselors assist GTR with an inspection tour of all Section 23 housing within the state in order to train them in inspections crucial to Quality Control.
June 24-25	HUD representatives meet with LHAs for preliminary discussion on Section 23 transfers.
July	Satellite centers closed. Counselor and director of housing services hold office hours every other week in the local ASSCs in Stutsman and Stark counties.
	Counseling staff continues Section 23 housing inspection tour.
	New draft of transition plan prepared by GTR.
July 24	Meeting with housing authorities to discuss transition plan.
July 26	On-site observer leaves site.
August	Forms and survey instruments completed by agency for QC and annual re-determination of eligibility.

August	Research design formulated by agency.
	Annual redetermination of eligibility begins.
September	Quality Control begins with counseling staff interviewing selected households, contact with grant sources and banks via letter.
October	Agency's analysis of data from QC begins with keypunching of cards.
November	Final approval of transition plan delayed.
	Special questionnaire printed by agency to test participant satisfaction with units.
December	Approval of transition plan given. Transfer of units to LHAs begins. Restrictions placed on LHAs to insure that financial feasibility of contract will not be endangered by too many high payment families.
January, 1975	Questionnaires mailed out to participants.
	HUD auditors visit site.
	Field visit by evaluation contractor.
	First checks issued to LHA families in vacated EHAP slots.
	Quality control continued.
February	Restrictions relaxed on LHAs as financial feasibility assured.
	Questionnaires returned by EHAP participants.
	Trend toward decreases in payments continues.

February	Director meets with Social Services Board to discuss possibility of them running a Section 8 program in state.
March	HUD auditors' report issued.
April	EHAP director meets with legislative research council to get approval for the Social Services Board to become a public housing agency.
	LHAs have ninety active cases.
May	Field visit by evaluation contractor.
	Quality control completed; analysis underway.
	GTR announces tentative resignation.
	New budgets prepared for final year of project operation.
	Meeting with LHAs to discuss phaseout of experiment and transfer of families who complete program to LHAs.
	End of case study coverage.

PERSONNEL CONNECTED WITH THE NORTH DAKOTA
EXPERIMENTAL HOUSING ALLOWANCE PROJECT

Name	Title	Background
MANAGERS		
Gottfried J. Kuhn	Director of Project Planning, Development and Administration	Most senior employe in the North Dakota welfare system. Co-author of the agency plan.
Robert (Bob) Barr	Assistant Director of Project Planning, Development and Administration (July, 1973-April, 1974). Thereafter, Director of Housing Services.	Member of the original planning team. Long-time employee of the North Dakota Department of Social Services.
Gregory (Greg) Simonson	Director of Research and Fiscal Management	Member of original planning team. M.S in economics. Limited experience in social programs.
HUD PERSONNEL		
Arnold Nelson	Government Technical Representaive (GTR) to April, 1974.	Based in HUD Region VIII headquarters in Denver, Colo.
Joe Queenan	Assistant to GTR to May, 1974. GTR thereafter.	Based in Denver, Colorado. Specialist in statistics.

Name	Title	Background
CLERICAL		
Jane Will	Assistant Director of Research and Fiscal Management from Sept. 1973 onward.	Bookkeeping experience in financial institutions.
Paula Ovre	Secretary (July–October 1973)	Member of original planning team. Wife of the retired former Executive Director or the North Dakota Social Services Board and close friend of G. Kuhn.
Elizabeth (Betty) Throndset	Eligibility Control Technician (July, 1973--).	Most senior Eligibility Control Technician in the welfare system.
Delores Hummel	Steno-Secretary (July, 1973--April, 1974) half-time thereafter.	Former secretary of G. Kuhn.
COUNSELORS		
Robert (Bob) Olsen	Housing Counselor (July, 1973--) Bismarck site office.	Former counselor with Vocational Rehabilitation.
Kris Sundberg	Housing Counselor (July-Sept., 1973) Bismarck site office	B.A. degree in Social Work, Briefly employed as a caseworker in Crookston, Minn.
Peggy Jo Mickels	Housing Counselor (August, 1973-February, 1974) Dickinson site office.	Recent graduate of the University of North Dakota.

Name	Title	Background
VOLUNTEER		
Joseph (Joe) Heiser	Outreach Volunteer (August-October, 1973)	Retired former director of Stark County Welfare Office. Long-standing colleague of G. Kuhn.

Appendix B

Selected Forms and Documents

EHAP

EXPERIMENTAL
HOUSING
ALLOWANCE
PROJECT

219 N. 7th Street
Room B-1
Bismarck, North Dakota
58501

Telephone 224-3420

Administered by
SOCIAL SERVICE BOARD OF NORTH DAKOTA

lowance Project decision that affects their participation in the project.

Applicants have the right to file an appeal (a specialized type of complaint) when they are dissatisfied with an Experimental Housing Allowance Project decision or action taken concerning their case. Appeals may be filed by letter or an appeal form which is available at the Experimental Housing Allowance Project office.

Enrollees Responsibilities: To report information accurately on the application and recertification forms.

To promptly inform the Experimental Housing Allowance Project of any changes in circumstances such as household size or income which would necessitate a change in the housing allowance payment.

The enrollee has the responsibility of using the housing allowance payment for the prompt payment of rent.

Experimental Nature of Project

The Experimental Housing Allowance Project (EHAP) is a research project designed to test the concept of channeling Federal assistance directly to people in need of housing. An administrative agency experiment in North Dakota is being funded by the Department of Housing and Urban Development to test the methods of delivering housing allowance payments to recipients in a non-metropolitan area.

The goals of the Experimental Housing Allowance Project are to achieve equal housing opportunity for participants, regardless of race, color, religion or national origin, and to provide supplemental income to participants, enabling them to enjoy the wide range of housing choices enjoyed by persons of similar income.

Approximately 400 households in the four-county area of Stark, Morton, Burleigh and Stutsman will receive housing allowance payments. The project is designed to assist renter households by subsidizing them the difference between 25% of their adjusted gross income and the cost of standard housing in the community.

Project Requirements

ELIGIBILITY FACTORS: In order to participate in the program, certain eligibility criteria must be met. They are:

Assets (defined as liquid assets and real property): Assets may not exceed $12,000 at time of application for elderly (age 62 or over) households, or for families with a disabled individual as head of the household. If the head of the household is under age 62, the asset limitation is $5,000.

Disqualifying Transfer: Any person who for a period of 2 years before or who, after making application, gives an assignment or conveys or makes a transfer of property for the purpose of rendering himself eligible for a housing allowance payment shall be ineligible.

Income Limits: Income for enrollment in the project is based on adjusted gross income. Income may be declared either through the use of 1972 income tax forms or by declaring current income received from all sources during the month. The upper income limits for each household size are as follows:

HOUSEHOLD SIZE	ADJUSTED GROSS INCOME LIMIT
1	$4,400
2	5,200
3 - 4	7,000
5 - 6	7,800
7 - 8	8,500
9 +	9,000

Public Housing: Households already receiving Federal housing subsidies are ineligible unless they terminate from the other program.

Housing Inspection: Prior to receiving a housing allowance payment, it shall be determined that the enrollee is residing in standard housing. If the dwelling is not up to standard, an enrollee may wish to negotiate with the landlord to get the dwelling rehabilitated. If this is not possible or if the enrollee decides to move, he or she has 60 days to locate standard housing.

Enrollees must complete an inspection report of the dwelling they reside in or plan to move to. The purpose of the inspection form is to determine if the dwelling meets minimum standards. Experimental Housing Allowance Project personnel will be available to counsel enrollees on housing inspection.

Lease Agreement: Lease agreements between the enrollee and the landlord are required before certification for payment can take place. The lease must include certain provisions required by the Experimental Housing Allowance Project. A model lease agreement may be obtained from the Experimental Housing Allowance Project office upon request.

Interviews: Potential enrollees must participate in three counseling sessions with Experimental Housing Allowance Project personnel. In addition, the experimental nature of the project requires that enrollees agree to participate in up to three interviews with an evaluation contractor whose responsibility it is to overview various aspects of the experiment.

Project Limitations - Durational Limit: Eligible enrollees may receive housing allowance payments for a maximum of 24 months.

Enrollee Rights: Enrollees have the right to fair and equal access to housing and the freedom to choose any dwelling they wish, provided it meets the requirements of standard housing.

Enrollees have the right to receive notice of any Experimental Housing Al-

345

EHAP
EXPERIMENTAL
HOUSING
ALLOWANCE
PROJECT

RENTER HOUSEHOLDS
APPLY NOW

If your gross household income is within the maximum shown in the following table, you may be eligible for a *monthly cash payment* to be applied toward the cost of *Rent and Utilities*. The amount of the payment will be the difference between 25% of your adjusted gross income and the cost of standard Housing and Utilities.

If you are enrolled in the Project, you will receive *24 monthly cash payments* through the Experimental Housing Allowance Project, after which you will be referred to the Local Housing Authority for continued housing assistance for 8 years -- making it a *10-year program!*

Maximum Income Limits for Eligibility by Household Size:

No. of Persons in Household	Maximum Gross Income Limits
1	$ 4,400
2	5,790
3 - 4	8,157
5 - 6	9,628
7 - 8	10,995
9 +	12,000

Asset Limits (defined as liquid assets and real property): Assets may not exceed $12,000 at time of application for elderly (age 62 or over) households, or for families with a disabled individual as head of the household. If the head of the household is under age 62, the asset limitation is $5,000.

FOR APPLICATION FORMS AND INFORMATION

Call Siri Ellisen, Housing Counselor.

Phone No. 225-5698

FOR OFFICE USE ONLY   NO. _____
                                      (Identification Number)

Return Completed Form To:

            Date of Request for Assistance   Date Application Returned
            _____   _____

            After review of all eligibility factors on this form, it is recommended that the Experimental Housing
            Allowance Project applicant:

            DECISION: 1. Be approved as eligible.
                        2. Be denied as ineligible because _____

            The application was withdrawn because (if known) _____

   _____   _____   _____
   Signature of Eligibility Worker   Signature of Director or Supervisor   Date

Please read Program Pamphlet Before Completing Form

START HERE

APPLICATION FOR HOUSING ALLOWANCE
or
RECERTIFICATION OF ELIGIBILITY

_____ *APPLICATION* _____ *RECERTIFICATION*

You are applying for a housing allowance to help meet shelter costs. Your answers will largely determine whether you are eligible. You may ask other persons or the Experimental Housing Allowance Project personnel for help in completing the form if you wish.

Your answers must be complete, clear, and correct. If they are not, the form will be returned to you for more information. Under penalty of perjury, your answers must give a true and complete statement of facts. Cases will be selected by the Experimental Housing Allowance Project personnel for complete review. If your case is selected, you will be asked to prove the accuracy of all your statements.

PLEASE PRINT   A. *General Information About Applicant (s)*

1. Name: _____   _____   _____
         First   Middle Initial   Last

2. Mailing Address: _____   _____
                    Street, Box No., or RFD No.   Town or City, State, and Zip Code

3. Telephone Number: _____   Directions for reaching home, if located in the country _____

347

B. Personal Information About Application (s)

4. How did you first hear of this program? (Please check only one)

___ Referral from Public Housing waiting list ___ TV ___ Printed Pamphlet ___ Other (specify):
___ Referral from another agency ___ Newspaper ___ Community Bulletin Board
___ Friend or relative ___ Radio ___ At a meeting

_____

5. What is the sex of the head of your household? ___ Male ___ Female

6. What is the race of the head of your household? (Please check only one)

___ White ___ Negro/Black ___ American Indian ___ Spanish American ___ Oriental ___ Other

7. Please circle the category which indicates the age of the head of your household:

Under 18 years   18 to 24 years   25 to 44 years   45 to 61 years   62 to 64 years   65 years or older

8. What is the total number of persons in your household? _____ If you are the only person in the household and you are less than 62 years of age, are you handicapped or disabled? ___ Yes ___ No

9. List names, relationship, date of birth, and sex for you and for all members of your household. You must list Social Security numbers for all those age 18 or over.

Name	Relationship to you	Birthdate	Sex	Social Security Number
1) _____	_____	_____	_____	_____
2) _____	_____	_____	_____	_____
3) _____	_____	_____	_____	_____
4) _____	_____	_____	_____	_____
5) _____	_____	_____	_____	_____
6) _____	_____	_____	_____	_____
7) _____	_____	_____	_____	_____

10. Is the head of the household, or the spouse, a full-time student? ___ Yes ___ No

11. Is the head of the household, or the spouse, employed by the Armed Forces? ___ Yes ___ No

C. Living Arrangement

12. I/We live in: (check only one)
    ___ Own Home   ___ Rented Home   ___ Rented Room   ___ First Floor Apartment
    ___ In Home of Relative   ___ Board and Room   ___ Basement Apartment   ___ Other, Describe _____
    ___ Second Floor Apartment   ___ Mobile Home   ___ Public Housing

    Cost by month of my living arrangement. (Include only cost of rent) $ _____

    Does rent include any of these utilities. Heat ___ Yes ___ No   Lights ___ Yes ___ No
                                                Water, sewer, and garbage ___ Yes ___ No

D. Income

13. You must declare the income for all members of your household age 18 and over except roomers. You may declare your income in either of two ways: (1) Declare your current income from all sources which you anticipate receiving during the month, or (2) Use your 1972 income tax forms to declare income. If you choose to use your income tax form, you may either: (1) send a copy along with this application (leave Section D below blank), or (2) Use your 1972 income tax form to complete Section D below.

Examples of types of income which must be declared are listed below. This should be the income which is expected to be received during the month or year.

   Earned Income - wages, salaries, and other compensation for services; fees; commissions; bonuses; tips; vacation and leave pay; severance pay; business income whether owned individually, in a partnership, or in some other form; farm income.
   Grant Income - Social Security benefits, both state and federal; unemployment benefits; Railroad Retirement; Veterans benefits; Civil Service benefits; teacher retirement; Public or General Assistance payments (welfare); State, County, or City retirement.
   Income from Assets - Interest; dividends; payment from roomers; rental of land or buildings.
   Other Income - Child support payments; alimony; foster care payments; training program; contributions from relatives.

SECTION D.

First and Last Name of Person Receiving Income or Money	Employer or Source of Income	How often is the money received? (Monthly, quarterly, annually, etc.)	Line 16 Form 1040 or Amount of Gross Income

14. What was your total medical expense last year which was not covered or paid by insurance? $ _____ Medical expenses should include actual payments made for physician or dental services, hospitalization, prescription drugs, health insurance, nursing care in and out of the home, and transportation as would normally be allowed by Internal Revenue Service. (currently six cents per mile).

15. Did your family incur expenses for child care (babysitting) or for the care of sick or incapacitated family members during the year? ___ Yes ___ No
    If yes, were these expenses work related? ___ Yes ___ No
    If yes, what was the total expense last year? $ _____

E. Assets

16. I/We own or are purchasing real property other than a home. ____ Yes ____ No If yes, give legal description (see tax statement)

Assessed value $ _____ Balance owed $ _____

I/We own the following personal property (check each item "Yes" or "No")

Cash on hand	___ Yes	___ No	Amount $ _____
Checking account in bank	___ Yes	___ No	Amount $ _____
Savings or certificates of deposit in bank, savings and loan association, credit union, etc.	___ Yes	___ No	Amount $ _____
U.S. Savings Bonds or other bonds	___ Yes	___ No	Amount $ _____
Stocks	___ Yes	___ No	Amount $ _____

Livestock . . . . ___ Yes ___ No If yes, estimated value $ _____ Balance owed $ _____
Machinery and/or tools . . . ___ Yes ___ No If yes, estimated value $ _____ Balance owed $ _____
Life Insurance . . . . ___ Yes ___ No If yes, give total face value of all policies $ _____
   Date(s) policies purchased _____
   Name(s) and address(es) of company(ies) _____
Other personal property ___ Yes ___ No If yes, describe _____

F. Transfer of Property

17. In the past two years, I and/or my spouse (if married) gave away, sold, or deeded items of value such as money, savings, livestock, shares of stocks or bonds, land, a home, or other buildings to another person. ___ Yes ___ No

If yes, describe the property transferred _____
Date of transfer _____ Estimated value of Property transferred $ _____
What did you receive in return for the property? _____
What did you do with what you received? _____

G. Certification and Signature (Each applicant must read and sign)

18. I understand that whoever, in any matter within the jurisdiction of any department or agency of the United States or of the State of North Dakota, knowingly and willfully falsifies, conceals or covers up by any trick, scheme, or device, a material fact, or makes any false, fictitious or fraudulent statement or entry, shall be subject to a fine, imprisonment, or both.

I certify that the information given by me on this form is correct and complete to the best of my knowledge. I agree to inform the Experimental Housing Allowance Project personnel immediately of any change in income, resources, number of persons in my household, address, or living arrangement which might affect my right to receive a housing allowance. I further agree that if my case is selected for review, my signature below constitutes my consent to obtain verifying information from any necessary source.

_____   _____   _____
Signature (or mark) of applicant   Date   Signature (or mark) of spouse if living with you

_____   _____
Name   Signature and address of person, if any, who helped complete this form
                                    Address

If applicant signed with a mark "X" or fingerprint, there must be two witnesses to mark or fingerprint.

_____   _____
Witness   Witness

350

WORKSHEET

A. 1. Name_____ 2. No._____

3. Age of H/H head_____ 4. Disabled_____ 5. H/H Size_____ 6. C*_____

7. Amount of Rent Family pays _____ B. Income reporting method: Form 1040_____
                                                                                       Monthly_____
                                                                                       Weekly_____

		MONTHLY	ANNUAL
B.	GROSS INCOME	$_____	$_____

C. DEDUCTIONS   Monthly

    1. 5 or 10% $_____

    2. Medical $_____

    3. Occupational $_____

    4. Child Care $_____

    5. No. of minors_____ x $25. $_____

    6. Secondary wage earners_____ x $25 $_____

    7. TOTAL DEDUCTIONS . . . . $_____
       (lines C1 thru C6)

D. ADJUSTED GROSS . . . . $_____
   (line B less line C7)

E. ENTRY FROM PAYMENT MATRIX TABLE. . . . . $_____

F. ACTUAL HOUSING ALLOWANCE PAYMENT . . . . $_____
   (lesser of line A7 and line E)

Date_____   Signature_____

Supervisor_____

INSPECTION FORM

No._____
　　　　　　　　　　　　　　　Identification Number

Name:_____
　　　　　Last　　　　　　　　First　　　　　　　　　　Initial

Address of Inspected Unit:_____
　　　　　　　　　　　　No.　　　　Street　　　　　　　　Apt.

_____
County　　　　　City　　　　　　State　　　　　　　Zip Code

Date of Inspection:_____
　　　　　　　　　　Month　　　Day　　　Year

Type of housing being inspected: (Check appropriate one)

　　　_____ Basement apartment　　　　_____ Second floor apartment

　　　_____ First floor apartment　　　_____ Rented home

　　　_____ Mobile home　　　　　　　　_____ Other, specify_____

If you are inspecting a basement apartment, how many rooms does it have?_____

Does each room have a window?_____ State the dimensions of the windows:

____inches x ____inches　　　____inches x ____inches　　　____inches x ____inches

Circle YES or NO to indicate the condition of the dwelling:

1. Does the dwelling have a city connected sewer and water system?　　Yes　　No

2. Does the dwelling have an adequate private water system?　　　　　 Yes　　No

3. Does the dwelling have an adequate private sewer system?　　　　　 Yes　　No

4. Does the dwelling have a safe and adequate central heating system?　Yes　　No

5. If the dwelling does not have a central heating system, does it have space heaters?　　　　　　　　　　　　　　　　　　　　　　　　　Yes　　No

6. Is the dwelling structurally safe and sound, weathertight and in good repair? (No structure should have defects such as sagging floors, walls, or roofs, unsafe foundations, holes, open cracks, or rotted materials.)　　　　　　　　　　　　　　　　　　　　　Yes　　No

7. Does the dwelling have electric lights and outlets?　　　　　　　　Yes　　No

BATHROOM

8. Does the dwelling have a bathroom for the household's use only?   Yes   No
9. Does the bathroom have either a bathtub or shower?   Yes   No
10. Does the bathroom have cold running water?   Yes   No
11. Does the bathroom have hot running water?   Yes   No
12. Does the bathroom have a flush toilet in good working order?   Yes   No
13. Does the bathroom have a window?   Yes   No
14. If not, does it have a ventilating fan?   Yes   No

KITCHEN

15. Does the kitchen have one or more windows?   Yes   No
16. Does the kitchen have a ventilation fan?   Yes   No
17. Does the kitchen have a sink?   Yes   No
18. Does the kitchen have cold running water?   Yes   No
19. Does the kitchen have hot running water?   Yes   No
20. Does the kitchen have cabinets for the storage of utensils and food?   Yes   No
21. Does the kitchen have a stove for cooking?   Yes   No
22. If not, does the kitchen have either an electrical outlet or a gas hook-up for a stove?   Yes   No
23. Does the kitchen have a refrigerator?   Yes   No
24. If not, does the kitchen have either an electrical outlet or a gas hook-up for a refrigerator?   Yes   No

LIVING ROOM AND BEDROOMS

25. Does the dwelling have a living room?   Yes   No
26. How many bedrooms does the dwelling have? (Check appropriate one)

    ____ Combination living room-bedroom   ____ 1 bedroom   ____ 2 bedrooms
    ____ 3 bedrooms   ____ 4 bedrooms   ____ more than 4 bedrooms

27. Is there a window in every bedroom?   Yes   No

MISCELLANEOUS

28. Does the dwelling have any adjoining health menaces such as junk-yard or a dump?   Yes   No
29. Is the dwelling free of insects, rodents and accumulation of refuse, garbage and debris?   Yes   No

_____
Signature of Person who completed this Report

Appendix C

Evaluation Contractor Forms

EXPERIMENTAL HOUSING ALLOWANCE PROGRAM – Application Form

PLEASE PRINT THE FOLLOWING INFORMATION ABOUT THE HEAD OF YOUR HOUSEHOLD:

1. Name: _____ last _____ first _____ initial   N⁰ 064402

2. Address: _____ no. _____ street _____ apt.   3 Phone _____ number

   _____ city _____ state _____ zip   Social Sec. No. ☐☐☐☐

COL 10=01

PLEASE ANSWER QUESTIONS 4–7 BELOW:

11-12

4. How did you *first* hear of this program? (Please check only one.)   N⁰ 064402 *Identification Number*
   - 01 ☐ Referral from Public Housing waiting list
   - 02 ☐ Referral from another agency
   - 03 ☐ Friend or relative
   - 04 ☐ TV
   - 05 ☐ Newspaper
   - 06 ☐ Radio
   - 07 ☐ Printed Pamphlet
   - 08 ☐ Community Bulletin Board
   - 09 ☐ At a meeting
   - 10 ☐ Other (specify:) _____

13

5. What is the sex of the head of your household? 1 ☐ Male 2 ☐ Female

14

6. What is the race of the head of your household? (Please check only one.)
   - 1 ☐ White
   - 2 ☐ Negro/Black
   - 3 ☐ American Indian
   - 4 ☐ Spanish American
   - 5 ☐ Oriental
   - 6 ☐ Other

15

7. What is the age of the head of your household?
   - 1 ☐ Under 18 years
   - 2 ☐ 18 to 24 years
   - 3 ☐ 25 to 44 years
   - 4 ☐ 45 to 61 years
   - 5 ☐ 62 to 64 years
   - 6 ☐ 65 years or older

PLEASE SEE THE APPLICATIONS CLERK WHEN YOU REACH THIS POINT.

16-17

8. What is the total number of persons in your household? _____

9. What is the annual income for your household?
   - 18-23 a) Earned Income _____
   - 24-29 b) Grant Income _____
   - 30-35 c) Other Income _____
   -        d) Total Income (a + b + c) _____
   - 36-41 e) Allowable Deductions _____
   - 42-47 f) Net Income (d−e) _____

48-53

10. The Net Income Limit for this household size is: _____

54

11. Is the head of the household, or the spouse, a full-time student? 1 ☐ Yes 2 ☐ No

   ASK THE FOLLOWING QUESTION IF THERE IS ONLY ONE PERSON IN THE HOUSEHOLD (ITEM 8) AND THE HEAD OF THE HOUSEHOLD IS UNDER 62 (ITEM 7)

55

12. Is the head of the household handicapped, disabled or displaced? 1 ☐ Yes 2 ☐ No

To the best of my knowledge, the above information is correct and accurate.

56-60

13. DATE ___ ___ 197___ SIGNATURE: _____
         month day   year

TO BE COMPLETED BY ELIGIBILITY STAFF:

61-62

14. Neighborhood code for above address: ☐☐

15. Eligibility Status

63

   - 1 ☐ Eligible
   - 2 ☐ Not Eligible – Over Income Limit for Household
   - 3 ☐ Not Eligible – Lives Outside Program Jurisdiction
   - 4 ☐ Not Eligible – Other (specify:) _____

64-68

16. DATE ___ ___ 197___ SIGNATURE: _____
         month day   year

EXPERIMENTAL HOUSING ALLOWANCE PROGRAM — Enrollment Form

1 Name _____
       last   first   initial   Identification Number

2 Address _____ 3 Phone _____
     no.   street   apt.

   _____
     city   state   zip

COL
1-10=03

*TO BE COMPLETED BY THE ENROLLMENT STAFF
AFTER THE APPLICANT'S ELIGIBILITY STATUS HAS BEEN VERIFIED*

11

4 What is the Applicant's Rental Status?

   1 ☐ Owner or Buyer
   2 ☐ Renter Occupied without Cash Rent

2-14, 15
   3 ☐ Renter, $ _____ per → 1 ☐ month 2 ☐ week 3 ☐ other (specify:) _____

Characteristics of Applicant's Current Dwelling:

16
5 Total rooms (including Kitchen and excluding Bathroom) _____

17
6 Number of rooms usually used for sleeping _____

18
7 Is there a full bathroom within this dwelling that is used by only this household? 1 ☐ Yes 2 ☐ No

19-28
8 Check all below that are included in the rent (Skip if item 4 is coded 1):

UTILITIES	APPLIANCES, SERVICES
19 ☐ Heat	24 ☐ Sink Garbage Disposal
20 ☐ Gas (not including heat)	25 ☐ Cooking Stove
21 ☐ Electricity (not including heat)	26 ☐ Refrigerator
22 ☐ Piped Water	27 ☐ Air Conditioning
23 ☐ Garbage/Trash Collection	28 ☐ Parking

29-32
9 Does the Applicant plan to move or to stay?

   1 ☐ Move → to which neighborhood? ☐☐ → Has he already selected a unit? 1 ☐ Yes 2 ☐ No
                                   COL 30-31   COL 32
   2 ☐ Move, but no neighborhood preference
   3 ☐ Stay
   4 ☐ Undecided

33-34
10 Neighborhood code for above address ☐☐

*THE APPLICANT HAS BEEN ADVISED
OF HIS RIGHTS AND OBLIGATIONS AS AN ENROLLEE IN THIS PROGRAM*

35-39
11 DATE OF ENROLLMENT __ __ __ 197__
                             month day year

SIGNATURE OF ENROLLED HEAD OF HOUSEHOLD _____

SIGNATURE OF ENROLLMENT STAFF MEMBER _____

EXPERIMENTAL HOUSING ALLOWANCE PROGRAM — (Re)certification Form

COL		
9-10=02		

1 Name _____ last _____ first _____ initial   Identification Number _____

2 Address _____ no. _____ street _____ apt.   3 Phone _____
_____ city _____ state _____ zip

TO BE COMPLETED BY THE (RE)CERTIFICATION STAFF

11-15   4 Date (Re)certification was initiated ___ ___ ___ 197__
                                              month day year   Identification Number _____

16   5 This form provides information on: (Please check only one.)
   1 ☐ Certification
   2 ☐ Recertification initiated by Participant — Income Change
   3 ☐ Recertification initiated by Participant — Household Size
   4 ☐ Recertification initiated by Agency — Periodic
   5 ☐ Recertification initiated by Agency, Other (specify:) _____

17-18   6 (Re)certification Method (Please check *one* for household size and *one* for income.)

   FOR HOUSEHOLD SIZE
   1 ☐ Spot Checking Data Items
   2 ☐ Checking All Data Items
   3 ☐ Signed Statement
   4 ☐ Signed Statement and Spot Checking Items
   5 ☐ Signed Statement and Checking All Items

   FOR INCOME
   1 ☐ Spot Checking Data Items
   2 ☐ Checking All Data Items
   3 ☐ Signed Statement
   4 ☐ Signed Statement and Spot Checking Items
   5 ☐ Signed Statement and Checking All Items

19-26   7 Source(s) used to verify Household Size (Please check all the sources that were used.)
   19 ☐ Birth Certificate   22 ☐ Contact with School(s)
   20 ☐ Tax Returns   23 ☐ Contact with Employer(s)
   21 ☐ Home Visit   24 ☐ Other (specify:) _____

27-34   8 Source(s) used to verify Income (Please check all the sources that were used.)
   27 ☐ Recent Paycheck Stub   30 ☐ Contact with Employer(s)
   28 ☐ Tax Records   31 ☐ Contact with grant source(s)
   29 ☐ Receipts, cancelled checks 32 ☐ Other (specify:) _____

35-36   9 (Re)certified Household Size is: _____

10 The following is the (Re)certified annual income for this household:

37-42   a) Earned Income   _____
43-48   b) Grant Income   _____
49-54   c) Other Income   _____
            d) Total Income (a + b + c)
55-60   e) Allowable Deductions   _____
61-66   f) Net Income (d − e)   _____

67-72   11 The Net Income Limit for This Household Size is: _____

73-74   12 Neighborhood code for above address: ☐

75   13 Eligibility Status
   1 ☐ (Re)certified eligible
                                   (Re)certified Ineligible because:
                                   2 ☐ Over Income Limit for Household
                                   3 ☐ Lives Outside Program Jurisdiction
                                   4 ☐ Other (specify:) _____

76-80   14
   DATE ___ ___ ___ 197__   SIGNATURE _____
        month day year

USE THIS FORM AFTER: APRIL 29, 1974

EXPERIMENTAL HOUSING ALLOWANCE PROGRAM — Recertification Form

1 NAME: _____ last _____ first _____ initial _____ Identification number _____

2 ADDRESS: _____ no. _____ street _____ apt. _____ **3** PHONE _____
_____ city _____ state _____ zip _____

4 DATE RECERTIFICATION WAS INITIATED _____ month _____ day _____ 197___ year _____ Identification number _____

5 type of recertification (check only one):

A Recertification initiated by Agency
1 ☐ annual recertification
2 ☐ special group recertification
3 ☐ correction of agency calculation
4 ☐ check of selected sample of households
5 ☐ other (Specify) _____

B Recertification initiated by Participant
1 ☐ income change
2 ☐ household size change
3 ☐ income and household size change
4 ☐ other (Specify) _____

6 If recertification is initiated by participants, did this count as annual recertification? ☐ Yes ☐ No

---
FILL OUT ONLY IF HOUSEHOLD SIZE IS RECERTIFIED

7 Sources used to recertify household size (Complete (A), (B) and (C))

A. Statement:
(Check one)
1 ☐ None
2 ☐ signed statement by participant

B. Written evidence:
(Check one or more)
1 ☐ none
2 ☐ birth certificate
3 ☐ tax returns
4 ☐ medicaid
5 ☐ divorce or separation papers
6 ☐ other (Specify) _____

C. Verification by Agency: (Check one or more)
1 ☐ none
2 ☐ home visit
3 ☐ contact with other member of household
4 ☐ contact with schools
5 ☐ contact with employer
6 ☐ contact with grant source
7 ☐ contact with IRS
8 ☐ other (Specify) _____

8 Recertified household size is: _____

FILL OUT ONLY IF INCOME IS RECERTIFIED

9 Sources used to recertify income and deductions (Complete (A) alone, or (B), (C) and (D))

A. Signed Statement only ☐ (Agency did not use any other sources of verification — go to Question #10)

B. Statement: (Check one or more for each source of income and deductions)

	Earned Income	Grant Income	Other Income	Deductions
none	☐	☐	☐	
signed by participant with written evidence and/or other verification also required	☐	☐	☐	☐

C. Written Evidence examined by Agency: (Check one or more for each source of income and deductions)

	Earned	Grant	Other	Ded.
none	☐	☐	☐	☐
recent paycheck stub, soc. security, or welfare check stub, etc.	☐	☐	☐	
tax records	☐	☐	☐	☐
bank books	☐	☐	☐	
receipts, cancelled checks, bills, etc.	☐	☐	☐	☐
letter (or form) from grant source or employer	☐	☐	☐	
other (Specify)	☐	☐	☐	☐

D. Verification By Agency: (Check one or more for each source of income and deductions)

	Earned	Grant	Other	Ded.
none	☐	☐	☐	☐
contact with employer(s)	☐			☐
contact with grant source (e.g., social security, or welfare)	☐	☐		☐
contact with IRS	☐	☐		☐
contact with other member of household			☐	☐
other (Specify)	☐	☐	☐	☐

10 The following is the recertified annual income for this household:

a) earned income _____
b) grant income _____
c) other income _____
d) total income (a + b + c) _____
31-35 e) allowable deductions _____
36-40 f) net income (d - e) _____

11 The net income limit for this household size is: _____

12 Eligibility status 1 ☐ Recertified eligible
(CHECK ONE ONLY)
Recertified Ineligible because:
2 ☐ over income limit due to increase in income
3 ☐ over income limit due to decrease in size
4 ☐ over income limit due to both of above
5 ☐ moved outside program jurisdiction
6 ☐ other (Specify) _____

13 Neighborhood code for above address: _____

14 Completed on _____ month _____ day _____ 197__ year
SIGNATURE _____
STAFF AGENCY MEMBER

359

EXPERIMENTAL HOUSING ALLOWANCE PROGRAM – TERMINATION FORM

1 Name _____
              last   first   initial

2 Current Address _____
              no.   street   apt.

3 Telephone No. _____

_____
city   state   zip

Identification Number _____

COL
9-10=05

11-15   **4** Date of Enrollment ___ ___ ___ ___ 197___
                          month   day   year

16-20   **5** Date of Termination ___ ___ ___ ___ 197___
                          month   day   year

Identification Number _____

21-22   **6** Neighborhood code for above address: [   ]

23-24   **7** Primary reason for termination (Please check only one)

       10 ☐ Income/Household Size
       11 ☐ Decided to move to subsidized housing
       12 ☐ Moved or moving from Program Area
       13 ☐ Bought or buying new home
       14 ☐ Moved -- new unit does not meet program requirements
       15 ☐ Present unit substandard -- will not move
       16 ☐ Present unit substandard -- could not find new unit
       17 ☐ Cannot be located
       18 ☐ Failure to provide recertification information
       19 ☐ Voluntary termination (Specify) _____

       20 ☐ Completed Program -- transferred to Section 23 housing
       21 ☐ Completed Program -- referred to other public housing
       22 ☐ Completed Program -- no further action
       23 ☐ Completed Program -- continued allowance

       Specify other reasons for termination in the "other" category

       24 ☐ Other _____

25-29   **8** Date: ___ ___ ___ ___ 197___   Signature: _____
                  month   day   year

Abt Associates Inc.
55 Wheeler Street
Cambridge, MA
02138

OMB NO. 63-S-73002
Approval Expires September 1974
9 April 1973

EHAP ID# ☐☐☐☐☐☐☐ 8-(4)
       1 2 3 4 5 6 7

EXPERIMENTAL HOUSING AGENCY SURVEY -
HOUSING EVALUATION FORM

CARD VI
9/10-(06)

1. NAME _____
        Last   First   Initial

2. ADDRESS _____ 3. Phone _____
        No.   Street   Apt.

        City   State   Zip

4. CENSUS TRACT _____ 11-16

5. NEIGHBORHOOD CODE FOR ABOVE ADDRESS ☐☐ 17-18
                                                                   19

6. HOUSING IS: One, single family house detached ( )-1
                from any other
                One, but attached to other houses ( )-2
                2 unit structure ( )-3
                3 ( )-4
                4 ( )-5
                5 or more ( )-6
                Unit is mobile home or trailer ( )-7

7. LOG OF PHONE CALLS TO MAKE APPOINTMENT:

Date of Call	Time of Call	Name of Caller	Time of Appointment Made?	No One Home

8. LOG OF HOUSE CALLS

		ATTEMPT			RESULT	
Date	Time	Inspector's Name	ID#	No one Home	Household Refused	Completed

H-2-5A
HUD Approval Date
30 March 1973

Date of Evaluation
Month ☐ Day ☐ Year 197☐
  20/21 22/23   24

Interviewer ID#
20/21/22
BLANK 23-30

HOUSING EVALUATION RATINGS

CARD VI cont. **CARD VII** 9/10—(07) **CARD VIII** 9/10—(08)   TIME: _____ Start

Part A. DWELLING UNIT INTERIOR

	LR	BDR	BTH	KCN	OTHER

1. Room Information
   - Presence ( )31— ( )50— ( )11— ( )31— ( )51—
   - Length 32-33 51-52 12-13 32-33 52-53-54
   - Width 34-35 53-54 14-15 34-35 55-56
   - Area 36-37-38 55-56-57 16-17-18 36-37-38 57-58-59
   - Regular ( )39— ( )58— ( )19— ( )39— ( )60—

2. Window Adequacy ( )40— ( )59— ( )20— ( )40— ( )61—
   - Ventilation ( )41— ( )60— ( )21— ( )41—
3. Ceiling ( )41— ( )60— ( )22— ( )42— ( )62—
4. Electricity ( )42— ( )61— ( )23— ( )43— ( )63—

	LR	BDR	BTH	KCN	OTHER

5. Ceiling Structure 43— 62— 24— 44— 64—
6. Wall Structure 44— 63— 25— 45— 65—
7. Ceiling Surface 45— 64— 26— 46— 66—
8. Wall Surface 46— 65— 27— 47— 67—
9. Floor Structure 47— 66— 28— 48— 68—
10. Floor Surface 48— 67— 29— 49— 69—
11. Window Condition 49— 68— 30— 50— 70—

CARD IX 9/10—(09)

12. Kitchen Sink [ ]11
13. Kitchen Accessories-Code Letters
    A ( )12   D ( )15
    B ( )13   E ( )16
    C ( )14   F ( )17

14. A Shower-Tub [ ]18—
    B Condition [ ]19—
    C Waterproof [ ]20—

15. Heating Equipment-Code Number [ ]21

362

CARD IX cont.

Part B. DWELLING UNIT EXTERIOR

16. Adequate Exits (Multi only) ( ) 22–
17. Passageways (Multi only) 23–
18. Exterior Wall Structure 24–
19. Exterior Wall Surface 25–
20. Yard Access 26–
21. Roof Structure 27–
22. Roof Surface and Drains 28–
23. Chimneys and Flues 29–
24. Overall Rating 30–

24A ( ) 31–
24B ( ) 32–
24C ( ) 33–
24D ( ) 34–

Part C. NEIGHBORHOOD

25 A Street Maintenance 35–
   B Street Lighting ( ) 36–
   C Pedestrian Walkways ( ) 37–
26. Street Litter 38–
27. Abandoned Buildings ( ) 39–
28. Abandoned Cars ( ) 40–

Time: _____ End

COMMENTS

41–
42–
43–
44–

45–
46–
47–
48–

49–
50–
51–
52–

53–
54–
55–
56–

363

Bibliography

Aaron, Henry, Shelter and Subsidies: Who Benefits from Federal Policies? (Brookings Institution, Washington, D. C., 1972).

Abt Associates Inc., *Agency Program Manual*, (Abt Associates Inc., Cambridge, 1972).

Abt Associates Inc., On-Site Observers' Manual, (xerox copy, 1972).

Abt Associates Inc., *Second Annual Report of the Administrative Agency Experiment Evaluation*, (Abt Associates Inc., Cambridge, 1974).

Abt Associates Inc., *Participation in a Direct Cash Assistance Program*, (Draft working paper, 1974).

Abt Associates Inc., *Third Annual Report of the Administrative Agency Evaluation*, (Abt Associates Inc., Cambridge, 1976).

Bennett, John W., *Northern Plainsmen*, (Aldine, Chicago, 1971).

Bismarck Chamber of Commerce, "North Dakota Community Data for Industry," (brochure, compiled: 1973).

Burns, Allen F., "An Anthropologist at Work," in (CAE Quarterly, Vol. VI, No. 4), pp. 28-34).

Clinton, Charles A., "The Anthropologist as Hired Hand," in: (*Human Organization*, Vol. 34, No. 2), pp. 197-204.

Drache, Hiram M., *The Day of the Bonanza*, (North Dakota Institute for Regional Studies, Fargo, 1964).

Foster, George M., *Traditional Cultures*, (Harper and Row, New York, 1962).

Frantz, Joe B., and J. E. Choate, *The American Cowboy*, (University of Oklahoma Press, Norman, 1955).

Gans, Herbert, "A Poor Man's Home is His Poorhouse," (New York Times Magazine, March 31, 1974).

Goffman, Erving, *Stigma*, (Prentice Hall, Englewood Cliffs, New Jersey, 1963).

Goodenough, Ward H., *Cooperation in Change*, (John Wiley & Sons, New York, 1963).

Gould, Peter and Rodney White, *Mental Maps*, (Pelican Books, London, 1974).

Handler, Joel F., and Ellen Jane Hollingsworth, *The Deserving Poor*, (Markham Publishing Co., Chicago, 1971).

Harrington, Michael, *The Other America*, (Penguin Books, London, 1964)

Heinburg, John F., Peggy W. Spohn, and Grace M. Taher, *Housing Allowances in Kansas City and Wilmington: An Appraisal*, (Urban Institute, Washington, D.C., 1975)

Helmer, O., *Social Technology*, (Basic Books, New York, 1966).

Holshouser, William, Jr., *Report on the Selected Aspects of the Jacksonville Housing Allowance Project*, (Abt Associates Inc., Cambridge, 1976).

Kazek, Melvin E., *North Dakota: A Human and Economic Geography*, (North Dakota Institute for Regional Studies, Fargo, 1956).

Kershaw, David N., and J. Fair, *Final Report of the New Jersey Graduated Work Incentive Experiment*, (Madison, Princeton, Princeton, New Jersey, 1973), Vol. IV.

Klose, Nelson, *A Concise Study Guide to the American Frontier*, (University of Nebraska, Lincoln, 1964).

Kraenzel, Carl Frederick, *The Great Plains in Transition*, (University of Oklahoma Press, Norman, 1955).

Leighton, Alexander, *The Governing of Men*, (Princeton University Press, Princeton, New Jersey, 1946).

Lokken, Rosco L., North Dakota: Our State, (Valley City College Press, Valley City, N. D., 1974)

Lunde, Richard M., "North Dakota and Its Immigrants," in (*The North Dakota Teacher*, August, 1972), pp. 16-29.

Margolis, Richard J., *Mobile Homes of the Rural Poor*, (Rural Housing Alliance, Washington, D. C., 1972).

Messerschmidt, Donald A., and Marilyn C. Richen, "Federal-Local Relations in Educational Change," (unpublished paper, 1976).

Niehoff, Arthur A., ed., *A Casebook of Social Change*, (Aldine, Chicago, 1966).

North Dakota Experimental Housing Allowance Project, *Strategic Plan*, (mimeo, 1973).

North Dakota Experimental Housing Allowance Project, *Detailed Plan*, (mimeo, 1973).

North Dakota Experimental Housing Allowance Project, Final Report of the North Dakota Experimental Housing Allowance Project, (xerox, 1976).

North Dakota State Planning Agency, *North Dakota Economic Atlas*, (n.p., Bismarck, 1969).

Phillips, Thomas G., "HUD Proposes Cash Allowance System as Link to Broad Welfare Reform," in (*National Journal Reports*, August 25, 1973).

Piven, Frances Fox, and Richard A. Cloward, *Regulating the Poor*, (Vintage Press, New York, 1971).

Piven, Frances Fox, and Richard A. Cloward, *The Politics of Turmoil*, (Vintage Press, New York, 1975).

Robinson, Elwynn B., *History of North Dakota*, (University of Nebraska Press, Lincoln, 1966).

Sevareid, Eric, *Not So Wild A Dream*, (Knopf, New York, 1946).

Sevareid, Eric, "You Can Go Home Again," in Brian R. Goodey and R. J. Eiden, eds., *Readings in North Dakota Geography*, (North Dakota Studies, Bismarck, 1968).

Severy, Bruce, *Crossing Into The Prairies*, (Scopcraft Press, Grand Forks, 1973).

Social Service Board of North Dakota, *Social Services in North Dakota* (First Annual Report of the Social Services Board of North Dakota for the period ending June, 1973.)

Spicer, Edward H., "Anthropology and the Policy Process," in Michael V. Agrosino, ed., *Do Applied Anthropologists Apply Anthropology?* (University of Georgia Press, Athens, Georgia, 1976).

Stack, Carol B., *All Our Kin*, (Harper and Row, New York, 1974).

Tiger, Lionel and Robin Fox, *The Imperial Animal*, (Dell Publishing Co., New York, 1972).

Toole, K. Ross, *The Rape of the Great Plains*, (Little, Brown and Co., Boston, 1976).

Trend, M. G., "The Anthropologist as Go-fer," (A paper read before the Society for Applied Anthropology, St. Louis, 1976).

Trend, M. G., "Income Certification Methods: The Importance of Different Administrative Configurations," (unpublished technical paper, 1976).

Turner, Frederick Jackson, "The Significance of the Frontier in American History," in George Taylor, ed., *The Turner Thesis Concerning the Role of the Frontier in American History*, (Little, Brown and Co., Boston, 1949).

U. S. Bureau of the Census, Census of Population, *General Population Characteristics*, Final Report PC (1)-B-36, *North Dakota*, (U. S. Government Printing Office, Washington, D. C., 1971).

U. S. Bureau of the Census, Census of Population, 1970, *General Social and Economic Characteristics*, Final Report PC (1)-C-36, *North Dakota*, (U. S. Government Printing Office, Washington, D. C., 1972).

U. S. Bureau of the Census, Census of Population, 1970, *Detailed Housing Characteristics*, Final Report, HC (1)-B-36, *North Dakota*, (U. S. Government Printing Office, Washington, D. C., 1972).

U. S. Bureau of the Census, Census of Population, 1970, *Subject Reports*, Final Report PC (2)-1-F, *American Indians*, (U. S. Government Printing Office, Washington, D. C., 1973).

U. S. Bureau of the Census, <u>Statistical Abstract of the United States</u>, (U. S. Government Printing Office, Washington, D. C., 1974).

U. S. Department of Health, Education and Welfare, <u>Administrative Review of Social Services</u>, (DHEW report for North Dakota, mimeo, 1965).

U. S. Department of Health, Education and Welfare, "Public Assistance Statistics," (DHEW Circular, SRS 75-03100, April, 1974).

U. S. Department of Health, Education and Welfare, "Quality Control," (DHEW Circular, n.n., December 20, 1973).

U. S. Department of Housing and Urban Development, "Analysis of the Bismarck-Mandan, North Dakota, Housing Market, (HUD, Washington, 1971).

U. S. Department of Housing and Urban Development, <u>Housing Allowances: The 1976 Report to Congress</u>, (U. S. Government Printing Office, Washington, D. C., 1976).

Vonnegut, Kurt, Jr., <u>Slaughterhouse Five</u>, (Dell Publishing Co., New York, 1971).

Weaver, Robert C., "Housing Allowances," in (Land Economics, LI 3, August, 1975), pp. 246-255.

Wilkins, Robert P., "The Non-ethnic Roots of North Dakota Isolationnism," in (Nebraska History, Vol. 44, No. 3, 1963), pp. 206-221.

Zais, James, P., et. al., <u>A Framework for the Analysis of Income Accounting Systems in EHAP</u>, (Draft copy The Urban Institute, Washington, D. C., 1975).

About the Author

M.G. Trend works for Abt Associates Inc., a private research firm. He received his training in social anthropology and studio art at the University of Minnesota. He lives with his wife and their two sons in Concord, Massachusetts. (Photo by J. Knoll)